新东方
NEW ORIENTAL

Model Essays for IELTS Writing

剑桥雅思写作高分范文

刘巍巍　方　林　编著

群言出版社
Qunyan Press

图书在版编目(CIP)数据

剑桥雅思写作高分范文 / 刘巍巍，方林编著. —北京：群言出版社，2009（2012.9 重印）

ISBN 978-7-80256-008-6

Ⅰ. 剑… Ⅱ. ①刘…②方… Ⅲ. 英语—写作—高等教育—自学参考资料 Ⅳ. H315

中国版本图书馆 CIP 数据核字(2009)第 080489 号

剑桥雅思写作高分范文

出 版 人	范 芳
责任编辑	孙春红
封面设计	大愚设计
出版发行	群言出版社(Qunyan Press)
地 址	北京东城区东厂胡同北巷 1 号
邮政编码	100006
网 站	www. qypublish. com
读者信箱	bj62605588@163. com
总 编 办	010－65265404 65138815
编 辑 部	010－65276609 65262436
发 行 部	010－62605588 62605019
经 销	新华书店
读者服务	010－65220236 65265404 65263345
法律顾问	中济律师事务所
印 刷	北京四季青印刷厂
版 次	2012 年 9 月第 1 版第 6 次印刷
开 本	787mm×1092mm 1/16
印 张	15. 5
字 数	274 千
书 号	ISBN 978-7-80256-008-6
定 价	38. 00 元

新东方图书策划委员会

主任 俞敏洪

委员 （按姓氏笔画为序）

王　强　　包凡一

仲晓红　　沙云龙

陈向东　　张洪伟

邱政政　　汪海涛

周成刚　　徐小平

谢　琴　　窦中川

序言 PREFACE

学在此，乐在此，爱在此

（代序）

“爱在此，乐在此”，是香港旅游发展局为“精彩香港旅游年”设计的口号。说起香港，很多人的心目中会首先想到的是高耸入云的中银大厦、碧波荡漾的维多利亚港、光怪陆离的夜中环和歌舞升平的兰桂坊，还有一些人会想到熙熙攘攘的人群、步伐匆匆的行人、礼貌而又高效的警官和日夜忙碌却又井然有序的街道。但是对于我而言，香港永远意味着温暖和感动、激情和奋斗。太平山下的这座充满活力的国际化大都市，无疑是我生命中最重要的驿站之一，在我的记忆中留下了永远不可磨灭的痕迹。在这里，我有幸获得了一笔金额不菲的奖学金，进入到亚太地区最著名的学府之一继续深造，衣食无忧、心平气和地研究自己从小就喜欢的课题，在科研和生活的点点滴滴中亲身体会六百万香港人最引以为豪的“香港效率”和“香港品质”。也正是在这里，我终于完成了《剑桥雅思写作高分范文》以及《剑桥雅思词汇掌中宝》这几本雅思辅导书的全部书稿。尽管这几本书的创作过程似乎远远没有达到“香港效率”，但是我自信，这两套书的质量绝对可以和“香港品质”媲美。

这两套书的历史要追溯到上个世纪末。当时我还在哈尔滨的一所工科院校的英语系读书。四周浓郁的理工氛围让当时踌躇满志、视学好英语为人生最高目标的我倍感压抑和绝望，甚至开始怀疑自己选择英语作为专业是不是一个美丽的错误。我喜欢学英语，也擅长学英语，这是我很小的时候就明白的事实；不该来到这里学英语，或者确切地说，来到这里就不该学英语，也是我不得不接受的事实。书本里，哲人说生活会因为一些突如其来的阴差阳错而变得幸福；现实中，我的生活却因为这样而变得痛苦。不过我很快在绝望中找到了希望。在阴差阳错地参加了一次当时报名费不低的雅思考试后，凭借着相当不错的考试成绩，我意外地在一家著名的雅思培训机构中觅得了一个兼职的机会，在 18 岁生日的前几天登上了雅思的讲台，在“暗无天日”的岁月里为自己打开了一扇通往自信和幸福的大门。我的教学从一开始就大获成功，学生和校方的反馈都极好，教授的科目也从最初的雅思阅读一直扩展到雅思考试的各个板块。事实证明，我在语言学习和语言使用方面的确是有过人的天赋的。在我人生的那个阶段，意识到这一点所带来的快感，远胜过手里揣着对于一个大学生而言几近天文数字的工资所带来的兴奋。于是，我无条件地爱上了教英语，疯狂地逃掉了大学里所有我觉得没有意义的课，义无返顾地投入到教学中，沉溺于其中，完全不能自拔。我的大学生活也因此而由原来的图书馆一个据点，变成了“图书馆——讲台”的两点一线。后来，这间培训机构有了将教师的教学心得整理成册正式出版的意向，于是就有了我写这几本书的初衷。当年我还满怀信心地盘算着，在自己20岁大学毕业的时候，怀里不仅要捧着毕业证和学位证，而且还要揣着几本自己写的书。

事实证明，我高估了自己的能力，低估了写书的难度。我自认是个做事相当努力和拼命的人，可惜生性平和，而生性平和的人做事情的效率往往就不会太高；我又很固执，坚决不愿意放弃品质来换取效率。于是乎，这套书一写就是好几年。在这个过程当中，我自己的生活发生了巨大的改变。2002年，我从白雪皑皑的冰城哈尔滨飞到了四季如春的花城广州，在这里开始了我在新东方的工作。新东方的日子，是我过去27年生命中最振奋人心的岁月。每天都全身心地投入、非常忘我地做事，全身的每个细胞都处于高度兴奋的工作状态，感觉非常亢奋，也很是尽兴和过瘾。常常是白天上10个小时的课，晚上回来还要备课、写文章，一直干到凌晨三四点。有时候合上笔记本电脑抬头看看闹钟已经是早上六点多了，就干脆再打开电脑继续写到七点多，然后冲个热水澡，直接出门，精神抖擞地上一天的课。后来我顺利地通过各轮面试拿到奖学金去香港继续深造，做的课题是我最感兴趣的方向，导师也是公认的这方面的权威，生活就变得更加充实和忙碌。有时甚至是上午在香港的大学课堂里做学生，晚上又要回到广州新东方的课堂里做老师，中间还在往来香港九龙和广州火车东站的KCR九广直通车上用笔记本电脑打书稿或博士论文。我没有详细统计过在这几本雅思辅导书的全部内容中，有多少是在KCR列车上完成的，但是我相信比例一定不低。这样的生活，让很多关心我的健康的人感觉到不可思议和惨不忍睹。但是，我却的确在这个过程中获得了巨大的满足感和成就感，也的确收获了很多的成绩。在过去的几年中，我连续三次被新东方评为“集团优秀教师”。虽然因为身在香港，最终未能去北京总部领奖，但是依然很得意于学生的认可；已经出版的《雅思阅读高分榜中榜》成绩也很喜人，业界的反响亦非常好，2006年更是被一家台湾的出版社成功引入海外市场，正式出版了繁体字的海外版；香港的学业也由始至终一直进展很顺利。更令人称奇的是，在这个过程中，我的健康状况也达到了历史最高水平。除了视力不幸下降外，我的各项健康指标都明显好过从前。“生命在于做事”，我常跟新东方的同事自嘲。

虽然这几本雅思辅导书中有不少内容是在九龙—广州的KCR列车上完成的，算是车轮上的作品，但是这几本书却绝对不是马虎之作。正式出版之前，我在香港参阅了大量国外出版的英文词汇、写作以及雅思备考方面的书籍，自认为和已经出版的数目繁多的雅思方面的书籍相比较，这几本雅思辅导书的确有不少自身所特有的优势，现列举如下：

1. 对词汇进行了语用学分析，确保单词使用的得体性

语用学是语言学的重要分支，主要研究词的使用方法和语言使用者所期望表达的真正含义。以往，大多数的雅思考生在学习英语的过程中，最关心的是如何用英语正确地交谈和写作，对语

言的认识停留在了语法这个层面。跨出国门、真正开始海外生活后，他们当中的很多人却发现，其实更需要关注的是如何得体地使用英语。外国同学和老师通常都会善意地原谅中国学生的语法错误，却无法接受和容忍一些因语言使用欠妥而引起的尴尬甚至是冒犯。《剑桥雅思写作高分范文》以及《剑桥雅思词汇掌中宝》这几本雅思备考用书中的很多单词，尤其是词汇掌中宝系列口语和写作分册中的绝大多数单词，都特别配置了用法方面的指导，请考生用心阅读。

2. 分类归纳词汇，配合"真题回放"环节，直接命中考点

《剑桥雅思词汇掌中宝》丛书将雅思词汇按照听、说、读、写四个考试部分进行归类，避免了机械地将各类词汇汇编于一册词汇书中的做法。同时，各分册的各个小节前，都特别设置了"真题回放" 环节，让考生直接了解到所记忆的词汇在雅思考试中的实际考查方向和出题方法，真正做到心中有数、有的放矢。

3. 严格区分书面语和口语

中国考生在雅思复习备考乃至整个英语学习的过程中，一个非常突出的问题，就是不能正确区分书面语和口语。很多学生在口语考试中直接照搬写作范文中的句子，然后又将不少口语课上学会的"口语"词汇写进了原本应该非常"书面"的雅思作文，导致了很低的得分。事实上，英语和汉语一样，口语和书面语有严格的区分，无论是《剑桥雅思写作高分范文》还是《剑桥雅思词汇掌中宝》，都在这方面有做特别的提醒，请广大考生用心体会。

4. 突出单词在实际生活中的运用，治标治本

在《剑桥雅思词汇掌中宝》各分册所收集的单词中，大多数都不仅是雅思考试中的核心词汇，而且还是英语国家人士日常生活中的常用词汇。希望考生利用复习备考雅思的机会，用心记忆这些词汇，真正提高自己的英文实力，为即将开始的海外生活打下坚实的基础。

5. 例句简短精练，适合自学

词汇书的例句一旦过于复杂，往往就会在彰显作者不俗的英语实力的同时，妨碍了考生的记忆。例句的功能在于辅助考生记忆单词。显然，一个生词众多、句式复杂的例句，是不可能帮助考生记忆单词的。《剑桥雅思词汇掌中宝》丛书除写作分册外，其他分册的例句均简短精练，适合雅思考生自学使用。复习备考的过程中，考生完全可以直接背诵丛书中的例句。《剑桥雅思写作高分范文》也特别配备了"词汇升级"栏目，提供了大量可供替换的同义词，方便考生快速积累写作词汇。

在多年的心血即将付诸出版之际，我想特别感谢很多人。感谢上海交通大学高级金融学院的 Golden Tsui 先生的大力支持。感谢我父母从小的言传身教。最后要特别感谢广州新东方的前任校长沙云龙先生、张隽女士和现任校长桂淳先生，以及我的博士导师 Dr. David Qian 和 Professor

Preface

Martin Warren，是他们的宽容、支持和协作，让我能够在一个相对比较宽松的环境中同时完成自己的工作和学业，在精神和物质的世界里找到了最好的平衡。感谢我的母校香港理工大学为我提供了全额奖学金并多次资助我远赴海外参加学术活动，让我在非常优越的环境中从事自己最感兴趣的课题研究，最大程度地挖掘了自己的学术潜力。我将会充分利用自己的学习所得，真正践行理大"开物成务，励学利民"的校训，以作为对母校资助和培养的感谢和回报。

需要特别向广大雅思考生说明的是，虽然我对这几本雅思词汇书以及写作书的词汇部分的品质充满了信心，它们却绝对代替不了词典。不论是单纯为了应付雅思考试，还是为了真正提高英语能力，词典都是必不可少的工具。无论你的英语处于哪个层次，词典都会是你的良师益友。这几本雅思词汇书无法代替词典，一般的电子词典更是无法代替词典。翻阅英文词典，不仅是很多语言大师和翻译大师的嗜好，也是英语学习的必由之路。在词典里认真地查找和阅读一个词条，可以获得很多相关的知识，自然会受益匪浅。日积月累，英语水平就必定会有很大的飞跃。我在本科、硕士和博士阶段的学习，一直都是以英语做为自己的专业。一路学过来，真的感觉其乐无穷。其实，英语和这个世界上的很多事情一样，只要你用心去学，用心去领悟，就一定会发现其中所蕴藏的巨大的乐趣，就会被它吸引，自然也就会爱上它。

"学在此，乐在此，爱在此"，与所有在英语学习的道路上奋勇向前的人共勉！

编者

2009年9月15日于香港红磡

如何使用本书
How to use this book

本书收集了近十年来在雅思A类和G类写作考试的Task 2中出现过的各类题材的议论文写作题，并且为每道雅思题目提供了高质量的范文。除了范文之外，每一道雅思题目的后面还附有单词注解、汉语译文、特别提醒、相关题目、写作点拨、词汇升级、句型升级、论据积累等自学辅导栏目。考生在阅读本书之前，请先了解各个自学辅导栏目的设置目的以及学习重点，结合自身情况对这些内容进行取舍，以提高学习效率、取得最佳的复习效果。

1. 单词注释

这个栏目归纳整理了范文中出现的难度相对较高的词汇，并附有音标和汉语释义。

- 如果考生的复习时间多于三个月，请记忆这些单词
- 如果复习时间在三个月至一个月之间，请选择性地记忆范文中出现的、打算在考场里使用的单词
- 如果复习时间少于一个月，请跳过这个栏目，直接进入“词汇升级”环节

2. 汉语译文

这个栏目提供了范文的汉语译文。为了方便读者的理解，大部分译文以直译为主，因而部分语句会略显生涩，望考生见谅。立志在雅思写作考试中夺取高分并且有较长复习时间的考生，可以在精读完范文以后，试着对照范文的汉语译文，将文章再译成英文。用心比较自己的译文和范文在文字方面的不同，可以让你的英语表达能力在短时间内有一个很大的提高。

3. 特别提醒

这个栏目将雅思写作中出现的题目按照题材进行了分类，并且指出了各类题材在雅思考试中出现频率的高低。由于雅思写作试题重复使用的几率很高，请考生特别留意那些在近几年的雅思写作考试中反复出现的热门题材。

4. 推荐指数

这个栏目用星号★标注了每道写作题目在将来的雅思考试中出现几率的高低，最高推荐指数为五星。

5. 相关题目

这个栏目提供了与各道雅思写作题目类似的其他雅思写作题目在本书中的编号。这些题材类似的雅思题目，组成了“相关写作题目组”，方便考生复习。

- 如果考生的复习时间多于三个月，请认真阅读“相关写作题目组”里的各篇范文，并用心体会这些范文在构思和表达方面的异同
- 如果复习时间在三个月至一个月之间，请在阅读了“相关写作题目组”里的各篇范文之后，选择性地精读其中的一篇
- 如果复习时间少于一个月，请直接从每组“相关写作题目组”里挑选一篇范文进行精读

6. 写作点拨

这个栏目对每一道雅思写作题目进行了点评，并将雅思写作题目按照提问方式的不同分成了若干个类型，从写作构思的角度对每种类型的作文的写作进行了指导。

7. 词汇升级

这个栏目从范文中挑选出大量在雅思写作中高频使用的词汇，并提供它们的同义替换以及常见搭配。“词汇升级”旨在将考生通常使用的普通词汇或搭配升级到有一定难度的词汇或搭配，同时也特意避免了难度过高、在文章中有可能显得突兀的表达方式。词汇量有限的考生，请特别留意这个栏目。

8. 句型升级

这个栏目中列举了大量原本句式结构平淡无奇的句子，并将它们进行“句式升级”，修改成中国考生往往不能驾驭或是不擅长使用的复杂句式，确保作文满足雅思写作高分所必备的“句式多变”的要求。

9. 论据积累

这个栏目以中英双语例举出雅思写作考试中常见话题的经典论据，帮助考生拓展思路、提高表达能力。考生可以在雅思考试中借鉴这些论据。需要提醒的是，为了避免文字内容的雷同，一定要将这些论据进行恰当的改写。

本书的编写理念，是以雅思写作题目为出发点，从词汇、句型、篇章、思想四部分全面提高考生的写作能力。如果考生的复习时间充裕，建议从第一篇文章开始精读，在备考雅思的同时，让自己的英文水平有一个整体的提高！

目录 CONTENTS

1. In the past, people spent their entire lives doing one job. But nowadays, they change their jobs frequently. Please give the reasons and your suggestions. 2

2. What are the main tasks of universities: to offer students knowledge and skills essential for their future career, or to provide students with access to knowledge itself? What do you think university education should contain? 4

3. Should government pay for medical care and education? Why? 6

4. What is it in the mass media that has negative effects on teenagers and what measures should governments take to solve this problem? 8

5. Nowadays computers are widely used in education. As a result, some people think teachers no longer play important roles in classrooms. To what extend do you agree or disagree? 10

6. Universities should accept equal numbers of male and female students in every subject. Do you agree or disagree? 12

7. Some people think that children should learn to compete, but others think that children should be taught to co-operate so that they could become more useful adults. State some reasons for both views and give your opinion. 14

8. The culture of different countries are becoming increasingly similar, so there is no point for people to go traveling abroad for they could have the same experience at home. Do you agree or disagree? 16

9. Some people think that people will forget their own tradition and history because they no longer wear their traditional costumes. Do you agree or disagree? 18

10. Traditional food is undergoing great changes and being replaced by new diets. What do you think are the reasons and what do you think about this phenomenon? 20

11. Some people think the Olympic Games will no longer play an important role in the 21st century, and the 2004 game should be the last one. Do you agree or disagree? 22

12. In most parts of the world, the volume of traffic is growing at an alarming rate. Discuss the main traffic problems in your country, their causes and possible solutions. 24

13. The world of work is changing rapidly. People today no longer take one job for life. Discuss the causes of these changes. What suggestions would you make for young people to prepare themselves for the work in future? 26

14. As science and technology contribute most to the development of society, science students should get more financial support from government than students in other fields (eg. business, language, etc.). To what extent do you agree or disagree with this statement? ······ 28

15. Nowadays people can use computers to talk, learn and communicate without leaving home. There is a danger that it will cause more isolation and a lack of communication among people. To what extent do you agree or disagree with this statement? ······ 30

16. Some people think that machine translation is highly developed in today's society. Therefore it is not necessary for children to learn a foreign language. What's your opinion? ······ 32

17. Some people say that the age of books has passed; information can be accessed via videos, computers, television, films and so forth. Other people think books and written words will still be essential for information dissemination and education. Discuss both sides and give your opinion. ······ 34

18. Television is dangerous because it destroys the family tie and community spirit. It is said by some that television absorbs so much of people's time that they have no time to talk to each other. To what extent do you agree or disagree? Give your opinion. ······ 36

19. People who do not know how to use computer will become more and more disadvantaged. State the disadvantages and what action governments should take. ······ 38

20. Scientific and technological advances bring benefits to our daily life. However, most scientists are no longer able to find the solutions to the problems they have created. To what extent do you agree or disagree? ······ 40

21. Intelligent robots will be more widely used in the future. Is this a blessing or a curse? What is your opinion? ······ 42

22. The reason why some families don't buy television set is that the parents want their children to spend more time on creative thinking or even inventions. Agree or disagree? ······ 44

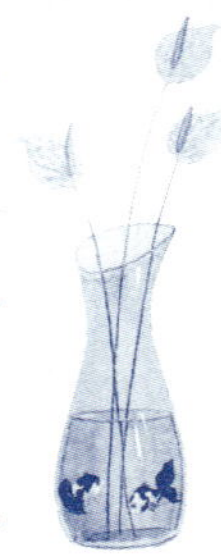

23. Newspaper, radio, television and computer each has its merits and drawbacks. What is the most efficient means of acquiring information? Give your reasons. ······ 46

24. Some people think science contributes more to the society; others believe subjects such as language or business make a bigger contribution. What's your opinion? ······ 48

25. Modern technology has greatly influenced people's ways of entertainment, making people less creative. Do you agree or disagree? ······ 50

26. Some parents maintain that co-education is better for their children while others believe it is better if boys and girls go to single-sex school. Discuss. ······ 52

27. Many schools are troubled by students' behavioral problems. What are the causes? What solutions do you recommend? ······ 54

28. Should the teacher in physical education class encourage the students to be more competitive or urge them to cooperate with one another? What is your opinion? ······ 56

29. Which is a better place for the aged, home or nursing home? ······ 58

30. It is said that life is becoming increasingly stressful for most people. What is the reason of this phenomenon and how could this problem be solved? ······ 60

31. Happiness is considered important by all people. Why is it hard to define happiness? What are the factors that are necessary to achieve happiness? ······ 62

32. Advertising adversely affects young people, so it should be strictly limited. Do you agree or not? ······ 64

33. More and more women go out to work. Hence, it is the governments' responsibility to provide daycare service for the children of working mother, free of charge. To what extent do you agree or disagree? ······ 66

34. Is it fair that sports professionals earn much more money than people in other important professions? Give reasons for both sides of the argument and your opinion. ······ 68

35. Discuss the advantages and disadvantages of people traveling abroad to work for a certain period of time. ······ 70

36. Waste disposal presents increasing problems, especially in urban areas. What do you think are the causes? Give some suggestion to the government and individuals on how to reduce the amount of rubbish. ······ 72

37. Statistics show that cities are increasing in size. What do you think are the causes and possible consequences? ······ 74

38. There are more and more cars in cities. Hence, pedestrians and cyclists are endangered by heavy traffic. Gardens and streets give way to car parks and highways. How can city planners satisfy all people's needs? ······ 76

39. Many people think that countries have a moral obligation to help each other, while others argue that the aid money is misspent by the governments that receive it, so international aid should not be given to the poor countries. Discuss. ······ 78

40. Creative artists should be given the freedom to express their ideas (through words, pictures, music or films). However, some people think government should impose certain restrictions on them. To what extent do you agree or disagree? ······ 80

41. Most countries spend large amount of money on weapons to defend themselves though they are not at war. Some believe those countries should spend the money to help poor countries. To what extent do you agree or disagree with this statement? ······ 82

42. How to measure a country's success? Some say it depends on the quality of citizens' life, but others say it means a prosperous economy. What's your opinion? ······ 84

43. Education is of vital importance to individual development and social progress. What should education consist of in order to fulfill both ends? …… 86

44. It is right that college graduates earn higher salaries than the less well-educated in the community. But they should also pay the full cost of their study. Do you agree or disagree with this statement? …… 88

45. Some people say that the positive effects of advertising outweigh its negative effects. Do you agree or disagree? …… 90

46. Many people are afraid of leaving their house because of crime. Some think more actions should be taken to prevent crime, but others think little can be done. What is your view? …… 92

47. Many people believe that subjects such as music or sports are not useful. Thus school should concentrate on subjects that offer better career prospect. What is your opinion? …… 94

48. Each year some languages die out. Some say this is good because fewer languages would make communication easier and relieve people of the burden of learning foreign languages. Do you agree or disagree? …… 96

49. Is distant learning as effective as school education? …… 98

50. Some say that children should obey their parents and teachers, while others believe that too much control will not help to prepare children for their adult life. Discuss both sides of the views. …… 100

51. Some think we can acquire knowledge from news reports. Others believe we cannot trust journalists. What do you think? What important qualities should a journalist have? …… 102

52. Each year, crime committed by young people is on the rise. What are the reasons? Suggest some solutions. …… 104

53. Some people think that traditional culture is being damaged as it is used as a tool to make money in the tourism industry. Others think it is the only way to preserve and protect culture and tradition. Discuss and state your opinion. …… 106

54. Some think students can learn more effectively in groups, while others think they should study alone. What are the benefits of each method? Which one do you think is more effective? …… 108

55. People are now able to perform everyday tasks such as shopping, banking and business transactions without meeting others face to face. What are the effects on both the individual and the society? …… 110

56. The government should control the amount of violence in films and on television in order to reduce the amount of violent crimes in the society. Do you agree or disagree? …… 112

57. Children are currently having extra classes after normal lessons. What are the positive and negative effects? What is your opinion? …… 114

58. Young children should stay in kindergartens or nursery schools so that their mothers can return to work earlier. Do you agree? …… 116

59. People now spend much time and money on their appearance and pay more attention to their dressing. Give reasons and your opinion on this. ············ 118

60. Many people believe that we have developed into a 'throw-away society' which is filled with plastic bags and rubbish. Do you agree or disagree? ············ 120

61. Some people agree that all kinds of jobs should be equally open to men and women. Others think that some jobs should only be suitable for men and women respectively. Discuss and give your opinion. ············ 122

62. Nowadays college students or even high school students start to work at a younger age. Do you think that it is a positive or negative development? ············ 124

63. Some people think that bicycle is the best way to travel from place to place. Discuss the advantages and disadvantages of the bicycle. ············ 126

64. Modern technology gives people more free time, but actually they are busier than before. Do you agree or disagree? ············ 128

65. Many people think that education is losing its value. Do you agree or disagree? ············ 130

66. Shopping has become a favorite pastime for some young people. Do we need to encourage the young to do something more useful in their free time? What is your opinion? ············ 132

67. Is it necessary to forbid smoking? State your opinion and reasons. ············ 134

68. Education used to be a period of schooling. But now people regard it as a lifelong process. Do you agree or disagree? ············ 136

69. People have different hobbies such as collecting stamps or wood carving. Why are hobbies important to us? How can we benefit from having hobbies? ············ 138

70. What are the advantages of marrying at an early and old age respectively? ············ 140

71. Should people doing different jobs have holidays at different time of the year? What is your opinion? ············ 142

72. Some people like to risk their lives in some dangerous sports such as mountain climbing. Some say rescuers need not risk their own lives to save those trapped on mountain peaks and that people should be responsible for their own lives. What is your opinion? ············ 144

73. Radio will be replaced by other forms of mass media such as TV or the Internet. Do you agree or disagree? ············ 146

74. What are the problems for people living and working in the countryside? What should the government do to solve them? ············ 148

75. Some people say that we should not encourage sports games among schools because they lead to competition rather than cooperation. To what extent do you agree with it? ············ 150

76. Some people regard animals as pets while others see them as a source of food and clothing. What is your opinion? ············ 152

77. Some people believe that damage to the environment is an inevitable consequence of the improvement of living standards. What is your opinion? 154

78. The spread of English and growth of international tourism have some negative effects on countries' languages and traditional culture. To what extent do you agree or disagree? 156

79. Traditional art is a sign of civilization. Do you think government should subsidize musicians, painters, actors or opera companies? What should the government do? 158

80. Many people think that painting and music do not directly improve the quality of people. Therefore, government should not spend too much money on artistic projects. Do you agree or disagree? 160

81. Today, many students take the course International News in secondary school. Some say it is a waste of time. Discuss and state your opinion. 162

82. If you have enough money, will you use it to buy a house or to start a business? 164

83. It is better to be a member of a group than to be the leader of a group. Do you agree or disagree with the statement? Give your reasons. 166

84. Some people say that children should spend their leisure time on educational activities. Some people believe it is dangerous to put too much pressure on children. What is your opinion? 168

85. Some people think that in order to improve the quality of education, high school students should be encouraged to evaluate and criticize their teachers, but other people maintain that such evaluation and criticism may cause loss of respect for teachers and discipline. What do you think? 170

86. Choosing a suitable career is a problem that faces many young people. What are the reasons? What suggestion would you give to them to help them make the right decision? 172

87. Many parents use punishment to teach their kids the differences between right and wrong. They think punishment is necessary in helping them learn the distinction. To what extent do you agree or disagree with these parents? What kind of punishments would you recommend? 174

88. Some people say that telling the truth is not always essential, and that it is necessary to tell lies sometimes. To what extent do you agree or disagree with this statement? Give specific reasons to support your ideas. 176

89. Some say that students with similar academic abilities should be put in one class. Others believe a class should include students with different academic performances. Discuss. 178

90. Some say it is impossible for a woman to work full-time and remain a good mother. So they should be paid by the government to stay at home to raise the children. What is your opinion? 180

91. Your character is strongly influenced by the place where you grew up. In what ways can growing up in a city or in the countryside influence one's character? Please give your view. ········ 182

92. Many people believe that women make better parents than men and that is why they have greater role in raising children in most societies. Others claim that men are just as good as women at parenting. State your point of view. ········ 184

93. There are lots of difficulties for the new students on the first day in a high school or college because they feel lonely. What are the difficulties they may face on the first day? What can the school or college do to solve these problems? ········ 186

94. Some people think that their children's life will be different from their own. What is your opinion? ········ 188

95. Today some people have to work away from their family. What are the advantages and disadvantages? ········ 190

96. Foods are produced more cheaply today by using improved fertilizers and machinery. However, some of the methods used in agriculture are dangerous to human health and local communities. To what extent do you agree or disagree with this view? ········ 192

97. Many old buildings are protected by law because they are part of a nation's history. However, some people think they should be knocked down to make way for new ones because people need houses and offices. How important is it to maintain old buildings? Should history stand in the way of progress? ········ 194

98. The mass media, including television, radio and newspapers, have great influence in shaping people's ideas. To what extent do you agree or disagree with this statement? Give reasons for your answer. ········ 196

99. Surveillance cameras are now installed in many shops and supermarkets to prevent shoplifting. But many people are against this because they think it is a disregard of privacy. What are your views about this? ········ 198

100. It is sometimes said that borrowing money from a friend can harm or damage the friendship. Do you agree? Why or why not? Use specific reasons to explain your view. ········ 200

101. If a five-year old commits a crime, should his/her parents take the responsibility and how should the parents be punished? What should be the age of a child when parents no longer take the responsibility for his or her behavior? ········ 202

102. Participating in a sport is as important for psychological health and social development as it is for physical conditions. What is your opinion? ········ 204

103. The threat of nuclear weapons maintains world peace. Nuclear power provides cheap and clean energy. The benefits of nuclear technology far outweigh the disadvantages. Give reasons for your answer. ········ 206

104. Are famous people treated unfairly by the media? Should they be given more privacy, or is the price of their fame an invasion into their private lives? ········ 208

105. Some countries allow women to join the armed forces, while some others think that armed forces such as navy or army don't suit women. Do you agree or disagree? 210

106. Many people think it's wrong to lock animals up in zoos because it is cruel and serves little purpose. But others think that the animals in zoos can bring happiness to people, especially the kids. What is your opinion? 212

107. Nowadays doctors can become very rich. Maybe they should not focus on profitable activities such as plastic surgery or looking after rich patients but concentrate more on all patients' health, no matter how rich they are. Give your view. 214

108. Should criminals be punished with lengthy jail terms or re-educated and rehabilitated, using community service programs for instance, before being reintroduced to society? 216

109. Many schools demand that the students should wear uniform. Some people think that such a practice undermines students' personality and individuality. What do you think? 218

110. Thanks to modern technology, people are living a longer life. Is it a good thing or a bad one? State your opinion. 220

111. What are the advantages and disadvantages of getting married with a foreigner? 222

112. Are women suitable to become police officers? Give your reasons and examples. 224

113. Some people think that it is the responsibility of the government to ensure that people in the country have healthy lifestyles. Other people believe that individuals should be free to decide their own lifestyles. Please give your own opinion. 226

IELTS

Model Essays

"Chance favors the prepared mind."

(Louis Pasteur)

ESSAY 1

In the past, people spent their entire lives doing one job. But nowadays, they change their jobs frequently. Please give the reasons and your suggestions.

Though the experience of moving from one job to another can sometimes be distressing or even traumatic, thousands of employees move from one job to another in rapid succession every year. Conventional reasons people give for job hopping include lousy bosses, miserable salaries and hostile work environments. Yet the fundamental reason has always been hidden and thus ignored by the general public.

The job hopping frenzy can be attributed mainly to the remarkable social changes taking place nowadays. The 21st century is characterized by the rapid rate of change. Nations around the world are experiencing dramatic shifts in their political, economic and social structures. These shifts have radically changed how people view job hopping. The days when being on a progressive career path meant staying at the same company for life are long gone. Neither employers nor employees directly link long service with loyalty now. Employers no longer think that the number of employers an individual has worked for provided the best measure of loyalty. Instead, they now place more emphasis on ensuring that employees are engaged and committed during the time they spend with them, believing this is more likely to deliver results. This means there is scope for employees to switch jobs with relative ease and take charge of their own progression and development at their own pace.

Despite the irresistible and irretrievable social change, there are things that HR managers can do to improve the current situation. It should be noticed that sometimes employees choose to leave because they find that the jobs or the workplaces are far from what they have expected. The working hours are not as promised, training or promotions don't come through, and managers may have misrepresented pay offers. To narrow expectations, HR managers should sample job experiences before the interview to give job candidates a more complete picture about working in the company.

单词注释

- distressing [dɪˈstresɪŋ] *adj.* 使苦恼的，使烦恼的
- traumatic [trɔːˈmætɪk] *adj.* 痛苦的
- succession [səkˈseʃən] *n.* 连续，连续性
- lousy [ˈlaʊzi] *adj.* 非常糟的，极坏的
- miserable [ˈmɪzərəbl] *adj.* 少得可怜的，太少的
- hostile [ˈhɒstaɪl] *adj.* 有阻碍的，不利的
- fundamental [ˌfʌndəˈmentl] *adj.* 根本的，基本的
- frenzy [ˈfrenzi] *n.* 疯狂
- progressive [prəˈgresɪv] *adj.* 稳步发展的，进步的
- irresistible [ˌɪrɪˈzɪstəbl] *adj.* 不可抵抗的，不能压制的
- irretrievable [ˌɪrɪˈtriːvəbl] *adj.* 不能挽回的，不能复原的
- come through 传出，公布
- misrepresent [ˌmɪsˌrepriˈzent] *v.* 歪曲，不如实地叙述
- sample [ˈsæmpl] *vt.* 取样，采样

过去人们往往一辈子从事同一份工作，而如今人们却频繁地更换工作。请给出造成这种现象的原因以及你的建议。

虽然有时更换工作会让人感到烦恼甚至痛苦，每年还是有成千上万的员工在短时间内连续更换工作。导致员工跳槽的常见原因包括可恶的老板、少得可怜的工资和恶劣的工作环境。然而，最根本的原因却往往被人们忽视了。

跳槽热在很大程度上是由当今社会所发生的巨大变革引发的。急剧的变化，是21世纪的最大特点。世界各国都经历着政治、经济、社会结构等方面的巨大转变。这些转变从根本上改变了人们对跳槽的看法。以往那种必须长期在一间公司工作才可以在职场获得提升的日子已经一去不返了。如今，无论是雇主还是雇员，都不会把长期供职于一间公司与忠诚度联系在一起。雇主们不再认为员工的雇主数目是衡量其忠诚度的最好方法。相反，他们更加看重的是员工是否在供职时全身心地投入工作，因为他们相信这样更有可能取得好的工作效果。这也就意味着，今天的雇员们可以相对容易地改变自己的工作，按自己的节奏来管理自己的职业发展。

虽然社会变化是不可抗拒也不可改变的，人事主管们仍然可以改善当前的状况。需要注意的是，有的时候员工决定离开，仅仅是因为他们觉得工作本身或是工作环境和自己原本所期待的有很大的差异。工作时间与原本承诺的不一样，培训或晋升的机会也迟迟未能公布，人事主管甚至在薪资方面撒谎。为了降低员工的期望值，人事主管应该在面试申请人之前，先做出符合现状的工作样本，让申请人能够更加全面地了解实际的工作情况。

特别提醒

工作的话题，是近几年来雅思考试最热门的话题之一。你现在看到的这篇作文，曾是2007年中国大陆考区第一场雅思考试的作文题。本书收集了以往雅思考过的全部8篇关于工作的文章，请认真参考并适当练笔！

推荐指数 ★★★★★　　**相关题目** 13, 35, 44, 71, 86, 95

写作点拨

这道雅思写作题不仅要求考生给出人们频繁更换工作的原因，而且还要求给出自己的建议，属于典型的“原因+建议”类的雅思写作题。这类文章通常可以如范文一样写成三段。第一段引入话题，第二段介绍原因，最后一段给出作者的建议。

词汇升级

change 的经典搭配：

普通版 The job hopping frenzy can be attributed mainly to the *great social changes* taking place nowadays.

升级版 The job hopping frenzy can be attributed mainly to the *remarkable social changes* taking place nowadays.

change: remarkable(显著的), considerable(相当大的), dramatic(戏剧性的), enormous(巨大的), extensive(广泛的), far-reaching(深远的), fundamental(根本的), momentous(重大的), profound(深刻的), radical(根本的), significant(显著的), irresistible(不可抵抗的), irretrievable(不能复原的)

ESSAY 2

What are the main tasks of universities: to offer students knowledge and skills essential for their future career, or to provide students with access to knowledge itself? What do you think university education should contain?

Universities around the world are now facing the problem of how to efficiently use their resources to serve a larger population of students that are more culturally and socially diversified. To solve the problem, universities should be perfectly aware of their main tasks: providing students with easy access to knowledge and, at the same time, encouraging them to make active contribution to the advancement of human knowledge.

Universities should, first of all, be learning communities where knowledge is not only disseminated but also advanced. As full-fledged members of this community, students should not be information recipients who learn the knowledge in a passive way. Instead, they should be challenged to achieve their potential and, indeed, to excel. Therefore, rather than focus merely on knowledge dissemination and transfer, universities should contrive to provide learning conditions that encourage students to remain curious, to value diversity in opinions and perspectives, and to think critically and communicate effectively. In this way, students can gain problem-solving experience and confidence.

Furthermore, universities will never attain their goals if they tailor all their courses or programs to meet the needs of specific employers or occupational sectors. Today's social environment is more dynamic and turbulent than ever before. Only those graduates who possess certain personality traits and can do well in diversified situations can distinguish themselves from other job applicants.

In order to fulfill the main tasks of universities, university education should contain amply opportunities for independent learning which can cultivate students who are more likely to adapt to the changing society. Students can also learn to exercise their autonomy more effectively, and they may clarify their own professional interests while learning in an independent way.

单词注释

- diversified [daɪˈvəːsɪfaɪd] *adj.* 多样化的
- perfectly [ˈpɜːfɪktli] *adv.* 很，完全，十分
- access to 有权使用
- advancement [ədˈvɑːnsmənt] *n.* 前进，进步
- disseminate [dɪˈsemɪneɪt] *v.* 散布，传播
- full-fledged *adj.* 完全合格的
- passive [ˈpæsɪv] *adj.* 被动的
- excel [ɪkˈsel] *v.* 超越，胜过他人
- perspective [pəˈspektɪv] *n.* 观点，看法
- tailor [ˈteɪlə(r)] *v.* 专门为…制作
- dynamic [daɪˈnæmɪk] *adj.* 动态的
- turbulent [ˈtɜːbjələnt] *adj.* 动荡的
- autonomy [ɔːˈtɒnəmi] *n.* 自主，自主权

大学的主要功能是什么：为学生提供职场必备的知识和技术，还是为学生提供获取知识的途径？你认为大学教育必须包括什么？

如今大学的在校学生人数远胜从前，而且学生的社会、文化背景也比过去更多样化。世界各国的大学都面临着如何有效利用自己的资源来为这些学生提供服务的问题。为了解决这个问题，大学应该明确自身的主要任务：为学生提供接触到知识的便捷方式，同时鼓励他们为人类知识的进步做出贡献。

首先，一所大学应该是一个学习社区。在这里，知识不仅得到传播，而且还被进一步发展。大学生作为这个社区完全合格的成员，他们不应该被动地接受知识。相反，他们应该不停地挑战自己的潜能甚至超越自己的潜能。大学不应该仅仅注重知识的传播，而应致力于为学生提供一个良好的学习环境，鼓励学生保持好奇心、重视不同的意见和观点、批判性地思考以及有效地沟通。通过这种方式，学生可以积累解决问题的经验，并且获得自信。

此外，如果大学设计自己所有课程以满足某一个行业或是某一个雇主的招聘要求，大学将永远无法达成目标。今天的社会环境，风云变幻、难以预测。只有那些个人素质突出、能够在不同的环境下都表现良好的毕业生，才可能从应聘者中脱颖而出。

为了完成自身的主要任务，大学应该为学生们提供充足的自主学习的机会。自主学习可以培养学生更能够适应社会变化。自主学习让学生学会有效地行使自主权，而且让他们逐渐发现自己的职业兴趣所在。

特别提醒

大学教育，是雅思写作考试中出现频率最高的话题，是考生绝对不可以不重视的话题。每一年的雅思写作考试中，大学教育的话题都会出现若干次。本书收集了以往雅思考试里出现过的关于大学教育的文章，其中大多数都在雅思考试中多次出现，请用心阅读这些范文！

推荐指数 ★★★★★

相关题目 6, 14, 24, 43, 44, 49, 65, 68, 93

写作点拨

这道雅思写作题目不仅要求考生给出大学的主要功能，还要求考生指出大学教育的必备内容。考生首先需要决定将写作重点放在“功能”还是“必备内容”上。范文分成四段：第一段引入话题；第二、三段介绍大学的各种主要功能；第四段叙述大学教育的必备内容。考生也可以把文章写成三小段，分别为话题引入、主要功能和必备内容；当然也可以写成四段，用两段来叙述大学教育的各类必备内容。

词汇升级

knowledge的经典搭配：

普通版 Universities should, first of all, be learning communities where *knowledge is not only spread* but also advanced.

升级版 Universities should, first of all, be learning communities where *knowledge is not only disseminated* but also advanced.

knowledge: disseminate（传播）, acquire（获取）, gain（获取）, demonstrate（展现）, parade（夸耀）, flaunt（夸耀）, apply（运用）

ESSAY 3

Should government pay for medical care and education? Why?

State officials and general public have been for years pondering the pros and cons of relying solely on the government for the funding of medical care and education without reaching any definite conclusion. As far as I'm concerned, we should contrive to achieve an appropriate balance of government and personal funding for medical care and education.

First of all, funding of medical care solely by the government can lead to adverse consequences. The advent of the aging society has been accompanied by an increasing demand for medical care. Apparently the government alone can shoulder the onerous financial burden imposed by the medical care of the elderly. As a matter of fact, the balance of cost sharing will inevitably shift dramatically toward the young tax payers, as the government will definitely resort to tax revenue. The sole funding system of the government thus translates into more taxes paid to the government.

Second, the cost of education should be balanced between the individual and the government, as education drives out progress toward a better life both personally and collectively. One of the most important outcomes of education is learning how to learn continuously. Well-educated individuals are not only prepared for well-paying jobs, but they are also able to cope with changes. When a country undergoes change and growth, it relies on its people to adapt and prepare themselves for new opportunities. Every country thus counts on the existence of a pool of civilized citizens to lead the social and economic development. Without a large number of well-educated people in a country, the collective capacity to grow would be severely diminished.

To sum up, the cost of medical care and education should be distributed between the government and the citizens. What is of ultimate importance is that the government make this decision thoughtfully and ensure that the proportion is appropriate.

单词注释

- ponder [ˈpɒndə(r)] *v.* 沉思，考虑
- pros and cons 正反面，事物的利与弊
- contrive [kənˈtraɪv] *v.* 设法做…
- adverse [ˈædvɜːs] *adj.* 不利的，有害的，反面的
- consequence [ˈkɒnsɪkwəns] *n.* 结果
- advent [ˈædvent] *n.* 出现，到来
- apparently [əˈpærəntli] *adv.* 表面上
- onerous [ˈəʊnərəs] *adj.* 繁重的，费力的
- collectively [kəˈlektɪvli] *adv.* 全体地，共同地
- continuously [kənˈtɪnjuəsli] *adv.* 不断地，持续地
- undergo [ˌʌndəˈgəu] *vt.* 经历，经受
- severely [sɪˈvɪəli] *adv.* 十分严重地
- diminish [dɪˈmɪnɪʃ] *v.* (使)减少，(使)变小
- thoughtfully [ˈθɔːtfəli] *adv.* 深思地，仔细地

政府是否应该支付医疗和教育的费用？为什么？

很多年以来，政府官员和普通老百姓都在考虑由政府来支付医疗和教育费用的利与弊，却从来没有得到一个确切的结论。在我看来，医疗和教育的开销应该由政府和百姓以一定的比例来共同承担。

首先，仅仅由政府来支付医疗费用，会引起一些负面的效果。老龄化社会的到来，意味着医疗需求的增加。表面上，政府可以依靠自身力量解决老年人医疗所带来的巨大财务负担。事实上，当政府采取提高税收的方法来解决医疗问题时，这些费用会不可避免地转移到年轻的纳税人身上。单凭政府力量解决医疗费用的制度，最终会导致纳税人需要交更多的税。

其次，教育不仅让个人的生活质量得到提高，同时还提高了社会整体的生活质量。因此，教育的费用应该由政府和个人来分摊。教育最突出的成效之一就是让人们获得了持续学习的能力。接受过良好教育的人，不仅可以获得薪资优厚的工作，而且还可以应对社会的变化。当一个国家经历变革或是发展的时候，它需要依靠自己的国民来适应新的机遇。因而每个国家都需要大量有素质的国民来引领社会和经济的发展。缺少受过良好教育的国民，国家的整体发展能力会受到严重的影响。

总而言之，医疗和教育的费用应该由政府和百姓来分摊。最重要的问题是政府应该谨慎地做这个决定，并确保分配的比例是恰当的。

特别提醒

政府应该如何合理地分配资金，是雅思写作考试中最传统的话题之一，在移民类的考试中出现的频率相对较高。雅思写作考试中出现的这类话题，不仅涉及教育和医疗，而且还涉及艺术发展、传统文化保护等等。这篇内容中的观点比较新颖，值得参考和改写！

推荐指数 ★★★★　　**相关题目** 29, 107, 113

写作点拨

这道雅思写作题目要求考生就“政府是否应该支付医疗和教育的费用”给出自己的观点，属于典型的“观点”类的雅思写作题，代表了雅思中最主要的一种作文题目类型。这类文章有很多种写法，其中剑桥雅思出版的由考官所写的范文中使用最频繁的方法，恰恰是中国考生最容易学会的方法，即如同这篇范文一般“一边倒”。第一段开门见山地摆出自己的观点，然后在文章的主体段落中立场鲜明地给出各种理由，最后一段再次重申观点，同时给出自己的建议。

句型升级

由对立观点引入话题：

普通版 Some people think that...others believe that...

升级版 1. ...and...have been for years pondering the pros and cons of...without reaching any definite conclusion.

2. A major debate in the field of...revolves around the issue of....

例 句 A major debate in the field of children education revolves around the issue of the appropriate time for children to start the learning of a foreign language. 在儿童教育界，关于小孩什么时候适合开始学习外语，有不同的观点。

ESSAY 4

What is it in the mass media that has negative effects on teenagers and what measures should governments take to solve this problem?

The 20th century has witnessed unprecedented advancement in virtually all fields of daily life, and the mass media is no exception. However, everything comes at a price. While we enjoy all the conveniences brought by new ways of disseminating information, our teenagers are adversely affected. There is too much in the media that is harmful to young people.

To begin with, the mass media has become a source of violent scenes and gruesome reports. Today's television programs, for example, are filled with violence and gory sights. Studies have shown that by the age of 18, children, on average, have watched 7000 robberies, 5000 murders and 3000 car chases on TV. What is more, crimes and criminals are often glorified; the victims and sufferings are usually ignored in those programs, for audiences are more interested in the fighting action than the dire consequences.

Also, the availability of adult-only videos and sexually explicit pictures on magazines and various websites contributes greatly to the increase in teenage sexual activities and abortion rate. Girls, as well as boys, are now influenced by stories where teenagers fell in love at first sight and enjoyed passionate love affairs without any commitment, responsibility or health concerns. As a result, they start to experiment with sex at an ever-earlier age.

Impulsive and easily influenced as young people are, they are constantly tricked by advertisements in all forms of media to purchase unnecessary products or spend hours practicing some new ways of keeping fit, which leads to a vast waste of time and money. Moreover, the omnipresent adverts tempt youngsters to pursuit luxurious lifestyles, which are not only unrealistic but also likely to lead teenagers astray.

Prompt measures should be taken to minimize the harmful effects of the media. Stricter censorship code should be implemented regarding the content of television programs and other forms of media. Besides, access to pornography is to be strictly controlled. For instance, children should be barred from Internet cafés and denied access to certain websites. Most importantly, governments should conduct massive educational programs to inform teenagers of the truth about sex, crimes and advertising. Children need to be taught how to distinguish realities from illusions.

单词注释

- witness [ˈwɪtnəs] *v.* 见证
- unprecedented [ʌnˈpresɪdəntɪd] *adj.* 空前的
- advancement [ədˈvɑːnsmənt] *n.* 前进，进步
- virtually [ˈvɜːtʃuəli] *adv.* 事实上，实际上
- exception [ɪkˈsepʃn] *n.* 除外，例外
- convenience [kənˈviːniəns] *n.* 便利，方便
- disseminate [dɪˈsemɪneɪt] *v.* 散布，传播
- teenager [ˈtiːneɪdʒə(r)] *n.* 十几岁的青少年
- adversely [ˈædvɜːsli] *adv.* 不利地，有害地
- violent [ˈvaɪələnt] *adj.* 暴力的，强暴的
- gruesome [ˈgruːsəm] *adj.* 可怕的，恐怖的，令人厌恶的
- gory [ˈgɔːri] *adj.* 血淋淋的，残暴的
- violence [ˈvaɪələns] *n.* 暴力，暴虐
- chase [tʃeɪs] *n.* 追赶，追击
- criminal [ˈkrɪmɪnl] *n.* 罪犯，犯罪者
- glorified [ˈglɔːrɪfaɪd] *adj.* 美其名的，变荣耀的
- audience [ˈɔːdiəns] *n.* 听众，观众
- dire [ˈdaiə] *adj.* 可怕的
- availability [əˌveɪləˈbɪləti] *n.* 可获得性
- explicit [ɪksˈplɪsɪt] *adj.* 外在的，清楚的，不隐晦的
- abortion [əˈbɔːʃən] *n.* 流产，堕胎
- passionate [ˈpæʃənət] *adj.* 充满激情的
- commitment [kəˈmɪtmənt] *n.* 许诺，承担义务
- impulsive [imˈpʌlsɪv] *adj.* 冲动的
- omnipresent [ˌɔmnɪˈpreznt] *adj.* 无所不在的
- luxurious [lʌgˈʒuəriəs] *adj.* 奢侈的，豪华的
- astray [əsˈtreɪ] *adv.* 迷途地，入歧途地
- censorship [ˈsensəʃip] *n.* 审查
- implement [ˈɪmplɪmənt] *v.* 贯彻，实施，执行
- pornography [pɔːˈnɒgrəfi] *n.* 色情文学，淫秽作品
- illusion [ɪˈluːʒn] *n.* 幻想

大众媒体中的哪些内容对青少年产生了负面影响？政府应该采取什么措施来解决这些问题？

在20世纪，我们日常生活的每个方面都得到了史无前例的改进，大众媒体也不例外。但是，这是有代价的。我们在享受信息传播的新方式所带来的种种便利时，我们的青少年却受到了很多负面影响。媒体当中有太多有害于青少年的东西。

首先，媒体是暴力场面和不良报道的来源之一。如今的电视节目充斥着暴力和血腥场面。研究显示，到18岁时，青少年在电视中平均观看了7000场抢劫，5000场凶杀和3000场追车场面。而且，节目当中的犯罪和犯罪分子常常被美化，而受害者及其痛苦却被忽略了，因为观众往往更喜欢看动作场面，而不是其带来的可怕后果。

此外，现在的青少年受到成人影碟、色情杂志和网站的影响，青少年性行为和堕胎率不断增加。现在的男孩和女孩受到浪漫故事的影响，喜欢一见钟情，然后享受性爱激情，完全没有考虑承诺、责任或者身体健康。结果，青少年开始尝试性行为的年龄越来越小。

年轻人容易冲动，容易受影响，所以他们常常上各种媒体广告的当，去购买那些不必要的产品，或者是每天花几个小时去实践某些新的健身方法，浪费了时间和金钱。另外，无处不在的广告还引诱青少年们去追求奢侈的生活方式。这不仅不现实，而且还容易将青少年引入歧途。

我们应该立即采取措施将媒体的负面作用减到最少。电视节目及其他媒体的内容应该进行更加严格的审查。此外，我们应该严格限制色情内容的传播，例如禁止小孩进入网吧，或是禁止他们登录某些网站。最重要的是，政府应该对青少年进行性知识、犯罪、广告知识的普及和教育，应该教会孩子们如何区分真实与幻想。

特别提醒

这道雅思写作题所涉及的儿童教育以及大众传媒两大话题，是雅思中最热门的两个话题。本书收集了近20篇关于儿童教育的文章，以及近10篇关于大众传媒的文章。这两类话题的雅思作文题，不仅数量明显多于其他类话题，而且很多题目还曾多次出现，请考生认真准备！

推荐指数 ★★★★ **相关题目** 17, 23, 32, 45, 51, 56, 73, 98

写作点拨

这道雅思写作题既要求考生给出媒体的危害（观点），又要求考生指出政府应该采取的措施（建议），属于"观点＋建议"类雅思写作题。考生动笔写这类文章之前，应该考虑是把写作的重点放在"观点"上，还是放在"建议"上。由于"建议"会随着不同的作文题而发生很大的变化，对考生的词汇量以及英文表达能力要求比较高，所以建议考生将重点放在"观点"上。范文分为五段：第一段引入话题；第二、三、四段阐述媒体对青少年的危害；第五段指出政府应该采取的措施。

句型升级

so...that...句型

普通版 Young people are so impulsive and easily influenced that they are constantly tricked by advertisement in all forms of media.

升级版 Impulsive and easily influenced as young people are, they are constantly tricked by advertisements in all forms of media.

注释：将原本十分普通的so...that句型改成倒装句，可以让句型结构变得更加多样化，满足"句式多变"这条雅思高分作文必须满足的要求。

ESSAY 5

Nowadays computers are widely used in education. As a result, some people think teachers no longer play important roles in classrooms. To what extend do you agree or disagree?

Invented less than a hundred years ago, computers are now used everywhere, even inside classrooms. While teachers remain more or less the same, computers are doubling in speed and capability every four years. In light of the increasing presence and importance of computers in classrooms, people can't help wondering whether teachers are as important as they once were. As far as I am concerned, teachers still play a major role and are still of great importance.

It is well known that computers are better at repetitive work but incapable of creative thinking. However advanced they may be, computers are nothing more than human contrivances, programmed to perform certain tasks. They are unable to deal with students with different background. Needless to say, a classroom is a place where individual attention and creativity matter most. Therefore, computers are no better than other tools used by teachers and couldn't possibly undermine the roles played by them.

It might be argued that in terms of accuracy and the amount of information, computers outshine humans; but to make a good teacher means far more than being an encyclopedia where one can access all relevant information. Indeed, a good teacher organizes and inspires the students, putting them into different groups and sharing with them his or her own experience and understanding of a certain subject. Instead of being the source of knowledge, a teacher is more like a guide who shows students the right path towards their destination.

Besides, the interaction between students and teachers is vital for the learning. According to most education authorities, real learning occurs during the discussion and sharing of ideas with one's teacher and classmates, which is a task beyond the power of computers. Moreover, a teacher is there to monitor every slight change in students' attitude, to respond to and encourage them whenever they show signs of frustration and impatience. Without this kind of interaction, education is unimaginable.

In conclusion, despite the increasing presence of computers inside classrooms, teachers are just as essential, if not more so, as instructors were in the past. Some inherent drawbacks make it impossible for computers to replace teachers in classrooms where creative thinking and interpersonal skills are vital to ensure success.

单词注释

- repetitive [rɪˈpetətɪv] *adj.* 重复的，反复性的
- incapable [ɪnˈkeɪpəbl] *adj.* 无能力的，不能的
- contrivance [kənˈtraɪvəns] *n.* 发明物
- creativity [ˌkriːeɪˈtɪvəti] *n.* 创造力，创造
- undermine [ˌʌndəˈmaɪn] *v.* 破坏
- outshine [autˈʃaɪn] *v.* 比…更亮，使相形见绌
- encyclopedia [ɪnˌsaɪkləˈpiːdiə] *n.* 百科全书
- destination [ˌdestɪˈneɪʃən] *n.* 目的地
- frustration [frʌsˈtreɪʃn] *n.* 沮丧，懊恼
- unimaginable [ˌʌnɪˈmædʒɪnəbl] *adj.* 想不到的，不可思议的
- drawback [ˈdrɔːbæk] *n.* 缺点，不利条件
- inherent [ɪnˈhɪərənt] *adj.* 固有的，内在的
- interpersonal [ˌɪntəˈpɜːsənl] *adj.* 人与人之间的

如今，计算机已经在教育领域被广泛地运用。因此，有人认为课堂里教师不再发挥重要的作用。你是否同意这样的观点？

不到一百年前人类发明了计算机。如今，它无处不在，甚至已经渗入了我们的课堂。老师们基本没什么变化，可是计算机的速度和性能却每四年就提高一倍。计算机在课堂里越来越普及也越来越重要，人们不禁要问：老师的重要性是否和从前一样呢？在我看来，老师仍然扮演着很重要的角色。

众所周知，电脑擅长做重复性的工作，而不能进行创造性思维。不管有多先进，计算机只是人类的一项发明，通过程序来完成某些任务。计算机无法因人而异地对待不同背景的学生。显而易见，在课堂里，个性和创造力是最重要的。所以，计算机和其他工具一样，也只是教师用来辅助教学的，不可能危及教师本身的重要地位。

或许有人会说，在准确度和信息量方面，计算机要胜过人脑。但是一名好老师远远不只是一本随时能够查阅各种信息的百科全书。事实上，一名好的老师要能够组织学生、启发学生，并且和学生分享自己对某一问题的体验和理解。老师不仅仅是知识的源泉，还是一名向导，指引学生走上通向目的地的正确道路。

另外，教师与学生之间的互动对于学生的学习来说是非常重要的。据教育专家说，真正的学习发生于学生与老师或者学生与学生之间的讨论和交流之中，这是计算机无法做到的。而且，老师还可以察觉学生学习态度的细微变化，可以在学生表现出沮丧和不耐烦的时候及时地鼓励他们。没有这种互动，教育是无法实现的。

总之，尽管计算机已经越来越深入我们的课堂，但是和以前一样，教师的作用仍然是主导性的。由于一些内在的不足，计算机无法在课堂里取代老师。毕竟创造性思维和人际交流才是取得学习成功的重要因素。

特别提醒

计算机的利弊，曾经一度是雅思写作中最热门的话题。但是近年来，关于计算机的利弊的作文题，在雅思写作考试中出现的频率明显下降。如今雅思写作考试中所出现的计算机类的文章，更侧重于计算机是否可以代替教师、代替翻译人员等话题。

推荐指数 ★★★

相关题目 14, 15, 16, 20, 21, 25, 64, 103, 110

写作点拨

这道雅思写作题要求考生就“计算机是否可以取代老师”发表自己的看法，是典型的“观点”类的雅思写作题。范文采用了“观点”类的雅思文章最传统的写法。范文分为五段：第一段摆明观点；第二、三、四段给出论据；最后一段总结全文。这种构思方法虽然不够新颖，但的确是最受推崇的雅思议论文的写法。在Cambridge IELTS真题系列丛书中，由考官写的高分样本中使用最多的正是这种构思法。

句型升级

状语从句：

普通版 Computers were invented less than a hundred years ago.

Computers are now used everywhere, even inside classroom.

升级版 Invented less than a hundred years ago, computers are now used everywhere, even inside classroom.

注释：巧妙地使用状语从句，可以将两个原本句式结构平淡无奇的句子合并成一个句子。

ESSAY 6

Universities should accept equal numbers of male and female students in every subject. Do you agree or disagree?

Since the feminist movement, females have been enjoying increasingly equal opportunities as males do. They account for nearly half of college student population. Some people thus demand complete equality in all subjects in terms of student number. I am, however, strongly against this proposal.

To begin with, the enrolment of men or women in each major should be dependent upon their respective academic performances and overall abilities, rather than some unrealistic percentage quota. Girls usually don't do well in science and thus have little chance of competing against boys in the math department. Similarly, it is hard to find boys studying education, for many of them just don't have the verbal skills or patience to become qualified teachers. Given the differences in their inherent abilities, it is right to expect boys and girls to have separate academic pursuits.

Besides, the natural interests of both sexes should be taken into consideration when we approach this issue. By compelling some girls to study engineering merely to increase the female percentage, universities are forcing them to work against their natural inclination while denying other boys the chance of pursuing their real interests. In general, it is as hard, for example, to persuade male students to learn embroidery as it is to coax a girl to study anatomy. Therefore, students should be given the freedom as to what subjects they would like to learn.

Education being a preparation for their future careers, universities should mark the fact that certain jobs are gender-specific. Take most manual work for example. It is physically unrealistic for a woman to be a construction worker, a plumber or a firefighter. At the same time, men can hardly succeed as nurses or kindergarten teachers. Understandably, gender differences shall be taken into consideration while students are still in college.

It's neither realistic nor necessary to recruit the same number of male and female students. It is not an issue of equality but a matter of choice. Given the difference in abilities and preferences, students shall be given the right to choose for themselves rather than be subject to certain arbitrary quotas stipulating the number of students for each sex.

单词注释

- proposal [prəˈpəʊzl] *n.* 提议，建议
- enrolment [ɪnˈrəʊlmənt] *n.* 登记，入学
- dependent [dɪˈpendənt] *adj.* 依靠的，由…决定的
- respective [rɪsˈpektɪv] *adj.* 分别的，各自的
- quota [ˈkwəʊtə] *n.* 配额，限额
- verbal [ˈvɜːbl] *adj.* 口头的
- inherent [ɪnˈhɪərənt] *adj.* 固有的，内在的，与生俱来的
- pursuit [pəˈsjuːt] *n.* 追求
- compelling [kəmˈpelɪŋ] *adj.* 强制的，强迫的；引人注目的
- inclination [ˌɪnklɪˈneɪʃən] *n.* 倾斜，弯曲，倾度；倾向；爱好
- pursue [pəˈsjuː] *vt.* 追赶，追踪，追击，追求；继续；从事
- embroidery [ɪmˈbrɔɪdəri] *n.* 刺绣品，刺绣；粉饰，装饰
- coax [kəʊks] *v.* 哄；耐心使…
- anatomy [əˈnætəmi] *n.* 剖析，解剖学
- plumber [ˈplʌmbə] *n.* 水管工人
- firefight [ˈfaɪəfaɪt] *n.* 交火，火战，炮战
- kindergarten [ˈkɪndəgɑːtn] *n.* 幼儿园
- recruit [rɪˈkruːt] *n.* 新兵，新分子，新会员 *vt.* 使恢复
- equality [iˈkwɒləti] *n.* 等同性，同等，平等，相等，等式
- arbitrary [ˈɑːbɪtrəri] *adj.* 任意的；武断的，独裁的，专断的
- stipulate [ˈstɪpjuleɪt] *v.* 规定，明确要求

大学是否应该确保每个科目的男女学生数目一致?

自从女权运动兴起以来，妇女已经享有越来越多的与男性平等的机会了。大学里几乎一半的学生是女生。有些人进一步要求这种男女数量的平等，应当体现在所有学科当中。

首先，每个专业录取多少男生、多少女生，应该看学生的学习成绩和综合能力，而不能由一些不切合实际的指标来决定。女孩通常在自然学科方面较弱，因此在数学系里，女孩往往很难和男孩竞争。同样，很少有男孩学习教育学，因为大部分男孩语言能力不强，而且缺乏耐心，很难成为一名合格的教师。由于内在素质的差异，男孩和女孩在学术追求方面就自然会有所不同。

另外，我们还必须考虑男性和女性在兴趣方面的差异。如果为了追求男女数量平等而勉强一些女孩子来学习工程专业，那么就势必有违她们的兴趣，同时又使那些对此真正有兴趣的男孩们失去了学习机会。总之，就像很难劝男生去学刺绣一样，很难劝女生去学解剖。学生应该自由选择他们自己想学的科目。

教育是为学生将来就业做准备的。大学的教育应该要体现这样一个事实：有些工作是有性别倾向性的，例如某些体力活。我们很难想象女性去当建筑工人、水管工，或者消防员。同样，让男性去做护士或者幼儿园教师也不现实。很明显，这些性别差异在大学里就应该被注意到。

保持每个学科的男女数量均衡，这样做既不现实，又没有必要。这并不是男女平等问题，而是个人选择问题。由于两性之间的能力和兴趣的差异，学生们应该有选择的自由，而不是用一些武断的指标来限定男女生的数量。

特别提醒

这道雅思写作题涉及男女性别及大学教育两大话题。大学教育，是雅思中的传统热门话题之一，如今依然是雅思考试中的大热门；男女性别问题，则是近年来雅思考试中新出现的话题。很多考生感觉对男女性别这个话题有点“无话可说”，因此请特别留意范文中出现的各种论据。

推荐指数 ★★★★★

相关题目 2, 14, 24, 43, 44, 49, 65, 68, 93

写作点拨

这道雅思写作题要求考生就“大学是否应该确保每个科目的男女学生数目一致”发表自己的看法，属于“观点”类的雅思写作题。范文的写法比较“冒险”，可以给大家提供一种写作的不同思路。文章的第一段引入话题，却没有直接给出观点。第二、三、四、五段依次给出了反对男女生数目一致的四个理由，结尾段也没有再次重申观点。值得注意的是，写作水平有限的考生应该慎重选择这种方法。

论据积累

大学如何处理男女生比例:

1. 大学录取应该以成绩作为基础，而不是性别。

   The enrollment of men or women in each major should be dependent upon their respective academic performances and overall ability, rather than upon some unrealistic quota.

2. 男女生在兴趣方面本身就有差异。

   The natural interests of both sexes should be taken into consideration when we approach the issue.

3. 很多工作是有职业倾向性的，因此更适合某一种特定的性别。

   Education being a preparation for their future careers, universities should mark the fact that certain jobs are gender-specific.

ESSAY 7

Some people think that children should learn to compete, but others think that children should be taught to co-operate so that they could become more useful adults. State some reasons for both views and give your opinion.

Growing up in a world with ever-increasing population, many children are taught to compete with each other from their earliest memory so as to surpass others. Although this practice is embraced by many, others remain unconvinced of its merits. They insist that for children to achieve greater things in their adulthood they should learn how to co-operate with others.

Those in favour of the ‘competition approach’ argue that competition skills have to be instilled into the children from an early age if they are to merely survive in their future life. Indeed, fierce competition starts from primary school where all students vie to get better grades in order to enter a prestigious university later on. This is followed by constant pressure to outshine one’s co-workers if career advancement is to be achieved. Moreover, instead of being an unavoidable nuisance, competition should be embraced, for it is the driving force behind all our progress. Understandably, people tend to perform better when they strive to beat their opponents, which is the very reason why most athletes run faster in critical races than they do in their training.

On the other hand, opponents of this view also have their reasons. To begin with, to survive and prosper, either at school or in society, co-operation is essential. No one can solely rely on his own talents to achieve academic success. In fact, many key factors that contribute to one’s scholastic achievement such as the instruction from teachers and the exchange of ideas with classmates require co-operation and interpersonal skills. The need to work with and assist each other is also reflected in every organization, be it a company or a laboratory, where teamwork is a prerequisite for all job seekers. Furthermore, if children are taught how to cooperate well with others, they are more likely to establish rapport wherever they go. By helping each other toward the same goal, people form genuine friendship.

Personally, I encourage kids to co-operate with each other. In a world where people become increasingly interdependent, it is imperative to teach our children how to work with rather than against each other.

单词注释

- surpass [sə'pɑːs] *vt.* 超越，胜过
- embrace [ɪm'breɪs] *vt.* 拥抱，欣然接受
- unconvinced [ˌʌnkən'vɪnst] *adj.* 不信服的
- merit ['merɪt] *n.* 优点，价值 *v.* 有益于
- adulthood ['ædʌlthʊd] *n.* 成人期
- fierce [fɪəs] *adj.* 凶猛的，猛烈的，暴躁的
- primary ['praɪməri] *adj.* 第一位的，主要的，初步的
- vie [vaɪ] *v.* 竞争
- prestigious [pre'stɪdʒəs] *adj.* 享有声望的，声望很高的
- nuisance ['njuːsns] *n.* 讨厌的人或东西
- strive [straɪv] *v.* 努力，奋斗
- opponent [ə'pəʊnənt] *n.* 对手，反对者
- prosper ['prɔspə] *v.* 成功，兴隆，昌盛
- essential [ɪ'senʃl] *adj.* 本质的，实质的，基本的
- solely ['səʊlli] *adv.* 独自地，单独地
- scholastic [skə'læstɪk] *adj.* 学校的，学校教育的
- prerequisite [ˌpriː'rekwəzɪt] *n.* 先决条件 *adj.* 首要必备的
- seeker ['siːkə] *n.* 搜索者，探求者
- genuine ['dʒenjuɪn] *adj.* 真实的，真正的
- interdependent [ˌɪntədɪ'pendənt] *adj.* 相互依赖的，互助的
- imperative [ɪm'perətɪv] *adj.* 绝对必要的

有人认为儿童应该学会竞争，而别的人却认为我们应该教会儿童如何互相合作，因为这样他们才能够成为对社会有用的人。请就两个观点给出你的理由和见解。

在如今这样一个人口不断增长的世界里，孩子们还在刚刚开始记事的时候，就被教育要同别人竞争，要出人头地。尽管很多人赞成这种做法，但有些人却表示怀疑。他们认为，要想孩子在长大成人时取得成就，就必须从小教他们学会如何与人合作。

那些赞成“竞争教育法”的人认为，要想孩子在将来社会中生存，必须从小就灌输竞争精神。事实上，人们从小学开始就有了激烈的竞争，学生们互相竞争，想要得到更好的成绩，以便将来考上名牌大学。参加工作后，又要和同事竞争，以争取职业生涯的发展。而且，竞争不是一种挥之不去的烦恼，而是我们进步背后的推动力量。不难理解，人们在和对手竞争的时候，总是发挥得更好些。这也就是大部分运动员在重大比赛时的成绩要比平时好的原因。

另一方面，反对这种观点的人也有他们自己的理由。首先，不管是在学校，还是在社会上，要生存就必须要学会合作。没有人能够仅靠自身的才能取得学业成就。事实上，对取得学业成就至关重要的很多因素，比如来自老师和同学的帮助，都需要学生具备合作和人际交往的能力。在任何机构里，不管是公司还是实验室，都需要大家互相帮助和协作，团队精神是所有工作者都需要具备的。如果教会了孩子们如何与人合作，不管他(她)走到哪里，都很容易形成一种亲和力。为了共同的目标互相帮助，在此过程中，人们还能够培养真诚的友谊。

从我个人来讲，我鼓励孩子们相互合作。在如今这样一个人与人之间越来越相互依赖的世界里，要教会孩子们互相合作，而不是互相恶性竞争，这一点是很必要的。

特别提醒

儿童教育，是雅思中最热门的话题之一，在雅思写作考试中占据了最大的比例。本书收集了近20道儿童教育方面的雅思写作题。事实上，考生现在看到的这道作文题，在雅思考试中就曾出现过4次，请用心整理这类话题的作文中常用的论据！

推荐指数 ★★★★★　　**相关题目** 5, 26, 27, 28, 47, 49, 50, 54, 57, 75, 81, 84, 85, 87, 89, 109

写作点拨

这道作文题给出了两种完全不同的观点，要求考生就两种观点分别进行论证，而且还要给出自己的观点，属于“论述＋观点”类的雅思作文题。这类作文题最安全的写法就是范文中的四段式：第一段引入话题，第二段和第三段分别给出正、反观点的理由，最后一段亮出自己的观点。

词汇升级

competition 的经典搭配：

普通版 Indeed, strong competition starts from primary school where all students vie to get better grades in order to enter a prestigious university later on.

升级版 Indeed, fierce competition starts from primary school where all students vie to get better grades in order to enter a prestigious university later on.

competition: cut-throat (凶狠的), intense (激烈的), keen(强烈的), serious(严重的), severe (残酷的), stiff (强烈的), tough(严酷的)

ESSAY 8

The culture of different countries are becoming increasingly similar, so there is no point for people to go traveling abroad for they could have the same experience at home. Do you agree or disagree?

Granted that cultures in various countries start to resemble one another, which is by no means to a large extent, it is still worthwhile to travel to other countries to appreciate what can only be obtained on a foreign soil.

Superficially, the world's culture is merging faster than we expected or could tolerate. That is partly why people get the same experience no matter where they go. If travel means to get on a plane, to stay in some hotel, to go to some museums and to do some shopping, then it could be quite alike in all the major cities around the world. But traveling should not be limited to this narrow sense. It means much more and therefore renders each trip a new experience.

To travel is to get to know the local people. People may wear the same kind of clothes, eat the same kinds of food and do similar jobs, but they are different from country to country. An ordinary Chinese could hardly believe that a totally stranger in America will dismantle his own bike and replace your ruptured tyre with one of his own if he has never been to that country. Media reports and second-hand information can never compare with your personal interaction with the local people during your stay there.

Apart from knowing the people, traveling affords you incomparable opportunities to appreciate the natural beauties of a foreign country. Admittedly, the Internet, satellite TV and multi-media technology are bringing the world closer to us. It is now easy to view exotic landscapes on a screen in the comfort of your home; virtue reality technology promises three dimensional experiences at the touch of a fingertip. However, is this vicarious experience really satisfying? Hardly. Travel brings us closer to nature, the wonders of which can only be truly appreciated first hand.

There is hope that technology will one day supply all the experiences we ever wish to have, which sounds exhilarating yet perhaps also disconcerting—it reminds me of the movie *The Matrix*. Also people will remain unique enough to excite our desire to meet them in person.

单词注释

- resemble [rɪˈzembl] *vt.* 像，类似
- worthwhile [ˌwɜːθˈwaɪl] *adj.* 值得做的，值得出力的
- obtain [əbˈteɪn] *v.* 获得
- superficially [ˌsuːpəˈfɪʃli] *adv.* 浅薄地
- tolerate [ˈtɔləreɪt] *vt.* 忍受，容忍
- render [ˈrendə] *vt.* 呈递，归还
- dismantle [dɪsˈmæntl] *v.* 拆除
- rupture [ˈrʌptʃə(r)] *v.* 破裂，裂开 *n.* 破裂
- incomparable [ɪnˈkɔmprəbl] *adj.* 无与伦比的，不能比较的
- admittedly [ədˈmɪtɪdli] *adv.* 公认地，诚然
- landscape [ˈlændskeɪp] *n.* 风景，山水画 *v.* 美化
- virtue [ˈvɜːtʃuː] *n.* 德行，美德
- dimensional [daɪˈmenʃnl] *adj.* 空间的
- vicarious [vɪˈkeəriəs] *adj.* 代理人的
- exhilarating [ɪɡˈzɪləreɪtɪŋ] *adj.* 令人喜欢的
- disconcerting [ˌdɪskənˈsɜːtiŋ] *adj.* 令人不安的，令人惊惶的
- excite [ɪkˈsaɪt] *vt.* 刺激，使兴奋

世界各国的文化正趋于同质化。因此，人们没有必要再出国旅游，因为可以在本国就获得同样的感受。你是否同意这样的观点？

即使不同国家的文化逐渐趋于同一(虽然目前这一趋势并不明显)，我们仍然应该去其他国家观光旅游，去感受一下当地特有的风土人情。

从表面上看，世界文化的融合速度之快超出了我们的预期，甚至让我们无法容忍。正因为如此，人们不管走到哪里，经历都大同小异。如果旅行仅仅意味着坐坐飞机、在旅馆里待待、去博物馆逛逛、到商场购购物的话，那么去全球各大城市旅游的感觉都会非常相似。但是旅行不应该这么狭义。旅行的含义很广，因此每次旅行人们都可能有新的体验。

旅行就是要去了解当地人。人们的衣着可能大同小异，吃的东西可能相差不大，做的工作也相似，但是不同国家的人是不同的。如果没有到过美国，一个普通的中国人可能很难相信，在美国，一个陌生人看到你的自行车轮胎破了，会拆下他自己的给你换上。很多东西通过媒体报道和二手资料是无法体会的，必须与当地人亲自交往才行。

旅行除了能让我们了解当地人，还提供了无与伦比的机会去领略外国的自然风光。不可否认，互联网、卫星电视和多媒体技术把我们与世界拉得更近。如今人们待在家里就能轻松地在屏幕上观赏到异国风光；虚拟现实技术让我们动动手指就能进行三维体验。然而这种间接体验真的能让人满意吗？很难。旅行使我们更加亲近大自然，它的奇妙只有亲自经历才能真正地体会到。

也许有一天科技可以为我们带来我们所希望的各种体验。这听起来振奋人心但同时也令人不安——这使我想到《骇客帝国》这部电影。人们总是彼此不同，各具特点，单这一点就值得人们不断去旅行。

特别提醒

文化问题，是雅思写作考试中最传统的话题之一，但是在近年的雅思考试中却少有涉及；旅游观光，反而在近几年雅思考试中时有涉及。考生可以将本篇范文的学习重点放在旅游题材的雅思文章的写作准备上。

推荐指数 ★★★　　**相关题目** 35, 53, 78

写作点拨

这道雅思作文题要求考生就“有没有必要出国旅游”发表自己的看法，属于“观点”类的雅思作文题，是雅思作文考试中最常见的题目类型。范文分成5段：第一段开门见山地亮出自己的观点；第二、三、四段分别叙述出国旅游的各个理由；最后一段总结全文。

论据积累

出国旅游的意义：

1. 不能狭义地认为旅游就是逛街、购物。
   Traveling should by no means be limited to the narrow sense of shopping.
2. 世界各国的人有很大的不同。
   People in different countries will remain unique enough to excite our desire to meet them in person.
3. 旅游让我们有机会体会到异国的自然风光。
   Traveling affords you incomparable opportunities to appreciate the natural beauties of a foreign country.

ESSAY 9

Some people think that people will forget their own tradition and history because they no longer wear their traditional costumes. Do you agree or disagree?

In cities around China, western style clothes of all sorts are worn by people, to the extent that many people under a certain age are no longer sure what constitutes our traditional costumes. This, however, doesn't indicate that they are losing touch with their history and tradition.

People's preference to certain kinds of apparel has little to do with their attachment to their history and tradition. Consumers' choices to purchase or wear certain clothes are often influenced by fashion. Each year, the fashion industry is coming up with new types of clothes, sometimes unnecessarily, to maintain the huge profits. Men, as well as women, fall victim to this enticement.

The abandoning of traditional clothes is sometimes necessitated by the changing lifestyle. As far as China is concerned, the gowns worn two hundred years ago would certainly get in the way in our daily life today. The hectic life most people lead nowadays requires costumes that can offer comfort and convenience. This is more a matter of practicality than of preference.

Therefore, people forgo traditional costumes solely out of other considerations; it hardly contributes to forgetting their history and custom. Traditional costume is only one reminder of one's tradition, nothing more. Education plays a far more important role in enhancing one's understanding of one's history and culture. Sometimes, the more we let go, the more we can retain.

Thus, we need not to be alarmed that traditional clothes don't find favor with many people, especially the young. It is by no means a betrayal of the past or tradition. History and tradition should be borne in mind rather than merely put on our body.

单词注释

- constitute [ˈkɒnstɪtjuːt] *vt.* 组成，任命
- indicate [ˈɪndɪkeɪt] *vt.* 指出，显示，象征
- preference [ˈprefərəns] *n.* 偏爱，优先选择
- apparel [əˈpærəl] *n.* 衣服，装饰
- attachment [əˈtætʃmənt] *n.* 附件，依恋，拥护
- influence [ˈɪnfluəns] *n.* 影响，感化 *vt.* 影响，改变
- enticement [ɪnˈtaɪsmənt] *n.* 诱惑，怂恿，引诱
- necessitate [nəˈsesɪteɪt] *v.* 成为必要
- hectic [ˈhektɪk] *adj.* 脸上发红 *n.* 脸红
- practicality [ˌpræktɪˈkælətli] *n.* 实用性
- forgo [fɔːˈgəu] *vt.* 作罢，放弃
- reminder [rɪˈmaɪndə(r)] *n.* 提醒的人，暗示
- enhance [ɪnˈhɑːns] *vt.* 提高，增强 *v.* 提高
- betrayal [bɪˈtreɪəl] *n.* 出卖，辜负

有人认为，因为人们不再穿传统服装，所以他们会忘记自己的传统和历史。你是否同意这样的观点？

在中国的很多城市，西式服装非常流行，很多一定年龄层以下的年轻人甚至不知道什么是我们的传统服装。然而这并不能表明他们正在忘记历史和传统。

人们对服饰的偏好与拥护历史传统几乎没有什么联系。消费者选择购买的服装常常受到时尚的影响。不管有没有必要，时装界每年都会设计出各种新式服装以保持巨大的利润。男人也和女人一样，成为时尚诱惑的牺牲品。

生活方式的变化有时必然导致人们放弃传统服装。就中国而论，两百年前流行的长袍无疑会妨碍我们今天的日常生活。现在多数人过着紧张忙碌的生活，他们需要舒适便利的服装。人们选择服装其实往往是出于实用考虑，而并非是个人偏好。

其实，人们放弃传统服装只是出于别的考虑；这不会令他们忘记历史和风俗。穿传统服装可以让我们想起传统，但也仅此而已。教育在增强人们对历史和文化的理解方面会起到更重要的作用。有的时候放弃得越多，获得的也越多。

由此可见，虽然传统服装不受到许多人尤其是年轻人的垂青，但我们不必惊慌。这绝不是对过去或传统的背叛。历史和传统应该记在心里，而不仅仅是穿在身上。

特别提醒

服装的问题，在雅思写作考试中属于比较冷门的话题，出现的频率很低。但是这道题目曾经难住了很多雅思考生，因为很多人词汇量不够，不认识题目中出现的costume这个单词。所以，在学习这篇范文之前，请你熟背单词costume(装束，服装)。

推荐指数 ★★★★　　**相关题目** 10, 53, 78, 97

写作点拨

这道作文题属于简单的“观点”类题目，是雅思作文考试中最常见的题目类型。范文第一段开门见山地亮出了全文的观点，第二、三、四段分别叙述各个论据，最后一段总结全文。

词汇升级

放弃

普通版 People give up traditional costumes solely out of other considerations.

升级版 People forgo traditional costumes solely out of other considerations.

放弃：abandon, abjure, abnegate, desert, discard, forsake

ESSAY 10

Traditional food is undergoing great changes and being replaced by new diets. What do you think are the reasons and what do you think about this phenomenon?

People in different countries have quite different traditional food. Even for people in the same region, the food they enjoy today is far from the same as those consumed by their grandparents. The trend is accelerating.

Scientific and technological development is the driving force behind this change. Our ancestors used to produce and preserve food without the benefit of modern technology, which often results in some ingenious ways of handling food. But with the demise of those special skills and the advance of food technology, food is produced quite differently nowadays. For example, whereas we now put a premium on fresh vegetables, people in the past often ate pickles because it was otherwise impossible to preserve vegetables for a long time.

The change in lifestyle also contributes to the change in traditional food. The fast-pacing modern life allows employees little time to cook meals. Thus, many choose fast foods for breakfast and lunch and eat a full meal for supper. As a result, those time-consuming traditional food is replaced by ready made, easy-to-cook convenient foods.

Lastly, the traditional food is also challenged by imported diets from other countries. Global economic integration has allowed restaurants to be opened in foreign countries. Restaurants catering to different nationalities provide city residents with a wide range of choices. Under the influence of exotic diet, traditional foods invariably experiences some changes and makes certain adjustments so as to have a broader appeal.

While it is a pity to lose some traditional foods to foreign imports, it is too sentimental if we hang on blindly to traditional food just for the sake of keeping the tradition. Change often means improvement. It is hardly wise to always eat the same food regardless of the changing lifestyle and technology.

单词注释

- consume [kən'sjuːm] *v.* 消耗
- accelerate [ək'seləreɪt] *v.* 加速
- preserve [prɪ'zɜːv] *v.* 保护
- ingenious [ɪn'dʒiːniəs] *adj.* 独特的
- demise [dɪ'maɪz] *n.* 死亡 *vt.* 让渡
- premium ['priːmiəm] *n.* 额外费用，奖金
- pickle ['pɪkl] *n.* 腌渍品 *vt.* 腌，泡
- lastly ['lɑːstli] *adv.* 最后，终于
- integration [ˌɪntɪ'greɪʃn] *n.* 综合
- resident ['rezɪdənt] *n.* 居民 *adj.* 居住的
- influence ['influəns] *n./vt.* 影响
- exotic [ɪg'zɒtɪk] *adj.* 异国情调的
- adjustment [ə'dʒʌstmənt] *n.* 调整，调节
- appeal [ə'piːl] *n.* 吸引力
- sentimental [ˌsentɪ'mentl] *adj.* 感伤的
- blindly ['blaɪndli] *adv.* 盲目地

传统的食物发生了巨大的变化，同时也正逐步被新的食物代替。你认为造成这种现象的原因是什么？你如何看待这种现象？

每个国家的传统食品都不尽相同。即使是在相同的地区，如今人们享用的食物与祖辈们的佳肴也相差甚远。这一趋势正日渐明显。

科学技术的发展为人们的饮食变化推波助澜。在以前，我们的祖先没有现代科学技术，所以常常使用一些独特的方法来生产和保存食物。随着这些特殊工艺的失传以及食品科技的发展，现在的食品生产加工方式与以前已经大不相同了。例如我们现在强调吃新鲜蔬菜，但是过去人却常常吃咸菜，因为当时人们只有把蔬菜腌制起来才能长期保存。

生活方式的改变也促进了传统食物的变化。由于现代生活的节奏很快，工薪阶层们很少有时间自己下厨做饭。很多人早饭和中饭都选择吃快餐，晚餐则吃一顿丰盛的。结果，费时的传统食物渐渐被现成的、容易烹饪的方便食物取代。

其次，传统食品也受到其他国家的进口食物的挑战。全球经济一体化为人们在国外开设饭店提供了方便。如今各大城市都拥有各种国家的特色饭店，为城市居民提供了多种选择。在外来食物的影响下，传统食品总会发生一些变化，做出一些调整，以吸引更多的消费者。

虽然一些传统食物被外来食物替代有点可惜，但是如果我们仅仅为了保存传统而盲目地坚持传统食物那就太感情用事了。毕竟，变化常常意味着进步。不顾及生活方式和科技的变化而总吃相同的食物是很不明智的。

特别提醒

食物的问题，在雅思写作考试中属于比较冷门的话题，出现的频率很低。这篇范文介绍了食物的变化，同时阐述了这些变化背后的原因，考生做一般了解即可。

推荐指数 ★★

相关题目 96

写作点拨

这道雅思写作题不仅要求给出饮食发生变化的原因，同时还要求考生给出自己对这一现象的看法，属于“原因＋观点”类型的作文题。这类作文题是雅思作文考试中最新的作文题目类型之一，在近年的雅思考试中占据了较大的比例。范文分为五段：第一段引入话题；第二、三、四段分别介绍了引起食物发生变化的各个原因；第五段对该现象进行评论，给出作者自己的看法。

词汇升级

盲目坚持

普通版 It is too sentimental if we *stick to* traditional foods *in a unwise way* for the sake of keeping the tradition.

升级版 It is too sentimental if we *hang on blindly to* traditional foods just for the sake of keeping the tradition.

盲目坚持：cling blindly to sth., grasp sth. tightly, hang on blindly to sth.

ESSAY 11

Some people think the Olympic Games will no longer play an important role in the 21st century, and the 2004 game should be the last one. Do you agree or disagree?

The Olympic Games has been with us for centuries. It was only interrupted by the world wars. Despite all its imperfections, it never fails to catch the heart and imagination of millions around the globe. It will and should last for centuries to come.

People get to know each other through the Olympic Games. There is a saying, if people can meet on the field of sports they won't want to meet on the battle field. Every four years, athletes from five continents get together to participate in the summer games. Billions around the world tune in to watch those athletes compete more against themselves than against their rivals in their unrelenting drive towards personal best. It is one of those rare occasions when people from different nations and backgrounds are engaged in the same activities and able to form genuine friendship.

In addition, enormous economic benefits are generated by the Olympic Games, not only for the host nations but other countries as well. A country's tourism, international trade and global status can get a tremendous boost by hosting the Olympic Games, which partly explains the intensity of the competition as countries vie for the right to host the Olympic Games. For the world at large, the game also serves to promote business in related fields, such as advertising, sports wears and soft drinks.

Admittedly, critics may be upset by the problems related to these international events, bribery, drug abuse, unfair competition, to name but a few. However, these are by no means inherent, and can be remedied. There is nothing wrong with the game itself; it's the management that leaves much to be desired.

In short, the Olympic Games is going to play even greater roles in the coming century. We shall have the Games as long as we play sports. There is, of course, no end to the improvement of the Olympic Games.

单词注释

- imperfection [ˌɪmpəˈfekʃn] *n.* 不足，缺陷
- continent [ˈkɒntɪnənt] *n.* 大陆，陆地
- rival [ˈraɪvl] *n.* 竞争者 *v.* 竞争
- unrelenting [ˌʌnrɪˈlentɪŋ] *adj.* 不宽恕的
- genuine [ˈdʒenjuɪn] *adj.* 真实的，真正的
- tourism [ˈtʊərɪzəm] *n.* 观光事业，游览
- status [ˈsteɪtəs] *n.* 身份，地位，情形
- tremendous [trəˈmendəs] *adj.* 极大的，巨大的
- boost [buːst] *n.* 增长，提高
- intensity [ɪnˈtensəti] *n.* 强烈，亮度
- bribery [ˈbraɪbəri] *n.* 行贿，受贿，贿赂
- abuse [əˈbjuːz] *v.* 滥用[əˈbjuːs] *n.* 滥用，虐待
- unfair [ˌʌnˈfeə(r)] *adj.* 不公平的
- inherent [ɪnˈhɪərənt] *adj.* 固有的，内在的
- remedy [ˈremədi] *v.* 治疗，补救

有人认为奥运会在21世纪将不会再发挥重要的作用，因此2004年的奥运会应该成为最后一届奥运会。你是否同意？

奥林匹克运动的历史可以追溯到一千多年以前。除了在世界大战期间中断过以外，奥林匹克运动一直延续至今。尽管奥运并不完美，但它总是能赢得全球无数人的心。奥运会一定而且也应该持续发展、常盛不衰。

通过奥林匹克运动人们可以彼此认识。俗话说：如果人们能在运动场上相见，他们就不会想刀兵相见了。每隔四年，来自五大洲的运动员们齐聚一堂，参加夏季奥林匹克运动会。全球数十亿观众通过电视看到的是这些运动员们的自我拼搏、挑战极限，而不是他们与对手之间的残酷竞争。奥运会提供了为数不多的机会让来自不同国家和背景的人们参与同一项活动，并由此建立真正的友谊。

此外，奥林匹克运动会能为东道国和其他国家带来巨大的经济效益。通过举办奥林匹克运动会，东道国的旅游、经贸和全球地位会得到极大的提升。这也正是为什么奥运会主办权的竞争会如此激烈。从全球范围来看，奥运会促进了相关领域的发展，例如广告、运动服饰和饮料等等。

诚然，批评家可能会因为奥运引起的一些问题而懊恼。贿赂、滥用药物、不公平竞争就是其中的几例。然而这些都不是奥运会的必然产物，都是可以避免的。奥运本身没有问题，不过其管理和操作还有很多有待改善之处。

总之，奥运会在未来将发挥更大的作用。只要我们还热衷运动就会有奥运会。当然奥运会的改进工作是永无止境的。

特别提醒

今天回头看这道昔日的雅思写作题，难免感觉有点荒谬。虽然因为时限的原因，这道题目不可能再次出现在雅思考试中，但体育类的话题却在雅思考试中时有涉及。本书的雅思真题库里收集了5道关于体育类话题的雅思真题。此外，本篇范文里出现了“让步段”，请认真参考！

推荐指数 ★★★

相关题目 34, 72, 102

写作点拨

这道雅思题要求考生就“奥运会是否应该停办”给出自己的观点，属于“观点”类的作文题。范文分为五段：第一段立场鲜明地指出了奥运会的必要性，确定了全文的思路；第二、三段指出了支持奥运会的各种理由。整篇范文最值得借鉴的是第四段。这一小段为“让步段”。在全文已经确立“支持奥运会”的这一背景下，用一小段文字来指出奥运会的缺点，让观点更加全面。第五段总结全文，再次重申了作者的观点。

论据积累

体育比赛的意义：

1. 通过体育比赛，人们互相了解。

   People get to know each other through sport games.

2. 体育比赛带来了巨大的商业利益。

   Sport games generate enormous economic benefits, not only for the host nations but other countries as well.

3. 体育比赛避免了战争和民族冲突。

   If people can meet on the field of sports, they won't want to meet on the battle field.

ESSAY 12

In most parts of the world, the volume of traffic is growing at an alarming rate. Discuss the main traffic problems in your country, their causes and possible solutions.

As the largest developing country, China is enjoying rapid economic growth, the evidence of which can be seen in all major cities whose streets are teeming with thousands of vehicles of all kinds. Unfortunately, traffic problems invariably ensue.

City dwellers are most vexed by traffic congestion. One can be stuck in the traffic for hours during rush hours in Guangzhou where I live. Cars and buses often advance at a snail pace even outside rush hours because there are always some cars ignoring traffic rules, holding up hundreds of cars. Worse still, accidents are increasing daily. With more cars on road, it becomes harder to navigate your vehicle out of a collision course with other cars, bikes, or people. Each year thousands die or get injured in traffic accidents, not to mention the incalculable property damage.

Traffic accidents and congestion need not to be a necessary evil. Something can be done to reduce them. To begin with, measures should be taken to reduce private car ownership. Increased taxes on gasoline will do well to dampen many people's enthusiasm for buying a car. In addition, most traffic wardens need to be posted in busy intersections to regulate the flow of traffic. Most accidents occur because people start to take chances when there isn't a policeman around. Accidents can be vastly reduced if all of us abide by traffic rules. A well developed public transport system is the ultimate solution. Cheap and reliable, public transport offers comfortable rides to everyone. It is the most energy and space efficient way to travel in cities unless all people choose to walk or ride bikes, which seems unlikely.

Progress often has its casualties and prices to pay. The promise of speed and safety offered by private cars is becoming harder to fulfill each day. Sound planning and measures are required to tackle traffic problems.

单词注释

- teem [tiːm] *v.* 充满
- ensue [inˈsjuː] *v.* 随之而来
- vex [veks] *v.* 激怒
- snail [sneɪl] *n.* 蜗牛
- navigate [ˈnævɪgeɪt] *v.* 航行
- congestion [kənˈdʒestʃən] *n.* 堵塞
- dampen [ˈdæmpən] *v.* 泼冷水
- abide [əˈbaɪd] *v.* 遵守
- casualty [ˈkæʒuəlti] *n.* 死亡

在很多国家，汽车的总量正在以令人担忧的速度增加。请论述你所在国家的主要交通问题以及这些问题产生的原因和解决方法。

作为最大的发展中国家，中国的经济正飞速发展。在各大主要城市，成千上万的车辆挤满了街道。然而不幸的是，令人头疼的交通问题也接踵而至。

交通堵塞令城市居民非常头疼。在我所居住的广州，如果遇上交通高峰期，你可能会被困在车里一两个小时。即使不在高峰期，车辆也只能以蜗牛的速度缓慢行驶，因为总有些车辆无视交通规则继而导致塞车。更糟糕的是，交通事故几乎每天都在增长。由于道路上的车辆日益增加，避开别的车辆、自行车甚至是行人，都变得越发困难起来。每年都有几千人在交通事故中死亡或是受伤。更不要说由此带来的财产损失。

交通事故和交通堵塞并非不可避免。我们可以采取相应的措施来加以防范。首先，我们应该采取措施减少私家车的数量。提高汽油税可以有效地遏制人们购车的热情。此外，应该在繁忙的十字路口配置更多的交警以疏导交通。大部分的交通事故都是因为没有交警在场而导致人们违规冒险所致。如果我们所有人都遵守交通规则，那么就能够大幅度减少交通事故。发达的公共交通系统是解决问题的最终办法。公共交通给人们提供了既廉价又舒适的乘车服务。除非人人都骑车或者走路（这是不可能的），否则公共交通就是最节约能源和最节约空间的交通方式。

进步总是伴随着伤亡和代价的。私家车越来越难以做到既快速又安全。要解决交通问题，就必须合理地规划并采取有效的措施。

特别提醒

交通问题，曾经一度是雅思写作考试中最热门的话题之一；这道作文题就曾经在雅思考试中出现过 6 次。但是近年来，交通的话题在雅思考试中却少有涉及，仅需要作一般了解。

推荐指数 ★★★　　**相关题目** 38, 63

写作点拨

这道写作题要求考生叙述所在地区的主要交通问题，并且给出这些问题的原因和解决方法，属于“叙述 + 原因 + 建议”类的作文题。动笔写这类规定内容较多的文章前，应该仔细考虑内容的分配问题，即如何尽可能地在照顾到各个板块的内容的同时突出文章的重点。范文分为四段：第一段引入话题；第二段具体介绍了现存的交通问题；第三、四段给出了原因和相应的解决方法。

句型升级

定语从句

普通版 China is the largest developing country and is enjoying rapid economic growth. As a result, in the streets of major cities in China, there are thousands of vehicles of all kinds.

升级版 As the largest developing country, China is enjoying rapid economic growth, the evidence *of which* can be seen in all major cities *whose* streets are teeming with thousands of vehicles of all kinds.

解析：巧妙地两次使用定语从句，可以将若干个原本句型结构非常普通的句子连接成一个句式巧妙的句子。

ESSAY 13

The world of work is changing rapidly. People today no longer take one job for life. Discuss the causes of these changes. What suggestions would you make for young people to prepare themselves for the work in future?

Job hopping is more common in developed countries like America or France. But even in countries traditionally renowned for job security or life-long employment, people are getting used to employment change. The causes are manifold.

On the employers' side, many of them no longer offer adequate pensions and fringe benefits to their long-time employees. Thus, employees see no point in working there all the time and are ready to leave because the financial loss will be inconsequential. Besides, long-time employees are no longer highly valued by the management. Many companies prefer a 'change of blood' from time to time to maintain their competitiveness and vitality. Older workers are replaced because they long lost their enthusiasm for work and hamper innovation by always doing things the old way.

However, employees also have their reasons to seek new employment. Most of them would leave a job when they feel there is nothing to learn doing that job. Due to intense competitions, people see the need to improve their abilities and competitiveness by acquiring as much work experience as possible. Moreover, people nowadays are more concerned about their interest in work. The first job they find may be boring but an indispensable stepping stone towards worthier employment. More often than not, they never know what they are after until they find it. The promise of better things to come keeps them hopping from one job to another.

My advice to young people would be to follow your heart. Life is very long; there is no point sticking to one job unless you really enjoy it. Try until you get the job where your interest lies. Besides, everything changes over time, including you and your interest. So when you feel the urge to change, go for it.

单词注释

- hop [hɒp] *v.* 单脚跳，(鸟、蛙等)跳跃
- job hopping 跳槽
- renowned [rɪˈnaʊnd] *adj.* 著名的
- fringe [frɪndʒ] *n.* 边缘
- inconsequential [ɪnˌkɒnsɪˈkwenʃl] *adj.* 无足轻重的
- competitiveness [kəmˈpetɪtɪvnɪs] *n.* 竞争力
- vitality [vaɪˈtæləti] *n.* 活力，生命力
- enthusiasm [ɪnˈθjuːziæzəm] *n.* 狂热，热心
- hamper [ˈhæmpə] *vt.* 妨碍
- innovation [ˌɪnəˈveɪʃən] *n.* 创新
- indispensable [ˌɪndɪsˈpensəbl] *adj.* 不可或缺的

职场正发生着巨大的变化。今天的人们不再一辈子只做一份工作。请讨论这些变化产生的原因并给准备参加工作的年轻人一些建议。

跳槽在美国和法国等发达国家更为普遍。但是如今，即使是在以稳定工作或终生雇佣而闻名的国家，人们对于换工作也逐渐变得习以为常了。造成这种现象的原因是多种多样的。

从雇主的角度来说，越来越多的雇主不再为老员工提供充足的养老金和其他福利。因此，员工们觉得在一个地方工作一辈子并没有太大的意义。由于跳槽的经济损失不大，人们更加倾向于换工作。此外，管理层也不像以前那样非常看重老员工。许多公司喜欢经常"换血"以保持自身的竞争力和活力。老员工失去了对工作的激情，做事往往墨守成规而妨碍了创新，所以常常被新员工取代。

但是，员工也有自己跳槽的原因。大部分人在感觉一份工作已经没有什么东西可学的时候，就会跳槽了。由于竞争很激烈，人们往往觉得有必要积累尽可能多的工作经验以提高自己的能力和竞争力。而且，现在的人更讲究工作的兴趣。第一份工作很可能索然无味，但却是通向更好的工作的必不可少的过渡阶梯。人们经常是遇到自己需要的，才知道自己真正想要什么。为了追求更好的，人们总是不断地跳槽。

我给年轻人的建议是：听从内心的声音。人生漫长，没有必要只干一份工作，除非你真的喜欢它。不断寻找，直到找到你感兴趣的工作。另外，事情总会不断变化，你自己和你的兴趣也不例外。所以，当你感觉想有所改变的时候，不妨大胆去改变。

特别提醒

工作的话题是近几年来雅思写作考试的大热门。你现在看到的这篇作文，曾经以不同形式在雅思考试中出现过 7 次。本书收集了以往雅思考过的近 10 篇关于工作的文章，其中有若干道作文题与这道题目仅仅是在文字表述方面有所不同，意思则一模一样，请认真复习！

推荐指数 ★★★★★　　**相关题目** 1, 44, 71, 86, 95

写作点拨

这篇文章不仅要求给出人们频繁更换工作的原因，而且还要求给出建议，属于"原因 + 建议"类的雅思作文题。范文分成四段：第一段引入话题；第二、三段介绍不同的原因；最后一段给出作者的建议。这类文章亦可以写成三段：第一段引入话题，第二段写原因，最后一段写建议。

论据积累

人们更换工作的原因：

1. 社会变化使得雇员可以轻松地找到新工作，按自己的节奏来管理自己的职业发展。

   Remarkable social changes mean that there is scope for employees to switch to jobs with relative ease and take charge of their own progress and development at their own pace.

2. 更换工作与否不再是衡量员工忠诚度的标准。

   Employers no longer think that the number of employers an individual has worked for provides the best measure of loyalty.

3. 工作环境和原本所期待的有很大的差异。

   Employees find that the jobs or the workplaces are far from what they have expected.

4. 公司倾向于不停地更换员工来保持活力。

   Many companies prefer a "change of blood" from time to time to maintain their competitiveness and vitality.

ESSAY 14

As science and technology contribute most to the development of society, science students should get more financial support from government than students in other fields (eg. business, language, etc.). To what extent do you agree or disagree with this statement?

Never in history was science and technology so emphasized as in modern society. One is most likely to get a scholarship for graduate study overseas if he or she majors in science or technology. However, this lopsided emphasis seems ungrounded.

It is quite debatable that science and technology contribute more to human progress. Notwithstanding the achievements and miracles made possible by science, numerous issues cannot be solved by science or technology. Social issues such as juvenile delinquency, racial discrimination and moral degradation are all beyond the scope of science. Modern people are more often plagued by problems of the heart, instead of the body. The material wealth generated by science and technology often pales against the peace of mind brought by art or literature.

Besides, the amount of financial aid should be based on the students' academic performance. How much financial support a student is to receive should be determined on an individual basis. Grants or scholarships should not be lavished upon those without real interest in or dedication to a scholarly pursuit, whereas those with real potential should be offered adequate financial support lest they get distracted by working part time to pay for their education. No matter what major they are in, the foremost criteria for receiving financial aid should be their academic potential. Thus, it is not justified to favor science majors more than other students.

In a larger sense, all subjects are vital to human progress. It will be a hopeless attempt to compare the importance of each subject. Financial support should be granted to those with real potential.

单词注释

- lopsided [ˈlɒpˈsaɪdɪd] *adj.* 不平衡的
- debatable [dɪˈbeɪtəbl] *adj.* 可争议的
- notwithstanding [ˌnɒtwɪθˈstændɪŋ] *prep.* 虽然，尽管
- miracle [ˈmɪrəkl] *n.* 奇迹，奇事
- juvenile [ˈdʒuːvənaɪl] *adj.* 青少年的
- delinquency [dɪˈlɪŋkwənsɪ] *n.* 行为不良
- discrimination [dɪˌskrɪmɪˈneɪʃn] *n.* 歧视
- degradation [ˌdegrəˈdeiʃən] *n.* 堕落
- plague [pleig] *vt.* 折磨；使苦恼
- lavish [ˈlævɪʃ] *v.* 浪费
- dedication [ˌdedɪˈkeɪʃən] *n.* 投入
- lest [lest] *conj.* 唯恐，以免，免得
- distract [dɪˈstrækt] *vt.* 分散，转移
- foremost [ˈfɔːməust] *adj.* 最先的；最重要的
- criteria [kraɪˈtɪəriə] *n.* 标准

科技为社会进步做出的贡献最大，所以学科技的学生应该比别的专业(例如商业、语言等)的学生获得更多的财政支持。你是否同意这样的观点?

有史以来，科学技术从来没有像现在这样受到重视。如果所学的专业与科技有关，学生获得奖学金到国外深造的机会就会大幅增加。但是，这种过分的重视似乎并没有根据。

科技是否对人类的进步做出了更大的贡献是很值得商榷的。尽管科技取得了很多成就，甚至很多的奇迹，但仍然有很多问题是科技无能为力的。青少年犯罪、种族歧视、道德败坏等社会问题都是科学不能解决的。现代人更多的时候是为心理问题所困扰，而不是生理问题。科技所带来的物质财富在艺术和文学给人们带来的心灵宁静面前显得苍白无力。

此外，一个学生能得到的经济援助应该由其学业成绩来决定，而且应该单独对待、因人而异。奖学金或助学金不应该发给那些对学术追求没有真正兴趣、缺乏奉献精神的人，而应该发放给那些有学术潜力的学生，以免其为了付学费而做临时工影响学业。不管是什么专业，考虑给学生发放经济援助与否的最重要标准应该是他们的学术潜力。所以，不应该偏向于科学专业的学生。

从更高的意义上来说，对于人类进步而言，所有的学科都是重要的。我们无法比较究竟哪个学科更重要些。经济援助应该发放给那些真正有潜力的学生。

特别提醒

科技和艺术，孰轻孰重，是这道雅思写作题向广大考生提出的问题。科技和艺术之间，社会资源如何才能恰当地分配，是雅思写作考试中最常见的话题之一。这篇范文中使用了一种不太常见的方法来展开论证，请认真体会和学习。

推荐指数 ★★★★★

相关题目 2, 6, 24, 43, 44, 49, 65, 68, 93

写作点拨

这篇范文的观点提炼以及对应的论证方法，与大多数中国考生的写法有所不同。题目中给出了一个“因果”型的观点：因为科技对社会进步做出的贡献最多，所以科技类学生应该获得更多的财政资助。考生往往会从“果”，即科技类学生应该获得更多的财政资助来展开论证。范文却首先提出题中给出的“因果”观点的“因”本身就有问题，即科技并没有做出最多的贡献，进而展开论证。这种论证的方法，很值得写作思路不够开阔的考生借鉴。

词汇升级

重要的

普通版 All subjects are *important* to human progress.

升级版 All subjects are *vital* to human progress.

All subjects are *vitally* important to human progress.

重要的：weighty, of great importance, notable, noteworthy, fateful, critical, momentous

修饰“重要的”的副词：critically, crucially, enormously, extremely, hugely, terribly, vitally

Many parents believe that preschool education is critically important yet overlooked in today’s society.

很多家长认为学前教育是极其重要的，而今天的社会却恰恰忽视了学前教育。

ESSAY 15

Nowadays people can use computers to talk, learn and communicate without leaving home. There is a danger that it will cause more isolation and a lack of communication among people. To what extent do you agree or disagree with this statement?

Invented some 60 years ago, computers have already transformed the way most of us live. The advent of the Internet opens up the possibility of communicating and interacting via the computer. With more time spent on computers and less with each others, people start to fear the dehumanizing effect of this wonderful human contrivance. This inordinate concern is quite groundless.

One doesn't necessarily become isolated if he spends most of his time alone using a computer. Isolation only occurs when one is obsessed by his own affair and cares nothing about anything else. Indeed, many feel isolated and lonely in the midst of crowds or even while talking to others because they are trapped in their own world or because others are in theirs. Alienation of people is not caused by how little they talk or meet each other but by the lack of interest in our fellow creatures and the world at large. Hence, computers actually help to prevent isolation by bringing every possible field of interest onto the screen. Everything is at the touch of a fingertip. You can broaden your interests and enrich your life by accessing whatever and whoever you are interested in.

As far as communication is concerned, the using of computers is by no means detrimental. In primeval times our ancestors communicated by a simple system of shouts and gestures. Then spoken and written languages developed. We now prefer emails to ordinary letters. Our mode of communication is forever changing. Why should computers be singled out as particularly deleterious? What matters is not whether or not we communicate in the orthodox or traditional ways but the very fact that we do communicate. Indeed, computer technology facilitates the exchange of ideas and information. The Internet keeps us linked to each other all the time. Apart from the usual emails, chat rooms and forums, tele-conferencing is being employed daily to enhance communication. Communication is made easy by technology, which promises infinite possibilities ahead.

Thus, communication and isolation must not be defined in a narrow sense. Problems arise not from technological development but from people themselves. Computer is but a tool, the misuse of which it is not responsible for.

单词注释

- transform [træns ˈfɔːm] *vt.* 改变
- advent [ˈædvənt] *n.* 出现，到来
- via [ˈvaiə; ˈviːə] *prep.* 通过，经由
- dehumanize [diː ˈhjuːmənaɪz] *vt.* 使失掉人性，使成兽性
- contrivance [kən ˈtraɪvəns] *n.* 发明
- inordinate [ɪn ˈɔːdɪnət] *adj.* 过量的
- isolation [ˌaɪsə ˈleiʃən] *n.* 分离
- obsess [əb ˈses] *vt.* 迷住，使困扰
- alienation [ˌeɪliə ˈneɪʃən] *n.* 疏远
- detrimental [ˌdetri ˈmentl] *adj.* 有害的
- primitive [prɪmətiv] *adj.* 原始的，远古的
- ancestor [ˈænsestə] *n.* 祖先，祖宗
- deleterious [ˌdeləˈtɪəriəs] *adj.* 有害的
- orthodox [ˈɔːθədɔks] *adj.* 正统的，传统的
- infinite [ˈɪnfɪnət] *adj.* 无限的

如今，人们使用电脑足不出户就可以进行交流和学习。这有可能会造成人和人之间的隔阂，使得人与人之间缺乏交流。你是否同意这样的观点？

人类在六十年前发明的计算机已经改变了大多数人的生活方式。互联网的出现则使得人们能够利用计算机进行沟通和交流。人们花在电脑上的时间多了，花在同他人交往上的时间少了，于是人们开始对这项人类伟大发明所带来的非人性效果感到恐惧。这种过度的担忧其实是杞人忧天。

即使一个人花了很多时间在电脑上，也不一定就会与世隔绝。真正的隔绝其实是指一个人过分专注于自己的事情，对其他一切都置之度外。事实上，很多人即使身处人群当中，甚至在和别人谈话的过程中，仍感到孤独寂寞，因为他已经深深陷入了自己的世界当中，或者因为他周围的人陷入了他们自己的世界当中。总的来说，人与人之间的疏远不是因为人们交谈或见面的时间少了，而是因为人们对他人、对世界失去了兴趣。所以，计算机其实有助于防止这种人与人的隔绝，因为计算机把大家在各种领域的可能的共同兴趣都集中到了屏幕上。一切都可以在指尖上实现。不管你对什么事情、什么人物感兴趣，你都可以通过计算机接近你感兴趣的人和事，进而拓宽你的兴趣爱好，丰富你的生活。

从沟通的角度来看，使用计算机也没有任何坏处。在远古时代，我们的祖先通过一套简单的喊叫和手势来交流。然后，出现了语言和文字。现在我们更喜欢用电子邮件代替传统邮件。我们的沟通方式在不断地改变。为什么要单单指责计算机的害处呢？重要的不是我们是否通过传统的方式沟通，而是我们是否真正地进行沟通。事实上，计算机技术为我们交换想法和信息提供了方便。互联网使我们时时刻刻都相互联系在一起。除了电子邮件，我们每天还使用聊天室、论坛、远程会议等来加强我们之间的沟通与交流。科技使我们的沟通变得容易了，为我们开辟了无限的机会。

所以，不能狭隘地看待沟通与交流。相关的问题不是技术发展带来的，而是产生于人们自身。计算机只是工具，它的滥用不能归咎于计算机本身。

特别提醒

这篇范文所涉及的计算机的问题，曾经一度是雅思考试中最热门的话题，但是近年来，关于计算机的优缺点的文章，在雅思考试中出现的频率明显下降。阅读本篇范文时请将学习的重点放在词汇上，因为本篇范文的词汇难度非常适合，既杜绝了过于低级的词汇，也没有出现过于生僻的难词，非常符合雅思高分作文的要求。

推荐指数 ★★★ **相关题目** 18, 55

写作点拨

这道作文题属于传统的“观点型”写作题，要求考生就一个问题给出自己的看法。范文的第一段一针见血地指出了题目中的观点是 groundless(没有根据的)，第二、三段指出反驳该观点的理由，第四段总结全文，属于比较稳妥的写作方法。

论据发散

电脑是否阻碍交流制造隔阂：

1. 不能狭隘地理解交流和隔阂，在电脑屏幕前花很多的时间不等于缺乏交流、与世隔绝。
   Communication and isolation must not be defined in a narrow sense. Alienation of people is not caused by how little they talk or meet each other but by lack of interest in our fellow creatures or the world at large.
2. 计算机让大家有了共同的兴趣，促进了人们之间的共鸣。
   Computers help to prevent isolation by bringing every possible field of interest onto the screen.
3. 不同的时代有不同的交流方式，电脑就是最新的交流工具。
   Our mode of communication is forever changing and computers represent the latest way of communication.

ESSAY 16

Some people think that machine translation is highly developed in today's society. Therefore it is not necessary for children to learn a foreign language. What's your opinion?

It will be good news for school children when they are told that foreign language is no longer a required subject because translation can all be done by machines. But is it wise to be so optimistic even after taking account of the advance in machine translation? Personally, I rather doubt it.

Computer-aided translation is far from doing a satisfactory job at the present stage of development. Machine translation has encountered seemingly insurmountable obstacles when dealing with written language. For example, it is having a hard time recognizing rhetorical expressions such as metaphors, puns and irony, which, it must be admitted, can sometimes present problems to common readers as well. When it comes to interpreting spoken languages, machine translation is further crippled by the mediocre performance of speech recognition technology. Thus, translators and interpreters are in no danger of losing their jobs in the foreseeable future.

Moreover, even if machine translation were able to eradicate all the language barriers between peoples, would there be no point in learning foreign languages? By no means, in the process of studying a language, one gets interested in its people, its culture, and its society. By understanding their language, we start to understand the people, for the language often exerts a subtle influence upon its people. What's more, each language is unique. The beauty of a language is what fascinates the students. French is known to be a romantic language; Chinese is renowned for its flexibility; Japanese for its politeness. All those distinctions would be lost if they are translated into one's own language.

The happy scenes in *Star Trek* where people from different planets can communicate comfortably with a 'translation machine' still belong to science fiction. And I would still encourage students to learn foreign languages even after such machines are made available.

单词注释

- required [rɪ ˈkwaɪəd] *adj.* 必需的
- optimistic [ˌɒptɪ ˈmɪstɪk] *adj.* 乐观的
- insurmountable [ˌɪnsə ˈmaʊntəbl] *adj.* 不能克服的，不能超越的
- rhetorical [rɪ ˈtɒrɪkl] *adj.* 修辞的
- metaphor [ˈmetəfə] *n.* [修辞] 隐喻，暗喻
- pun [pʌn] *n.* 双关语
- irony [ˈaɪərənɪ] *n.* 反语，讽刺
- cripple [ˈkripl] *vt.* 削弱
- mediocre [ˌmiːdɪ ˈəukə] *adj.* 不太好的，平庸的
- foreseeable [fɔː ˈsiːəbl] *adj.* 可预知的，能预测的
- eradicate [ɪ ˈrædɪkeɪt] *vt.* 根除
- exert [ɪg ˈzɜːt] *vt.* 施加(影响等)
- subtle [ˈsʌtl] *adj.* 难以捉摸的，微妙的
- flexibility [ˌfleksə ˈbɪlətɪ] *n.* 灵活性
- distinction [dɪs ˈtiŋkʃən] *n.* 特征；差别

有人认为，如今机器翻译已经达到了很高的水平，所以小孩没有必要学习外语。请给出你的看法。

外语不再是必修课(因为可以使用机器翻译)，这对于在校的学生来说将是一个好消息。尽管机器翻译取得了一些突破，但是由此便如此乐观是明智之举吗？就我个人而言，这是很不明智的。

现阶段的计算机辅助翻译还远远不能令人满意。在进行书面翻译的时候，机器翻译会遇到似乎不可逾越的障碍。例如，它难以识别修辞手法如比喻、双关和讽刺，当然也必须承认，这些手法有时也会给普通读者带来问题。在翻译口头语言时，机器翻译由于性能平平的语音识别技术而愈发无能为力。因此在今后很长一段时间内，笔译和口译译员们没有失业的危险。

此外，即使机器翻译真的能清除人们之间所有的语言障碍，学习外语就完全没有意义吗？当然不是。在学习语言的过程中，你会对整个民族、文化和社会产生兴趣。通过理解他们的语言，我们可以渐渐了解某个民族，因为语言往往对人们有潜移默化的影响。更重要的是，语言是独一无二的。各种语言的魅力往往让语言学习者为之着迷。法语是众所周知的浪漫语言；汉语以其灵活性而著称；日语因礼貌而闻名。如果将所有的外语都翻译成母语，那么我们就无法体会外语本身的种种特点。

影片《星际旅行》中来自不同星球的人们可以使用“翻译机”进行自由交流，这些情景仍是科学幻想。即使这种机器真的出现，我还是会鼓励学生们继续学习外语。

特别提醒

这篇范文所涉及的儿童教育的问题，一直是雅思考试中最热门的话题，在每年的雅思写作考试中都占据了相当的比例。同时，这篇文章所提及的“机器翻译”的问题，在一些关于计算机的雅思写作题中也有所涉及。

推荐指数 ★★★　　**相关题目** 5, 14, 15, 20, 21, 25, 64, 103, 110

写作点拨

这道作文题要求考生就“机器翻译高度发达的今天小孩子是否有必要学外语”这一问题给出自己的看法，属于传统的“观点型”写作题。范文采用了最稳妥的写作方法，第一段开门见山地提出观点，第二、三段给出理由，第四段总结全文。

句型升级

设问句

普通版 Even if machine translation were able to eradicate all the language barriers between peoples, learning foreign languages still makes sense.

升级版 Even if machine translation were able to eradicate all the language barriers between peoples, would there be no point in learning foreign languages? By no means, ...

点评：Cambridge ESOL 提供的雅思写作评分标准中清楚地指出，句式多样化是高分作文必备的条件。在不妨碍表达的情况下，考生应该在文章中使用尽可能多的句型，向阅卷人展示自己驾驭各类句式结构的能力。

ESSAY 17

Some people say that the age of books has passed; information can be accessed via videos, computers, television, films and so forth. Other people think books and written words will still be essential for information dissemination and education. Discuss both sides and give your opinion.

Books have been with us for thousands of years. Are they going to become obsolete like so many other products once deemed indispensable? Under the onslaught of technology progress, books seem increasingly outdated. However, the total numbers of books published each year is increasing defiantly.

It must be admitted that books are increasingly being replaced by other types of storage devices. Books are not suited for the storage of video and audio materials. Besides, compact disks and other new storage devices outstrip books in terms of storage capacity, cost effectiveness and user friendliness. It is said that all the books in an average library can be stored in dozens of compact disks, which also allow the user to search, copy, and paste, all with a few strokes of the keyboard. Interaction between the reader and material is also made possible by computer technology.

Meanwhile, there are strong signs that books are going to remain with us for a long time. Books are by far the most convenient way to disseminate information. Just count the number of magazines published each day around the world. They are cheap, easy to carry and don't require electricity. Besides, a book allows you to read at your own pace: you can pause to ponder when necessary or you can skip some tedious parts. Books are tangible and give you a sense of achievement when you finish one whereas the completion of an e-book affords less satisfaction.

We can rest assured that books would and should not be replaced by some novel electronic devices. We have seen the folly of such doom day predictions for the radio with the advent of television. The fact remains that different types of media actually complement rather than replace each other. There is every possibility that books will remain and improve as time goes by.

单词注释

- obsolete [ˈɒbsəliːt] *adj.* 荒废的，陈旧的
- indispensable [ˌɪndɪsˈpensəbl] *adj.* 不可缺少的
- onslaught [ˈɒnslɔːt] *n.* 冲击
- defiantly [dɪˈfaɪntli] *adv.* 挑战地，对抗地
- compact [kəmˈpækt] *adj.* 紧凑的，紧密的
- outstrip [autˈstrɪp] *vt.* 超过
- paste [peɪst] *vt.* 粘贴
- keyboard [ˈkiːbɔːd] *n.* 【计】键盘
- disseminate [dɪˈsemɪneɪt] *vt.* 散布
- ponder [ˈpɒndə] *vt.* 沉思，考虑
- tedious [ˈtiːdɪəs] *adj.* 单调乏味的，沉闷的
- tangible [ˈtændʒəbl] *adj.* 切实的
- whereas [(h)weərˈæz] *conj.* 然而，反之
- folly [ˈfɒlɪ] *n.* 愚蠢，荒唐事
- complement [ˈkɒmplɪmənt] *vt.* 补充，补足

有些人认为书籍的时代已经一去不复返了；人们可以通过音像、电脑、电视、胶片等各种方式获得信息。还有些人认为书籍以及书面文字在信息传播以及教育过程中仍是不可或缺的。请论证这两种观点，并给出你自己的观点。

书籍的历史可以追溯到数千年前。它们会不会像其他许多曾被认为不可或缺的产品一样被历史淘汰？随着科技的不断发展，书籍似乎变得日益过时了。然而，书籍的年出版总量却在不断增加。

必须承认书籍正日益被其他形式的存储设备所替代。书籍不适合存储图像及声音素材。此外，电脑光盘及其他新的存储设备在存储容量、成本和用户操作便利性等方面都超过了书籍。据说一个中型图书馆的全部书籍都可以保存在几十张电脑光盘里，这样用户只需要敲一敲键盘就能够查找、拷贝和粘贴了。计算机技术的发展使得读者和资料间的互动成为可能。

与此同时，书籍也很有可能在很长一段时期内被人们广泛使用。书籍是传播信息最便利的方式。算算全球每天杂志的发行量吧。它们便宜，便于携带且不耗电。而且书籍允许你按自己的速度阅读：必要时你可以停下来思考，或者跳过一些乏味的部分。书籍是有形的，你读完一本书便能获得很大的成就感，而读完一部电子书却不会让人感到太大的满足。

我们可以大放宽心，因为书籍不会、也不该被某些新潮的电子设备所代替。人们曾经预言收音机会因为电视的出现而遭淘汰，我们已经看到了这些预言的荒唐可笑。事实表明不同的媒介是相互补充而不是彼此替换的。随着时间的流逝，书籍将不断改良，长盛不衰。

特别提醒

这篇范文所涉及的大众传媒以及信息传播的问题，是雅思考试中的传统热门话题，在每年的雅思考试中都有涉及。范文中的很多观点具有很强的可迁移性，可以应用到其他的雅思作文中。例如：范文中列举的图书的各种优势，也可以用于另外一道雅思真题中来论证为什么电子邮件不可以代替手写书信。

推荐指数 ★★★★★ **相关题目** 4, 23, 32, 45, 51, 56, 73, 98

写作点拨

这道作文题要求考生就两个相反的观点进行论证，并且给出自己的观点，属于“正反观点＋个人观点”类型的作文题。这类作文题通常可以使用这篇范文所采纳的写作构思，第一段引入话题，第二、三段分别论证正反两个观点，最后一段提出自己的观点。

词汇升级

不仅没有减少，反而增加

普通版 increase rather than decrease

升级版 increase defiantly

increase: considerably（相当地）, dramatically（戏剧性地）, defiantly（对抗地）, significantly（明显地）, enormously（非常地）, sharply（急剧地）, steeply（险峻地）, substantially（充分地）, exponentially（成倍地）

ESSAY 18

Television is dangerous because it destroys the family tie and community spirit. It is said by some that television absorbs so much of people's time that they have no time to talk to each other. To what extent do you agree or disagree? Give your opinion.

Ask someone what he did last night and you will often get the answer that he or she was watching television. Yes, TV has made itself seemingly indispensable in the modern society, providing hours of entertainment each day. However, all these recreations come at a price.

Contrary to what people expect, TV alienates family members by absorbing their time and attention which can otherwise be given to each other. Superficially, the parents and children who sit in front of a TV are supposed to spend some quality time together. But in fact, they are glued to the screen, receiving passively what is offered by the producers. There is no lively discussions, no exchange of views, but only occasional fights over which channel to watch. The time spent watching TV could have been used far more effectively to communicate with each other and strengthen family ties.

People's social life is also affected by the advent of television. Before the age of television, people used to socialize more in the community. After dinner, men would get together to discuss work and politics while women exchanged gossips. Close community ties often can't withstand the onslaught of TV programs, which induces people to shut the door, sit on the couch and stare at the screen. People become less likely to play a game of chess or basketball with their neighbors. TV has robbed them of other more worthwhile activities.

Television by itself is not detrimental to improving family ties and community spirit. However, our undue dependency upon it alienates us from our loved ones and neighbors. Nothing would please me more than to see TV be given its proper treatment.

单词注释

- indispensable [ˌɪndɪsˈpensəbl] *adj.* 不可缺少的
- recreation [ˌrekrɪˈeɪʃ(ə)n] *n.* 消遣，娱乐
- contrary [ˈkɒntrərɪ] *adj.* 相反的
- alienate [ˈeɪljəneɪt] *vt.* 疏远
- superficially [ˌsuːpəˈfɪʃəli] *adv.* 表面上地
- glue [gluː] *vt.* (全神贯注地)盯着看
- occasional [əˈkeɪʒnəl] *adj.* 偶然的
- strengthen [ˈstreŋθən] *vt.* 加强，巩固
- advent [ˈædvənt] *n.* 到来
- socialize [səʊʃəlaɪz] *v.* 使社会化
- gossip [ˈgɔsɪp] *n.* 闲话，闲谈
- withstand [wɪðˈstænd] *vt.* 抵挡，经受住
- onslaught [ˈɒnslɔːt] *n.* 冲击
- induce [inˈdjuːs] *vt.* 劝诱，促使
- detrimental [ˌdetrɪˈmentl] *adj.* 有害的
- undue [ˈʌnˈdjuː] *adj.* 不适当的

电视是危险的，因为它破坏了家庭成员之间的联系以及团体精神。据说电视占据了人们大多数的时间，以至于人们无暇交谈。你是否同意这样的观点？

如果问某人昨晚做了些什么，他的回答往往是看电视。没错，在现代社会中电视似乎变得必不可少了，因为它每天都为人们提供数小时的娱乐。然而这一切都是有代价的。

让人们始料未及的是，电视占据了人们大量的时间和精力，导致家庭成员间没有时间交流，关系变得疏远。表面上看起来父母与子女坐在电视前，共同渡过了无数的美好时光。但实际上，他们总是两眼直盯着电视机，被动地接受制片商们制作的各种节目。他们之间没有激烈的讨论，没有观点的交流，只会偶尔为看哪个频道而发生争执。花费在看电视上的时间本来可以更有效地用于相互沟通、增强家庭成员的联系。

人们的社交生活也受到电视的影响。在电视时代之前，人们常常更多地参加社会活动。晚餐后男人们会聚在一起讨论工作和政治，而妇女们会聚在一起闲聊。紧密的邻里关系无法抵挡电视节目的冲击。有了电视以后，人们总是关上房门，坐在沙发上盯着电视屏幕看。人们渐渐不去和邻居下一盘象棋或打一场篮球赛了。因为电视，他们不再去参加更有价值的社会活动。

电视本身并不会损害家庭关系和团体精神。然而我们对电视的过度依赖使得我们与爱人和邻居渐渐疏远。如果人们能恰当地对待电视，我将欣喜无比。

特别提醒

这篇范文所涉及的大众传媒的问题，是雅思考试中的传统热门话题之一。雅思写作题目不仅有关于电视的题目，还有关于互联网、报纸等其他媒体的文章。关于各种媒体的优缺点的文章，其实有不少相通的观点和论据，请注意收集和整理。

推荐指数 ★★★★★ **相关题目** 22, 55

写作点拨

这道作文题要求考生就给定的观点进行论证，属于“观点论证”型的作文题，是雅思中最传统和最常见的作文类型。这类作文题通常可以使用这篇范文所采用的写作构思，第一段给出观点，第二、三段分别给出论据，最后一段再次重申自己的观点，并在可能的情况下给出建议。

论据收集

电视破坏人际关系、家庭关系：

1. 电视占据了人们大量的时间和精力，导致家庭成员间没有时间交流，关系变得疏远。
   TV alienates family members by absorbing their time and attention which can otherwise be given to each other.
2. 有了电视以后，人们总是关上房门，坐在床上盯着电视屏幕看，紧密的邻里关系无法抵挡电视节目的冲击。
   Close community ties often can't withstand the onslaught of TV programs, which induces people to shut the door, sit on the couch and stare at the screen.
3. 看电视的时候，人们之间没有激烈的讨论，没有观点的交流，只会偶尔为看哪个频道而发生争执。
   There is no lively discussions, no exchange of views, but only occasional fights over which channel to watch.

ESSAY 19

People who do not know how to use computer will become more and more disadvantaged. State the disadvantages and what action governments should take.

It has been predicted by some futurists that people in future will be divided into two categories: the technologically savvy and the technologically illiterate. Needless to say, the latter will become underprivileged and manipulated. Notwithstanding some exaggeration, this is true for the computer illiterate.

Without adequate computer skills, finding employment may prove increasingly challenging. Invented just 50 years ago, the computer is becoming an integral part in all fields of business, from banking to shoe making. Computers are used to write reports, analyze data and design products. No wonder computer skills are now taken for granted by employers just as the ability to read and write. Apart from a few manual jobs, most positions require a fair command of computer.

Additionally, the computer illiterate will encounter problems in daily life. So extensively are computers used that it is impossible not to come into contact with them in everyday life. When you go to an ATM to withdraw some money, you have to operate on a computer. When you want to find a book in a library, you are faced with a computer. Lacking computer skill, you can't even send an email, which leads us to the most alarming consequence of being a computer illiterate.

Lagging behind your peers is the most devastating result. The ignorance of computer severely curtails your chances for personal development. Your education and job will get nowhere if you fail to tap into the enormous potentials offered by computer. Even your personal relationship will suffer because you can't use the Internet to keep in touch with your friends. While others are making progress, you are standing still.

Much needs to be done by the government to help this disadvantaged group. Education is the best medicine. Preferably, computer training should be made compulsory and free of charge for the students and enough training centers should be set up to provide low-cost training for adults.

单词注释

- predict [prɪˈdɪkt] *vt.* 预知，预言
- futurist [ˈfjuːtʃərɪst] *n.* 未来学家
- category [ˈkætəgərɪ] *n.* 类别
- savvy [ˈsævɪ] *n.* 实际知识，技能
- illiterate [ɪˈlɪtərɪt] *adj.* 不识字的，文盲的
- underprivileged [ˈʌndəˈprivɪlɪdʒd] *adj.* 被剥夺基本权力的
- manipulate [məˈnɪpjʊleɪt] *vt.* (熟练地)操作
- exaggeration [ɪgˌzædʒəˈreɪʃən] *n.* 夸张，夸大之词
- integral [ˈɪntɪgrəl] *adj.* 完整的，整体的
- additionally [əˈdɪʃənəlɪ] *adv.* 加之，又
- encounter [ɪnˈkauntə] *v.* 遭遇，遇到
- extensively [ɪksˈtensɪvlɪ] *adv.* 广阔地
- alarming [əˈlɑːmɪŋ] *adj.* 惊动人的，令人担忧的
- peer [pɪə] *n.* 同等的人，同辈
- devastating [ˈdevəsteɪtɪŋ] *adj.* 毁灭性的，破坏力极强的
- curtail [kɜːˈteɪl] *vt.* 缩减，减少(经费等)
- enormous [ɪˈnɔːməs] *adj.* 巨大的
- disadvantaged [ˌdɪsədˈvɑːntɪdʒd] *adj.* 弱势的，处境不利的
- preferably [ˈprefərəbli] *adv.* 更适宜
- compulsory [kəmˈpʌlsərɪ] *adj.* 必须做的，必修的

不会使用电脑的人将会越来越处于劣势。请指出他们的劣势以及政府应该采取的措施。

一些未来学家已经做出预言，未来的人们将被分为两类：科技能手和科技文盲。不用说，后者将处于劣势，被人操纵。尽管这种说法有些夸张，但是对于电脑盲来说事实的确如此。

如果人们对电脑一无所知，找工作会越来越难。虽然从发明到现在仅50年，电脑已经在所有商业领域(从银行业到制鞋业)广泛使用，成了不可或缺的一部分。人们用电脑来写报告、分析数据和设计产品。难怪现在雇主理所当然地认为(雇员)应该像具备读写能力那样具备电脑技能。除了一些体力工作之外，大部分职位都要求精通电脑。

此外，电脑盲将会在日常生活中遇到问题。电脑应用如此广泛，人们在日常生活中不可能不接触到它们。当你去自动取款机提款时，你不得不操作电脑。当你想在图书馆找一本书时，你也要面对电脑。不懂电脑你甚至都不会发送电子邮件。这常常给电脑盲带来最为严重的后果。

不懂电脑带来的最大问题就是落后于同辈。对电脑一无所知会严重影响个人的发展机会。如果你不会利用电脑带来的大量的潜在机会，你的工作和学习将停滞不前。甚至连你的人际关系也会受到损害，因为你不会用互联网和朋友们保持联系。当别人进步的时候你仍然停滞不前。

政府需要采取相应措施来帮助这个弱势群体。教育是最好的办法。计算机教育应该成为学生的必修课程并且免费提供，政府应该开设大量的培训中心，为成人提供低价的电脑培训。

特别提醒

计算机曾经一度是雅思中最热门的话题，但是近年来，关于计算机的优缺点的文章，在雅思考试中出现的频率明显下降。如今的雅思考试里出现的计算机类的文章侧重于计算机是否可以代替教师、翻译人员等话题。

推荐指数 ★★★　　**相关题目** 5, 15, 16

写作点拨

这道作文题属于“观点 + 建议”类题，既要求给出不懂计算机的人所处的劣势(观点)，又要求给出政府应该采取的措施(建议)。动笔写这类文章之前，应该考虑写作的重点是放在“观点”上，还是放在“建议”上。由于“建议”会随着不同的作文题而发生很大的变化，对考生的词汇量以及表达能力要求比较高，所以通常建议考生将重点放在“观点”上。范文分为五段：第一段引入话题，第二、三、四段叙述电脑盲所面临的问题，最后一段给出政府应该采取的措施。

论据收集

不懂电脑可能引发的问题：

1. 不懂电脑就很难找到工作。

   Without adequate computer skills, finding employment may prove increasingly challenging.

2. 不懂电脑会很难处理很多日常生活中的问题。

   So extensively are computers used that it is impossible not to come into contact with them in everyday life.

3. 不懂电脑会阻碍个人的发展。

   The ignorance of computer severely curtails your chances for personal development.

4. 不懂电脑就会落后于同时代的人。

   Lagging behind your peers is the most devastating result.

ESSAY 20

Scientific and technological advances bring benefits to our daily life. However, most scientists are no longer able to find the solutions to the problems they have created. To what extent do you agree or disagree?

Time and again, science and technology has created wonders and even miracles, thus fortifying our belief in it. But is this belief sometimes so taken for granted as to blind us to its limits? Can science solve everything? I am afraid there might not be a simple answer.

It must be realized that in the process of solving problems, scientists also create problems, the solutions of which are often beyond their reach. To do them justice, it is not always possible to predict the results and bring everything under control. For example, after setting up a nuclear power plant, scientists are unable to find an ideal way to treat nuclear waste, nor are they able to eliminate the threat posed by radio activity. Thus in many fields, science and technology is far from providing perfect solutions.

However, given enough time, science will prevail. Numerous examples can be found in favour of this argument. Notwithstanding some failures, what people created by employing science and technology is beyond the wildest dreams of our ancestors. We have split the atoms; we have landed on the moon. Numerous diseases are eradicated thanks to modern medical science. What baffles scientists today would be tackled in the future.

Of course, there are limits and scientists are not omnipotent. There will always be problems waiting to be tackled because of the very nature of our infinite universe. But without resort to divine power, science is the best tool in our quest for the understanding and mastering of the world. Failure is only temporary and a step towards the ultimate success.

单词注释

- miracle [ˈmɪrəkl] *n.* 奇迹，奇事
- fortify [ˈfɔːtɪfaɪ] *vt.* 加强
- process [prəˈses] *n.* 过程
- justice [ˈdʒʌstɪs] *n.* 正义，正当
- ideal [aiˈdɪəl] *adj.* 理想的
- eliminate [ɪˈlɪmɪneɪt] *vt.* 排除，消除
- pose [pəuz] *vt.* 造成，引起
- prevail [prɪˈveɪl] *vi.* 流行，盛行
- ancestor [ˈænsɪstə] *n.* 祖先，祖宗
- eradicate [ɪˈrædɪkeɪt] *vt.* 根除
- baffle [ˈbæfl] *vt.* 困惑，阻碍
- tackle [ˈtækl] *vt.* 处理，应付
- omnipotent [ɔmˈnɪpətənt] *adj.* 全能的，无所不能的
- infinite [ˈɪnfɪnɪt] *adj.* 无穷的
- resort [rɪˈzɔːt] *vi.* 求助，诉诸
- divine [dɪˈvaɪn] *adj.* 神的，神圣的
- ultimate [ˈʌltɪmɪt] *adj.* 最后的，最终的

科技的进步给人们的日常生活带来了便利。但是与此同时，科学家已经无法解决很多由他们自己制造的问题。你是否同意这样的观点？

科学技术为人类创造了无数壮举，带来了无数奇迹，增强了我们对它的信念。但是，这种信念有时候是否过于想当然，使得我们看不到它的局限？科学能解决所有的问题吗？我认为答案恐怕并不简单。

人们必须认识到在解决问题的过程中，科学家也制造了很多问题，面对这些问题他们又常常束手无策。当然客观来讲，人们不可能每次都对结果做出准确的预测并且控制一切客观因素。例如，建立起核电站以后，科学家往往找不到理想的办法来处理核废料，也不知道该如何消除核辐射。在很多领域，科技还远远不能提供完美的解决方案。

然而如果给予足够的时间，科学迟早能够解决问题。很多例子都能证明这一点。尽管存在一些失败，人们利用科技所创造的成绩远远超出了祖先们的梦想。我们能分割原子，我们登上了月球，现代医学根除了众多疾病。目前困扰科学家的难题将来都会得到解决。

当然，科技的力量是有限的，科学家也不是无所不能的。宇宙本身是无穷无尽的，所以总会有问题等待我们解决。但是在不依靠神力帮助的情况下，科学就是我们了解和控制世界的最好工具。失败是暂时的，失败一次就又朝最后的成功迈进了一步。

特别提醒

科技发展的问题虽然不是雅思写作考试中最热门的话题，但是却在每年的雅思考试中都有所涉及。这道雅思写作题就曾经在雅思考试中出现过5次，而且是为数不多的雅思A类和G类的在大作文里都出现过的作文题。

推荐指数 ★★★★　　**相关题目** 5, 14, 15, 16, 21, 25, 64, 103, 110

写作点拨

这篇文章采取了"折衷"的写法，既不反对题目所给出的观点，也不完全同意该观点。文章分为四段：第一段引入话题，第二段指出题目所给观点的合理性，第三段则反驳该观点的一些漏洞，最后一段总结前文。使用这类折衷法写出的文章，往往结构比较松散，观点也不够鲜明，因而对考生的文字水平要求比较高。英文功底不太扎实的考生应该慎用这种方法。

词汇升级

困扰(某人)，难住(某人)

普通版 What *puzzles* scientist today would be solved in the future.

升级版 What *baffles* scientist today would be tackled in the future.

困扰(某人)，难住(某人)：puzzle, perplex, confound, mystify, bewilder, addle, muddy, stump, riddle

ESSAY 21

Intelligent robots will be more widely used in the future. Is this a blessing or a curse? What is your opinion?

Robots in science fictions and movies are depicted as either our servants or our enemies, but seldom our friends. Though I don't believe they will rebel against or win a war against us, the using of robots could lead to rather undesirable consequences.

As has happened when industrial machinery was first introduced, the extensive use of intelligent robots is likely to cause vast unemployment. Numerous workers, not only those working with their hands but also those working with their brains, will lose their jobs when robots learn to handle their work. Other things being equal, robots are preferred by employers on account of their reliability, cost effectiveness and the unlikelihood of going on strikes. Assemble lines and computers, for instance, have already taken jobs from thousands of employees. Thus, people in the future will have to vie with robots in their quest for a job.

Having said all that, it must be pointed out that mankind will always find its way. In a large sense, robots are just another human invention, nothing more. There is no sound reason that we would be overwhelmed by this contrivance. The benefits robots can bring are enormous. To begin with, robots can be assigned to work in dangerous and harsh environments. With their physical and mechanical superiority over humans, robots are suited for exploring deep oceans, the moon and even human blood vessels, which offers infinite possibilities for medical treatment. Moreover, the reliability and incorruptibility of intelligent robots are invaluable in our fight against corruption. To err is human, but rarely robots. Bribery and peer pressure don't work for robots.

As I see it, robots are not different from other human inventions, which are never perfect. Someone will always be adversely affected, but the benefits far outweigh its damages. Thus we should learn to adapt.

单词注释

- fiction [ˈfɪkʃən] *n.* 虚构，编造，小说
- depict [dɪˈpɪkt] *vt.* 描述，描写
- undesirable [ˈʌndɪˈzaɪərəbl] *adj.* 不受欢迎的
- consequence [ˈkɔnsɪkwəns] *n.* 结果
- reliability [rɪˌlaɪəˈbɪlɪtɪ] *n.* 可靠性
- effectiveness [ɪˈfektɪvnɪs] *n.* 效力
- unlikelihood [ˌʌnˈlaɪklɪhʊd] *n.* 未必有，不可信
- vie [vai] *v.* 竞争
- overwhelm [ˈəuvəˈwelm] *vt.* 彻底击败，击溃
- contrivance [kənˈtraɪvəns] *n.* 发明物
- harsh [hɑːʃ] *adj.* (条件)艰苦的，恶劣的
- mechanical [mɪˈkænɪkl] *adj.* 机械的，机械制的
- superiority [sju(ː)pɪərɪˈɔrɪtɪ] *n.* 优越
- vessel [ˈvesl] *n.* 管
- incorruptibility [ˈɪnkəˌrʌptəˈbɪlətɪ] *n.* 不腐败，清廉
- invaluable [ɪnˈvæljuəbl] *adj.* 无价的，价值无法衡量的
- corruption [kəˈrʌpʃən] *n.* 腐败，贪污
- bribery [ˈbraɪbərɪ] *n.* 贿赂
- peer pressure 同辈间的压力，同龄人间的压力
- adversely [ˈædvɜːslɪ] *adv.* 逆地，反对地
- outweigh [aʊtˈweɪ] *vt.* 在重量(或价值等)上超过
- adapt [əˈdæpt] *vi.* 适应

智能机器人在将来会被更加广泛地使用。这究竟是一件好事情，还是一件坏事情？

科幻小说和电影中的机器人有时被描绘成我们的佣人，有时被描绘成我们的敌人，但很少被描绘成我们的朋友。虽然我不相信他们会反抗人类或战胜我们，但是使用机器人可能会导致不良后果。

就像当初工业机械被大规模使用那样，广泛使用智能机器人很可能导致大面积的失业。在机器人学会如何工作以后，大量的体力和脑力劳动者将面临失业。在同等条件下，雇主们更愿意雇用机器人，因为它性能可靠、成本低而且不会罢工。比如流水生产线和电脑已经夺走了成千上万名雇员的工作。因此，未来的人们将不得不与机器人竞争工作。

话虽如此，我们必须指出人类总能够另辟蹊径，解决问题。广义来讲，机器人只是人类的又一项发明，仅此而已。说我们会被这项发明打败，这是毫无道理的。机器人可以带来巨大的利益。首先，机器人可以在恶劣的环境下从事危险的工作。它们在物理和机械方面拥有超人的优势，机器人适合于探测深海、月球甚至人的血管，这为人类医疗带来了无限的可能。此外，智能机器人廉洁可靠，可以在我们的反腐斗争中发挥重要作用。犯错误是人之常情，但机器人很少犯错误。贿赂和同伴的压力对机器人不起作用。

在我看来，机器人和人类的其他发明大同小异，并不完美。总会有人身受其害，但是其利远远大于弊。所以我们应该学会适应。

特别提醒

雅思写作题目中，关于机器人的写作题很少。但是这道关于机器人的写作题，却曾经在雅思写作考试中出现过若干次。对于英文基础不太好的考生来说，首先需要解决的问题，是必须认识题目中出现的 blessing（幸事）和 curse（祸害）两个单词。

推荐指数 ★★

相关题目 5, 14, 15, 16, 20, 25, 64, 103, 110

写作点拨

这篇文章采取了“折衷”的写法，既承认机器人给人类构成的威胁，又指出机器人的确给人类带来不少的好处。文章分为四段：第一段引入话题，第二段指出机器人对人类的威胁，第三段则指明机器人对人类的益处，最后一段总结全文，指明机器人利大于弊。

词汇升级

描述

普通版 Robots in science fiction novels and movies are *described* as either our servants or our enemies, but seldom our friends.

升级版 Robots in science fiction novels and movies are *depicted* as either our servants or our enemies, but seldom our friends.

描述：represent, portray, describe, delineate, picture, illustrate, characterize

ESSAY 22

The reason why some families don't buy television set is that the parents want their children to spend more time on creative thinking or even inventions. Agree or disagree?

All parents want the best for the children. Some of them make every decision for their kids to the extent that they don't even allow their children to watch TV with the hope that they might be more creative. I can hardly endorse this kind of practice.

In the first place, the right to watch TV should not be denied by the parents in this fashion. Notwithstanding their good intention, those parents fail to take into consideration the opinions of their children. More likely than not, youngsters enjoy watching TV. By depriving kids of this right enjoyed by most other children, the parents are at the risk of creating tension within the family. Backlashes might be expected when kids are forced to engage in some creative activities while others are watching TV. In their eagerness to guide their children every step of the way, parents sometimes ignore the kids' natural inclination. Unfortunately, it is always a bad idea to work against one's nature.

Secondly, it is a dubious claim that watching TV damages one's creativity. Actually, TV plays a positive role in the intellectual and mental development of children. Of course, many programs are not suited for children, but there are numerous others which help to develop kids' imagination and creativity. Cartoons and commercials, to name just two. Indeed, many artistic and creative people attribute their success partly to what they watched as a child. What's more, TV programs often become the topics of mutual interest when kids talk with each other. With no knowledge of any TV program, one is likely to feel isolated from his peers.

It is always wise not to impose too much upon one's children, especially when it comes to something so close to their heart as watching TV. Contrary to common belief, a proper selection of programs is conducive to the development of creativity.

单词注释

- endorse [ɪnˈdɔːs] *vt.* 赞同，支持
- notwithstanding [ˌnɒtwɪθˈstændɪŋ] *prep.* 虽然，尽管 *adv.* 尽管
- consideration [kənˌsɪdəˈreɪʃən] *n.* 体谅，考虑
- youngster [ˈjʌŋstə] *n.* 青年，少年
- deprive [diˈpraɪv] *vt.* 剥夺，使丧失
- tension [ˈtenʃən] *n.* 紧张(状态)，不安
- backlash [ˈbæklæʃ] *n.* 强烈反对
- eagerness [ˈiːgənɪs] *n.* 热心
- inclination [ˌɪŋklɪˈneɪʃn] *n.*（思想或行为的）倾向
- dubious [ˈdjuːbɪəs] *adj.* 可疑的
- intellectual [ˌɪntɪˈlektʃʊəl] *adj.* 智力的
- numerous [ˈnjuːmərəs] *adj.* 众多的，许多的
- imagination [ɪˌmædʒɪˈneɪʃən] *n.* 想像
- cartoon [kɑːˈtuːn] *n.* 卡通片
- commercial [kəˈməːʃəl] *n.* 商业广告
- artistic [ɑːˈtɪstɪk] *adj.* 艺术的
- attribute [əˈtrɪbju(ː)t] *vt.* 归因于
- mutual [ˈmjuːtjuəl; ˈmjuːtʃuəl] *adj.* 相互的
- isolated [ˈaɪsəleɪtɪd] *adj.* 隔离的，孤立的
- conducive [kənˈdjuːsɪv] *adj.* 有益于

很多家庭并不购买电视，因为父母希望小孩用更多的时间来进行创造性思维甚至是发明。你是否同意这样的做法？

所有的父母都是为了孩子好。有些父母所有事情都替孩子做主，他们甚至不让孩子们看电视，希望孩子能够因此而变得更有创造力。我不认同这种做法。

首先，父母无权这样随意剥夺孩子看电视的权利。尽管出于好意，父母这样做完全没有考虑到孩子的想法。孩子们大都喜欢看电视。如果父母剥夺这项其他大多数孩子都享有的看电视的权利，家庭关系可能会变得紧张。如果别的孩子在看电视，而自家孩子却被迫参与某些创造性的活动，他们可能会产生对抗情绪。父母如果太热衷于指导孩子的每一步，他们往往会忽视孩子的天性。不幸的是违背天性、拔苗助长往往是行不通的。

其次，"电视会损害创造力"这一说法也让人怀疑的。实际上电视对孩子的智力发展有积极作用。当然，有很多节目不适合孩子观看，但是也有很多节目可以帮助孩子发展想像力和创造力。卡通和商业广告就是两个很好例子。事实上，很多富有艺术气质和创造力的人士都将他们的成功部分地归功于儿童时代看过的节目。此外，电视节目常常成为孩子们的共同话题。不了解电视节目，你可能会感到与同龄人存在隔阂。

父母应该明智一些，不要过度压抑孩子的喜好，尤其是像看电视这样他们喜欢做的事。与普遍的看法相反，恰当的电视节目有益于创造力的发展。

特别提醒

电视的利和弊以及儿童教育，是雅思写作考试中最热门的话题之一。雅思写作题目里有大量关于这两类话题的考题。这道关于电视对儿童教育的影响的写作题，曾经在不同的年份里，在雅思写作考试中出现过若干次。

推荐指数 ★★★★　　**相关题目** 18

写作点拨

这道写作题属于典型的"观点"类题目，要求考生就一个给定的观点给出自己的意见。范文采取了最常用的写法，第一段开门见山地给出观点，第二、三段分别给出两条不同的理由，最后一段总结全文，再次重申作者的观点。

词汇升级

权利

普通版 By *not giving kids the right* to watch TV, parents are at the risk of creating tension within the family.

升级版 By *depriving kids of the right* to watch TV, parents are at the risk of creating tension within the family.

right（权利）：deny（否认、不给与），deprive of（剥夺），abdicate（放弃），relinquish（放弃），renounce（放弃），forfeit（丧失），defend（维护），safeguard（捍卫），grant（授予），exercise（行使），enforce（行使）

ESSAY 23

Newspaper, radio, television and computer each has its merits and drawbacks. What is the most efficient means of acquiring information? Give your reasons.

Modern people are blessed with so many means of acquiring information that some of us feel overwhelmed by the outpouring of vast amount of information. Once so promising, the Internet has not replaced all other types of media because it is not superior to others under all circumstances. Efficiency depends on many factors.

Newspaper certainly requires the least of its readers. So long as you can read you can pick up a newspaper and enjoy. It can be read in the office, on the bus or even in the bathroom. It also offers in-depth report on various events which can rarely be found on radio or TV. Being printed on paper, newspaper is friendly to eyes.

However, if one wants to see as well as to read about the events, TV is the best choice. After all, one sight is worth a thousand words. Sometimes it is hard to really comprehend something until one sees it with his own eyes. Take last year's tsunami for example. The TV coverage brought the terror of the catastrophe to the hearts of millions, prompting the international community to take urgent relief measures.

Of course, computer is the most efficient if one wants to search for something that happened two weeks ago. Unlike newspaper, radio or TV, which is usually devoted to recent events, a computer provides access to a wealth of information. Virtually everything is accessible at the touch of a fingertip.

Thus we see that different types of media complement each other. Each has its strength and weakness and is most efficient in some way.

单词注释

- acquire [əˈkwaɪə(r)] *vt.* 获得，学到
- overwhelm [ˌəʊvəˈwelm] *vt.* 淹没，覆没
- outpouring [ˈaʊtpɔːriŋ] *n.* 倾泻，流出
- promising [ˈprɒmisiŋ] *adj.* 有希望的，有前途的
- superior [sjuːˈpiəriə(r)] *adj.* 较高的
- circumstance [ˈsɜːkəmstəns] *n.* 环境，情况
- various [ˈveərɪəs] *adj.* 不同的，各种各样的
- comprehend [ˌkɒmpriˈhend] *vt.* 领会，理解
- tsunami [tsuːˈnɑːmi] *n.* 海啸
- catastrophe [kəˈtæstrəfɪ] *n.* 大灾难，大祸
- relief [rɪˈliːf] *n.* (痛苦等的)减轻
- virtually [ˈvɜːtjʊəli] *adv.* 事实上，实质上
- accessible [əkˈsesəbl] *adj.* 易接近的，可到达的
- fingertip [ˈfɪŋgətɪp] *n.* 指尖
- media [ˈmiːdɪə] *n.* 媒体
- complement [ˈkɒmplɪmənt] *n.* 补足物 *vt.* 补助
- efficient [ɪˈfɪʃnt] *adj.* (直接)生效的，有效率的

报纸、广播、电视以及电脑都有各自的优缺点。你认为获取信息的最有效方法是什么？请给出你的理由。

现代人非常幸运，可以通过多种方式获取信息，但同时也有人面对扑面而来的大量信息感到不知所措。人们曾经一度确信互联网会取代所有其他形式的媒体，可是直到现在各种媒体依然存在。这是因为互联网并非在任何环境下都胜过其他形式的媒体。媒体传递信息的效率取决于很多因素。

人们阅读报纸是最方便的。只要不是文盲，任何人都可以拿起报纸就看。在办公室里、公车上甚至厕所里都可以看报纸。报纸经常提供各种事件的深度报道，这些是很难在电视上看到或广播里听到的。而且阅读报纸不会引起眼睛疲劳。

然而，如果既想听又想看，电视则是最好的选择。毕竟，百闻不如一见。有的时候除非亲眼目睹，否则我们很难想像到底发生了什么。以去年的海啸为例，电视新闻报道让人们身临其境，感受到这场灾难的可怕。国际社会也因此紧急动员，迅速采取了救援措施。

当然，如果你想查找两个星期前发生的事情，电脑是最快的方法。报纸、广播和电视通常只注重时事，但电脑却不一样。除时事外，电脑还提供包罗万象的资讯。事实上，只要动动指头就什么都能找到。

由此我们可以看到所有的媒体其实是相辅相成的。每种媒体都有长处和短处，而且每种媒体都会在某个方面独占鳌头。

特别提醒

广播、电视、互联网等各种传媒形式的优缺点是雅思考试中出现频率最高的话题之一。这篇范文里提到了报纸、电视以及互联网三种传媒形式各自的优点，请用心整理一些有用的论据。

推荐指数 ★★★★★ **相关题目** 4, 17, 32, 45, 51, 56, 73, 98

写作点拨

这道写作题要求考生介绍自己心目中最有效的传媒方式。范文采取了“中立”的立场，指出各类传媒都有自己的优缺点，不同的情况下应该使用不同的传媒方式来获取信息。文章分为五段，第一段引入话题，第二、三、四段分别介绍报纸、电视以及电脑的优点，最后一段指出各种传媒相辅相成，各有优缺点。在雅思考试中，这种“中立”的方法属于安全系数比较高的写作方法。

论据积累

各类传媒的优点：

电视：1. 可以随时看。So long as you can read you can pick up a newspaper and enjoy.

2. 不会引起眼疲劳。Being printed on paper, newspaper is friendly to eyes.

3. 提供深度报道。Newspapers offer in-depth reports on various events, which can rarely be found on radio or TV.

电视：1. 百闻不如一见。One sight is worth a thousand words.

2. 眼睛看到了，才会更加了解。Sometimes it is hard to really comprehend something until one sees it with his own eyes.

网络：1. 提供搜索功能。Computer is the most efficient if one wants to search for something that happened two weeks ago.

2. 网络提供大量可获得的信息。A computer provides access to a wealth of information.

ESSAY 24

Some people think science contributes more to the society; others believe subjects such as language or business make a bigger contribution. What's your opinion?

Science is a rather broad category. In this essay, science refers to natural science as opposed to social science, which also includes economic and business theory. While all subjects contribute to the progress of mankind, science should get the most credits.

Without doubt, social science, such as philosophy, language, and economics, is of great importance to civilization. Natural science, in its modern sense, came into being only in the past few decades. Before that, philosophy provided explanation for most natural occurrences. Basic theories and practices in business and trade did much to increase the material wealth of our society. Of course, spoken and written languages made possible the development of all other subjects.

However, all these cannot be compared with the wonders and miracles created by natural science. As per its very definition, natural science deals with nature. It is our ways to understand and tap our mother nature. Through science and technology, we made numerous inventions that vastly improve and facilitate our daily life, from cars, computers, to cell phones. It is beyond the wildest dreams of our ancestors, who didn't enjoy the benefits of modern science, that men can see each other thousands of miles apart.

What is even more important is that scientific method is transforming our ways of thinking. We are becoming more objective in our assessment of issues we encounter in our life. Science is the weapon against superstition and tyranny. It has taught people the right way to approach a problem—no supposition or assertion can be valid unless it can be proved by experiments. This way of thinking can assure continuing progress in all our undertakings.

Thanks to science, mankind keeps making progress both materially and spiritually. Natural science and social science are both employed in our everlasting quest toward the total understanding of the world, neither of which can be discarded.

单词注释

- category [ˈkætəgəri] *n.* 种类，类别
- opposed [əˈpəʊzd] *adj.* 反对的，敌对的
- credit [ˈkredɪt] *n.* 信任，信用
- philosophy [fɪˈlɒsəfi] *n.* 哲学，哲学体系
- occurrence [əˈkʌrəns] *n.* 发生，出现
- practice [ˈpræktɪs] *n.* 实行，实践
- compare [kəmˈpeə] *v.* 比较，相比 *n.* 比较
- miracle [ˈmɪrəkl] *n.* 奇迹，奇事
- definition [ˌdefɪˈnɪʃn] *n.* 定义，解说
- numerous [ˈnjuːmərəs] *adj.* 众多的，许多的
- vastly [ˈvɑːstli] *adv.* 广大地，许多
- facilitate [fəˈsɪlɪteɪt] *vt.* 推动，帮助
- ancestor [ˈænsɪstə] *n.* 祖先，祖宗
- apart [əˈpɑːt] *adv.* 分离，相距
- scientific [ˌsaɪənˈtɪfɪk] *adj.* 科学的
- transform [trænsˈfɔːm] *vt.* 转换，改变
- assessment [əˈsesmənt] *n.* 估价，评估
- superstition [ˌsjuːpəˈstɪʃn] *n.* 迷信
- supposition [ˌsʌpəˈzɪʃn] *n.* 假定，假设
- assertion [əˈsɜːʃn] *n.* 主张，断言
- valid [ˈvælid] *adj.* 有效的，有根据的
- experiment [iksˈperimənt] *n.* 实验，试验
- undertaking [ˌʌndəˈteɪkɪŋ] *n.* 事业
- spiritually [ˈspɪrɪtʃʊəli] *adv.* 精神上地
- everlasting [ˌevəˈlɑːstɪŋ] *adj.* 永恒的，持久的
- discard [dɪsˈkɑːd] *vt.* 丢弃，抛弃

有人认为科学对社会做出的贡献比语言、商业等学科要大，其他人持相反的观点。请给出你的观点。

科学是个广义的范畴。本文中"科学"指代的是与社会科学相对的自然科学。社会科学包括经济和商业等学科。所有的学科都促进了人类的发展，但是(自然)科学的贡献最大。

毫无疑问，社会科学，如哲学、语言、经济学等对人类文明的进步起到了重要作用。自然科学，现代意义的自然科学，只有短短几十年的历史。在那之前，人们总是通过哲学来解释绝大部分的自然事件。基本商贸理论的形成以及商贸活动的发展极大地促进了社会物质财富的增长。当然口头和书面语言的形成及发展为其他学科的发展奠定了基础。

然而，这些与自然科学创造的壮举和奇迹相比就显得相形见绌了。顾名思义，自然科学就是要研究自然。它是我们理解和开发自然界的方法。我们运用科学技术实现了无数的发明创造，例如汽车、电脑、手机等等。这些发明给我们带来了诸多便利，极大地改善了我们的日常生活。在我们祖先的时代，现代科学技术还尚未出现，所以他们连做梦也不可能想到现代人运用科学技术真正实现了天涯若比邻。

更重要的是科学方法在改变我们的思维方式。我们处理问题的方式变得更加客观了。科学是反对迷信和专制的有效武器。在科学上，除非通过实验证明，否则所有的假设和命题都是不成立的。这种科学的思维方式正在潜移默化地影响着我们。它是我们事业获得持续发展的保障。

科学使得人类在物质和精神方面不断取得进步。我们不断探索世界的奥秘，希望能彻底了解整个世界。这需要自然科学和社会科学，两者缺一不可。

特别提醒

科技与人文学科哪个更加重要，是雅思考试中出现频率最高的话题之一。与这道题目相似的其他雅思写作题往往要求考生指出政府应该在哪方面投入更多的资金。这篇范文里提出了一些比较新颖的观点，请用心参考。

推荐指数 ★★★★ **相关题目** 2, 6, 14, 43, 44, 49, 65, 68, 93

写作点拨

这篇范文的第一段开门见山地指出作者的观点(即科技比人文科学贡献更大)后，并不急于证明。文章最大的特点在于第二段。这一段指出人文科学也做出了很大的贡献，起到"让步"的作用。第三、四、五段则从不同方面阐述科技所做出的贡献更大，有力地支持了全文的主题。需要指出的是，雅思考试中，只有考生拥有非常有说服力的论据，才可以考虑将第二段写成让步段。

词汇升级

改变

普通版 What is even more important is that scientific method is *changing* our ways of thinking.

升级版 What is even more important is that scientific method is *transforming* our ways of thinking.

改变：alter, vary, fashion, inflect, remodel, shift, transfer, transform

ESSAY 25

Modern technology has greatly influenced people's ways of entertainment, making people less creative. Do you agree or disagree?

Entertainment has undergone enormous change since the advent of modern science and technology. Reading, watching traditional operas and playing chess no longer have much appeal. The latest science and technologies are employed to satisfy our ever increasing desire for sensual pleasure. While enjoying unprecedented thrills brought by technology, we are becoming less creative as an unfortunate result.

Take the most popular form of recreation among younger people—computer games for example. It must be admitted that there are all sorts of games catering to people of different ages and gender and some even claim to be educational. But the truth remains that people are attracted to games mainly because of the graphic and audio effects. Swiftly abandoned are those games that demand too much cerebral activities because games are meant to be relaxing and entertaining. Thus, to play most games one only has to use his reflects; there is hardly any thinking involved, let alone creative thinking.

TV does an even better job at diminishing our creativity. The average amount of time devoted to watching TV makes it a major factor in our intellectual and mental development. When people watch TV, they just passively take in what is presented on the screen. Their eyes are riveted on the screen; their minds go blank. Besides, there is no time for them to pause to reflect and think. Gradually, the habit of passively taking in everything without thinking is reinforced. The appeal of TV lies in the fact that it asks almost nothing of its audience.

Traditional recreation, on the other hand, helps to develop our creativity. Reading is a case in point. To read a book one has to not only comprehend the sentences but also take in the real meaning. The reader is not distracted by unnecessary pictures or sounds but focused on the writer's chain of thoughts. He can read at his own pace, constantly evaluating, accepting or rejecting the author's ideas. It is a really thought-provoking process. Moreover, reading excites our imagination. When reading a novel for example, the reader has to conjure up pictures based on the written words; it is like 'watching a silent film' in one's mind. The director of that 'film' is the reader himself.

People's creativity is essential to any society. The decline in creativity can be partly attributed to modern ways of entertainment. By providing almost everything, they leave no room for the audience to think for themselves.

单词注释

- undergo [ˌʌndəˈɡəʊ] *vt.* 经历，遭受
- opera [ˈɒpərə] *n.* 歌剧
- appeal [əˈpiːl] *n.* 吸引力
- desire [dɪˈzaɪə] *vt./n.* 愿望，期望
- sensual [ˈsenʃuəl] *adj.* 肉欲的，色情的
- unprecedented [ʌnˈpresɪdəntɪd] *adj.* 空前的
- thrill [θrɪl] *n.* 刺激
- recreation [ˌrekrɪˈeɪʃn] *n.* 消遣，娱乐
- educational [ˌedʒuˈkeɪʃənl] *adj.* 教育的，教育性的
- graphic [ˈɡræfik] *adj.* 绘画似的，图解的
- swiftly [ˈswɪftli] *adv.* 很快地，即刻
- cerebral [ˈserɪbrəl] *adj.* 脑的，大脑的
- reflect [rɪˈflekt] *n.* 反射，反映
- passively [ˈpæsɪvli] *adv.* 被动地，顺从地
- riveted [ˈrɪvɪtɪd] *adj.* 用铆钉钉牢的
- reinforce [ˌriːɪnˈfɔːs] *vt.* 加强，使…加强
- evaluate [ɪˈvæljueɪt] *v.* 评价，评估
- reject [riˈdʒekt] *vt.* 拒绝
- provoke [prəˈvəʊk] *vt.* 使…产生；引起(某种情感等)
- conjure [ˈkʌndʒə(r)] *v.* 召唤，使…呈现于脑中，想起
- decline [dɪˈklaɪn] *n.* 下降，下倾
- creativity [ˌkriːeɪˈtɪvəti] *n.* 创造力

现代科技极大地改变了人们的娱乐方式，削弱了人们的创造力。请给出你的观点。

现代科技的出现使人们的娱乐方式发生了巨大改变。人们不再醉心于读书、看戏、下棋了。最新科技满足了我们日益增长的感官刺激需求。在享受科技带来的无限快乐的同时，我们的创造力却遭到了损害。

以年轻人最喜欢的娱乐方式电脑游戏为例。电脑游戏多种多样，可以迎合不同年龄、性别人士的需要，有些甚至有一定教育性。但是不可否认的是：吸引玩家的主要是游戏的图像和声音效果。那些很花脑筋的游戏很快就被丢在一边，因为游戏就应该轻松有趣。人们在玩游戏时只用到简单的条件反射，几乎用不着思考，更不必说创造性思维了。

电视对我们创造力的损害更为巨大。因为我们每天花大量的时间看电视，所以电视对我们的智力和心理发展影响最大。当人们看电视时，他们只是被动地接受荧屏上呈现的内容。他们的眼睛紧紧盯着电视，脑子一片空白。此外，他们也没有时间停下来反应和思考。久而久之，人们便渐渐养成了不加思考、被动接受的习惯。人们之所以喜欢看电视就是因为看电视不费吹灰之力。

相反，传统娱乐有助于发展我们的创造力。读书就是典型的例子。阅读的时候你不仅要理解句子还要领会它的真正含义。读者不会被多余的图画和声音干扰，可以很好地把握住作者的思路。他可以按自己的速度进行阅读，边读边想，对作者的思想进行评价，进而决定接受或是反驳。阅读往往能够引发人们的思考，并且激发我们的想像力。在读小说的时候，读者不得不根据书面语言在脑海中想像相应的图画，这就像是"在心中观赏一部无声电影"。"电影"的导演便是读者自己。

创造力对任何社会都是必不可少的。人们创造力水平的下降可以部分归因于现代的娱乐方式。它们包罗万象、图文并茂，但是却没有给观众留下思考的空间。

特别提醒

科技的负面影响，是雅思考试中出现频率最高的话题之一。这道题目要求考生指出现代科技所带来的现代娱乐方式是否削弱了人们的创造力。由于这类话题在雅思考试中出现的频率甚高，考生应该用心积累这篇范文里提出的一些比较新颖的论据。

推荐指数 ★★★★★

相关题目 5, 14, 15, 16, 20, 21, 64, 103, 110

写作点拨

这篇范文从正反两面证明了作者的观点。范文的第一段提出了作者的观点——现代娱乐方式的确削弱了人们创造力，第二、三段分别以电脑游戏和电视为例，阐述了现代娱乐方式对人们的负面影响，从正面证明了作者的观点；第四段阐述了传统娱乐方式对创造力的正面影响，从反面证明了作者的观点。在雅思写作考试中，这种正反两面的论证法往往更具说服力。

词汇升级

降低，减少

普通版 TV does an even better job at *reducing* our creativity.

升级版 TV does an even better job at *diminishing* our creativity.

改变：decrease, lessen, curtail, abate, diminish, allay

ESSAY 26

Some parents maintain that co-education is better for their children while others believe it is better if boys and girls go to single-sex school. Discuss.

There is almost no single-sex school in China where male and female are equal under most circumstances. However, there have been schools catering exclusively to boys or girls in most western countries. Experience in both types of school can be rewarding.

Co-education seems the natural mode of education. Males and females are not separated unless absolutely necessary. They can ride on the same bus, eat at the same restaurant and work in the same company. There is no justification to set up separate schools. Besides, co-ed schools help to reduce the prejudice against the opposite sex. By mingling with one another on a daily basis, boys and girls can relinquish the stereotype view about the other sex. They will find that a girl can be as brave as any boy and that gossiping is also common among boys. Thus, we are equal. Lastly, co-education is usually preferred because it resembles the real world. After their graduation, those students won't have difficulty adjusting to a world where the opposite sex also exists because they have learnt how to tolerate, appreciate and cooperate with each other in school.

On the other hand, single-sex schools have their unique appeals as well. Safety is regarded as the foremost reason for choosing those schools, especially girls' schools. It is safe to send one's kids to a place where they won't be seduced, molested or even assaulted by the other sex. Of course, this is to assume that none of the teachers and staff is criminally inclined. In addition, the students can focus more on their study. Free from the burden of co-existing harmoniously with the opposite sex, boys and girls often turn their attention to scholarly pursuits. This might explain why many prominent scientists went to single-sex school at one time or another. Last but definitely not the least, single-sex school bars the possibility of the much-dreaded puppy love among students. This is reassuring as long as the parents have no qualm about their children being driven to homosexuality.

It might be gathered from the above that each type of school has its strength and weakness. Co-ed school seems a nature choice for many, while single-sex school may be more suited for some. It rather depends on the individual.

单词注释

- maintain [meɪnˈteɪn] *vt.* 维持，维修；继续；供养；主张
- circumstance [ˈsɜːkəmstəns] *n.* 环境，境况
- rewarding [rɪˈwɔːdɪŋ] *adj.* 有益的，值得的
- justification [ˌdʒʌstɪfɪˈkeɪʃn] *n.* 认为有理，认为正当；理由；辩护
- prejudice against 对…偏见
- mingle with 和…混合
- stereotype [ˈsteriətaɪp] *n.* 陈腔滥调，老套
- gossip [ˈɡɒsɪp] *n.* 闲话，闲谈
- resemble [rɪˈzembl] *vt.* 像，类似
- seduce [sɪˈdjuːs] *v.* 诱使堕落
- molest [məˈlest] *vt.* 骚扰，调戏
- assault [əˈsɔːlt] *v.* 攻击，袭击
- inclined [ɪnˈklaɪnd] *adj.* 倾向…的
- harmoniously [hɑːˈməuniəsli] *adv.* 和谐地，调和地
- prominent [ˈprɔmɪnənt] *adj.* 卓越的，显著的，突出的
- dread [dred] *n.* 恐惧，恐怖；可怕的人(或物) *v.* 惧怕；担心
- reassuring [ˌriːəˈʃʊərɪŋ] *adj.* 安心的，可靠的
- qualm [kwɑːm; kwɔːm] *n.* 顾虑，不安
- puppy love 早恋
- homosexual [ˌhəʊməˈsekʃuəl] *adj.* 同性恋的 *n.* 同性恋者

一些父母认为男女混合教育对儿童更有利，其他人却认为儿童应该上单一性别的男校或女校。请讨论这个问题。

在中国几乎没有同性学校，在绝大多数情况下男女都是平等的。而在大部分西方国家，就存在许多专门的女子或男子学校。不管在哪种学校里学习，其学习经历都可以让人受益匪浅。

男女混合教育似乎是更自然的一种教育模式。除非特别有必要，男女都不会被分开。男女可以同坐一辆公共汽车，同在一个餐厅里用餐，同在一家公司里工作。设立男女分开的学校是没有什么必要的。而且，男女混合教育有助于减少两性之间的歧视。每天在一起交往，男孩和女孩会放弃固有的两性之间的成见。他们会发现女孩也可以像男孩子一样勇敢，而很多男孩子也很长舌。所以，男女都是一样的。其次，男女混合教育更接近我们现实世界的情况，所以人们通常更倾向于选择这种教育模式。由于他们在学校的时候，就已经学会了如何去容忍、欣赏异性，如何去与异性合作。因此，等到他们毕业后，这些学生就能够很容易适应这个两性同时存在的世界。

另一方面，同性学校也有其独特的优点。安全因素是选择同性学校的首要原因，尤其是女子学校。把子女送到同性学校往往更安全。因为在那里，他(她)不会受到异性的引诱、骚扰、甚至是攻击。当然，这要以学校的教职员工没有犯罪倾向为前提。此外，学生们能够把精力更多地放在学习上。由于不用把心思花在如何与异性和睦相处上，学生们可以把注意力更多地用于学业追求。这也许可以说明为何有许多著名的科学家都曾经就读过同性学校。最后一点，但绝不是最次要的一点，同性学校防止了最让父母担心的学生早恋现象。只要父母不担心子女会发展成同性恋，家长们就没有什么可担心了。

从上面的论述可以看出，这两种学校都各有优缺点。男女混合学校对许多人来说是一种更合乎自然的选择，但对有些人来说，同性学校则更适合些。就读何种学校更多地取决于个人的选择。

特别提醒

这道关于"男女学生是否应该分开接受教育"的作文题，是雅思写作考试中历史最悠久的题目之一，曾连续很多年在雅思考试中出现。目前，儿童教育的话题，依然是雅思考试中高频出现的话题。

推荐指数 ★★★★

相关题目 5, 7, 27, 28, 47, 49, 50, 54, 57, 75, 81, 84, 85, 87, 89, 109

写作点拨

这道题目要求考生就一个给定的问题展开讨论，属于"discussion"类的写作题。这类作文一般建议考生从正反两面展开论述，分别指出正反两面的优缺点。范文的第一段提出混合教育和单一性别教育各有优点；第二、第三段分别介绍混合教育和单一性别教育各自的优点；最后一段指出因为两种教育形式各有利弊，因此不同人应该有不同的选择。

论据积累

混合教育 VS 单一性别教育

混合教育：

1. 更加符合自然的教育模式。Co-education seems the natural mode of education because males and females are not separated in real life unless absolutely necessary.
2. 有利于减少两性之间的歧视。By mingling with one another on a daily basis, boys and girls can relinquish the stereotype view about the other sex.
3. 男女一起工作和学习才符合社会现状。Co-education is usually preferred because it resembles the real world.

单一性别教育：

1. 杜绝性骚扰的可能，更加安全。It is safe to send one's kids to a place where they won't be seduced, molested or even assaulted by the other sex.
2. 学生更加专注于学习。Free from the burden of co-existing harmoniously with the opposite sex, boys and girls often turn their attention to scholarly pursuits.
3. 防止学生早恋。Single-sex school bars the possibility of the much-dreaded puppy love among students.

ESSAY 27

Many schools are troubled by students' behavioral problems. What are the causes? What solutions do you recommend?

According to my former teacher from America, China probably boasts the best students in terms of orderly behavior. But I still find it hard to tolerate some students both in and outside the classroom. The situation seems to be deteriorating in China. The causes are many folds.

In the first place, children today are generally spoiled. Since China implemented the one-child policy, most families are allowed only one kid, who is usually regarded as the apple of parents' eye. Together with two maternal and paternal grandparents, parents go too far in the attempt to provide their child with everything. Hence, the kid is used to getting what they want. Taking their parents' love for granted, those kids become unappreciative and self-centered. They tend to show little respect for their teachers, regarding them as nothing more than paid employees hired by their parents.

Being an only child, he or she is also likely to have trouble dealing with classmates in school. With no experience of sharing and compromising with one's siblings, one lacks the necessary interpersonal skill to get along with one's classmates in school, where dozens of students mingle with each other on a daily basis. Had they been taught to be more considerate of others' needs and rights, they would not engage so readily in arguing or fighting with each other.

Peer pressure is by no means the smallest reason for students' behavior problems. A boy is often jeered at and called mummy's boy by other boys if he is obedient and causes no trouble. In their mind, teenagers, boys at least, should be rebellious and follow no orders. Therefore, many of them assume an indifferent air towards their teachers, parents and classmates. Study becomes unimportant for them; they are too engrossed in getting a few cheers from their peers for being manly, daring, and cool. No wonder they intentionally cause some trouble from time to time. Attention and admiration is what they are after.

It will always be hard to shape the younger generation according to the standards of the older. However, some steps can be taken to address those problems. Giving the youth more responsibility and less privilege would certainly help. Having them work together on a more regular basis can help enhance the understanding and harmony between students.

单词注释

- boast [bəʊst] *v.* 自夸，以有…而自豪
- tolerate [ˈtɒləreɪt] *vt.* 忍受，容忍
- deteriorate [dɪˈtɪəriəreɪt] *v.* (使)恶化
- implement [ˈɪmplɪmənt] *vt.* 贯彻，实现，执行
- maternal [məˈtɜːnl] *adj.* 母亲的，像母亲的，母性的
- paternal [pəˈtɜːnl] *adj.* 父亲的，像父亲的
- unappreciative [ˌʌnəˈpriːʃətɪv] *adj.* 不赏识的，不欣赏的
- compromise [ˈkɒmprəmaiz] *n.* 妥协，折衷 *v.* 妥协，折衷
- interpersonal [ˌintəˈpɜːsənl] *adj.* 人与人之间的，关于人与人之间关系的
- mingle with 和…混合
- considerate [kənˈsɪdərɪt] *adj.* 考虑周到的，体贴的
- peer [pɪə(r)] *n.* 同龄人
- jeer [dʒiə] *v.* 嘲笑
- obedient [əˈbiːdiənt] *adj.* 服从的，顺从的
- rebellious [rɪˈbeljəs] *adj.* 反叛的，叛逆的
- indifferent [ɪnˈdɪfrənt] *adj.* 漠不关心的
- engrossed [ɪnˈgrəʊst] *adj.* 全神贯注的
- manly [ˈmænli] *adj.* 男子气概的，果断的 *adv.* 具有男子气概地
- address [əˈdres] *v.* 设法解决，处理，对付
- enhance [inˈhɑːns] *vt.* 提高，增强

很多学校都为学生的行为问题所困扰。导致这些问题的原因是什么？你有什么解决方法可以推荐？

据我以前的美国外教说，中国学生可能是世界上最遵守规矩的学生。但是我仍然发现有些学生在课堂内外的行为令人无法忍受。而且这种情况在中国有愈演愈烈的趋势。其原因是多方面的。

首先，在中国，如今的孩子都备受溺爱。自从中国实施了独生子女政策，大部分家庭都只有一个孩子。独生子女往往都成了父母的掌上明珠。再加上爷爷奶奶、外公外婆，父母尽量做到孩子要什么给什么。所以，孩子总是能得到他们想要的。这些孩子把父母对他们的溺爱看作是理所当然的，变得不懂得感激，以自我为中心。他们对老师没有充分的尊重，认为老师只不过是他们父母花钱请来的雇员而已。

独生子女往往在学校更难处理同学关系。由于没有和兄弟姐妹分享和妥协的经历，在学校这样一个每天都要和几十个同学相处的地方，独生子女缺乏和同学相处所必需的人际交往技巧。如果他们能学会要更多地体谅别人的需要和权利，那么他们就不会轻易地和别人发生争执和冲突了。

同伴的压力往往也是导致学生行为问题的重要原因。一个男孩如果太听话也从不惹事的话，他的同伴就会笑话他是妈妈的乖宝宝。在他们的心目中，十几岁的孩子，至少男孩子应该是叛逆的，不听话的。因此，许多青少年就会对他们的老师、父母、同学不屑一顾。学习对他们来说无足轻重。他们关心的是如何显得有气概，勇敢，够酷，得到同伴的喝彩。怪不得他们总是故意时不时地惹些事端出来。他们追求的是别人的注意力和羡慕。

想要以老一代的标准来塑造新一代，这是很难办到的。但是，总还是有些措施可以用来解决这些问题。给青少年多一些责任，少一些优待，是很有效的方法。让他们多合作能增进学生之间的相互理解及和睦相处。

特别提醒

这道雅思写作题所涉及的儿童教育的问题是雅思写作中出现频率最高的话题之一。这道题目不仅要求考生给出学生行为问题的原因，而且还要求给出可能的解决方法，属于"原因＋建议"类的作文题。请留意这类作文题的写法。

推荐指数 ★★★★★ **相关题目** 5, 7, 26, 28, 47, 49, 50, 54, 57, 75, 81, 84, 85, 87, 89, 109

写作点拨

这道题目不仅要求考生给出学生行为问题的原因(causes)，而且还要求给出可能的解决方法(solutions)，是典型的"原因＋建议"类雅思作文题。范文分为五段：第一段引入话题；第二、三、四段分别介绍了导致学生出现行为问题的各种原因；第五段提出作者的建议。

句型升级

状语从句

普通版 Children tend to regard teachers as merely paid employees hired by their parents and show little respect for their teachers.

升级版 Children tend to show little respect for their teachers, regarding them as nothing more than paid employees hired by their parents.

普通版 Today's children are the only child in their families and they are also likely to have trouble dealing with classmates in school.

升级版 Being an only child, he or she is also likely to have trouble dealing with classmates in school.

ESSAY 28

Should the teacher in physical education class encourage the students to be more competitive or urge them to cooperate with one another? What is your opinion?

Competition is everywhere. We can get a most vivid taste of it when we watch the Olympic Games, where the best of athletes try their utter most to outdo each other. So it seems natural that students should learn to compete at an early age.

A sense of competition can certainly bring about improvement, which explains why one can run faster when he is running with other runners. Most people are lazy by nature and easily contented. They require some kind of incentives in the form of victory over others or humiliation when defeated. Without competition they will lose their drive to better themselves.

However, competition is not the sole driving force toward excellence. Cooperation is more essential to success. Most sports require cooperation between all team members, football, basketball, for example. To defeat another team, all team members must work together, adjusting to and communicating with each other. The total synergy is far more important than the strength of an individual player. A case in point is the Chinese National Football Team. It is generally agreed that its chronic poor performance is more due to its collective strategy than the skills of individual player. After all, rarely can one accomplish much all by himself.

Besides, compared to competition, cooperation gives a greater impetus to progress. Whereas the urge to improve provided by competition is based on personal gratification, i.e. the seeking of glory and victory and the avoidance of pain and humiliation, that of cooperation is grounded on one's devotion to a common goal. To put it simply, to compete one often works for himself; to cooperate one works for others. One will try his uttermost because his performance will affect others' and because he can't bear the thought of letting others down.

Indeed, aside from physical education classes, students are daily engaged in competition and cooperation. While giving competition its due credits, we should encourage students to cooperate with each other because success is not achieved by defeating others but improving ourselves.

单词注释

- competitive [kəm'petətɪv] *adj.* 竞争的
- cooperate with 与…合作
- improvement [ɪm'pruːvmənt] *n.* 改进，进步
- contented [kən'tentɪd] *adj.* 满足的，心安的
- incentive [ɪn'sentɪv] *n.* 动机
- humiliation [hjuːˌmɪli'eɪʃn] *n.* 羞辱，蒙羞
- excellence ['eksələns] *n.* 优秀，卓越；优点，美德
- synergy ['sɪnədʒi] *n.* 协同作用，配合
- chronic ['krɒnɪk] *adj.* 慢性的；延续很长的
- performance [pə'fɔːməns] *n.* 成绩，表现
- strategy ['strætɪdʒi] *n.* 策略
- accomplish [ə'kɒmplɪʃ] *vt.* 完成，达到，实现
- impetus ['ɪmpɪtəs] *n.* 推动力；促进
- whereas [weər'æz] conj. 然而，反之；鉴于
- gratification [ˌɡrætɪfɪ'keɪʃn] *n.* 满意
- devote to 把…献给；把…专用于
- uttermost ['ʌtəməʊst] *n.* 极端，最大限度
- due [djuː] *n.* 应得物；应有的权利 *adj.* 应得的，应付的
- credit ['kredɪt] *n.* 优点；信用；声望，荣誉

体育老师应该鼓励小孩去竞争，还是促进他们之间的合作？请给出你的看法。

竞争无处不在。我们在观看奥运会比赛时最能够体会到这一点了。在奥运赛场上，各国运动员中的精英，都竭尽全力，一决高下。所以，学生似乎很自然地应该在很小的时候就学会竞争。

竞争意识一定会带来进步，这就是为什么一个人在和别人一起跑步的时候，能够跑得更快些。大多数人天性是懒惰的，很容易满足。他们需要一些外部刺激，比如超过别人所带来的胜利感，或者被打败时所蒙受的羞耻感。没有竞争，他们就失去了自我改善的驱动力。

然而，竞争不是通向完美的唯一动力。合作对于成功来说更为关键。大部分的体育项目都需要队员之间通力合作，比如，足球、篮球皆是如此。要想打败对方，所有队员就必须同心协力，相互调整，相互交流。整体协同比个人力量重要得多。中国国家足球队就是一个很好的例子。大家普遍认为国家队长期的不佳表现更多源于集体策略的问题，而不是单个队员的水平问题。毕竟，一个人的力量是很难取得多大的成就的。

相对于竞争而言，合作是进步的更大动力。竞争所带来的进步动力，主要是基于个人的满足，即追求胜利和荣誉，避免失败的痛苦和羞辱，而合作所带来的动力，则是基于个人对于集体共同目标的追求。简单地说，竞争是为了自己，而合作则更多是为了别人。一个人会为了集体竭尽所能，因为他知道他的表现会影响别人，他不愿意让别人失望。

事实上，除了上体育课以外，学生们每天都处在竞争和合作之中。我们在合理评价竞争的作用的同时，应该同时鼓励学生相互合作，因为成功不是靠打败别人，而是靠完善自我取得的。

特别提醒

“竞争还是合作”，是雅思写作考试中的热门话题，雅思写作题目中有若干类似的作文题。这道作文题所涉及的儿童教育的问题，同样也是雅思写作中出现频率最高的话题之一，请认真阅读。

推荐指数 ★★★★★　　**相关题目** 5, 7, 26, 27, 47, 49, 50, 54, 57, 75, 81, 84, 85, 87, 89, 109

写作点拨

这道题目要求考生就“竞争还是合作”给出自己的观点，是典型的观点类雅思作文题。范文分为五段：第一段引入话题；第二段为让步段，指出了竞争带来的好处；第三、四段分别介绍了合作的好处，从侧面证明了合作优于竞争；第五段重申作者的观点。

论据积累

竞争 VS 合作

竞争：1. 可以克服惰性，带来进步。A sense of competition can certainly bring about improvement.

2. 没有竞争，就失去了自我改善的驱动力。Without competition, people will lose their drive to better themselves.

合作：1. 合作产生的集体力量远远大于个人的力量。The total synergy of a team is far more important than the strength of an individual player.

2. 合作带来进步的动力，而且这种动力是基于个人对于集体共同目标的追求。Whereas the urge to improve provided by competition is based on personal gratification, i.e. the seeking of glory and victory and the avoidance of pain and humiliation, that of cooperation is grounded on one's devotion to a common goal.

ESSAY 29

Which is a better place for the aged, home or nursing home?

In light of the growing number of senior citizens in many countries, the caring for elderly people is becoming harder to tackle. Some aged people can afford paid nurses and maids to look after their needs at home, but many others are not so fortunate. To them, a nursing home seems an ideal place.

To begin with, staying at a nursing home makes good financial sense. Some state-owned nursing homes are free of charge. Even for those that do require a small admission fee, the cost is low when you take into consideration the daily expenses incurred when one lives all by oneself. At the nursing home, everything can be purchased at wholesale prices. You don't have to do your own shopping or pay the electricity bill.

More importantly, a nursing home can provide professional care for those having trouble looking after themselves. Elderly people are prone to sudden attacks of various diseases. There is no telling when they would require help. If they live alone or even with their partners, there is every likelihood that they won't react effectively enough to an emergency. The stakes are too high to allow for even one mistake. Thus, it is wise to go to a nursing home where you will be monitored and attended to by professionals.

An even stronger argument in favor of nursing homes is the sense of community created there. Living alone, the aged usually feel lonely and sad. Even those living with their children often find themselves depressed because of the generation gap. By living in a nursing home, one can meet and talk to people of one's own age. There is a wealth of shared memory and common interest. They can take their mind off their own troubles and concerns and become part of the community, which means a lot to their mental health.

Staying at home is a good choice only for some people. For the vast majority of the senior citizens, nursing homes are ideal places to spend the rest of their lives in. Of course, much needs to be done to improve the conditions of the numerous poorly-managed nursing homes.

单词注释

- tackle [ˈtækl] *vt.* 应付(难事等)，处理，解决
- maid [meɪd] *n.* 女仆
- fortunate [ˈfɔːtʃənɪt] *adj.* 幸运的
- admission fee 入会费
- wholesale [ˈhəʊlseɪl] *n.* 批发 *adj.* 批发的；[喻]大规模的
- be prone to 有…的倾向，易于
- likelihood [ˈlaɪklihʊd] *n.* 可能，可能性
- emergency [iˈmɜːdʒənsi] *n.* 紧急情况，突然事件，非常时刻
- argument [ˈɑːgjumənt] *n.* 争论；辩论，论据，论点
- depressed [dɪˈprest] *adj.* 沮丧的
- generation gap 代沟
- community [kəˈmjuːnəti] *n.* 公社，团体；社会；(政治)共同体；共有，一致
- mental health 心理健康
- numerous [ˈnjuːmərəs] *adj.* 众多的，许多的，无数的

老年人待在家里更好，还是去养老院更好？请给出你的观点。

在许多国家，老年人的数目在不断增加，老年人的护理问题变得越来越棘手。有些老年人可以雇佣护士和保姆来照顾他们在家的日常生活，但是许多老年人没有这个经济能力。对于他们来说，养老院似乎是更理想的去处。

首先，待在养老院在经济上更划算。有些国家设立的养老院是免费的。即使有些养老院要收取一小笔入院费，但是相比老年人独自生活的成本，养老院的开销还是很低的。在养老院，任何东西都是以批发价购买的。你不必自己去购物或是交电费。

更重要的是，养老院可以给那些照顾自己有困难的老年人提供专业的照料。老年人很容易突发各种疾病。不知道什么时候他们就需要帮助。如果他们自己一个人住，或者是和老伴一起居住，就有可能不能够对紧急情况做出有效的反应。这很重要，必须要万无一失。所以，去养老院是一个明智的选择。在那里，你可以得到专业的看护。

选择养老院的更为重要的一点理由是在那里你会有一种集体的感觉。老年人如果一个人住的话很容易感到孤独和伤感。即使是那些和儿女一起住的老人，也会因为代沟的原因而感到忧郁压抑。在养老院，老年人则可以和同龄人互相交流。他们有着许多共同的兴趣和回忆。他们可以放开自己的烦恼，成为集体的一部分。这对于老年人的心理健康来说是很重要的。

住在家里只是适合一些老年人。对于大部分老年人来说，养老院是他们安度晚年的理想场所。当然，我们还需要做很多工作来改善那些管理混乱的养老院的居住条件。

特别提醒

医疗卫生问题，是近年来雅思写作考试中的热门话题，在移民类的考试中出现频率较高。这篇关于老年人是否应该选择养老院的雅思写作题，曾经在雅思写作考试中出现过多次，但是近几年出现的频率较低。

推荐指数 ★★★　　**相关题目** 3

写作点拨

这道题目要求考生就“老年人应该在家还是去养老院”给出自己的观点，是典型的观点类雅思作文题。范文采取了最正统的议论文写作方法，全文分为五段：第一段开门见山给出观点；第二、三、四段分别介绍养老院的各种优势，有力地证明了作者的观点；第五段再次重申作者的观点。

论据积累

养老院的优势：

1. 从经济的角度来说比较合算。

   You will find that staying at a nursing home makes good financial sense if you take into consideration the daily expenses incurred when one lives all by oneself.

2. 提供专业水准的护理。

   A nursing home can provide professional care for those having trouble looking after themselves.

3. 给老人集体的感觉。

   A strong argument in favor of nursing home is the sense of community created there.

ESSAY 30

It is said that life is becoming increasingly stressful for most people. What is the reason of this phenomenon and how could this problem be solved?

Most people would say life is improving, expect those in Africa or living in the throes of regional conflicts. But at the same time, life is becoming ever more stressful, leading to ten of thousands of suicides each year. It is high time that we pinpoint the causes and come up with some solutions.

Work is a main source of stress for most people. With the unemployment rate running high in even the most affluent countries, job security is becoming less and less guaranteed. To keep their jobs, people are compelled to work longer hours and achieve better performances. Getting ahead in the workplace becomes our priority, to the extent that we think about it all the time and can never really relax or take a break. Even for those with secure jobs, promotions and better salaries are irresistible, forever coaxing them to try their uttermost.

The relationship with one's fellow human being also adds to one's stress. People are becoming more isolated nowadays, not only from strangers but even from close relatives and friends. Everyone is engrossed in his or her own affair with no energy for or interest in what happens to other people. Real communication between people is on the decline. As a result, emotions get bottled up. People are more linked by economic interests than emotional needs. Genuine friendship becomes hard to find; even marriages are purely based on financial considerations. It seems that we face the world alone every day. No wonder people tend to feel the whole weight of the world on their shoulders.

While the right amount of pressure is often beneficial, the stress experienced by most people is detrimental both physically and mentally. Work and material wealth are far overrated and need to be put into its proper perspective. In addition, people need to improve their relationship with others around them, be it a colleague, a loved one, or a total stranger by really communicating with and caring for each other.

单词注释

- stressful [ˈstresfl] *adj.* 产生压力的，使紧迫的
- phenomenon [fɪˈnɒmɪnən] *n.* 现象
- throe [θrəu] *n.* 剧痛
- in the throns of 正处于，正忙于
- regional [ˈriːdʒənl] *adj.* 地方的，地域性的
- suicide [ˈsʊɪsaɪd] *n.* 自杀
- pinpoint [ˈpɪnpɔɪnt] *v.* 准确解释
- unemployment [ˈʌnɪmˈplɔɪmənt] *n.* 失业，失业人数
- affluent [ˈæfluənt] *adj.* 富裕的
- compel [kəmˈpel] *v.* 强迫，迫使，强要
- priority [praɪˈɒrɪti] *n.* 最重要的事，首要事情，优先，优先权
- irresistible [ˌɪrɪˈzɪstəbl] *adj.* 不可抵抗的，极诱人的
- uttermost [ˈʌtəməʊst] *n.* 极端，最大限度
- coax [kəʊks] *v.* 哄骗
- isolated [ˈaɪsəleɪtɪd] *adj.* 隔离的，孤立的
- engrossed [ɪnˈgrəʊst] *adj.* 全神贯注的
- detrimental [ˌdetrɪˈmentl] *adj.* 有害的
- mentally [ˈmentəli] *adv.* 精神上；智力上

大多数人的生活压力都变得愈来愈大。导致这种现象的原因是什么？这个问题应该如何解决？

除了那些生活在非洲或者战火纷飞地区的人，大部分人都会说现在的生活比以前改善了很多。但是与此同时，生活也变得越来越有压力。这导致每年有成千上万的人自杀。现在是找出原因、拿出解决办法的时候了。

对大部分人来说，工作是压力的主要来源。在大部分国家，甚至是最富裕的国家，失业率都居高不下，工作的稳定性越来越得不到保障。为了保住饭碗，人们被迫工作更长时间，努力达到最佳工作业绩。我们最关注的是如何在职场上有所发展，以至于我们时时刻刻都在想着工作，根本无法真正地放松或者休息一下。即使对于那些有稳定工作的人来说，由于受到升职、加薪的诱惑，他们也总是在竭尽全力努力工作。

人与人之间的关系也给我们带来压力。如今，人们变得更加孤立了，不仅是同陌生人，和亲戚、朋友也是一样。每个人都只关注自己的事情，没有更多的精力和兴趣去关心别人。相互间的交流少了。其结果是情感得不到释放。人们之间更多的是经济利益关系，而不是情感需求。真正的友谊变得难以寻觅，甚至连婚姻也仅仅是基于经济因素的考虑了。我们似乎每天都在独自面对这个世界。难怪人们越来越感到整个世界的重担都压在了自己的肩上。

尽管适量的压力是有益的，但大多数人承受的压力，都会造成生理上和心理上的危害。人们过于看重工作和物质财富，人们应该用合理的角度对它们重新进行审视。另外，人们应该改善同周围人的关系，不管他是同事、爱人或者陌生人。人与人之间要相互交流和关心。

特别提醒

现代人的压力问题是近年来雅思写作考试中新出现的话题之一。这篇范文探讨了现代人面临巨大压力的原因，同时提出了相应的解决方法。范文中的很多论据值得考生参考。

推荐指数 ★★★　　**相关题目** 18, 55

写作点拨

这道题目不仅要求考生给出现代人日益面临巨大压力的原因（reason），而且还要求给出可能的解决方法（how could this be solved），是典型的“原因＋建议”类雅思作文题。范文分为四段：第一段引入话题；第二、三段分别介绍了导致现代人日益面临巨大压力的各种原因；第四段提出作者的建议。

句型升级

压力

普通版 Nowadays people are *under great pressure*.

升级版 Nowadays people have to *cope with considerable pressure*.

压力：*adj.* acute（剧烈的）, considerable（相当大的）, extreme（极度的）, severe（严重的）, excessive（过分的）
v. suffer from（遭受）, cope with（应付）, handle（处理）, manage（应付）, stand（经受）, relieve（减轻）, remove（去除）, reduce（减少）

ESSAY 31

Happiness is considered important by all people. Why is it hard to define happiness? What are the factors that are necessary to achieve happiness?

Upon reading this essay question, I recalled the article learned in Grade Three entitled 'What Is Happiness', in which the author presents various interpretations of happiness by different people. Alas, happiness still defies definition even today. The reasons are quite obvious.

Happiness means different things for different people. It is not the same as pure pleasure, which may be brought by eating when you are hungry or taking a rest when you are tired. Happiness is more related with the individual's set of mind. One can be happy while enduring great physical pain or he may still feel sad even though he is the king. Thus, for a doctor, happiness means curing his patients; for a scientist, finding the truth; a criminal, getting away with his crime. There is no single definition.

Besides, happiness takes on different meaning as people progress through life. As a child, one regards vacations or holidays as the happiest days. For a grown-up, career success and personal achievement can bring the most happiness. When one gets old, he or she will be the happiest to watch their grand children grow up. It is hard to define something that changes all the time.

By and large, all people can be happy. Contrary to common belief, happiness depends very little on material wealth. Rather, it depends on our attitude. If we are content with who we are and what we already have, we can be happy no matter how unlikely it seems according to worldly standards. Unrealistic goals (often unworthy goals) and our failures to achieve them are the ultimate causes for unhappiness. Peace of mind is essential to achieving happiness.

单词注释

- factor [ˈfæktə] *n.* 因素，要素
- recall [rɪˈkɔːl] *vt.* 回忆，回想，记起
- interpretation [ɪnˌtɜːprɪˈteiʃn] *n.* 解释，阐明
- defy [dɪˈfaɪ] *vt.* 不服从，挑衅，违抗
- obvious [ˈɒbviəs] *adj.* 明显的，显而易见的
- criminal [ˈkriminl] *n.* 罪犯，犯罪者
- definition [ˌdefɪˈnɪʃn] *n.* 定义，释义
- contrary to 与…相反
- attitude [ˈætɪtjuːd] *n.* 态度，看法，意见
- worldly [ˈwɜːldli] *adj.* 世俗的，世间的
- unworthy [ʌnˈwɜːði] *adj.* 不值得的
- ultimate [ˈʌltɪmət] *adj.* 最后的，最终的；根本的
- be essential to 对…必要的

人人都觉得幸福很重要。为什么幸福如此难以定义？获得幸福最重要的因素是什么？

看到这个作文题目时，我想起了三年级学的一篇课文《幸福是什么》。在这篇课文里，作者列举了不同人对幸福的不同理解。唉，幸福到今天仍然是难以定义的。其原因是很明显的。

对于不同的人来说，幸福意味着不同的内容。它与饥饿的时候吃顿美餐、困倦的时候睡个好觉所带来的愉悦感不同。幸福更多的是与个人的心境有关。一个人可以在承受巨大的肉体痛苦的同时感到幸福，也可能即使当上了国王，但还是感到悲哀。所以，对于一个医生来说，幸福就是治愈他的病人；对于一个科学家来说，幸福就是找到真理；对于一个罪犯来说，幸福就是能够逍遥法外。幸福没有统一的定义。

此外，在人生的不同阶段，幸福也会有不同的幸福的定义。在儿童时期，假期和节日是最幸福的日子。长大以后，职业成功和个人成就则能够带来最大的幸福。而老年人最大的幸福就是看着孙子孙女们长大。幸福是一个不断变动的概念，因此很难定义。

总的来说，人人都可以得到幸福。与通常看法相反，事实上幸福与物质财富联系不大，它更多地取决于我们的心态。如果我们满足于做自我，满足于自己所拥有的，那么我们就可以是幸福的，不管我们离世俗的幸福标准相差多远。不切合实际的目标（通常也是没有意义的目标）以及达不到目标的失败感，是导致忧愁的最大因素。心境的平和是获得幸福的关键所在。

特别提醒

幸福是什么？这是一个生活中人们经常讨论的话题，却是英语写作考试作中很少涉及的话题。或许这也就是为什么这道雅思写作题当年难倒不少考生的原因。虽然这道作文题在雅思里出现的频率并不高，阅读这篇范文的时候，请顺便学习这一类型的雅思作文题应该如何写。

推荐指数 ★★★　　**相关题目** 42, 88, 94, 100

写作点拨

这道题目不仅要求考生给出幸福难以定义的原因（reason），而且还要求给出获取幸福必备的因素（essential factors），属于“原因＋观点”类雅思作文题。范文分为四段：第一段引入话题；第二、三段分别介绍了导致幸福难以定义的各种原因；第四段指出作者心目中获取幸福因素的必备。

句型升级

幸福

普通版 A doctor can *get great happiness* from curing his patients while a scientist can *get great happiness* from finding the truth.

升级版 A doctor can *derive sheer happiness* from curing his patient while a scientist *achieves eternal happiness* from finding the truth.

happiness: *adj.* deep（深的）, perfect（全然的）, pure（纯粹的）, sheer（纯粹的）, true（真正的）, eternal（永恒的）, lasting（持久的）

v. achieve（获得）, acquire（获得）, obtain（获得）, derive from（从…获得）, glow with happiness（幸福得满脸红光）, be filled with happiness（充满幸福）, cry with happiness（喜极而泣）

ESSAY 32

Advertising adversely affects young people, so it should be strictly limited. Do you agree or not?

Advertising is ubiquitous. Wherever you go, you are likely to see or hear some forms of advertising, usually for a certain product or service. In fact, some adverts are used to raise public awareness or to educate people. As I see it, most commercial adverts should be placed under strict control or banned.

For one thing, advertisements often withhold the truth from the public. In order to sell more products, advertisements are designed with no concern for the truth. Some of them are outrageous lies, while most of them exaggerate the benefits and hide or downplay the drawbacks of a certain product. Consumers can't see the whole picture. Being given to impulsive actions and inexperienced in worldly affairs, young people are often the first to fall victim to those misleading adverts.

For another, most adverts advocate an unhealthy way of life. In most newspaper advertisements or TV commercials people are depicted as leading an exciting and romantic life. Attractive men and women can transform their lives after they used such and such products. But real life is not like that. Daily life is apt to be much simpler and uneventful. As it often happens, young people often get too carried away by the daily onslaught of advertising and become unsatisfied with their lives. They start to try out various products, imitate the trendy lifestyle portrayed in commercials and squander time and money on luxuries.

Additionally, advertising adds to the anxiety of the young. Already under lots of pressure, the young are being told all kinds of problems they are to have if they don't use certain products or services. You are going to lose your attraction to your husband if you don't use our perfume; you are going to lose your health if you don't take our calcium tablets three times a day. What a bunch of lies! Indeed, it is widely agreed that many so called 'diseases' are created by advertisers—they try to find some problems with us at first and then offer the solution with their products. It is nothing more than a tricky business strategy.

Although credits should be given to commercial advertisements for informing the public, strict control should be imposed to rid them of the usual misrepresentation of the truth. Adverts must be truthful or banned altogether.

单词注释

- adversely [ˈædvɜːsli] *adv.* 负面地
- ubiquitous [juːˈbɪkwɪtəs] *n.* 广告
- advert [ədˈvɜːt] *n.* 广告
- withhold [wɪðˈhəʊld] *vt.* 拒绝给，不给
- outrageous [aʊtˈreɪdʒəs] *adj.* 骇人的，无法容忍的
- exaggerate [ɪɡˈzædʒəreɪt] *v.* 夸大，夸张
- drawback [ˈdrɔːbæk] *n.* 缺点
- impulsive [ɪmˈpʌlsɪv] *adj.* 冲动的
- depict [dɪˈpɪkt] *vt.* 描述，描写
- such and such 某种
- be apt to 倾向于
- uneventful [ˌʌnɪˈventfl] *adj.* 平淡的，平凡的
- carry away 运走，使失去自制力
- onslaught [ˈɒnslɔːt] *n.* 冲击
- imitate [ˈɪmɪteɪt] *vt.* 模仿，仿效
- commercial [kəˈmɜːʃl] *n.* 商业广告
- squander [ˈskwɒndə] *v.* 浪费
- anxiety [æŋˈzaɪəti] *n.* 忧虑，焦急
- perfume [ˈpɜːfjuːm] *n.* 香水
- calcium tablet 钙片
- tricky [ˈtrɪki] *adj.* 狡猾的
- impose [ɪmˈpəʊz] *vt.* 强制实行，强加
- rid [rid] *vt.* 使摆脱，使去掉

广告给年轻人造成了不良影响，所以应该被严格限制。你是否同意这种说法？

广告无处不在，不管你走到哪里，你都很有可能听到或者看到某种形式的广告。这些广告通常都是宣传某种产品或者服务。事实上，也有一些广告是用来提高大众意识或者教育大众的。但是，我认为大部分的商业广告应该受到严格的控制或者予以禁止。

一方面，广告经常向公众隐瞒真相。为了销售更多的产品，厂家在设计广告的时候，根本就没有考虑是否符合事实真相。有些广告通篇都是假话，有些则夸大产品优点，掩饰或者轻描淡写其缺点。消费者无法了解真相。年轻人做事冲动、不谙世事，所以很容易成为这些误导性广告的牺牲品。

另一方面，大部分广告都宣扬不健康的生活方式。大部分的报纸或电视广告总是渲染充满激情和浪漫的生活。广告力图使人们认为使用了他们的产品后就可以改变生活面貌。但是现实生活不是那样的。日常生活通常是简单和平淡的。而年轻人通常会被这些每天轮番轰炸的广告所影响，对现实的生活不满。他们开始尝试不同的产品，模仿广告所描述的时尚的生活方式，把大量的时间和金钱浪费在奢侈品上。

另外，广告还加剧了年轻人的焦虑心理。年轻人本来就处在很多压力之下了，广告还告诉年轻人，如果不用某某产品或某某服务，就会产生这样或那样的不良后果。如果你不用我们的香水，你会在你丈夫面前失去吸引力；如果你每天不服用三次我们的钙片，你的健康就得不到保证。简直是假话连篇！其实很多所谓的"疾病"都是广告策划人发明的。他们首先尽量找到我们的"毛病"，然后给我们提供解决方案也就是他们的产品。这只不过是一种狡猾的商业手段而已。

尽管广告在给公众提供信息方面有着积极的作用，我们应该对广告进行严格的控制以防止广告扭曲事实真相。广告应该是真实的，否则就应该被完全禁止。

特别提醒

大众传媒的问题是历年雅思写作考试中的热门话题。在各种传媒形式中，互联网和广告在雅思写作考试中出现的频率最高。这道关于广告是否应该受到严格限制的写作题曾经在雅思写作考试中出现过多次。虽然近年来广告类作文出现的频率有所下降，这篇范文中出现的不少精彩论据依然值得考生用心整理和归纳。

推荐指数 ★★★★★

相关题目 4, 17, 23, 32, 45, 51, 56, 73, 98

写作点拨

这道题目要求考生就"广告是否应该受到严格限制"给出自己的观点，是典型的观点类雅思作文题。范文采取了最正统的议论文写作方法，全文分为五段：第一段开门见山给出观点；第二、三、四段分别介绍广告所带来的各种不良影响，有力地证明了作者的观点；第五段再次重申作者的观点。

论据积累

广告的负面影响：

1. 广告经常向公众隐瞒真相。
   Advertisements often withhold the truth from the public.
   In order to sell more products, advertisements are designed with no concern for the truth.
2. 大部分广告宣扬不健康的生活方式。
   Most adverts advocate an unhealthy way of life.
3. 广告还加剧了年轻人的焦虑心理。
   Advertising adds to the anxiety of the young by telling them all kinds of problems they are to have if they don't use certain products or services.

ESSAY 33

More and more women go out to work. Hence, it is the governments' responsibility to provide daycare service for the children of working mother, free of charge. To what extent do you agree or disagree?

China is one of those countries where women usually work fulltime after marriage. The caring for the children in those families can sometimes be a problem. But as of today, there has not been any childcare centers providing free service. I see no justification for those centers.

There is no point in treating working mothers differently from other workers. Some would say that working mothers are burdened by both the family and the work. But that is something they should sort out for themselves. They can choose to work shorter hours and ask their husbands to help take care of the children. By choosing to work while being a mother, they should be prepared to make extra efforts. After all, their hard work will pay off because working mothers are always looked upon with admiration and respect.

Besides, it won't be fair for non-working mothers if their children cannot enjoy the same free service. Mothers should be treated equally no matter whether they work or not. It might be argued that working mothers pay taxes and should therefore enjoy some privileges. But should non tax-payers be denied those benefits? Shouldn't the unemployed receive any money from the government? Social welfare should be extended equally to those who are in need, regardless of their tax contribution.

Therefore, I am in favour of providing free child care for all the children, not just those of working mothers, if the government can afford it. Otherwise, the caring of the children remains to be the responsibility of individual families.

单词注释

- hence [hens] *adv.* 因此，从此
- responsibility [rɪˌspɔnsəˈbɪləti] *n.* 责任，职责
- justification [ˌdʒʌstɪfɪˈkeɪʃn] *n.* 辩护，认为有理，认为正当；理由
- burdened [ˈbɜːdnd] *adj.* 负荷的，受重负的
- sort out 挑选出，想出解决办法
- pay off 报复，赢利
- admiration [ˌædməˈreɪʃn] *n.* 钦佩，赞美，羡慕
- privilege [ˈprɪvəlɪdʒ] *n.* 特权，特别待遇
- deny [dɪˈnaɪ] *v.* 否认，拒绝
- benefit [ˈbenɪfɪt] *n.* 利益，好处
- social welfare 社会福利
- in favour of 支持…的活动
- otherwise [ˈʌðəwaɪz] *adv.* 否则的话

如今越来越多的女人参加工作。因此，政府有责任免费替职业妇女照顾小孩。你是否同意这样的观点？

在中国，大部分女性婚后仍然全职工作。这样的国家为数不多。在这些家庭中照看孩子就成了一个问题。到目前为止，还没有出现一个免费的托儿所。我认为没有必要设立这样的机构。

没有理由把职场母亲和其他工作者区别对待。有些人会说职场母亲肩负家庭与工作的双重重担。但是，那是这些职场母亲自己应该考虑好的事情。她们可以选择缩短工作时间，并且让丈夫帮助照看孩子。既然选择了做职场母亲，她们就应该做好额外付出的准备。毕竟，人们对职场母亲总是报以羡慕和尊敬的目光。她们的辛勤工作总能得到回报。

而且，如果不工作的母亲的孩子不能享受免费的服务的话，就不公平了。不管工作与否，母亲们都应该受到同等对待。可能有人会说，职场母亲缴了税，所以应该享受些特权。但是，非纳税人就不应该得到这些福利吗？失业人员就不该从政府领到救济金吗？社会福利应该平等地提供给每一个需要的人，不管他(她)是否有纳税贡献。

所以我主张如果政府能够承担的话，那就为所有孩子提供免费托儿所服务，而不仅仅局限于职场母亲的孩子。否则的话，照看孩子就还是每个家庭自己的责任。

特别提醒

职业妇女的问题是近年来雅思写作考试中新出现的话题，在移民类的考试中出现的频率较高。这道关于政府是否应该向职业妇女提供免费的儿童看管的作文题，曾经在雅思写作考试中出现过多次，请认真阅读。

推荐指数 ★★★

相关题目 58, 61, 90, 92, 105, 112

写作点拨

这道题目要求考生就“政府是否应该提供免费的儿童看管服务”给出自己的观点，是典型的观点类雅思作文题。范文采取了最正统的议论文写作方法，全文分为五段：第一段开门见山给出观点，即反对政府无偿提供这类服务；第二、三段分别阐述了政府无需向职业妇女提供儿童看管服务的两条理由；第四段总结全文，同时再次重申作者的观点。

词汇升级

负担

普通版 Working mothers *have two burdens*—the work and the family.

升级版 Working mothers *are burdened with* both the work and the family.

burden： *adj.* onerous(繁重的), weighty(沉重的), crippling(极限的), intolerable(无法忍受的)

v. carry(承受), bear(负担), assume(承担), shoulder(肩负), take on (承担、接受), impose(施加), ease(减轻), lighten(减轻), relieve(减轻), remove(减轻)

ESSAY 34

Is it fair that sports professionals earn much more money than people in other important professions? Give reasons for both sides of the argument and your opinion.

It is often reported that one or another sport star just signed a multi-million dollar contract shooting a TV commercial. Those reports often fill someone with admiration and others with indignation. 'That guy gets millions by kicking a ball!' you will often hear people say. But is the money earned really that easily?

It is by no means easy money. The astronomical salaries are only enjoyed by a tiny portion of all athletes. The competition is fierce, even brutal, among the professionals. To get ahead one has to undergo years of systematic training and even then one will find himself far from succeeding. For every Olympic champion, there are countless others who tried almost as hard but failed to make their names known. Besides, sport is not a life long career and an athlete's professional life is often shortened by injuries and accidents. One can only maintain his peak performance and salary for a certain period. They do their jobs at the risk of their health and limbs. Profession sport is demanding both physically and mentally.

However, it is also argued that professional athletes as a group are paid too much and the exceptionally high salaries for top athletes cannot be justified. Competition is intense in all professions. Sports should not be singled out as particularly demanding. Indeed many jobs require years of education and training. To become an expert usually requires life-long dedication. But we don't see top police officers, professors or even doctors paid in the millions. In addition, objectively speaking, sport is less important than many other professions. It serves no practical purposes other than providing entertainment. The salary and attention enjoyed by athletes are out of proportion.

From my point of views, those sports professionals don't deserve what they get. Undue attention and importance have been given to sports. I would like to see other more important professions get more recognition and financial rewards.

单词注释

- professional [prəˈfeʃənl] *n.* 专业人员
- argument [ˈɑːgjumənt] *n.* 争论，辩论；论据，论点
- shooting [ˈʃuːtɪŋ] *n.* 拍摄
- astronomical [ˌæstrəˈnɔmɪkl] *adj.* 庞大无法估计的
- portion [ˈpɔːʃn] *n.* 一部分；一份
- athlete [ˈæθliːt] *n.* 运动员
- brutal [ˈbruːtl] *adj.* 残忍的，兽性的
- undergo [ˌʌndəˈgəʊ] *vt.* 经历，遭受，忍受
- injury [ˈɪndʒəri] *n.* 伤害
- limb [lim] *n.* 肢，臂，腿
- demanding [dɪˈmɑːndɪŋ；(US)dɪˈmændɪŋ] *adj.* 过分要求的，苛求的
- exceptional [ɪkˈsepʃənl] *adj.* 例外的；异常的
- dedication [ˌdedɪˈkeɪʃn] *n.* 贡献，奉献
- objectively [əbˈdʒektɪvli] *adv.* 客观地
- entertainment [ˌentəˈteɪnmənt] *n.* 娱乐，娱乐表演
- proportion [prəˈpɔːʃn] *n.* 比例，均衡
- undue [ˌʌnˈdjuː] *adj.* 不适当的
- recognition [ˌrekəgˈnɪʃn] *n.* 赞誉，承认

职业运动员往往拿到了比其他重要行业的从业人员高很多的收入。这是否合理？请从正反两方面给出原因以及你的看法。

我们经常听到这样的报道：某某体育明星拍了个电视广告就挣了几百万。这些报道让有些人看了羡慕不已，而有些人看了则义愤填膺。“那个家伙就靠踢踢球就赚了几百万！”，可以经常听到人们这样议论。但是这天价的收入来得真的这么容易吗？

这钱绝对不是这么好赚的。只有极少一部分运动员能够享受天文数字般的高收入。职业运动员之间的竞争是非常激烈的，甚至是残酷的。为了出人头地，你必须通过多年的系统训练，即使这样你仍然会发现自己离成功还很遥远。对于每一个奥运冠军来说，总有无数的几乎和他(她)一样付出的运动员以失败而告终，默默无闻。体育不是一项终生职业，而且运动员还经常因为受伤和事故被迫缩短职业生涯。顶级运动员的最佳状态和高收入也只能维持一段时期而已。他们是冒着健康和身体受损的危险来从事体育这项职业的。职业体育运动对生理和心理都有极高的要求。

但是，也有人认为运动员作为一个整体收入过高，而且顶级运动员的超高收入更是很不合理。所有行业的竞争都很强烈，不应该只把体育看作是要求特别高的职业而加以区别对待。事实上，很多工作都要求很多年的训练和教育，要成为专家通常要付出一生的努力。但是我们发现，没有哪个特级的警官、权威的教授、著名的医生的收入是以百万计算的。而且客观地说，体育的重要性不如许多其他行业。除了能够为人们提供娱乐以外，体育并没有什么实际作用。 运动员们受到了过多的关注，享受了过高的收入。

依我看，职业运动员得到的太多了。人们给了体育过高的关注，把它看得太重。我希望那些更重要的行业能够得到人们更多的认可，以及更高的经济回报。

特别提醒

运动员或名人是否应该拿高薪的问题是多年来雅思写作考试中热门的话题，在移民类的考试中出现的频率较高。这道题曾经在雅思写作考试中出现过多次，请认真阅读。

推荐指数 ★★★　　**相关题目** 11, 34, 72, 102

写作点拨

这道题目要求考生就“运动员比其他行业从业人员薪资高是否合理”这个问题从正反两面展开论证，并给出自己的观点，是典型的“正反两面叙述”类的雅思作文题。由于要求从正反面同时论证，这类作文题对考生思想的深度有比较高的要求。这类文章建议采用这篇范文的写法，全文分为四段：第一段引入话题；第二、三段分别从支持和反对的角度论证；第四段提出作者自己的观点。

词汇升级

气愤的

普通版 Those reports often fill someone with admiration and others with *anger*.

升级版 Those reports often fill someone with admiration and others with *indignation*.

气愤的： wrathful, wroth, irate, ireful, incensed, enraged, raging, infuriated, furious, livid, heated, mad, sore, provoked, indignant

ESSAY 35

Discuss the advantages and disadvantages of people traveling abroad to work for a certain period of time.

Going abroad to study and work has become the dream of most students in China. In fact, the reason for taking this exam is to meet the admission requirement of most British universities. However, when I take a moment to reflect the prospect of working abroad upon graduation, I see challenges as well as opportunities.

For most Chinese, working abroad means a better salary. The average income in China is only one tenth of that enjoyed by employees in most western countries. We often hear stories that so and so also made millions abroad. Financial consideration is certainly on the mind of those working overseas. Apart from the financial reward, there is the added benefit of improving one's overall ability. Western countries are leading the world in science and management. By mingling and cooperating with one's colleagues on a daily basis, one gets to really understand the people and culture. Besides, working experience in a foreign country is often highly valued, at least in China. To put it in a Chinese way, to work abroad is to be gilded. You will be treated as a foreign expert when you return home. In fact, that is why most oversea students choose to advance their career at home.

However, it is not without its drawbacks. The separation from family members can be most trying for many people working in a foreign land. Only very few people go abroad with their wives and kids; most of them went by themselves. Having few friends, expatriates often feel lonely and some even suffer nervous breakdown. Besides, immigrant workers are not often treated friendly. The local people sometimes blame unemployment on those workers. Resentment and hostility are not uncommon in countries like France and Japan. It is hard for foreign workers to fit in. They will always be regarded as outsiders.

Having said all that, I still look forward to working abroad, should there be the chance. All the inconveniences are to be put up with because the experience is a rewarding one.

单词注释

- disadvantage [ˌdisəd'vɑːntidʒ] *n.* 不利，不利条件；缺点，劣势
- reflect [ri'flekt] *v.* 反省，细想；反射；反映；表现
- prospect ['prɒspekt] *n.* 景色；前景，前途
- overall ['əuvərɔːl] *adj.* 全部的，全面的
- advance [əd'vɑːns] *v.* 前进；提前；预付
- gilded ['gɪldɪd] *adj.* 镀金的
- trying ['traɪɪŋ] *adj.* 难受的；费劲的；令人厌烦的
- expatriate [ˌeks'pætriət] *vt.* 逐出国外，脱离国籍，放逐 *n.* 亡命国外者
- nervous breakdown ［医］神经失常
- resentment [rɪ'zentmənt] *n.* 怨恨，愤恨
- hostility [hɒ'stɪləti] *n.* 敌意，恶意，不友善，敌对，对抗，反对
- fit in 融入
- outsider [ˌaut'saidə] *n.* 外来者
- inconvenience [ˌɪnkən'viːniəns] *n.* 麻烦，不方便之处

请讨论出国工作一段时间的利与弊。

到国外去工作或者留学是大部分中国学生的梦想。事实上，参加雅思考试的目的也是为了达到大部分英国大学的入学要求。但是，当我仔细想想在国外留学毕业后的工作前景时，我既看到了机会，也看到了挑战。

对于大部分中国人来说，在国外打工就意味着更高的工资。中国的平均工资只有大部分西方国家的十分之一。我们经常听到某人在国外赚了几百万。那些在国外务工的中国人，首要考虑的当然是经济因素。除了经济上的好处之外，出国工作还有助于提升个人素质。西方国家的科学管理水平是世界先进的。每天和国外的同事相处，工作在一块，就能够真正地了解外国人民和文化。而且，国外工作经验很受重视，至少在中国是这样的。中国人通常把到国外工作称作是镀金。当你回国的时候，别人就把你当外国专家看待。实际上，这就是为什么许多留学生选择回国创业的理由。

但是，到国外工作也有其缺点。和家人远隔重洋，这对于很多在国外工作的人来说是很难忍受的。只有很少数人和妻子孩子一起出国，大部分人都是孤身前往。由于没有什么朋友，这些异乡客经常感到孤独，有些甚至精神崩溃。而且，移民工人在国外有时还会受到不友好的对待。当地人有时候把失业问题归咎于这些外来移民。在有些国家，比如法国和日本，对外来移民的憎恨和敌意屡见不鲜。外来移民很难融入当地社会。他们总是被看作是外来者。

说了这么多，如果有机会，我个人还是盼望能够出国。所有的不便之处都可以克服，因为出国的经历实在是太令人受益匪浅了。

特别提醒

或许是因为雅思本身就是一个准备出国的人才参加的语言考试，雅思作文考试中充斥着各类与出国有关的话题，例如出国旅游的利和弊以及这道雅思写作题所涉及的出国工作的利弊问题。这道题目曾经在雅思考试中多次出现。范文中提出了一些比较朴实但是却很新颖的观点，请仔细阅读。

推荐指数 ★★★★

相关题目 8, 53, 78

写作点拨

这道题目要求考生就“出国工作一段时间的利与弊”展开讨论，属于典型的“优点＋缺点”类的雅思作文题。尽管这类作文题要求考生同时指出特定事务的利和弊，实际考试中考生一定要在文章的结尾处点明自己的看法，指出究竟是利大于弊还是弊大于利。范文分为四段：第一段引入话题；第二、三段分别介绍出国工作的利弊；第四段介绍作者自己的选择。

词汇升级

思考

普通版 However, when I take a moment to *think about* the prospect of working abroad upon graduation, I see challenges as well as opportunities.

升级版 When I take a moment to *reflect* the prospect of working abroad upon graduation, I see challenges as well as opportunities.

思考：reflect, ponder, contemplate, deliberate, meditate, muse, mull over

ESSAY 36

Waste disposal presents increasing problems, especially in urban areas. What do you think are the causes? Give some suggestion to the government and individuals on how to reduce the amount of rubbish.

I didn't have a clear idea of how much garbage we produce each day until I saw a landfill on television where truckloads after truckloads of rubbish were dumped each day. If things go on without control, there will be no place for mankind in the future.

All the garbage is man-made. The extensive use of dispensable items is the main culprit. Recent decades have seen a ten-fold increase in the amount of waste produced in major cities around China. Fifty percent of that garbage is dispensable items such as plastic bags and food boxes, most of which are not biodegradable. In our quest for convenience, we give no thoughts to environmental friendliness.

The problem is compounded by the poor efforts we made at recycling. Many of the things we throw out can be recycled, which not only reduced the amount of rubbish we produce but make sound economic sense. Actually, huge profits could be made by reclaiming waste products. However, many people don't see the importance of recycling or bother to throw a recyclable item to the garbage bin marked 'recyclable'.

Lastly, rapid population growth in urban areas is also responsible for the increase of garbage. Each year, millions of immigrant workers from rural areas swarm into big cities in search of work. Not regarding the city as their home, they often have no qualm doing some damage to the environment by throwing rubbish everywhere, which often made garbage collection and disposal impossible. Consequently, some garbage is left unattended for months.

Measures can and should be taken to address this issue. People should be educated to increase their environmental awareness. Incentives should be given by the government to encourage citizens to reduce the use of disposable items and recycle as much as possible. If possible, more factories and companies should move to the countryside to prevent the influx of immigrant workers to the cities. While these may cause some inconveniences, we will be amply rewarded with a better environment.

单词注释

- disposal [dɪˈspəʊzl] *n.* 处理，处置，布置
- present [prɪˈzent] *vt.* 提出，呈现
- individual [ˌɪndɪˈvɪdʒʊəl] *n.* 个人，个体 *adj.* 个别的，单独的
- truckload [ˈtrʌkləʊd] *n.* 一货车的容量
- landfill [ˈlændfɪl] *n.* 垃圾场
- dispensable [dɪˈspensəbl] *adj.* 不是必要的；一次性的
- decade [ˈdekeɪd] *n.* 十年，十
- biodegradable [ˌbaɪəʊdɪˈgreɪdəbl] *adj.* 生物所能分解的，能降解的
- compound [kəmˈpaund] *v.* 使…严重，使…恶化
- profit [ˈprɒfɪt] *n.* 利润，益处，得益
- reclaim [r(ɪ)ˈkle(ɪ)m] *vt.* 要求归还，回收
- recycle [ˌriːˈsaikl] *v.* 使再循环，反复应用 *n.* 再生，重复利用
- immigrant [ˈɪmɪgrənt] *n.* 移民，侨民
- swarm into 涌入
- rural [ˈrʊər(ə)l] *adj.* 乡下的，田园的
- qualm [kwɑːm; kwɔːm] *n.* 疑虑，考虑
- consequently [ˈkɒnsɪkwəntli] *adv.* 从而，因此
- unattended [ˌʌnəˈtend(ɪ)d] *adj.* 没人照顾的；未被注意的
- influx [ˈ(ɪ)nflʌks] *n.* 流入

垃圾给我们造成了越来越多的问题。这种情况在城市里尤为严重。你认为出现这种情况的原因是什么？请就如何减少垃圾排放量的问题，向政府以及个人提出你的建议。

我以前对我们每天制造多少垃圾没有一个清晰的概念，直到有一天我在电视上看到一个垃圾站，每天都有一卡车一卡车的垃圾倒在那里。如果事情得不到控制的话，那么将来人类就可能没有生存空间。

所有的垃圾都是人类自己制造的。一次性用具的滥用是罪魁祸首。最近几十年来，中国主要城市的垃圾总量几乎翻了十倍。其中百分之五十都是一次性用具，比如塑料袋、塑料饭盒，而且大部分都是不能降解的。我们为了追求方便，一点也没有考虑到对环境的影响。

由于我们的回收再利用工作不得力，垃圾处理问题变得更加严重。我们抛弃的很多东西其实都是可以回收再利用的，这样不仅能够减少我们的垃圾量，而且还可以产生可观的经济效益。事实上，废物的回收利用可以带来巨大的利润。但是，许多人看不到垃圾回收利用的重要性，甚至不愿费事把可回收的垃圾扔入标有“可回收”标志的垃圾筒。

城市人口的快速增长也是垃圾量增加的原因之一。每年有几百万外地民工涌入城市打工。因为没有把城市当作自己的家，这些外来民工根本不会在意对环境的破坏，他们会到处乱扔垃圾，这给垃圾的清理和处理工作带来困难。结果有些垃圾几个月都没有人处理。

我们应该而且也能够采取相应的措施解决这个问题。我们应该教育人们提高环境意识。政府应该提供一些激励措施，以鼓励公众减少一次性用具的使用，而且尽可能地进行回收利用。如果可能的话，更多的工厂和公司应该搬到郊区，以避免外来民工涌入城市。尽管这些措施会带来一些不便，但是我们会得到很好的回报，那就是一个更佳的生存环境。

特别提醒

环境保护问题，是历年雅思写作考试中的热门话题；在关于环保的话题中，环境被破坏的原因以及政府应该采取的措施在雅思写作考试中出现的频率最高。这道关于垃圾排放的写作题就不仅要求考生给出原因，而且要求考生向政府和个人提出建议。这道题目曾经在雅思写作考试中出现过多次，请用心准备。

推荐指数 ★★★★

相关题目 74, 91

写作点拨

这道题目不仅要求考生给出垃圾问题日益严重的原因（reason），而且还要求向政府以及个人提出建议（suggestion），属于典型的“原因＋建议”类雅思作文题。范文分为四段：第一段引入话题；第二、三段分别介绍了垃圾问题日益严重的各种原因；第四段给出了作者的建议。

词汇升级

加剧，使…恶化

普通版 The problem is *made worse* by the poor efforts we made at recycling.

升级版 The problem is *compounded* by the poor efforts we made at recycling.

加剧，使…恶化：compound, aggravate, deprave, deteriorate, exacerbate, exasperate, worsen

ESSAY 37

Statistics show that cities are increasing in size. What do you think are the causes and possible consequences?

Most cities are expanding in terms of population and land area. City residents are daily reminded of this growth by the erection of new high-rise buildings and the extended bus routes. Generally a good thing, the expansion of a city is not often welcomed.

The influx of immigrant workers is the biggest reason behind city expansion. Lured by the prospect of employment and a better life in big cities, people from poorer regions come in millions. In order to accommodate an increasing number of people, cities are forced to expand. In addition, the expansion is also necessitated and fuelled by rapid economic growth. Most cities are also centers for trade and industry, the development of which requires the use of land. Vast stretches of land has to be used to improve the infrastructure.

This kind of growth may lead to dire consequences. Population growth almost invariably causes traffic congestion. The building of new roads often lags far behind the increase in the number of cars and city dwellers. As a result, people can be trapped in cars for up to an hour during rush hours. Worse still, a huge population often puts too much pressure on city's infrastructure. Many newly arrived immigrant workers live in appalling conditions, sharing a room with four or five people. The local people also experience a decline in public service because it was designed only for a certain number of people. Last but not least, urban sprawl often causes severe environmental damage. Trees, fields and even villages have to be sacrificed because of the unrelenting pace of urban sprawl. The only defensive against it is a balanced development of all regions, both urban and rural.

单词注释

- expand [ɪkˈspænd] *vt.* 扩张 *vi.* 张开；发展
- extend [ɪkˈstend] *v.* 扩充，延伸
- erection [ɪˈrekʃn] *n.* 直立，竖起；建筑物
- high-rise *adj.* (建筑物)超高层的，高楼的
- resident [ˈrez(ɪ)dənt] *n.* 居民
- influx [ˈ(ɪ)nflʌks] *n.* 流入
- lure [lʊə] *v.* 诱惑
- prospect [ˈprɒspekt] *n.* 前景；前途；期望
- accommodate [əˈkɒmədeɪt] *v.* 容纳
- necessitate [nəˈsesɪteɪt] *v.* 成为必要
- dire [ˈdaɪə(r)] *adj.* 可怕的
- decline [dɪˈklaɪn] *v.* 下降
- unrelenting [ˌʌnrɪˈlentɪŋ] *adj.* 毫不留情的

数据表明，城市的规模在不断扩大。你认为这个现象的原因和后果分别是什么？

大部分城市人口不断扩张，面积不断扩大。城市居民每天都能感觉到这一点，因为有高楼大厦不断拔地而起，公交路线不断增加。虽然总的来说是一件好事，但城市的扩张还是带来了些问题。

民工的涌入是城市扩张背后的最大原因。由于认为来到城市就能找到工作，改善生活水平，来自贫困地区的民工数以百万计地涌入城市。为了容纳更多的人，城市不得不扩张。而且，经济的快速增长也加速了城市的发展，使得城市的扩张成为必然。大部分城市还是贸易和工业中心，其发展需要大量用地。基础设施的建设也需要大量用地。

这样的扩张带来了不良后果。人口增长带来了交通堵塞。道路的增长总是赶不上车辆和人口增长。其结果是，在交通高峰时间，人们可能因为塞车而被困在车里长达一个小时。更糟糕的是，过多的人口给城市的基础设施带来太大的压力。许多刚刚来到城市的民工，其居住条件令人震惊，往往是四五个人挤在一间小房间里。本地人享受到的公共服务也不断减少，因为这些公共服务当初就是设计为一定数量的人享用的。最后一点，但并非不重要的一点是城市扩张还带来了严重的环境破坏。树木、田地、甚至村庄都成了无情的城市扩张的牺牲品。现在唯一的解决方法就是要使得城市和乡村地区平衡发展。

特别提醒

城市化的起因和后果，是近年雅思写作考试中的热门话题。近几年的雅思考试，每年都有若干道作文题涉及城市化的问题。这道题目不仅要求考生给出城市化的原因，而且还要求给出城市化的危害，曾经在雅思写作考试中出现过多次。请用心归纳和整理范文中的论据。

推荐指数 ★★★★

相关题目 74, 91

写作点拨

这道题目不仅要求考生给出城市化规模扩大的原因，而且要求给出其所造成的危害。范文采用了最简单的写法，分为三段：第一段引入话题，第二段介绍了城市规模日益扩大的各种原因，第三段指出城市规模扩大所带来的后果。

词汇升级

结果

普通版 This kind of growth may lead to *very bad consequences*.

升级版 This kind of growth may lead to *dire consequences*.

consequence（结果）：*adj.* far-reaching（深远的）, profound（深刻的）, adverse（不利的）, catastrophic（灾难的）, damaging（破坏性的）, devastating（破坏性的）, dire（可怕的）, disastrous（灾难的）, fatal（致命的）, tragic（悲惨的）, severe（严重的）

ESSAY 38

There are more and more cars in cities. Hence, pedestrians and cyclists are endangered by heavy traffic. Gardens and streets give way to car parks and highways. How can city planners satisfy all people's needs?

Each day tens of thousands of people die from traffic accidents in cities worldwide, a regrettable and wasteful loss of human lives. With cars increasing daily, new roads and parking lots are forever taking the place of gardens and streets. Careful planning and necessary measures can best serve the interest of all people.

A well-developed public transport system is the ultimate way to reduce the number of cars on the road. Extensive and efficient subway systems and bus services could provide cheap and comfortable drives for everyone even in rush hours, vastly reducing the total number of cars on the road. Besides, environmental damages are also kept at the minimum, for it is the most energy-efficient method to convey huge numbers of people from place to place.

In addition, there is often room for improvement when it comes to city planning. Better planning could make the best use of existing roads without further encroachment on the already scarce parks, gardens or squares. For instance, more underground car parks and overpasses should be built in order to reserve the ground for trees and gardens.

Lastly, more traffic wardens should be posted and traffic lights set up so as to regulate the flow of traffic, the result of which could be a decrease in the number of traffic incidents because most accidents occur when the drivers decide to take chances as there is no policeman around. Pedestrians also need to be reminded to observe traffic rules by keeping to pavements and sidewalks.

Most of the human loss and property damage caused by traffic accidents are avoidable if people choose to give up a little bit of their convenience for the sake of others. Harmony can only be achieved by balancing the needs of all people.

单词注释

- reduce [r(ɪ)ˈdjuːs] *v.* 减少
- ultimate [ˈʌltɪmət] *adj.* 最后的，最终的；根本的
- minimum [ˈmɪnɪməm] *adj.* 最小值
- convey [kənˈveɪ] *v.* 运送
- encroachment [ɪnˈkrəutʃmənt] *n.* 侵蚀；侵犯
- scare [skeə(r)] *adj.* 缺乏的，不足的；稀有的
- overpass [ˈəuvəpɑːs] *n.* 天桥
- regulate [ˈregjule(ɪ)t] *vt.* 管制，控制
- pavement [ˈpe(ɪ)vmənt] *n.* 人行道
- property [ˈprɒpəti] *n.* 财产

都市里的汽车数量日益扩大，行人以及骑自行车的人的安全受到威胁。花园和街道被停车场以及高速公路取代。城市规划者应该如何满足所有人的需求？

在全世界的各大城市，每天都有成千上万的人死于交通事故，这是多么令人遗憾，多么无谓的生命损失呀。由于汽车的不断增多，总是有越来越多的花园和街道被公路和停车场所取代。因此政府需要谨慎规划，采取必要的措施，最大化地维护公众的利益。

一个完善的公共交通系统是减少路上车辆数量的最终方法。发达而高效的公交、地铁系统即使在交通高峰时期也能够为人们提供廉价、舒适的乘车服务，从而大大减少了道路上车辆的数量。另外，对环境的影响也由此被控制到最低限度，因为公共交通对能源的利用率最高，可以经济地运送大批人群。

此外，城市规划总是有改进的空间。合理的规划可以最大限度地利用现有的道路，而不必去侵占那些本来就很稀少的公园、花园和广场。例如，我们可以建筑更多的地下停车场和立交桥，这样就可以节约地面土地使用，从而为种植树木、修建公园提供更多的土地。

最后，我们应该设置更多的交警执勤点和红绿灯，以更好地协调交通。这样就能减少交通事故的发生。因为大部分的交通事故都是在司机认为没有交警在场而试图铤而走险的情况下发生的。我们同时也应该提醒行人遵守交通规则：行人应该走人行道。

只要人们愿意为了他人的安全牺牲一点点自己的便利，大部分因交通事故造成的生命财产损失都是可以避免的。只有平衡所有人的需要，才能达到和谐。

特别提醒

公共交通的问题，是历年雅思写作考试中的热门话题；在各种关于交通工具的雅思写作题中，关于如何减少交通危害的作文题出现的频率最高。这道雅思写作题就曾经在雅思写作考试中出现过多次。范文中出现不少精彩论据，请你用心整理和归纳。

推荐指数 ★★★★

相关题目 12, 63

写作点拨

这道题目要求考生就“城市规划者如何满足所有人的需求”给出自己的建议，是典型的建议类雅思作文题。范文采取了最传统的写作方法，全文分为五段：第一段引入话题；第二、三、四段分别介绍城市规划者应该采取的各种措施，回答了这道作文题所提出的问题；第五段总结所有的措施。

论据积累

如何改善城市的交通状况：

1. 建立完善的公共交通系统。

   A well-developed public transport system is the ultimate way to reduce the number of cars on the road.

2. 合理的城市规划，最大限度地利用现有的道路。

   Better planning could make the best use of existing roads without further encroachment on the already scarce parks, gardens or squares.

3. 应该设置更多的交警执勤点和红绿灯，以更好地协调交通。

   More traffic wardens should be posted and traffic lights set up so as to regulate the flow of traffic.

ESSAY 39

Many people think that countries have a moral obligation to help each other, while others argue that the aid money is misspent by the governments that receive it, so international aid should not be given to the poor countries. Discuss.

Billions of dollars each year are given out as aid to poor countries in the hope of relieving the sufferings of their people. Whenever and wherever natural disasters strike, people from all countries never hesitate to offer help and assistance to the victims. However, some people fear these kinds of good will and generosity are being abused by some governments.

There is no point in giving aid because aid money is misused and never reaches the intended recipients. It is the poor that need help. Unfortunately, due to their social and economic status, they have no access to foreign aid once it is brought in through official channels. North Korea, for instance, receives millions of dollars each year, but thousands still starve to death. The cause of this, as revealed in some independent studies, is that a large portion of the donation was spent on the army and very little went to the poor. More alarmingly, international aid sometimes, instead of alleviating sufferings, backfires on the people if the money were used by the dictators to consolidate their rule. The government might use the money to build its army and police force; those with close ties with government officials might use a portion of it to seek profits for themselves, often at the expense of public interest.

However, notwithstanding possible misuses, abuses or side effects, rich countries are morally responsible for assisting poor nations. Developed countries accumulate great wealth not only by the hard work and ingenuity of their people but, to some degree, at the expense of other countries' economic well-being. For instance, many former colonies were exploited economically by former empires such as Britain and France and are still plagued by unfair trade relations, whereby they serve as suppliers of natural resources and markets for expensive end products. Besides, rich countries often call themselves civilized nations. If they are to really live up to their names, how could they refuse to aid the poor who are suffering in poverty and languishing in misery? Creatures of a kind often help each other wherever possible, which is happening in the animal world all the time. As human beings, how can we stand by when other people are struggling merely to survive? Our human decency forbids it!

As Bertrand Russell puts it: there are two kinds of tragedy, one caused by nature and the other by ourselves. We are now in a position to conquer most natural disasters if the rich and powerful nations choose to do so. Also, I'd like to see measures taken to prevent the misuse of international aid.

单词注释

- relieve [r(ɪ)ˈliːv] *v.* 减轻
- strike [stra(ɪ)k] *vt.* 到达；侵袭
- hesitate [ˈhez(ɪ)te(ɪ)t] *v.* 犹豫，踌躇；不愿
- victim [ˈv(ɪ)kt(ɪ)m] *n.* 受害人；牺牲者
- generosity [ˌdʒenəˈrɒsəti] *n.* 慷慨，宽大
- abuse [əˈbjuːz] *v.* 滥用
- recipient [rɪˈsɪpiənt] *n.* 领取人
- alleviate [əˈliːvie(ɪ)t] *v.* 缓解
- dictator [dɪkˈteɪtə(r)] *n.* 暴君
- consolidate [kənˈsɒlɪdeɪt] *v.* 加强
- backfire [ˌbækˈfaɪə(r)] *v.* 起反作用
- portion [ˈpɔːʃn] *n.* 部分
- accumulate [əˈkjuːmjəleɪt] *v.* 积累
- plague [ple(ɪ)g] *v.* 困扰
- languish [ˈlæŋgwɪʃ] *v.* 受苦

一些人认为国家之间出于道义应该互相帮助，而另外一些人却认为援助款目往往被滥用，因此不应该向贫穷的国家提供国际援助。请讨论这个问题。

每年都有几十亿美元作为援助投向了贫困国家，以期减少那些国家的人民的痛苦。每当发生自然灾难时，全世界人民总是毫不犹豫地向受难者伸出援助之手。但是，有人担忧，这些善意和慷慨可能会被有些国家的政府利用。

如果援助资金被滥用，不能到达受灾者手中，那么援助就失去意义了。穷人才是真正需要援助的人，但是由于他们的社会经济地位低下，援助资金通过官方渠道进入国内后，往往到不了他们的手中。例如，朝鲜每年都接受几百万美元的援助，但每年仍然有几千人饿死。有些独立研究表明，这是因为大部分的援助资金都被军队挪用，只有很小一部分能到达穷人手中。更令人不安的是，有时候国际援助不仅不能减轻人们的痛苦，反而被独裁者们用来加强独裁统治。政府把援助用来加强军队和警察力量，那些和政府官员勾结的人还用其来谋取一己私利，其结果通常都是牺牲公众的利益。

但是，尽管有这些滥用和挪用，尽管有这么多副作用，富裕国家在道义上仍然有义务帮助贫困国家。发达国家的富裕并非仅仅依靠本国人民的勤劳和智慧，在某种程度上，他们积累的财富是以牺牲别国经济利益为代价的。例如，许多前殖民地被他们的宗主国如英国、法国等在经济上残酷剥削，被当作是原材料的提供者和昂贵成品的销售市场。另外，富裕国家通常自诩为文明国度。如果他们想名副其实的话，他们怎么可以拒绝援助那些在痛苦和贫困中挣扎的穷人呢？在动物世界里，同种动物都经常尽可能地相互帮助。作为人类，看到有人在生存线上挣扎的时候，我们怎能坐视不理呢？人性不允许我们这样做。

正如罗素所说：世上有两种悲剧，一种是自然造成的，一种则是我们自己造成的。如果那些富裕强大的国家积极参与的话，我们能够战胜大部分的自然灾害。我也希望我们能采取有效措施来防止国际援助遭到滥用。

特别提醒

国家之间是否应该互相帮助，是近年雅思写作考试中新出现的热门话题，近年来在雅思写作考试中出现过多次。很多考生缺乏对国际政治的了解，因此在雅思考场里面对这道作文题时，往往感觉无话可说。如果你有这样的问题，那么请你用心归纳和整理范文中的论据。

推荐指数 ★★★ **相关题目** 41

写作点拨

这道题目要求考生讨论“国家之间是否应该互相帮助”的问题，属于典型的“discussion”类的雅思作文题。对于这类讨论型的作文题，建议考生从正反两面来展开讨论，同时指出题目所给观点的合理和不合理处。范文采用了这类作文题最正统的写法，分为四段：第一段引入话题，第二、三段分别介绍国家之间互相帮助的不合理性和合理性，第四段引用罗素的名言，巧妙地抒发了作者自己的期望。

词汇升级

受苦，遭受困难

普通版 If they are to really live up to their names, how could they refuse to aid the poor who are *suffering* in poverty and misery?

升级版 If they are to really live up to their names, how could they refuse to aid the poor who are *languishing* in poverty and misery?

受苦，遭受困难：agonize, ail, moan, writhe, languish

ESSAY 40

Creative artists should be given the freedom to express their ideas (through words, pictures, music or films). However, some people think government should impose certain restrictions on them. To what extent do you agree or disagree?

In a real democracy people should enjoy the freedom of speech. Everyone should be able to freely express his or her ideas and views. This kind of freedom must not be curtailed when it comes to artistic creations.

Freedom of speech is a basic right for all citizens, more so for artists. The ideas of an artist are often expressed not in his speeches but through his artistic work. Everyone should have the right to tell the truth and his true feelings. The denying of freedom is a kind of oppression. Only a government without the mandate of its people would fear free speech. All dictators, for examples, never allow the people to criticize the government.

Art is all but impossible without the freedom of expression. Art is a reflection of the real world: artists reproduce the world as they see it. An artist may choose any part of the world as his subject and approach from his unique angle. No two artists perceive the world in quite the same way. If restrictions are imposed on certain areas and subjects, if artists can only approach an issue in ways approved by the authority, and if they are in fear of being thrown into prison by truly expressing their ideas, art ceases to be art.

Of course, artists should abide by the law while enjoying the freedom of expression. Therefore, their art work cannot be pornographic for example. They must not slander other people or spread vicious lies. Freedom doesn't mean doing whatever you like but doing whatever you like so long as you don't infringe on others' freedom or rights.

Therefore, governments should not impose censorship or restrictions on artistic creation. Artist should have their freedom of expression as long as this freedom is not used as an excuse for illegal activities.

单词注释

- curtail [kəː'teɪl] *v.* 削减
- oppression [ə'preʃn] *n.* 压迫
- criticize ['krɪtɪsaɪz] *v.* 批评，责备
- reflection [rɪ'flekʃn] *n.* 反映
- unique [jʊ'niːk] *adj.* 独特的
- perceive [pə'siːv] *vt.* 察觉 *v.* 感知，感到
- approve [ə'pruːv] *v.* 批准
- pornographic [ˌpɔːnə'græf(ɪ)k] *adj.* 淫秽的
- slander ['slɑːndə] *n.* 诽谤
- vicious ['v(ɪ)ʃəs] *adj.* 恶意的
- infringe [(ɪ)n'fr(ɪ)ndʒ] *v.* 侵犯

艺术家在进行创作时应该被允许通过文字、图片、音乐或电影等方式来自由地表达自己的思想。有人却认为政府应该对此进行一定的限制。你是否同意？

在一个真正民主的国家，人们有言论自由。人人都能自由表达意见和想法。在艺术创作领域，这种自由也不应该受到限制。

言论自由是每一个公民的基本权利，对艺术家来说更是如此。艺术家的观点通常都不是通过其言论，而是通过其作品表达的。每个人都有说出真理和自己真实感受的权利。剥夺这种自由就是一种压迫。只有不是人民当家作主的国家才害怕言论自由。比如，所有的独裁者都不让其人民批评政府。

艺术是绝对离不开自由表达的。艺术是真实世界的反映。艺术家把自己看到的世界用艺术的形式再现出来。艺术家可以选择世界的任何一部分作为对象，然后用自己独特的视角进行观察。没有两位艺术家对世界的认知是完全一样的。如果对艺术的领域和对象加以限制，如果艺术家只能用政府批准的方法来表现艺术，如果他们害怕因表达真实想法而被投入监狱的话，艺术就不再是艺术了。

当然，艺术家在自由表达的同时也要遵守法律。他们的艺术作品不能包含淫秽内容。他们不能诽谤他人，或者传播谣言。自由并不是为所欲为，而是要在不侵犯他人自由和权利的情况下，做自己想做的事情。

所以，政府不应该对艺术创作加以限制。艺术家应该享有自由表达的权利，只要这种自由没有被当作从事非法活动的借口。

特别提醒

艺术创作问题曾经是雅思写作考试中的热门话题；在各种关于艺术的雅思写作题中，关于艺术的价值以及艺术创作是否需要绝对自由的文章出现的频率最高。这篇范文中出现不少精彩论据，请你用心整理和归纳。

推荐指数 ★★★　　　　**相关题目** 79, 80

写作点拨

这道题目要求考生就“艺术创作是否需要绝对自由”给出自己的观点，是典型的观点类雅思作文题。范文有别于最传统的写作方法，添加了一个让步段。全文分为五段：第一段亮出作者的观点；第二、三段分别介绍摆出各种论据，支持作者的观点；第四段是让步段，指出在某些时候艺术家应该规范自己的行为；第五段总结全文，重申作者的观点。雅思考试中，让步段往往起到“以退为进”的作用，使得文章的论证思路更为缜密。

论据积累

艺术创作为什么需要自由：

1. 言论自由是每一个公民的基本权利，对艺术家来说更是如此。
   Freedom of speech is a basic right for all citizens, more so for artists.
2. 艺术是真实世界的反映，是绝对离不开自由表达的。
   Art is a reflection of the real world.
3. 如果人人表达的观点一样，艺术就不再是艺术了。
   If restrictions are imposed on certain areas and subjects, and if artists can only approach an issue in ways approved by the authority, art ceases to be art.

ESSAY 41

Most countries spend large amount of money on weapons to defend themselves though they are not at war. Some believe those countries should spend the money to help poor countries. To what extent do you agree or disagree with this statement?

Last year, the defense expenditure of the United States exceeds 200 billion US dollars. If half of that money were used to help the poor, we would see a vast increase in the quality of their life. Alas, most countries are lukewarm in their efforts to help the poor, which is most deplorable to me.

People around the world have a moral obligation to help each other. Even animals often do this. As civilized men, can we stand by and do nothing while our fellow creatures are struggling in misery? National defense is given priority in most countries, which is a clear indication of our mutual hostility towards each other—we feel the need to guard and fight against one other. How ironic it is that instead of helping, we spend vast amount of money and resource on making sure that we will not be harmed by others. Granting some historical reasons, religious or ideological differences, human decency requires us to look after the interest of all people on earth, not just that of ourselves.

What's more, the assistance given to other countries by us often proves beneficial to ourselves in the long run. Economic globalization and integration makes nations increasingly interdependent. Rarely can one country develop all by itself. Any nation relies on others for raw materials or markets for end products. It is in the interest of rich countries that poor nations achieve economic growth because the increased purchase power in those countries may in turn give a boost to world economy. Therefore, aiding the poor makes economic as well as moral sense.

In short, peace and development is certainly the theme of this century. Priority should be given to assisting the poor both at home and abroad rather than national defense.

单词注释

- expenditure [ɪkˈspendɪtʃə(r)] *n.* 支出
- exceed [(ɪ)kˈsiːd] *v.* 超过
- lukewarm [ˌluːkˈwɔːm] *adj.* 微热的
- deplorable [d(ɪ)ˈplɔːrəbl] *adj.* 可叹的
- obligation [ˌɒblɪˈgeɪʃn] *n.* 责任
- priority [praɪˈɒrəti] *n.* 优先，重点
- hostility [hɒˈstɪləti] *n.* 敌意
- ideological [ˌaɪdiəˈlɒdʒɪkl] *adj.* 意识形态的
- integration [ˌɪntɪˈgreɪʃn] *n.* 一体化
- interdependent [ˌɪntədɪˈpendənt] *adj.* 相互依赖的，互助的

尽管并不处于战争状态，大多数国家还是在武器和国防方面花费了大量的经费。有人指出这些国家应该将这些钱用于援助贫穷国家。你是否同意？

去年，美国的国防开支超过了2000亿美元。如果将其中的一半用以帮助穷人，他们的生活水平将得到极大的提高。唉，可惜的是，大部分国家对帮助穷人都表现得比较冷淡。

世界上的所有人在道义上都有互相帮助的义务，即使动物都经常这样做。作为文明的人类，我们怎么能在同伴痛苦挣扎的时候坐视不管呢？大多数国家都非常注重国防，这明显地反映出人类之间存在着相互敌视的情绪：我们感觉必须彼此提防、争斗。具有讽刺意味的是，我们不是互相帮助，而是花大量的钱和资源来保证自己不被他人伤害。虽然存在一些历史的原因以及宗教和意识形态的差异，但是人类的本质要求我们考虑全人类的利益，而不仅仅是自己的利益。

另外，帮助别人，从长远来说，对自己也是有好处的。经济全球化和一体化使得国家间的相互依赖程度加深。一个国家仅靠自己是很难发展的。每个国家都会在原材料、成品市场方面依赖别国。如果贫穷国家经济发展了，这对富裕国家来说也是有利的，因为这些国家的购买力增加了，对世界经济有促进作用。所以，帮助穷人不仅在道义上有必要，在经济方面也是有意义的。

总之，和平与发展是这个世纪的两大主题。我们应该高度重视对穷人的援助，而不能过分注重发展国防。

特别提醒

国家之间是否应该互相帮助，是近年雅思写作考试中新出现的热门话题，在雅思写作考试中出现过多次。本书收集了若干道关于国际援助的题目，虽然形式各异，但是实质问题却大同小异。请用心归纳和整理范文中的论据，为这类作文题的写作打下坚实的基础。

推荐指数 ★★★ **相关题目** 39

写作点拨

这道题目要求考生就“国家应该将经费用于国防还是用于国家援助”的问题发表自己的看法，属于典型的观点类的雅思作文题。范文采用了这类作文题最正统的写法，分为四段：第一段开门见山地给出作者的观点，第二、三段分别列举不同的理由来证明该观点，第四段总结全文。

词汇升级

冷淡的，不热心的

普通版 Most countries are *indifferent* in their efforts to help the poor, which is most deplorable to me.

升级版 Most countries are *lukewarm* in their efforts to help the poor, which is most deplorable to me.

冷漠的，不热心的：nonchalant, unconcerned, tepid, lukewarm

ESSAY 42

How to measure a country's success? Some say it depends on the quality of citizens' life, but others say it means a prosperous economy. What's your opinion?

Success is a universal goal for all people and nations. It often defies definition. It is hard to measure personal and national success. A nation's success in particular depends on many factors.

Equality is a main factor in measuring a nation's success. A nation may enjoy great material wealth yet remains a failure. Indeed, inequality exists in all countries to some degree. There is an old Chinese saying which goes: trouble is caused not by poverty but inequality. If people are discriminated against because of their gender, income or social status, resentment and hostility between different classes will grow. The oppressed and underprivileged will struggle for equality, culminating often in social unrest or even civil wars. A sound political and judicial system is required to ensure equality among the people. It should be considered the proudest achievement of any nation.

Apart from that, success should be gauged by a country's contribution to the international community. Ours is a global village whose villagers are all interrelated and interdependent. Each nation is just one member of the global family. One is supposed to look after the interest of one's relatives. However, many a time we have witnessed aggression and war against other nations in the quest for power and money. However mighty those invaders become, their history will forever be tinted with wickedness and humiliation. The luxury enjoyed by the conquerors or exploiters inspires no admiration, only contempt and hatred. Truly noble are those nations who extend a helping hand to others with no strings attached and no ulterior motives.

Success is forever pursued by nations as well as individuals. All too often people mistake success for economic success, which is rather deplorable. Among the factors contributing to real success, a booming economy is an inconsequential one.

单词注释

- defy [dɪ ˈfaɪ] *v.* 抗拒
- inequality [ˌɪnɪ ˈkwɒləti] *n.* 不平等
- discriminate [dɪ ˈskrɪmɪneɪt] *v.* 歧视，区别
- resentment [rɪ ˈzentmənt] *n.* 反感
- underprivileged [ˌʌndə ˈprɪvəlɪdʒd] *adj.* 被剥夺基本权利的；穷困的；下层社会的
- culminate [ˈkʌlm(ɪ)ne(ɪ)t] *v.* 达到顶峰
- gauge [geɪdʒ] *v.* 衡量
- aggression [ə ˈgreʃn] *n.* 扩张
- quest [kwest] *n.* 寻求
- invader [ɪn ˈveɪdə(r)] *n.* 侵略者
- tint [t(ɪ)nt] *v.* 给…着色
- wickedness [ˈwɪkɪdnɪs] *n.* 邪恶，不道德
- humiliation [hjuːˌmɪli ˈeɪʃn] *n.* 羞辱，蒙羞
- contempt [kən ˈtempt] *n.* 鄙视
- hatred [ˈheɪtrɪd] *n.* 憎恨，敌意，仇恨
- ulterior [ʌl ˈt(ɪ)əriə] *adj.* 隐秘的
- inconsequential [ɪnˌkɒnsɪ ˈkwenʃl] *adj.* 不合逻辑的，不合理的

如何衡量一个国家的成功？有人认为国家成功与否取决于百姓的生活水平，其他人认为国家成功意味着经济繁荣。请给出你的看法。

成功是所有人和所有国家共同的目标。但成功却很难定义。我们很难衡量个人和国家的成功。一个国家的成功受到各种因素的影响。

平等是衡量一个国家是否成功的重要因素。一个国家可能拥有大量的物质财富但仍然不成功。事实上，任何国家都存在不同程度的不平等。中国有句古话：不患贫而患不均。如果存在性别、收入或者社会地位等方面的歧视，那么不同阶级之间就会产生憎恨和敌意。受压迫的下层人群就会为平等而战，严重的话甚至会导致社会动乱和内战。一个完善的政治和司法体系是保证人与人之间平等的重要手段。平等对任何一个国家来讲都是最值得骄傲的成就。

除了上述因素，一个国家对国际社会的贡献也是衡量其成功与否的标准之一。我们的世界是一个地球村。村民们都互相关联、互相依赖。每个国家都是全球大家庭里面的一名村民。我们应该互相照顾，就像亲戚一样。但是，我们看到，为了金钱和权力，侵略和战争时有发生。不管侵略者有多么淫威，他们的历史将永远地留下了污点和羞辱。那些征服者、剥削者所享受的奢靡带来的不是羡慕，而是蔑视和憎恨。只有那些无条件、无险恶用心、主动帮助他人的国家才是真正高尚的国家。

个人和国家都将永远地追求成功。但是人们往往把成功错误地等同于经济上的成功。这是很令人叹息的。在所有影响成功的因素当中，经济因素并不是最重要的。

特别提醒

如何定义成功？如何定义幸福？如何定义友谊？这些看似属于哲学的问题，近年来却成了雅思写作考试中的热门话题。这道关于国家的成功应该如何衡量的作文题就曾经在雅思写作考试中出现过多次。请用心体会这类作文题应该如何展开论证。

推荐指数 ★★★

相关题目 31, 88, 94, 100

写作点拨

这道题目要求考生就“国家的成功应如何衡量”这一问题发表自己的看法。很多考生在动笔写这篇作文之前，往往未能正确理解题目的意思。虽然题目中列举了两种衡量国家成功的方法，但是题目却并不是要求考生就这两种方法发表自己的看法，而是要求考生提出自己心目中的衡量国家成功的方法。范文分为四段：第一段引入话题，第二、三段分别列举不同的方法用来衡量一个国家成功与否，第四段总结全文。

词汇升级

测量，衡量

普通版 Apart from that, success should also be *measured* by a country's contribution to the international community.

升级版 Apart from that, success should also be *gauged* by a country's contribution to the international community.

测量，衡量：fathom, survey, plumb, assess, appraise, rate, estimate

ESSAY 43

Education is of vital importance to individual development and social progress. What should education consist of in order to fulfill both ends?

Educational expenditure in most developed countries, the United States, for instance, often outstrips that in other areas. From this we can see the importance attached to education. Teachers and educators in China are enjoying better salaries as people start to reap the benefits from a highly educated workforce. Ideally, education should contribute to personal advancement and social development.

To achieve personal growth and success, one needs in-depth knowledge in a certain discipline. Every branch of knowledge is worth pursuing provided that you don't merely scratch the surface. No real interest can be fostered by just dipping into a subject. Without interest, learning becomes not a pleasure, but a burden to be endured for the sake of getting a diploma, which is often a prerequisite to a decent job. To really develop one's abilities, one needs to focus on his or her major. Enormous amount of time and energy are required to pursue a discipline or a perfect skill. Unfortunately, college students in China are often distracted by taking many irrelevant courses in which they are not remotely interested. It is the experts and specialists that prevail in the increasingly competitive society. Of course, it is also essential to have a general knowledge of relevant subjects because many disciplines are interrelated.

To promote social progress, schools need to provide moral and ethical education. The development of a society calls for genuine cooperation and harmony among its people. No society can develop if all its citizens are engaged in a rat race for personal gains with no regard for each other. With a lowering of moral and ethical standard, people start to scramble for their personal interest at all cost. Fraud, bribery and corruption become rampant. Therefore, people need to be educated morally, ethically and psychologically. It is not enough for one to become powerful; one should be a good man above anything else. Just think about the untold atrocities caused by those evil men wielding enormous power.

Education is a lifelong process, the importance of which can be hardly exaggerated. As things stand now, there is always room for improvement. A well-balanced education will be most conducive to individual and social progress.

单词注释

- vital [ˈva(ɪ)tl] *adj.* 生命的；很重要的
- advancement [ədˈvɑːnsmənt] *n.* 前进；促进
- contribute [kənˈtr(ɪ)bjuːt] *v.* 贡献；资助
- in-depth [inˈdepθ] *adj.* 深入的；彻底的
- discipline [ˈdɪsəplɪn] *n.* 纪律；训练；学科
- diploma [d(ɪ)ˈpləumə] *n.* 文凭，毕业证书
- scratch [skrætʃ] *vt.* 抓；擦伤
- endure [(ɪ)nˈdjuə] *v.* 忍受；持久，耐久
- prerequisite [ˌpriːˈrekwəzɪt] *n.* 先决条件，前提
- decent [ˈdiːsnt] *adj.* 正当的，正经的
- ethical [ˈeθɪkl] *adj.* 伦理的，道德的
- scramble [ˈskræmbl] *vi.* 爬；争夺
- harmony [ˈhɑːməni] *n.* 协调，和睦；调和
- fraud [frɔːd] *n.* 欺骗，骗人的事
- rampant [ˈræmpənt] *adj.* 繁茂的；蔓生的；蔓延的；猖獗的；猛烈的
- psychologically [ˌsaɪkəˈlɒdʒɪkli] *adv.* 心理上地
- wield [wiːld] *vt.* 支配；控制；挥动，使用，熟练地操作，有效地运用
- atrocity [əˈtrɒsəti] *n.* 凶恶，暴行

教育对个人发展以及社会进步都极其重要。为了兼顾个人发展和社会进步的需要，你认为教育应该包含哪些要素？

以美国为首的大多数世界上最发达的国家的教育开支往往超过其他方面的开支。其对教育的重视，由此可以见一斑。在中国，受过高等教育的人才给社会带来了价值，因此教师和教育者的工资待遇也日益优厚。教育理应为个人的进步和社会的发展做出贡献。

要取得个人的成长和成功，一个人需要对某些学科进行深入的研究。只要你不只是浅尝辄止，每一门学科都值得人们去研究。浅尝辄止是不可能培养兴趣的。没有了兴趣，学习就不是乐趣，而成为一种包袱，只是为了得到文凭。文凭往往是获得一份体面工作的前提。要想真正地发展能力，我们应该把注意力放在自己的专业上。研究一个学科或者完善一项技能需要大量的时间和精力。不幸的是，中国的大学生却经常被很多无关紧要的、他们一点儿也不感兴趣的课程分散了精力。在这个竞争日益激烈的社会，只有专家才能胜出。当然，拥有相关学科的广泛知识也是很重要的，因为很多学科之间都是相互联系的。

要推动社会进步，学校需要提供道德教育。社会的发展呼唤人与人之间真诚合作，和谐相处。如果一个社会的公民只忙于个人得失而不关心他人，这样的社会是不能发展的。在低下的道德标准下，人们不惜一切攫取个人利益。欺骗、贿赂和腐败由此得以泛滥。因此，人们需要道德和心理教育。将一个人培养成有用之才还不够；一个人应该首先是一个好人。那些拥有巨大权力的邪恶分子给人类带来了无尽的灾难。

教育是一辈子的事，它的重要性再强调也不为过。在当前的情况下，我们还有改进的空间。全面平衡的教育对个人和社会的进步都是有益的。

特别提醒

教育问题历来都是雅思写作考试中的热门话题。关于教育的雅思写作题目，大致可以分为教育的内容（教育应该包含什么、应该重点传授职业技能还是人文知识）、教育的方式（混班教学 VS 男女分校、集体学习 VS 单独辅导）以及教育的意义三大类。

推荐指数 ★★★★

相关题目 2, 6, 14, 24, 44, 49, 65, 68, 93

写作点拨

这道题目要求考生就"教育应该包含哪些要素"这一问题发表自己的看法。与一般的作文题不同，这道题目并没有给出对立的观点，并不要求考生就已经给出的观点发表自己的看法，而是要求考生独立地提出自己心目中教育应该包含的要素，对学生思想的深度和广度有一定的要求。范文分为四段：第一段引入话题，第二、三段分别从个人发展以及社会进步两方面来探讨教育应该包含哪些要素，第四段总结全文。

词汇升级

从…获利

普通版 Teachers and educators in China are enjoying better salaries as people start to *benefit from* a highly educated workforce.

升级版 Teachers and educators in China are enjoying better salaries as people start to *reap the benefits from* a highly educated workforce.

ESSAY 44

It is right that college graduates earn higher salaries than the less well-educated in the community. But they should also pay the full cost of their study. Do you agree or disagree with this statement?

College graduates in China are having a hard time getting employed, more often than not, even on quite unappealing terms. It began to dawn on people that college education is no guarantee for decent jobs. Besides, even if the assumption that better education means better jobs were true, it is still wrong not to provide any financial assistance to students.

In reality, college graduates are far from enjoying higher salaries than those without a diploma. Actually, an employee should be rewarded as per his or her contribution to the company, which should be measured by using objective criteria as much as possible. Besides, one's performance at work often doesn't have much to do with the amount of education one receives except in some knowledge-intensive fields. All too often, skilled blue collar workers who haven't finished high school are paid much better than degree holders. Work experience, interpersonal skills and teamwork are far more valued by employers. Long gone are the days when college education guarantees enviable salaries.

Contrary to common belief, college education is much more than an investment made by the individual in the hope of getting higher return upon graduation. Education is essential to social progress. A university does not and should not act as a career training center, whose aim is merely to prepare students for the work ahead. Rather, college education cultivates the mind of the student and improves one's overall abilities. With more people receiving higher education, the whole nation benefits in numerous ways. This has been testified in the developed countries, all of which put a premium on education. Thus, it is fitting that gifted students with potentials not be barred from universities simply because they cannot foot the bill.

Although college education no longer automatically translates into decent salaries, its appeals to youngsters have never been stronger. Adequate grants and scholarships should be set aside to alleviate the financial burdens of those underprivileged students.

单词注释

- unappealing [ˌʌnəˈpiːl(ɪ)ŋ] *adj.* 不动人的，无魅力的
- terms [tɜːmz] *n.* 条件
- guarantee [ˌgærənˈtiː] *vt.* 保证，承诺；确定；保护
- assumption [əˈsʌmpʃn] *n.* 假定，设想
- reward [r(ɪ)ˈwɔːd] *vt.* 报答，酬劳，奖赏
- criteria [kraɪˈtɪəriə] *n.* 标准；准则；规律
- knowledge-intensive [ˈnɔlɪdʒɪnˈtensɪv] *adj.* 知识密集的
- interpersonal [ˌɪntəˈpɜːsənl] *adj.* 人与人之间的；人际关系的
- numerous [njuːmərəs] *adj.* 极多的，为数众多的
- essential [iˈsenʃəl] *adj.* 必要的，必不可少的，基本的；本质的
- testify [ˈtest(ɪ)faɪ] *vi.* 证实，证明；郑重宣言；提供证据
- premium [ˈpriːmiəm] *n.* 奖赏，酬金；保险金；额外费用
- bar [bɑː(r)] *vt.* 妨害；禁止
- foot the bill 支付费用
- automatically [ˌɔːtəˈmætɪklɪ] *adv.* 自动地
- appeal [əˈpiːl] *vi.* 有感染力
- grant [grɑːnt] *vt.* 赐予，授予特权
- scholarship [ˈskɒləʃip] *n.* 奖学金
- alleviate [əˈliːvie(ɪ)t] *vt.* 使减轻，缓和
- underprivileged [ˌʌndəˈprɪvəlɪdʒd] *adj.* 贫穷的，下层社会的

大学生比教育程度较低的人收入高是合情合理的，但是大学生应该自己承担全部的教育费用。你是否同意这样的观点？

中国大学毕业生面临着就业难的问题，很多人甚至连待遇一般的工作也找不到。这使人们开始认识到：大学教育并不是体面工作的通行证。另外，即使我们假定高等教育意味着更好的工作，不给学生提供任何经济帮助的做法也还是错误的。

在现实生活中，大学毕业生并不比那些没有学历的人享受更高的工资。实际上，一个员工应该按照他/她对公司的贡献来领取报酬，而这种贡献应该尽可能地用客观标准来加以评定。除非在一些专业知识性很强的领域，否则一个人在工作中的表现往往和他的教育程度无关。那些没有完成高中教育但技术熟练的蓝领工人往往会比持有学位的人拿到更高的报酬。雇主们更看重工作经验、人际交往技巧和团队精神。那个大学教育保证带来令人艳羡工资的时代已经不复存在了。

和大众观点相反的是，大学教育远不是个人为得到高额回报而进行的一项投资。教育对社会的发展十分重要。大学不是也不应该只是一个为学生将来就业提供培训的职业培训中心。大学教育应该陶冶学生的心智，培养学生的综合能力。越来越多的人接受高等教育，整个国家也以多种方式获利。这一点在所有的发达国家都得到证实，因为他们都重视教育。因此，有才华和潜力的学生不应该仅仅因为他们付不起学费而被拒于大学校门之外。

尽管大学教育不再等同于高薪工作，然而它对年轻人的吸引力却日益强烈。相关部门应该准备足量的助学金和奖学金来减轻贫困学生的经济负担。

特别提醒

教育问题历来都是雅思写作考试中的热门话题。本书收集了大量关于教育的雅思写作题目。这道雅思作文题讨论的是大学生是否应该独立承担全部教育费用的问题。在类似的关于高等教育的雅思作文题中，出现频率较高的还有大学教育应该侧重职业教育还是素质提高、各个专业是否应该招收同等数目的学生等问题。

推荐指数 ★★★★　　**相关题目** 1, 13, 71, 86, 95

写作点拨

这道题目要求考生就“大学生是否应该独立承担全部教育费用”这一问题发表自己的看法，属于非常典型的“观点”类的雅思作文题。范文采用了最正统的雅思议论文写法，文章分为四段：第一段开门见山地给出作者的观点，第二、三段分别从不同方面论证了作者观点的合理性，第四段在总结全文的同时再次重申了作者的观点。

词汇升级

工资

普通版 Although college education no longer automatically translates into *good salaries*, its appeals to youngsters have never been stronger.

升级版 Although college education no longer automatically translates into *decent salaries*, its appeals to youngsters have never been stronger.

工资：competitive(有竞争力的), generous(丰盛的), handsome(大方的), reasonable(合理的), pensionable(可领退休金的)

ESSAY 45

Some people say that the positive effects of advertising outweigh its negative effects. Do you agree or disagree?

Advertising is ubiquitous. Wherever you go and whatever you read, you are likely to be bombarded by adverts touting some products or services. Is the unsolicited, seemingly wholesome information beneficial or detrimental?

It would be wrong to deny advertising any credit. The yearly turnover of this industry indicates its importance in the business world. Without adverts, it would be much harder for consumers to learn about new products. Indeed, world economy would be much less developed.

Notwithstanding all that, advertising influence most people adversely. It advocates an unhealthy and wasteful lifestyle. In an attempt to cash in on every new product, copywriters are employed to come up with eye-catching adverts. Most of these ads portray the new product as trendy and almost indispensable. Sure enough, many people discard the old products and purchase the latest model, which often turns out only fractionally superior to the older one. The fashion industry is a case in point. Thanks to its advertising, women and some men are coaxed to throw out their clothes bought a year ago because they are out of style.

In addition, adverts may lead to inordinate anxiety and worries. There are two main tactics used in the advertising industry to persuade and convince people: one is to appeal to our desire for pleasure and the other is to take advantage of our fear. Many adverts solemnly assume a scientific tone and warn consumers of certain terrible but overlooked ailments and then offer the cure. In fact, it is agreed that many diseases are created by advertisement, many of which are without solid scientific basis. Apart from that, most adverts intentionally exaggerate or mislead the audience by implying dire consequences if their products are not used. A man is in danger of losing his job if he doesn't partake in a certain program; a woman is likely to lose the affection of her husband if she doesn't use certain kind of perfume. Adverts put strain on our already high-strung nerve by feeding us all kinds of potential or invented problems.

Despite its big role in modern society, advertising needs to be strictly regulated and restricted because the strategies employed in advertising is becoming increasingly insidious and vicious.

单词注释

- outweigh [ˌaʊtˈweɪ] *vt.* 重过，胜过
- ubiquitous [juːˈb(ɪ)kw(ɪ)təs] *adj.* 无所不在的
- bombard [bɒmˈbɑːd] *vt.* 炮轰；质问；攻击某人
- unsolicited [ˈʌnsəˈlɪsɪtɪd] *adj.* 多余的，多事的；自发的，主动提出的
- seemingly [ˈsiːmɪŋlɪ] *adv.* 表面上，看起来
- detrimental [ˌdetr(ɪ)ˈmentl] *adj.* 有害的，伤害的；不利的
- credit [ˈkred(ɪ)t] *n.* 名誉；赞同，赞许
- notwithstanding [ˌnɒtwɪθˈstændɪŋ] *adv.* 虽然，即使
- adversely [ˈædvɜːsli] *adv.* 有敌意地，不利地
- attempt [əˈtempt] *vt.* 尝试，企图
- cash in on 靠…赚钱；乘机利用
- copywriter [ˈkɒpiraɪtə(r)] *n.* 广告撰稿人
- eye-catching *adj.* 吸引目光的
- portray [pɔːˈtreɪ] *vt.* 描绘，描写
- indispensable [ˌɪndɪˈspensəbl] *adj.* 不可缺少的，必需的；义务的；不可避免的
- fractionally [ˈfrækʃənli] *adv.* 部分地，碎片地
- coax [kəuks] *vt.* 劝诱；哄骗，以劝诱取得
- inordinate [ɪnˈɔːdɪnət] *adj.* 过度的，无节制的
- partake [pɑːˈteik] *v.* 参与；分享；吃，喝
- affection [əˈfekʃən] *n.* 爱，爱好
- exaggerate [ɪgˈzædʒəreit] *vt.* 夸大，夸张
- insidious [ɪnˈsɪdiəs] *adj.* 狡猾的，阴险的

有人认为广告利大于弊。你是否同意这样的看法？

广告是无所不在的。不管你走到哪里，不管你读什么，你都有可能被宣传商品或服务的广告围攻。这种不请自来、看似无伤大雅的信息是否有利于大众呢？

否认广告的作用是错误的。广告工业的年营业额说明了它在商业世界中的重要性。没有广告，顾客要知道新的商品就更困难了，而且世界经济的发展步伐也会由此放慢。

尽管如此，广告对大多数人有不利的影响。广告鼓吹一种不健康的、奢侈浪费的生活方式。商家试图从每一种新商品中获取利润，因此他们雇用大量广告人设计出各种广告以吸引观众的眼球。大多数这类广告都把这些新商品描述成时尚的、不可缺少的东西。果然，许多人都丢弃旧的商品，去购买最新的型号。这些新型号其实往往与旧的型号相差无几。时装工业就是这样一个示例。由于广告的缘故，大部分女性和部分男性受到广告的影响，扔掉一年前的衣服，因为它们已经不再流行了。

此外，广告还会引起过度的焦虑和担忧。广告业使用两种主要的策略来说服观众：一是引诱我们对快乐的渴望，一是利用我们的恐惧感。很多广告都以一种严肃、科学的语气警告人们去关注一些严重的、被忽视的疾病，然后提出治疗方法。人们已经达成普遍共识：许多疾病都是广告创造出来的，而且很多都是没有确凿的科学依据的。除此之外，许多广告还故意误导观众，夸大产品效果或者暗示人们不使用他们的产品将有严重后果。如果男人不参加某项培训就有丢掉工作的危险；如果女人不用某种香水就会失去丈夫的宠爱。广告往往反复强调各种潜在的甚至是莫须有的问题，给我们本已高压的生活带来更多的压力。

尽管广告在现代社会扮演着重要的角色，但是由于广告中运用的策略变得越来越恶意和有害，广告需要受到严厉的限制和约束。

特别提醒

大众传媒的利弊问题历来都是雅思写作考试中的热门话题。本书收集了大量关于大众传媒的雅思写作题目。这道关于广告的利弊问题的雅思作文题，就曾经以不同的形式多次出现在雅思写作考试中。请用心积累这类高频出现于写作题中的常用论据。

推荐指数 ★★★★★　　**相关题目** 4, 17, 23, 32, 51, 56, 73, 98

写作点拨

这道题目要求考生就“广告利大于弊”这一观点给出自己的看法，是典型的观点类雅思作文题。范文最大的亮点是添加了一个让步段，从而使得文章的论证思路更为缜密。全文分为五段：第一段引入话题；第二段是让步段，指出广告的确有不少可取之处；第三、四段分别从不同角度指出了广告的弊端，有力地支持作者的观点；第五段总结全文，再次重申作者的观点。

词汇升级

有危害的

普通版 Is the unsolicited, seemingly wholesome information beneficial or *harmful*?

升级版 Is the unsolicited, seemingly wholesome information beneficial or *detrimental*?

有危害的：hurtful, baneful, pernicious, noisome, injurious, deleterious, damaging, prejudicial, destructive, disadvantageous, adverse, inimical

ESSAY 46

Many people are afraid of leaving their house because of crime. Some think more actions should be taken to prevent crime, but others think little can be done. What is your view?

Crime has been around since time immemorial. Like war, crime is not likely to be totally eradicated, if history is any judge. Some might even say that it is an integral part of our universe, where balance must be achieved by the co-existence of opposing forces. However, I see no reason why crime cannot be largely prevented, if not exterminated.

Education is the first thing we can do to reduce crime. Take China for example. Seventy per cent of criminal offences were committed by the poorly educated who often didn't realize that they were breaking the law. In some rural villages it is still common practice to settle disputes by force. The concept of law is far from self-evident or widely accepted even among city dwellers. People need to be taught what constitutes a crime and what penalty or punishment would follow. But more importantly, people need to form the habit of resorting to law when problems arise.

Apart from that, effective law enforcement can make a great difference. More often than not people get frustrated and take things into their own hands because the judicial system fails to protect them or solve their problems. Bureaucracy, inefficiency and corruption are not uncommon in most countries. If police brutality go on unchecked, if some policemen can be bribed to offer protection to petty criminals, if murderers can get away unpunished because of their powerful connections, people will lose heart. Law enforcement is as essential as law itself.

To ultimately prevent crime, we have to dive into the root of crime. Though Christians assert that all men are sinful, the supposedly inherent sin doesn't necessarily lead to crime. There is no such a thing as a born criminal. Most people turn to crime as a last resort. It is a gradual process, starting from bad behavior to misconduct, wrongdoing and culminating in felony. Poverty, social inequality and racial discrimination are often causes of criminal acts. Given a secure life, few people would risk their liberty or life.

It would seem optimistic to claim that crimes can be reduced at a time when the crime rates in most countries are actually rising. However, effective education and law enforcement can make a difference. The day will come when everyone is so provided for that there is no point to commit a crime.

单词注释

- immemorial [ˌɪmə'mɔːriəl] *adj.* 太古的，极古的；无法追忆的
- integral ['ɪntɪgrəl] *adj.* 整体的，不可或缺的
- eradicate [ɪ'rædɪkeɪt] *vt.* 根除，消灭
- co-existence *n.* 共存，同时存在，和平共处
- exterminate [ɪk'stɜːmɪneɪt] *vt.* 扑灭，消灭，根绝
- offence [ə'fens] *n.* 犯罪，冒犯，过错
- self-evident [ˌself'evɪdənt] *adj.* 自明的
- constitute ['kɒnstɪtjuːt] *vt.* 构成，组成；任命
- penalty ['penəlti] *n.* 刑罚，罚款；报应
- resort [rɪ'zɔːt] *vi.* 诉诸；常去；滞留
- enforcement [ɪn'fɔːsmənt] *n.* 执行，强制
- frustrated [frʌ'streɪtɪd，'frʌ-] *adj.* 挫败的，失意的
- bureaucracy [bjʊə'rɒkrəsi] *n.* 官僚，官吏
- inefficiency [ˌɪnɪ'fɪʃənsi] *n.* 无效率，无能
- brutality [bruː'tæləti] *n.* 残忍，无慈悲，野蛮的行为
- ultimately ['ʌltɪmətli] *adv.* 最后，终于
- misconduct [ˌmɪs'kɒndʌkt] *n.* 办错，渎职；行为不端
- wrongdoing ['rɒŋduːɪŋ; 'rɔːŋ-] *n.* 坏事，不道德行为
- culminate ['kʌlmɪneɪt] *vt.* 使到绝顶，使达到高潮
- felony ['feləni] *n.* 重罪
- discrimination [dɪˌskrɪmɪ'neɪʃn] *n.* 差别，歧视，辨别力
- optimistic [ˌɒptɪ'mɪstɪk] *adj.* 乐观的，乐观主义的，乐天的
- provide for 供养

犯罪活动让很多人不敢出门。有人认为我们应该采取更多的行动来防止犯罪，别的人却认为几乎没有什么行动可以防止犯罪。请给出你的观点。

犯罪古来有之。从历史中可以看出，和战争一样，犯罪是不可能完全消除的。一些人甚至会说犯罪是我们宇宙中不可缺少的一部分，因为宇宙的平衡必须通过对立力量的共存来实现。然而我认为犯罪就算不能根除也可以在很大程度上加以预防。

教育是减少犯罪的第一步棋。以中国为例，70%的犯罪分子的教育程度都很低，他们常常没有意识到他们违反了法律。在乡下，使用暴力解决纠纷仍然是常见的事情。即便在城市，法律的概念也远未达到不言自明或者被广泛接受的程度。政府应该教育人们哪些行为构成犯罪以及犯罪所带来的惩罚。更重要的是，人们要形成用法律来解决问题的习惯。

除此之外，有效的执法也能有效减少犯罪。由于司法系统在保护人民或解决问题上的不力，人们常常十分沮丧，不得不自己私下解决问题。官僚作风、效率低下和贪污腐败在许多国家都十分常见。如果警察暴力继续得不到控制，如果罪犯可以通过贿赂某些警察来获得保护，如果利用人际关系杀人犯就能够逍遥法外，人们就会失去信心。法律实施和法律本身一样重要。

要彻底预防犯罪，我们要深入到犯罪的根源。尽管基督教断言说所有的人都有原罪，但是所谓固有的罪孽并不必然导致犯罪，并没有人天生就是罪犯。许多人走向犯罪是由于穷途末路。犯罪是一个渐进的过程，从坏的习惯开始，到不规矩的行为，再发展到恶劣行径，最后酿成大罪。贫穷、不平等、种族歧视往往都是犯罪的原因。如果有安定的生活，很少有人会拿自己的自由和生命冒险。

在犯罪率普遍上升的时候大谈减少犯罪似乎过于乐观。然而，有效的教育和执法能够遏制犯罪。总有一天每个人都能安居乐业，犯罪将变得毫无必要。

特别提醒

社会治安以及违法犯罪的问题，是近年来雅思写作考试中新出现的热门话题。本书收集了若干道关于违法犯罪的雅思写作题目，其中大多数是关于如何减少犯罪行为以及青少年犯罪的原因两大话题。这道关于犯罪行为是否可以被减少的雅思作文题，就曾经以不同的形式多次出现在雅思写作考试中。

推荐指数 ★★★★

相关题目 52, 56, 99, 101, 108

写作点拨

这道题目要求考生就“犯罪行为是否可以被减少”这一问题给出自己的观点，是典型的观点类雅思作文题。范文使用了最传统的议论文的写法，全文分为五段：第一段亮出作者的观点；第二、三、四段分别介绍不同的减少犯罪行为的措施，有力地支持作者的观点，即犯罪行为是可以被减少的；第五段总结全文，再次重申作者的观点。

论据积累

如何减少犯罪活动：

1. 教育可避免很多人无意识地犯罪

   Education is the first thing we can do to reduce crime as many criminal offences were committed by the poorly educated who didn't realize that they were breaking the law.

2. 有效的执法

   Effective law enforcement can make a great difference.

3. 消除犯罪的根源

   To ultimately prevent crime, we have to dive into the root of crime.

ESSAY 47

Many people believe that subjects such as music or sports are not useful. Thus school should concentrate on subjects that offer better career prospect. What is your opinion?

In a few days' time, the yearly College Entrance Exam is to be held in China. Achieving a high score in the exam is no longer enough for the long-suffering students, who also face the task of choosing a suitable major. As might be expected, many universities are setting up new departments that offer job-oriented courses or expanding existing ones to enhance their enrollment. As far as I am concerned this lopsided emphasis is not justified.

Career prospect is on most people's mind when choosing a major, but this can hardly justify the overemphasis on certain disciplines. It is not the goal of education to provide job trainings to students. Education aims to improve one's all-round abilities. It is a gradual process, a cultivation of the mind, which is not easily measured or even perceived. It is short-sighted to concentrate on certain subjects that are supposed to be in great demand. More haste, less speed. There is no way one can acquire all the skills and expertise needed for work through college education. Internal training at workplace is always necessary.

Besides, profession skill is not the only thing valued by employers. Indeed, it is hardly the most important consideration. One's overall ability is more regarded. A successful candidate must possess the right personality, adequate interpersonal skills and the willingness to learn. Only a well-balanced education can ensure all-around development. Employers are increasingly bored and put down by those graduates who know very little outside their major. Music, sports and other neglected subjects can benefit us in ways we never expected.

Ironically, the overemphasis of certain subjects often backfires. In China, for example, fueled by steady economic growth, most universities rush to set up departments like Accounting, Finance, International Trade, Law and so on. As a result, the demand for those majors falls behind the supply—thousands of students fail to get employed. In the meantime, there is a shortage of highly-educated and qualified workers in some 'unpopular' fields.

Therefore, this kind of imbalance is doing damage to both the individual and society at large. In fact, each subject is just as important as any other. One can excel in any field if he is dedicated enough.

单词注释

- concentrate [ˈkɒnsntreɪt] *vi.* 集中，专心
- long-suffering [ˌlɒŋ ˈsʌfərɪŋ] *adj.* 坚忍的
- suitable [ˈsuːtəbl] *adj.* 适当的，适宜的，相配的
- enhance [ɪn ˈhɑːns] *vt.* 提高，加强，增加
- enrollment [ɪn ˈrəʊlmənt] *n.* 登记，注册，入伍
- lopsided [ˌlɒp ˈsaɪdɪd] *adj.* 倾向一方的，不平衡的
- emphasis [ˈemfəsɪs] *n.* 强调，加强
- overemphasis [ˌəʊvər ˈemfəsɪs] *n.* 过分的强调
- cultivation [ˌkʌltɪ ˈveɪʃn] *n.* 教化，培养，耕作
- all-around [ˌɔːlə ˈraʊnd] *adj.* 全面的，综合性的
- perceive [pə ˈsiːv] *vt.* 感觉，认知，理解
- short-sighted *adj.* 眼光短浅的
- acquire [ə ˈkwaɪə(r)] *vt.* 获得，学到
- expertise [ˌekspɜː ˈtiːz] *n.* 专家的意见，专门技术
- candidate [ˈkændɪdɪt] *n.* 候选人，投考者
- backfire [bæk ˈfaɪə(r)] *vi.* 产生事与愿违的不良效果
- ironically [aɪ ˈrɒnɪkli] *adv.* 讥讽地，反讽地
- excel [ɪk ˈsel] *vt.* 胜过，优于
- accounting [ə ˈkaʊntɪŋ] *n.* 会计学，清算账目
- dedicate [ˈdedɪkeɪt] *vt.* 献出，贡献

很多人认为诸如音乐和体育之类的课程并不实用，因此学校应该专注于那些有利于学生就业的科目。请给出你的看法。

再过几天，中国一年一度的大学入学考试就要开始了。在考试中取得高分对这些饱受折磨的学生来说还不够，他们还必须选择一个合适的专业。果然，很多大学都在通过建立新的学院或者扩建已有的学院来扩大就业不错的专业的招生。就我而言，这种对热门专业的过分重视是不合理的。

在选择专业的时候，大多数人想到的都是就业前景，但是这并不意味着应该对某些专业给予过分的重视。教育的目标不是给学生提供就业培训。教育的目标在于完善一个人的综合能力。教育是一个渐进的过程，是对人心智的培养。这是不易测量和察觉的。仅仅重视某些需求量大的专业是目光短浅的。欲速则不达。想通过大学教育获得所有的技能和专业知识是不可能的。工作当中的内部培训永远是必不可少的。

另外，顾主看重的并不只是专业技能。实际上，专业技能往往不是最重要的因素。雇主更加看重个人的综合能力。一个成功的候选人必须具有正直的个性、足够的人际交往技能以及学习的意愿。顾主们越来越对那些对专业外的知识了解甚少的毕业生感到厌烦。音乐、体育以及一些被忽略的专业能以我们想不到的方式使我们受益。

讽刺的是，对某些专业的过多重视反而适得其反。例如，中国经济稳步增长，多数大学都匆忙地设立会计、金融、国际贸易、法律等院系。结果对这些专业的需求远远小于供给：成千上万的学生找不到工作。而在同时，在一些不受欢迎的领域却出现了高学历和高素质人才的短缺。

因此，这种不平衡对个人和社会总体都造成了危害。实际上，每门学科都和任何其他学科一样重要。如果一个人能做到术业有专攻，那么他在任何领域都能做到优秀。

特别提醒

教育问题，历来都是雅思写作考试中的热门话题。雅思写作考试中，关于教育的雅思写作题目，大致可以分为三大类：1.教育的内容（教育应该包含哪些内容、教育应该重点传授职业技能还是人文知识）；2.教育的方式（混班教学 VS 男 / 女校、集体学习 VS 单独辅导）；3 教育的意义（为什么要接受教育）。这道关于学校是否应该专注于那些有利于学生就业的科目的雅思写作题，属于第一大类，曾经以不同的形式在雅思写作考试中多次出现。

推荐指数 ★★★★★

相关题目 2, 6, 14, 24, 43, 44, 49, 65, 68, 93

写作点拨

这道题目要求考生就“学校是否应该专注于那些有利于学生就业的科目”这一问题给出自己的观点，是典型的观点类的雅思作文题。范文使用了最中规中矩的议论文的写法，全文分为五段：第一段亮出作者的观点，即不应该专注于那些有利于学生就业的科目；第二、三、四段介绍了学校专注于那些有利于学生就业的科目有可能带来的弊端；第五段在总结全文的同时再次重申了作者的观点。

词汇升级

杰出，出众，优秀

普通版 One can *become outstanding* in any field if he is dedicated enough.

升级版 One can *excel* in any field if he is dedicated enough.

杰出，出众，优秀：*adj.* outstanding, eminent, prominent, illustrious, distinguished *v.* tower, overdo, surpass

ESSAY 48

Each year some languages die out. Some say this is good because fewer languages would make communication easier and relieve people of the burden of learning foreign languages. Do you agree or disagree?

It is said that sixty percent of the languages that ever existed have already become extinct. This would not be much lamented by most people except those linguists or archeologists. Indeed, some people regard this as a healthy sign that the world is integrating.

As far as learning foreign languages is concerned, it is indeed good news on the face of it. But, following the same logic, biologist would wish to have more extinct species because that means a lighter workload. The truth is far from it. They are advocating the protection of endangered species. Similarly, fewer languages don't necessarily mean better communication unless all languages are forsaken except a lingua franca. As long as several languages are used, there will always be language barriers.

The loss of languages is akin to that of history and culture. A nation's history and culture are largely recorded in its language, both verbal and written. With the demise of a language, the history and tradition are gradually forgotten, which is often irreparable. Scientists nowadays are trying in vain to decipher those ancient languages to get a glimpse at what life was like millenniums ago. How much easier it would become if the languages were still used today.

The loss is regrettable because languages are closely linked to people's ways of thinking. Our thoughts are described in our languages and hinted maybe in artistic works. People speak different languages and think in different ways. To really understand their way of thinking, one needs to comprehend their languages. Each language is unique. For instance, Chinese is known for its flexibility, Japanese for its politeness, French its beauty. Different languages really complement each other.

As that of dinosaurs, the extinction of certain languages is just as lamentable. As a language dies out, the door to a unique history, culture and beauty is closed. The world becomes much duller as a result.

单词注释

- lament [ləˈment] *vt.* 哀悼 *vi.* 悔恨，悲叹
- linguist [ˈlɪŋgwɪst] *n.* 语言学家
- archeologist [ˌɑːkiˈɒlədʒɪst] *n.* 考古学家
- integrate [ˈɪntɪgreɪt] *vt.* 使成整体，使一体化
- extinct [ɪkˈstɪŋkt] *adj.* 熄灭的，灭绝的
- advocate [ˈædvəkeɪt] *n.* 提倡者，鼓吹者 *vt.* 提倡，鼓吹
- forsake [fəˈseɪk] *vt.* 放弃，抛弃
- lingua franca 混合语，通用语
- akin [əˈkɪn] *adj.* 同族的，类似的
- verbal [ˈvɜːbl] *adj.* 口头的
- demise [dɪˈmaɪz] *n.* 死亡
- irreparable [ɪˈrepərəbl] *adj.* 不能挽回的
- in vain 徒然地
- decipher [dɪˈsaɪfə(r)] *vt.* 译解(密码等)，解释
- glimpse [glɪmps] *n.* 一瞥，一看
- regrettable [rɪˈgretəbl] *adj.* 可叹的，可惜的
- hint [hɪnt] *v.* 暗示，提示
- flexibility [ˌfleksəˈbɪləti] *n.* 灵活性
- dinosaur [ˈdaɪnəsɔː(r)] *n.* 恐龙
- lamentable [ˈlæməntəbl] *adj.* 令人惋惜的

每一年都有一些语言消失。有人认为这是件好事，因为语言的种类变少后，人们的交流可以变得更加轻松，同时人们学习外语的负担也减轻了。你是否同意这样的观点？

据说在地球上曾经存在过的所有语言中，60%已经消失了。除了语言学家和考古学家，其他人可能很少会为此感到悲哀。事实上，有人甚至认为这是件好事，标志着世界正在一体化。

从学习外语的角度来说，这件事情似乎的确是件好事。但是，按照这个逻辑，生物学家应该希望更多的物种灭绝才是。因为物种的灭绝，可以减轻他们的工作负担。事情却恰恰相反，生物学家们不遗余力地倡导人们保护濒临灭绝的物种。同样，语言种类的减少，并不意味着人们之间的交流可以变得更加容易，除非人们放弃所有的语言并开始使用世界通用语。只要还有不止一种语言在使用当中，语言障碍就一定会存在。

语言的消失，与社会和文明的消失基本一样。一个国家的历史和文化，往往主要靠口语或是书面语言来记录。随着语言的消失，相应的历史和传统也会逐渐为人们所淡忘。而历史和传统的失落，往往是不能挽回的。当代的科学家们努力地解密古代的语言，以期窥视几千年前人们的生活。然而，这种努力往往是徒劳的。如果这些语言依然存在，那么事情就会变得简单得多。

语言的消失落是非常令人叹息的，因为语言往往和人们的思维方式紧密相关。我们的思维方式往往在语言里有所描述，有的时候也会在艺术作品里有所体现。人们使用不同的语言，自然思维方式也不同。要想真正地了解一个民族的思维方式，我们必须理解他们所使用的语言。每一种语言都是独一无二的。比方说，汉语以灵活性著称，日语以敬语著称，而法语则以美丽动听著称。不同的语言其实有互补的作用。

一些语言的消失，就如同恐龙的灭绝一样让人叹息。随着一种语言的消失，人们了解一种独一无二的历史、文化和美丽的门被关闭了。世界也会因此而变得更加枯燥无味。

特别提醒

语言问题，是近年来雅思写作考试中新出现的话题。雅思写作考试中，关于语言的写作题，大致可以分为三类：1.语言的多样性的意义，即为什么要保护语言的多样性；2.学习外语的目的；3.人们是否应该学习外语。这道关于一些语言的消失是否会消除人们之间的沟通障碍的雅思写作题，虽然在雅思考试中出现的频率并不高，但是从写作构思的角度来说，的确有不低的难度。

推荐指数 ★★★★　　**相关题目** 8

写作点拨

这道题目要求考生就“一些语言的消失是否会消除人们之间的沟通障碍”这一问题给出自己的观点，是典型的观点类雅思作文题。范文采用了最传统的议论文的写法，全文分为五段：第一段引入话题；第二段亮出作者的观点——一些语言的消失不会消除人们之间的沟通障碍；第三、四段从不同的角度证明了作者的观点，第五段总结全文，将语言的消失比喻成恐龙的灭绝，再次重申作者的观点。

词汇升级

as...as...

普通版 The extinction of certain languages is just as lamentable as that of dinosaurs.

升级版 As that of dinosaurs, the extinction of certain languages is just as lamentable.

注释：将 as that of dinosaur 提前后，原本平淡无奇的句子不仅变得更加生动，而且还有效地强调了语言的消失正如恐龙的灭绝一样，起到了一箭双雕的作用。

ESSAY 49

Is distant learning as effective as school education?

Thanks to the development of the computer and the Internet, distant learning has been made available to most people. It does much to promote education in remote areas, where regular schooling is hardly possible. The possibilities opened up by distant learning seem infinite.

In some aspects, it even surpasses school education. Through e-learning, people can tap into a wider variety of courses which transcend the distance of time and space. It is indeed like universities without borders. Coupled with multi-media technology, distant learning can provide us with a virtue classroom, with the teacher lecturing from the podium and others sitting beside you. For those who cannot attend school it is the best choice.

However, at the present stage of development, distant learning is still inferior to school education. The freedom offered by distant learning actually backfires on the students. Many cannot follow through a course because they are not committed enough. Unlike school education, distant learning follows no strict schedule. Students themselves decide everything. Understandably, this kind of freedom is often abused. It is regrettable but true that most students lack perseverance and need to be constantly reminded or even goaded to finish a course.

Another drawback is the lack of face-to-face interaction. Researches have shown that people learn best not by cramming text books but by communicating with teachers and classmates. It is the discussion, the debates, and the exchange of ideas that really count. Through daily interaction, fellow students exert a subtle but significant influence over each other. People are less likely to get inspired or motivated when they take a course over the Internet. Besides, distant learning often adds to one's loneliness.

Though imperfect, distance learning has greatly benefited many people. But it is still a complement to normal education, at least for now.

单词注释

- available [əˈveɪləbl] *adj.* 有用的，可得到的
- remote [rɪˈməʊt] *adj.* 遥远的，偏僻的
- possibility [ˌpɒsəˈbɪləti] *n.* 可能性，可能的事
- surpass [səˈpɑːs] *vt.* 超越，凌驾，胜过
- variety [vəˈraɪəti] *n.* 多样，种类，品种
- couple [ˈkʌpl] *vt.* 加倍，使成双，使成婚
- multi-media 多媒体
- podium [ˈpəʊdiəm] *n.* 指挥台
- inferior [ɪnˈfɪəriə(r)] *adj.* 次等的，较低的 *n.* 低下的人，次品
- committed [kəˈmitid] *adj.* 致力（于某主义、主张）的，奉献的
- abuse [əˈbjuːs] *n.* 滥用，恶习，辱骂 [əˈbjuːz] *vt.* 滥用，辱骂，虐待
- constantly [ˈkɒnstəntli] *adv.* 不变地，不断地，时常地
- goad [gəʊd] *n.* 刺棒，激励物 *vt.* 用刺棒驱赶，激励，煽动
- drawback [ˈdrɔːbæk] *n.* 缺点
- interaction [ˌɪntərˈækʃən] *n.* 互动
- cram [kræm] *vt.* 塞满，填满，猛吃 *vi.* 贪吃
- subtle [ˈsʌtl] *adj.* 敏感的，精细的，狡猾的，细微的
- motivate [ˈməʊtɪveɪt] *vt.* 给与动机，刺激，促动
- debate [dɪˈbeɪt] *n.* 辩论，讨论

远程教育是否和学校教育一样有效?

由于电脑和互联网的发展,多数人都可以获得远程教育。这对推进偏远地区的教育帮助很大,因为那些地方常规教育往往无法进行。远程学习带来的机会似乎是无限的。

在某些方面远程教育甚至超过了校园教育。通过在线学习,人们可以选择多种多样的课程,跨越时间和空间的距离。远程教育就好像一所没有边界的大学。利用多媒体技术,远程教育给我们提供了一个虚拟的教室。教室里有老师在讲台授课,有他人坐在你旁边一起听课。对那些不能上学的人来说这是最好的选择。

然而就目前的发展阶段而言,远程教育还是比不上在校教育。远程教育提供的自由实际上对学生起着反作用。因为不够坚持,很多人往往不能完成全部课程。和学校教育不同,远程教育没有严格的日程可循,学生自己决定一切。不难理解,这种自由常常被人们滥用。大多数学生都缺乏毅力,需要旁人不断提醒甚至强迫才能完成整个课程。这一点令人遗憾但却千真万确。

远程教育的另一个不足之处在于缺少面对面的互动。研究人员发现,最好的学习方法不是死记硬背书本,而是和老师、同学进行交流。真正重要的是讨论、辩论和思想的交流。通过每日的互动,同学之间的相互影响虽然微妙但却举足轻重。人们在互联网上学习则不太可能受到激励和启发。此外,远程学习常常增加人的孤独感。

尽管远程学习能使很多人受益,但它并不完美,它仍然是正规教育的补充,至少目前是这样。

特别提醒

教育问题,历来都是雅思写作考试中的热门话题。雅思写作考试中,关于教育的雅思写作题目,大致可以分为三大类:1. 教育的内容(教育应该包含哪些内容、教育应该重点传授职业技能还是人文知识);2. 教育的方式(混班教学 VS 男 / 女校、集体学习 VS 单独辅导);3. 教育的意义(为什么要接受教育)。这道关于远程教育是否比课堂教育更有效的雅思写作题,曾经以不同的形式在雅思写作考试中多次出现,属于第二大类的教育题材雅思作文。

推荐指数 ★★★★ **相关题目** 2, 6, 14, 24, 43, 44, 65, 68, 93

写作点拨

这道题目要求考生就"远程教育是否比课堂教育更有效"这一问题给出自己的观点,是典型的观点类雅思作文题。范文最值得借鉴的地方,是添加了一个让步段,使文章的论证思路更为缜密。全文分为五段:第一段引入话题;第二段是让步段,指出远程教育的确有不少可取之处;第三、四段分别从不同角度指出了远程教育的弊端,有力地支持作者的观点;第五段再次重申作者的观点。

词汇升级

状语从句

普通版 Distant learning is coupled with multi-media technology and can thus provide us with a virtue classroom. In this room, the teacher is lecturing from the podium and others are sitting beside you.

升级版 Coupled with multi-media technology, distant learning can provide us with a virtue classroom, with the teacher lecturing from the podium and others sitting beside you.

注释:"升级版"的句子巧妙地使用两个状语从句,将两句话巧妙地合并成了一句话,体现了雅思高分作文所必备的"句式多变"的特点。

ESSAY 50

Some say that children should obey their parents and teachers, while others believe that too much control will not help to prepare children for their adult life. Discuss both sides of the views.

The relation between parents and children varies from time to time and place to place. But the general trend seems to be that children are becoming less likely to obey blindly. This has caused much uneasiness on the part of parents and teachers.

In their opinion, children have a duty to obey their elders. Raised and taken care of by their parents, children should do as they are told to show their gratitude and respect for the elders. This is a tradition in many cultures. Besides, the elders always want the best for their children. No parents would intentionally harm their kids and thus there is no point in objecting their bidding. More importantly, youngsters often cannot make informed decision on their own. Being young and inexperienced, children are prone to indiscretion. On many occasions, they need guidance and advice from their parents or teachers.

On the other hand, too much control is certainly detrimental to children's future development. Sooner or later children need to make decisions on their own. If they have been taught to obey orders since they can remember, they gradually lose the ability and desire to form their own opinion. Such kids would never be given positions with responsibilities because they are accustomed to following instead of issuing instructions. Besides, only a totalitarian society will demand total obedience. It is contrary to democratic principles which take account of all people's opinions and interests. Tyrannical parents are in danger of starting a vicious circle: when their children become parents themselves, they also become tyrants.

It is not easy to get along with one's parents or kids. It is unwise to be overprotective or overindulgent. As with most things, moderation seems the best policy. Any high-handed approach is likely to breed another generation of tyrannical parents.

单词注释

- blindly [ˈblaɪndli] *adv.* 轻率地，盲目地
- uneasiness [ʌn ˈiːzinəs] *n.* 不舒适，不安，局促
- gratitude [ˈɡrætɪtjuːd] *n.* 感激之情
- object [ˈɒbdʒɪkt] *n.* 物体，目标，目的
  [əb ˈdʒekt] *vi.* 反对，拒绝，抗议
- bidding [ˈbɪdɪŋ] *n.* 命令，邀请，出价
- informed [ɪn ˈfɔːmd] *adj.* 见多识广的
- inexperienced [ˌɪnɪk ˈspɪəriənst] *adj.* 无经验的，不熟练的
- indiscretion [ˌɪndɪ ˈskreʃn] *n.* 不慎重，轻率
- detrimental [ˌdetrɪ ˈmentl] *adj.* 有害的
- position [pə ˈzɪʃn] *n.* 位置，地位，身份
- totalitarian [təʊˌtælə ˈteəriən] *adj.* 极权主义的 *n.* 极权主义者
- obedience [ə ˈbiːdiəns] *n.* 服从，顺从，忠实
- vicious [ˈvɪʃəs] *adj.* 邪恶的，堕落的，品行不端的
- tyrant [ˈtaɪrənt] *n.* 暴君，暴虐统治者
- overindulgent [ˌəuvərin ˈdʌldʒənt] *adj.* 过度放任的，过分任性的，放纵的
- moderation [ˌmɒdə ˈreɪʃən] *n.* 缓和，适度，温和
- high-handed [ˌhaɪ ˈhændɪd] *adj.* 高压的，不容分说的，横暴的
- breed [briːd] *n.* 种类，品种 *vt.* 养育，引起，饲养
- tyrannical [tɪˈrænɪkl] *adj.* 暴虐的，压制的，残暴的

有人认为儿童应该处处服从老师和家长的命令，其他人却认为太多的控制不利于儿童长大成人后的生活。请从两方面讨论这些观点。

不同的时代，不同的国家，父母和子女之间的关系都不尽相同。现在的小孩似乎变得不像以前那样对父母言听计从。这让父母和老师感到很不安。

他们认为，小孩有义务遵从他们的长辈。子女由父母抚养照顾，理应听父母的话。在许多文化背景里都有这样的传统，听从长辈显示出子女对长辈的感激和尊敬。另外，长辈总是为子女着想。没有父母会故意伤害他们的子女，所以子女没有理由反对他们的命令。更重要的是，年轻人经常不能自己做出成熟的决定。由于年轻没有经验，小孩做事容易轻率。在很多场合，他们需要从父母和老师那里获得指引和建议。

另一方面，过多的管制对小孩将来的发展肯定是有害的。小孩迟早都得自己面对问题，做出决定。如果从他们记事起就被教育得唯命是从，他们就会渐渐失去自我判断的能力和意愿。这样的孩子是不可能走上领导岗位的，因为他们习惯了遵从而不是发布命令。另外，只有极权的社会才会要求完全的服从。这与民主的原则是背道而驰的。民主社会要考虑所有人的意见和利益。专制的父母很可能导致恶性循环：当他们的小孩成为父母的时候，他们也会成为暴君。

父母和子女相处是不容易的。过于庇护或者过于放任都是不明智的。和大多数事一样，适可而止似乎是上策。任何高压的方法都有可能滋生出另一代专制的父母。

特别提醒

儿童教育的问题，是历年来雅思写作考试中的热门话题，在留学和移民类的雅思考试中出现的频率都很高。这道关于小孩是否应该顺从父母和老师的作文题，曾经在雅思写作考试中出现过多次，请认真阅读。

推荐指数 ★★★★★

相关题目 5, 7, 26, 27, 28, 47, 49, 54, 57, 75, 81, 84, 85, 87, 89, 109

写作点拨

这道题目要求考生就“小孩是否应该顺从父母和老师”这个问题从两方面展开论证，并给出自己的观点，是典型的“正反两面叙述”类的雅思作文题。由于要求从正反面同时论证，这类作文题对考生思想的深度有比较高的要求。这类文章建议采用这篇范文的写法，全文分为四段：第一段引入话题；第二段从正面谈儿童应该顺从父母和家长的原因；第三段从反面指出过多地管制可能产生的负面影响；第四段在总结全文的同时，提出了作者自己的观点。

词汇升级

决定

普通版 More importantly, youngsters often cannot make *right decision* on their own.

升级版 More importantly, youngsters often cannot make *informed decision* on their own.

decision（决定）：*adj.* rational（理智的）, sensible（合理的）, wise（明智的）, key（关键的）, fateful（重大的）, crucial（至关紧要的）, momentous（重大的）

ESSAY 51

Some think we can acquire knowledge from news reports. Others believe we cannot trust journalists. What do you think? What important qualities should a journalist have?

It is estimated that seventy percent of what we read is newspaper. We get most of the information from reporters and journalists. However, they are not doing a good job at present.

News reports often don't show us the whole picture. All too often news coverage must bow to political pressure. Take the coverage of the Iraqi War for example. In the United States, American victories are always reported, with only brief mentions of American and Iraqi civilian casualties. In Europe, where most people are against the war, on the contrary, news reports are focused on civilian casualties and rebel activities. It is hard to remain completely impartial even for the most independent news agencies. As a result, some facts are suppressed while others are highlighted. The readers are being sold journalists' preferences and views, rather than objective information.

Worse still, in order to survive in this intensely competitive industry, reporters often seek to captivate rather than inform the readers. Consequently, sensationalism prevails. The readers are daily fed with reports about celebrities: their divorces, their dresses, their diets and so on. Trivialism invariably ensues. Do the public really need to know who is dating who? Apart from that, news events often get dramatized. Journalists are catering to our sensual desire for excitement and entertainment. Thus, most reports involve some violence or conflicts. Many newspapers read like a litany of disasters. The really informative reports are cut out.

A real journalist should be objective. He has the duty to report the truth and only the truth. He must not be swayed by pressure or bias. Additionally, he should not give way to commercialism. An event should only be reported if it is worthy and informative.

单词注释

- bow [baʊ] *v.* 鞠躬，弯腰；屈服
- casualty [ˈkæʒuəlti] *n.* 伤亡
- rebel [ˈrebl] *n.* 造反者，叛逆者
- impartial [ɪmˈpɑːʃl] *adj.* 公正的
- suppress [səˈpres] *vt.* 压抑
- highlight [ˈhaɪlaɪt] *vt.* 加亮，使显著
- preference [ˈprefərəns] *n.* 偏好
- captivate [ˈkæptɪveɪt] *vt.* 吸引
- sensationalism [senˈseɪʃənəlɪzəm] *n.* 耸人听闻
- prevail [prɪˈveɪl] *vi.* 流行
- celebrity [səˈlebrəti] *n.* 名人
- ensue [ɪnˈsjuː] *vi.* 紧随其后
- trivialism [ˈtrɪvɪəlɪzəm] *n.* 琐碎，平凡
- dramatize [ˈdræmətaɪz] *vt.* 戏剧地表现
- sensual [ˈsenʃuəl] *adj.* 肉欲的，色情的；世俗的
- litany [ˈlɪtəni] *n.* 冗长而枯燥的故事
- sway [sweɪ] *v.* 摇摆，摇动
- commercialism [kəˈmɜːʃəlɪzəm] *n.* 商业主义，重商主义

有人认为我们可以通过新闻报道来获取信息；别的人却认为我们不可以信任记者。你的观点是什么？你认为一个记者应该具备哪些重要的品质？

据估计，在我们阅读的资料中，报纸占据了70%。我们大部分的信息来源于新闻记者。然而，目前他们的工作并不令人满意。

新闻报道通常不够全面。它们往往要屈服于政治压力。就拿伊拉克战争的报道来说吧，美国媒体总是大肆宣扬胜利，而对平民伤亡的报道少之又少。相反地，在欧洲，由于大部分人反战，媒体则着重报道平民伤亡和反战活动。即使是最独立的新闻机构也很难保证绝对公正。因此，有些事实被隐瞒了，而有些事实又被大肆渲染。读者获取的不是客观信息，而是记者们的观点与倾向。

更糟糕的是，为了在激烈的竞争中存活，记者们关心的不是信息传达，而是如何吊起读者的胃口。因此，媒体无不追求轰动效应。报纸上每天充斥着名人们的报道，从他们的离婚、衣着，到他们的饮食，不一而足，八卦至极。大众真的有必要知道谁和谁在约会吗？除此之外，新闻报道还越来越戏剧化。记者们一味地迎合我们对刺激与娱乐的追求。因此，大部分报道都涉及一些暴力或冲突，许多新闻读起来像灾情报导。真正有价值的新闻却常常被砍掉。

一个真正的记者应该做到客观。报道真相是记者的职责。一个记者不应被偏见与压力所左右。此外，记者也不能向商业化屈服。是否报道一个事件的依据只能是看是否有价值以及是否有内容。

特别提醒

大众传媒的问题，是历年来雅思写作考试中的热门话题，在留学和移民类的雅思考试中出现的频率都很高。这道关于我们是否可以信任记者以及记者应该具备哪些品质的雅思作文题，虽然在雅思写作考试中出现的次数并不多，但是却代表了一大类的雅思作文题，请用心阅读范文。

推荐指数 ★★★★★

相关题目 4, 17, 23, 32, 45, 56, 73, 98

写作点拨

这道题目不仅要求考生就“我们是否可以信任记者”这一问题给出自己的观点，同时还要求考生指出“记者应该具备哪些品质”，是典型的“观点＋叙述”类的雅思作文题。由于这类作文题向考生提出了两个问题，因此考生在动笔前必须先考虑清楚文章将重点回答哪一个问题。建议采用这篇范文的写法，全文分为四段：第一段在引入话题的同时亮出作者的观点，即记者不可以信任；第二、三段从不同方面论证为什么记者不可以信任；第四段指出记者应该具备的品质，回答这道写作题提出的第二个问题。

论据积累

新闻报道的缺陷：

1. 屈服于政治压力，报导不够全面。

   News reports often don't show us the whole picture because all too often news coverage must bow to political pressure.

2. 读者获取的不是客观信息，而是记者们的观点与倾向。

   The readers are being sold journalists' preferences and views, rather than objective information.

3. 记者们关心的不是传达信息，而是如何吊起读者的胃口。

   Reporters often seek to captivate rather than inform the reader.

4. 新闻报道越来越戏剧化。

   News events often get dramatized.

ESSAY 52

Each year, crime committed by young people is on the rise. What are the reasons? Suggest some solutions.

In most countries, the crime rate among young people is rising. More alarmingly, youngsters are more involved in organized crimes and felonies. Something must be done to curb this trend.

Many juvenile delinquents commit crimes out of ignorance. Without due education at school or at home, teenagers often don't have the slightest idea of what constitutes a criminal offence. They regard it natural to settle a problem with violence. They are easily manipulated. For example, many are coaxed to sell drugs at discos, which seems to them a harmless part-time job. Not until they are caught by the police do they find out it is illegal.

The violence and crimes portrayed in the mass media certainly contribute to juvenile delinquency. Children are easily influenced. They imitate the people around them. Tuning on TV, they are daily exposed to vast amount of violence and bloodiness. Some programs even inadvertently teach people how to commit a crime because every step of the crime is described in detail. In addition, violence and criminals are often glorified in the mass media. The shooting and fighting seem manly and cool to the young. No wonder some of them have no qualm about trying it themselves.

Last but not least, many of those under-aged criminals go astray because of the lack of communication. They often have uncaring parents who don't bother to find out what is happening to their kids. Gradually, those kids learn to take things into their own hands. They usually become introvert and sensitive. By and by, they develop hostility towards most people except a few like-minded pals. Lonely and angry, they are apt to vent their wrath on their unhappy victims.

It can be seen from the above that most of the crimes can be prevented. The causes are largely man-made. Through adequate education and communication, the young can become law-abiding citizens. Also, stricter censorship should be enforced to cut out the unhealthy influence from the mass media.

单词注释

- felony [ˈfeləni] *n.* 重罪
- curb [kɜːb] *vt.* 压制
- juvenile [ˈdʒuːvənaɪl] *adj.* 青少年
- delinquent [dɪˈlɪŋkwənt] *n.* 失职者，违法者
- due [djuː] *adj.* 恰当的
- manipulate [məˈnɪpjuleɪt] *v.* 操纵
- coax [kəʊks] *v.* 教唆
- illegal [iˈliːgl] *adj.* 非法的
- portray [pɔːˈtreɪ] *v.* 描绘
- bloodiness [ˈblʌdɪnɪs] *n.* 残酷，残忍，血腥
- inadvertently [ˌɪnədˈvɜːtəntli] *adj.* 非故意的
- glorify [ˈglɔːrɪfaɪ] *vt.* 美化
- manly [ˈmænli] *adj.* 男子气概的
- qualm [kwɑːm, kwɔːm] *n.* 不安
- astray [əˈstreɪ] *adv.* 迷途地，入歧途地
- introvert [ˈɪntrəvɜːt] *n.* 性格内向的人
- hostility [hɒˈstɪləti] *n.* 敌意，恶意
- like-minded *adj.* 具有相似意向或目的的
- apt [æpt] *adj.* 易于…的，有…倾向的
- vent [vent] *v.* 放出，排出，发泄
- wrath [rɔːθ] *n.* 愤怒
- censorship [ˈsensəʃɪp] *n.* 审查机构，审查制度

青少年犯罪率在逐年上升。造成这种状况的原因是什么？请给出一些解决这个问题的建议。

在大部分国家，青少年犯罪比例正不断上升。更给我们敲响警钟的是，越来越多的青少年正卷入有组织的犯罪。我们必须采取措施来遏制这一趋势。

很多青少年罪犯因为无知而犯罪。由于在家里或学校没有接受相应的教育，很多年轻人对犯罪认识模糊不清。他们认为用武力来解决一个问题是顺理成章的事情。他们很容易就被人操纵。例如，很多年轻人被骗到舞厅里兜售毒品，而他们还以为那是正当的兼职。直到被警察逮捕后他们才认识到那样做是违法的。

媒体里面暴力及犯罪的镜头为青少年犯罪推波助澜。小孩容易受外界影响，他们会模仿身边人们的行为。每天打开电视，看到里面充斥着大量血腥与暴力镜头。很多节目在不经意之间教会了人们如何犯罪，因为犯罪的每一个具体步骤都被描绘得一清二楚。此外，暴力与犯罪在媒体上得到了美化。对年轻人来说，枪战与打斗是很酷、很有男人味的事情。难怪有些年轻人要毫不犹豫地把它们付诸实施。

最后很重要的一点，很多未成年人是因为缺乏沟通而误入歧途的。这些未成年人的父母往往疏于了解自己子女的事情。孩子们因此逐渐养成凡事都由自己拿主意的习惯。而这样的孩子，往往性格内向而敏感，对周围的大多数人心怀敌意，却喜欢和一些有同样问题的小孩混在一起。长此以往，这类孩子往往内心感觉愤怒和寂寞，喜欢找一些不幸的受害者当出气筒。

由此可见大部分犯罪是可以避免的，其根源在于人们自己。通过恰当的教育，年轻一代也可以成为遵纪守法的好公民。此外，必须对大众传媒实行严格的审查制度，删除有害社会的内容。

特别提醒

社会治安以及违法犯罪的问题，是近年来雅思写作考试中新出现的热门话题。本书收集了若干道关于违法犯罪的雅思写作题目，其中大多数是关于如何减少犯罪行为以及青少年犯罪的原因这两大话题的。这道关于青少年犯罪的雅思作文题，就曾经多次出现在雅思写作考试中。

推荐指数 ★★★★　　**相关题目** 46, 56, 99, 101, 108

写作点拨

这道题目不仅要求考生给出青少年犯罪行为日益增加的原因(reason)，而且还要求给出可能的解决方法(solutions)，是典型的“原因＋建议”类雅思作文题。范文分为五段：第一段引入话题；第二、三、四段分别介绍了导致青少年犯罪行为日益增加的各种原因；第五段提出作者的建议。

词汇升级

倾向于，有可能(做…事)

普通版 Lonely and angry, they *tend to* vent their wrath on their unhappy victims.

升级版 Lonely and angry, they *are apt to* vent their wrath on their unhappy victims.

倾向于，有可能：tend to, be apt to, be likely to, be prone to, be liable to

ESSAY 53

Some people think that traditional culture is being damaged as it is used as a tool to make money in the tourism industry. Others think it is the only way to preserve and protect culture and tradition. Discuss and state your opinion.

Many people today enjoy the pleasure of traveling around the world and appreciating exotic cultures and landscapes. Tourism industry generates billions of dollars each year. But this has sparked fear that traditional culture is being paid as a price.

Such concerns are not groundless. In pursuit of profit, local governments rush to set up more tourist attractions. Large stretches of land are being used to build amusement parks, hotels and restaurants, forcing thousands of aboriginal people out of their ancestral homes. Those who remained are often employed in the tourism industry, acting as guides for the sightseers. In addition, local tradition and culture are also under the onslaught of foreign cultures brought by the influx of tourists. Tourists bring with them their cultures and traditions which are often exotic and thus appealing. In order to appear trendy, many people start to imitate those travelers and lose interest in their own traditions.

However, others believe that instead of damaging, tourism actually promotes and protects traditional culture. The daily interaction between the locals and travelers will make them more aware of their unique cultures. They often start to appreciate and cherish their own traditions because outsiders are fascinated by their seemingly ordinary way of doing things. One fails to perceive the beauty if he sees it every day. Tourism often highlights the local custom. Besides, tourism contributes to local revenue. Money is required to maintain buildings of historical and cultural value. Traditional industries can also be subsidized by tourism income.

The way I see it, tourism can do much to promote tradition and culture. Indeed, what captivates tourists is not only the beautiful scenery but also the local tradition. Of course, everything should be done to keep the collateral damage at a minimum.

单词注释

- appreciate [əˈpriːʃieɪt] *vt.* 赏识，鉴赏；感激
- exotic [ɪɡˈzɒtɪk] *adj.* 异国情调的，外来的；奇异的
- landscape [ˈlændskeɪp] *n.* 风景，山水画；地形
- generate [ˈdʒenəˌreɪt] *vt.* 产生，发生
- spark [spɑːk] *n.* 火花，火星，闪光 *vi.* 闪烁 *vt.* 发动
- concern [kənˈsɜːn] *vt.* 涉及，关系到 *n.* (利害)关系；关心，关注
- groundless [ˈɡraʊndləs] *adj.* 无根据的，没有理由的
- pursuit [pəˈsjuːt] *n.* 追求
- stretch [stretʃ] *v.* 伸展，伸长 *n.* 一段时间，一段路程，伸展
- aboriginal [ˌæbəˈrɪdʒnəl] *adj.* 土著的，原来的 *n.* 土著居民
- ancestral [ænˈsestrəl] *adj.* 祖先的，祖传的
- sightseer [ˈsaɪtsiːə(r)] *n.* 观光客
- onslaught [ˈɒnslɔːt] *n.* 冲击
- influx [ˈɪnflʌks] *n.* 流入
- appealing [əˈpiːlɪŋ] *adj.* 吸引人的；哀诉似的，恳求似的
- trendy [ˈtrendi] *n.* 新潮人物，穿着时髦的人 *adj.* 流行的
- imitate [ˈɪmɪteɪt] *vi.* 模仿，仿效；仿制，仿造
- interaction [ˌɪntərˈækʃən] *n.* 交互作用，互动
- unique [juˈniːk] *adj.* 唯一的；独特的
- fascinate [ˈfæsɪneɪt] *vt.* 使着迷，使神魂颠倒
- perceive [pəˈsiːv] *vt.* 察觉，感知，感到，认识到
- subsidize [ˈsʌbsɪdaɪz] *v.* 资助，津贴
- captivate [ˈkæptɪveɪt] *vt.* 迷住，迷惑
- collateral [kəˈlætərəl] *adj.* 间接的

有人认为如今传统文化已经成为了旅游业获取暴利的工具，并因此受到了破坏。其他人却认为这是保护文化和传统的唯一方式。请讨论这个问题并给出你的观点。

如今许多人都喜欢环球旅行，欣赏异国的文化和风土人情。旅游业每年创造几十亿美元的收入。但是，这也引起了人们的担心，害怕传统文化的丢失会成为旅游业蓬勃发展的代价。

这种担忧并不是没有根据的。为了追求利润，地方政府常常急于建立旅游景点。大片的土地被用来建游乐场、酒店、餐厅，成千上万的原居民被迫搬离祖地。只有那些被旅游业雇作导游的少数人留了下来。另外，大量的游客所带来的外国文化也对当地的传统和文化产生了巨大的影响。游客所带来的文化通常具有异国情调，所以是很吸引人的。为了赶时髦，许多人就开始模仿那些游客，对自己的传统渐渐失去了兴趣。

但是，有些人认为，旅游业不仅没有损害，相反有助于保护传统文化。当地人每天和游客打交道，更有助于他们感觉到自己文化的独特之处。外来的游客对他们习以为常的生活方式表现出如此大的兴趣，这使得当地人开始珍视自己的传统。人们对每天都见到的东西容易产生审美疲劳。旅游业强调的重点之一就是地方传统。另外，旅游业对当地的财政收入也有很大帮助。保护历史文化遗产需要资金投入。旅游业还可以作为传统产业的一个补贴。

我认为，旅游业对于弘扬传统文化有很大帮助。事实上，吸引游客的不仅是美丽的风景，还有当地的传统文化。当然，我们必须采取一切措施把间接的负面影响减少到最小。

特别提醒

传统文化的保护和发展的问题，一直是雅思写作考试中的热门话题。本书收集了若干道关于此类话题的雅思写作题目，其中大多数都要求考生提出自己的建议。请考生认真参考范文中出现的论据。

推荐指数 ★★★★★ **相关题目** 78

写作点拨

这道题目不仅要求考生讨论旅游业和保护传统文化之间的关系，而且还要求给出自己的观点，是典型的"讨论+观点"类雅思作文题。范文分为四段：第一段引入话题；第二、三段分别从正、反面介绍了旅游业对传统文化的保护所造成的影响；第四段在整理全文思路的同时提出自己的观点。

词汇升级

吸引

普通版 Indeed, what *attracts* tourists is not only the beautiful scenery but also local tradition.

升级版 Indeed, what *captivates* tourists is not only the beautiful scenery but also local tradition.

吸引：allure, bewitch, charm, fascinate, enthrall, enchant

ESSAY 54

Some think students can learn more effectively in groups, while others think they should study alone. What are the benefits of each method? Which one do you think is more effective?

From kindergarten to college, students are always grouped together. Indeed, they spend so much time in groups that they long for some private moments. Some students prefer to study in a group, while others would like to study by themselves. It rather depends on the individual.

Group learning can profit those who are gregarious in nature. When you study in a group with your classmates by your side, you can consult them if you encounter any problem. Sometimes a word or two from others can save you hours of pondering. The exchange of ideas can benefit all parties involved. Additionally, one will be favourably influenced when she or he is put in a group. Seeing others working diligently, one will feel uneasy if she or he doesn't follow suit. This is especially helpful for those weak-minded students who need to be constantly reminded and encouraged.

On the other hand, it is also beneficial to study alone. Studying alone, one will not be distracted by others. Study is a mental activity, which requires high levels of concentration. Distraction is the bane of thinking. Someone even goes so far as to suggest the removal of all possible distractions: turning off cell phones, shutting doors and curtains and putting away all irrelevant items. Besides, it helps to develop our independent thinking. When there is no one to consult or confer with, one is forced to think for himself. Indeed, independent judgment and thinking are highly regarded these days. Moreover, when you are a lone wolf, you enjoy freedom. You can choose when and where to start your work. You can follow your own pace; no one would interfere. You can decide when and whether to take a break. In a word, you are your own boss.

Personally, I would like to study by myself whenever possible. In fact, I intentionally avoided evening study sessions during high school. I treasure the freedom when studying alone.

单词注释

- kindergarten [ˈkɪndəgɑːtn] *n.* 幼儿园
- gregarious [grɪˈgeəriəs] *adj.* 社交的，群居的
- consult [kənˈsʌlt] *v.* 商量，商议，请教
- encounter [ɪnˈkaʊntə] *v.* 遭遇，遇到
- ponder [ˈpɒndə(r)] *v.* 沉思，考虑
- exchange [ɪksˈtʃeɪndʒ] *n.* 交换，调换
- influence [ˈɪnfluəns] *vt.* 影响，改变
- diligently [ˈdɪlɪdʒəntlɪ] *adv.* 勤勉地，坚持不懈地
- beneficial [ˌbenɪˈfɪʃl] *adj.* 有益的，受益的
- distracted [dɪˈstræktɪd] *adj.* 心烦意乱的
- irrelevant [ɪˈreləvənt] *adj.* 不相关的
- bane [beɪn] *n.* 毒药；祸害
- independent [ˌɪndɪˈpendənt] *adj.* 独立自主的，不受约束的
- confer [kənˈfɜː] *vi.* 协商，交换意见
- lone wolf 喜欢单独行动的人，孤僻的人
- removal [rɪˈmuːvl] *n.* 移动；免职；切除
- interfere [ˌɪntəˈfɪə(r)] *vi.* 干涉，干预

有人认为集体学习的效果更好，别的人却认为学生们应该独立学习。两种方法的益处分别是什么？你认为哪一种更加有效？

从幼儿园到大学，学生们都是身在集体中的。事实上，学生们花在集体生活上如此多的时间，他们很渴望有一些私人的时间。有些学生喜欢集体学习，而有些则喜欢单独学习。这因人而异。

集体学习对于那些天性合群的学生比较适合。和同学一起学习的时候，如果你遇到了什么问题，可以向同学请教。有时候别人的一言两语就可以省得你自己思考几个小时。思想交流对各方都是有好处的。另外，一个人在集体中，会受到有益的影响。看见别人在努力学习，如果自己不学习的话，就会感到不安。这对于那些意志力差的学生来说尤其有帮助。他们往往需要被提醒和鼓励。

另一方面，单独学习也有好处。单独学习不会被人打扰。学习是一项脑力活动，需要精神高度集中。被打扰是极不利于思考的。有些人甚至建议在思考的时候要排除一切干扰因素。关掉手机、关上门、拉上窗帘，把所有无关的东西都移开。还有，独立学习有利于我们培养独立思考能力。当没有人可以商量时，人被迫开始独立思考。事实上，当今社会非常看重一个人的独立思考能力。而且，当你是一个人的时候，你有最大限度的自由。你可以选择在什么时候、什么地方开始学习。你可以选择自己的学习进度，没有人会干涉你。你可以决定什么时候休息，是否要休息。总之，一切都由自己决定。

从我个人来讲，只要有可能，我就会选择单独学习。事实上，在我上高中时，我就刻意避开晚自习。我特别喜欢单独学习时的自由感。

特别提醒

教育问题历来都是雅思写作考试中的热门话题。雅思写作考试中，关于教育的雅思写作题目大致可以分为三大类：1. 教育的内容（教育应该包含哪些内容、教育应该重点传授职业技能还是人文知识）；2. 教育的方式（混班教学 VS 男 / 女校、集体学习 VS 单独辅导）；3. 教育的意义（为什么要接受教育）。这道关于集体学习和独立学习的雅思写作题属于第二大类，曾经以不同的形式在雅思写作考试中多次出现。

推荐指数 ★★★★

相关题目 9, 10, 48, 78, 97

写作点拨

这道题目要求考生分别阐述集体学习和独立学习这两种方法的可取之处，并指出自己心目中更有效的方法，是典型的“叙述＋观点”类雅思作文题。范文使用了最中规中矩的议论文的写法，全文分为四段：第一段引入话题；第二、三段介绍了两种方法的可取之处；第四段指出作者自己的喜好。

词汇升级

珍惜

普通版 I *value* the freedom when studying alone.

升级版 I *treasure* the freedom when studying alone.

珍惜：appreciate, cherish, value, treasure

ESSAY 55

People are now able to perform everyday tasks such as shopping, banking and business transactions without meeting others face to face. What are the effects on both the individual and the society?

Things have really changed. Only six years ago I had to pay a typist to type my graduation paper because I couldn't use a computer. Today, I spend more than ten hours each day banging on the keyboard. The changes in our ways of doing things have far reaching implications.

On the individual side, technical advance brought unprecedented conveniences but also certain problems. Time is saved when people choose to shop online instead of roaming shopping malls. Distant learning brings online courses onto our computer screens, which benefits numerous people. By and large, people are better informed than before. However, all this comes at a price. To say the very least, the heavy reliance on computer printing leads to a decline in our handwriting. It is reported that 40 per cent of teenagers in Japan cannot write many commonly used Japanese characters because most homework is typewritten. Graver still is the alienation and estrangement between people caused by the extensive use of machinery. We gradually lose sight of the connection between people when most of our daily contacts are with a machine. We are connected with our humanity; we need to feel the presence of our fellow creatures.

Similarly the society as a whole also experiences this kind of mixed blessing. On one hand, science and technology contributes to economy growth, generating enormous material wealth. Machines are usually more reliable than humans. They are easier to monitor, maintain and manage. The society grows seemingly steadier as a result. However, problems are lurking. Identity crisis is occurring in most societies. Everything is so sterile that it is hard to find common ground between people. The sense of community is lost for many people because they rarely see or interact with each other.

Though exhilarating, changes can sometimes overwhelm us. At present, most technological developments only aim to address our physical needs. In fact, our mental and spiritual life need more attention.

单词注释

- typist [ˈtaɪpɪst] *n.* 打字员
- bang [bæŋ] *v.* 发巨响；重击
- implication [ˌɪmplɪˈkeɪʃən] *n.* 牵连；含意；暗示
- unprecedented [ʌnˈpresɪdentɪd] *adj.* 空前的
- mall [mɔːl] *n.* 购物商场，商业街
- reliance [rɪˈlaɪəns] *n.* 信任，依靠
- decline [dɪˈklaɪn] *vi.* 下倾；下降；下垂
- character [ˈkærɪktə] *n.* 特性，性质
- alienation [ˈeɪliəneɪʃn] *n.* 疏远，转让
- estrangement [ɪˈstreɪʌdʒmənt] *n.* 疏远
- extensive [ɪkˈstensɪv] *adj.* 广大的，广阔的，广泛的
- machinery [məˈʃiːnəri] *n.* 机器，机械
- humanity [hjuːˈmænəti] *n.* 人性；人类
- blessing [ˈblesɪŋ] *n.* 祝福
- reliable [rɪˈlaɪəbl] *adj.* 可靠的，可信赖的
- sterile [ˈsteraɪl] *adj.* 贫瘠的；不育的；毫无结果的
- interact [ˌɪntərˈækt] *vi.* 互相作用，互相影响
- exhilarating [ɪɡˈzɪləreɪtɪŋ] *adj.* 令人喜欢的，使人愉快的
- overwhelm [ˌəʊvəˈwelm] *vt.* 淹没，覆没；压倒
- spiritual [ˈspɪrɪtʃuəl] *adj.* 精神上的
- convenience [kənˈviːniəns] *n.* 便利，方便

如今人们不用见面，就可以完成诸如购物、去银行、商务交易之类的日常活动。这种现象对个人和社会的影响分别是什么？

世事变迁，仅仅六年前，我还必须花钱找打字员帮我打毕业论文，因为当时我还不会用电脑。今天，我每天花十小时以上的时间敲键盘。我们的生活和工作方式的改变有着深远的意义。

对个人来说，科技进步带来了前所未有的便利，但同时也带来了一些问题。人们选择用网上购物代替逛商场以节约时间。远程教育把学习课程呈现到了我们的电脑屏幕上，使无数人受益。总的来说，人们比以前要见多识广。但是，这些是需要付出代价的。举个最小的害处为例：人们如此依赖电脑打字，以至于人们的写字能力越来越差了。据报道，在日本有40%的青少年连一些常用的日本字都不会写了，因为他们的作业大部分都是打印的。更严重的是，人们过度使用机器，使得人与人之间的关系都疏远了。当我们的日常联系都是通过机器进行的时候，我们渐渐地忘却了人与人之间的联系。是人性使我们联系在一起，我们需要感觉到人与人之间的关系。

类似地，从整个社会的角度来看，科技进步带来的结果也是喜忧参半的。一方面，科技促进了经济增长，带来了大量物质财富。机器通常比人更可靠，而且更容易监控、维护和管理。表面上，社会因科技进步而稳步发展，但是事实上潜伏着很多问题。许多人都失去了社区的集体感，因为社区的人们相互之间很少交往。

尽管看起来令人欢欣鼓舞，但改变所带来的后果有时候会让我们难以承受。现在，大部分的技术发展都只是着眼于解决我们的物质需要。然而事实上，我们应该对人们的心理和精神需要给予更多的关注。

特别提醒

这道写作题是雅思考试中最新的试题之一。在以往的雅思考试中，也没有出现过与其话题相似的作文题。尽管雅思写作会不时推出一些新的话题，考生只要用心整理其他范文中出现的论据，再适当地加以包装，就完全可以以不变应万变！

推荐指数 ★★★　　**相关题目** 18

写作点拨

这道题目要求考生阐述一种现象对个人以及社会的影响，是典型的叙述类雅思作文题。由于题目要求分别讨论对个人和社会的影响，范文使用了最简单明了的写作方法，全文分为四段：第一段引入话题；第二、三段分别介绍这种现象对个人和社会的影响；第四段总结这种现象的所有影响并提出作者的看法。

词汇升级

令人兴奋的，令人鼓舞的

普通版 Though *exciting*, these changes can sometimes overwhelm us.

升级版 Though *exhilarating*, these changes can sometimes overwhelm us.

吸引人的，激动人心的：tempting, intoxicating, bewitching, enrapturing, appealing, ravishing, energizing, breathtaking

ESSAY 56

The government should control the amount of violence in films and on television in order to reduce the amount of violent crimes in the society. Do you agree or disagree?

On my way home last night I passed several boys apparently fighting and chasing each other in a backyard. A glance at the TV nearby told me that they were imitating a fight scene on TV. How unwholesome! People are daily bombarded by violence and crimes on TV or in films. Something must be done before it is too late.

Those TV and film producers may doggedly defend themselves, saying that their production is true to life. Violent crimes exist in daily life and it is wrong to keep a blind eye to them. It would do the public no good if the harsh realities and unpleasantness of the world were brushed away. They even claim credits for educating the public and depicting reality. But is it really so?

The effects of violent programs on people have been borne out by facts. Crime rate, especially juvenile delinquency, is on the rise. And criminals are becoming more ruthless and cruel. How can we account for all this? Violence on TV or in films is the main culprit. Just as romantic stories can induce gentle feelings, violence rouses our aggressiveness. By the age of 20, most young people have watched thousands of killings, robberies and shootings on TV. They become desensitized. They learn to regard violence as commonplace.

Not only should we reduce the amount of violence on TV but the way violence is portrayed should also be regulated. At present, some crimes and criminals are glorified. Criminals are often portrayed as highly capable and cool guys on the wrong side of the law. Some of them even excite admiration from the young. Fighting scenes are often shot in slow motion, always stylistic and thrilling, concealing the consequent sufferings and damages. No wonder some people resort to violence and crime. It is glorifying and consequence-free, which is by no meaning the real case.

Therefore, it is paramount that the amount of violence be reduced on TV and in films. There are numerous ways to attract audience without catering to the lowest desire for power and aggression.

单词注释

- bombard [bɒm ˈbɑːd] *vt.* 炮轰；轰击
- violence [ˈvaɪələns] *n.* 猛烈，强烈；暴力
- doggedly [ˈdɒgɪdli] *adv.* 固执地，顽强地
- harsh [hɑːʃ] *adj.* 粗糙的；荒芜的；苛刻的
- unpleasantness [ʌn ˈplezntnəs] *n.* 煞风景的事，不愉快的事
- depict [dɪ ˈpɪkt] *vt.* 描述，描写
- juvenile [ˈdʒuːvənaɪl] *adj.* 青少年的；幼稚的 *n.* 青少年
- delinquency [dɪ ˈlɪŋkwənsi] *n.* 行为不良，错失
- ruthless [ˈruːθləs] *adj.* 无情的，残忍的
- culprit [ˈkʌlprɪt] *n.* 犯人，罪犯
- aggressive [ə ˈgresɪv] *adj.* 好斗的；有闯劲的；侵略性的
- desensitize [ˌdiː ˈsensətaɪz] *vt.* 减少感光性；使不敏感
- commonplace [ˈkɔmənpleɪs] *n.* 平凡的事，平常话 *adj.* 平凡的
- regulate [ˈregjuleɪt] *vt.* 管制，控制；调节，校准
- glorified [ˈglɔːrɪfaɪd] *adj.* 美其名的，变荣耀的
- stylistic [staɪ ˈlɪstɪk] *adj.* 风格的，文体的
- thrilling [ˈθrɪlɪŋ] *adj.* 毛骨悚然的；颤动的，发抖的
- conceal [kən ˈsiːl] *vt.* 隐藏，隐瞒
- consequent [ˈkɒnsɪkwənt] *adj.* 作为结果的，随之发生的
- paramount [ˈpærəmaʊnt] *adj.* 首要的
- aggression [ə ˈgreʃn] *n.* 进攻，侵略

为了减少暴力犯罪，政府应该控制电视、电影中的暴力镜头。你是否同意这样的说法?

昨晚我在回家的路上看到几个小孩在院子里打打闹闹。我看了一眼附近的电视，原来这几个孩子是在模仿电视里的打斗镜头。多么不健康的节目!影视作品里充斥着暴力犯罪镜头，几乎要把人们给淹没了。在为时已晚之前，我们一定要采取一些措施。

影视制片人们肯定会顽固地为自己辩护，说他们的作品是忠于现实生活的。现实生活中存在着暴力犯罪，对他们视而不见不是一种明智的做法。如果把现实世界中的残酷事实和种种不和谐都掩盖掉，这对公众来说是没有好处的。他们甚至认为他们这样做是教育了大众、描述了事实。但真的是这样吗?

事实可以证明暴力影视节目对人们的危害。犯罪率，尤其是青少年犯罪率在上升。罪犯变得越来越无情和残酷。我们怎么解释这些呢?影视节目中的暴力就是罪魁祸首。正如浪漫故事可以勾起我们的柔情一样，暴力节目引得人们更加好斗。到 20 岁的时候，大部分青少年已经看了成千上万的杀戮、抢劫、激战的电视节目。他们都变得麻木了。他们把暴力已经看作是司空见惯的东西了。

我们不仅要减少电视上暴力节目的数量，而且还要调整表现暴力的方式。现在，影视节目经常美化犯罪和犯罪分子。影视节目中的犯罪分子通常都是站在法律对立面的、有才能、有气质的性格男女。有些甚至能引来青少年的崇拜。打斗场面通常用慢镜头拍摄，显得既有风格又震撼人心，掩盖了其带来的痛苦和破坏。难怪有些人喜欢动不动就诉诸暴力和犯罪，因为在影视节目里，暴力和犯罪显得如此荣耀，而且没有后果。在现实社会中，情况完全不是这样的。

所以，我们务必要减少影视节目中的暴力成分。吸引观众有很多方法，不一定要去迎合人们追逐权力和好斗的最低等欲望。

特别提醒

大众传媒的问题，历来是雅思写作考试中的热门话题，在留学和移民类的雅思考试中出现的频率都很高。这道关于政府是否应该控制电影和电视中的暴力镜头的雅思作文题，曾经在雅思写作考试中出现过多次，而且同时代表了一大类的雅思作文题，请用心阅读范文。

推荐指数 ★★★★

相关题目 46, 52, 99, 101, 108

写作点拨

这道题目要求考生就“政府是否应该出于减少犯罪行为的目的而控制电影和电视中的暴力镜头”这一问题给出自己的观点，是典型的观点类的雅思作文题。范文分为五段：第一段在引入话题的同时亮出作者的观点，即政府的做法是正确的；第二、三、四段从不同方面论证为什么电影和电视中的暴力镜头应该受到控制；第五段用很简单的语句总结全文，重申作者的观点。

词汇升级

遭遇或面临(困难等的)打击，受到(苦难等的)袭击

普通版 People *face* violence and crimes on TV and films every day.

升级版 People *are bombarded* by violence and crimes on TV and films.

遭遇或面临(困难等)的打击，受到(苦难等)的袭击：be bombarded by, be confronted by, encounter

ESSAY 57

Children are currently having extra classes after normal lessons. What are the positive and negative effects? What is your opinion?

In China, people have been talking about lightening learning load for years. Yet, the students' schoolbags are getting heavier by the year. It is common now for kids to spend six and a half days in school each week, sitting through one extra class after another.

Although banned by the Ministry of Education, extra classes are thought to be beneficial by most teachers and parents. To them, the more, the merrier. By spending more time in class, all students can improve their academic performances to some extent. Extra classes can be used for quizzes or exercises, to which there never seems to be an end. In addition, having extra classes at school prevent students from wasting their time. Released from school, many kids start to relax with a vengeance by playing computer games or watching TV all day. For those poorly motivated pupils, extra classes may prove particularly beneficial.

However, students often don't get much out of those classes. What counts here is quality rather than quantity. Indeed, many kids fall asleep during those classes, and others daydream half the time. The plethora of lessons only adds to their boredom. As we all know, the cultivation of one's interest is of great importance. Besides, students need some time to follow their own interest. The assembly-line-style education undermines their independent thinking. Individuality is ignored in classrooms because all students are taught the same thing. In fact, top students and average students learn at different paces. Thus, the former often feels underfed while the latter has difficulty digesting what is taught in class.

I am strongly against having extra classes. Indeed I would like students to have fewer classes. Interest is the best teacher. Hardly can interest be fostered by taking extra classes.

单词注释

- schoolbag [ˈskuːlbæg] *n.* 书包
- ban [bæn] *n.* 禁令 *vt.* 禁止，取缔(书刊等)
- ministry [ˈmɪnɪstri] *n.* (政府的)部门
- beneficial [ˌbenɪˈfɪʃl] *adj.* 有益的，受益的
- academic [ˌækəˈdemɪk] *adj.* 学院的；理论的
- performance [pəˈfɔːməns] *n.* 履行，执行；成绩；性能；表演，演奏
- vengeance [ˈvendʒəns] *n.* 复仇，报仇
- motivated [ˈməʊtɪveɪtɪd] *adj.* 有根据的；有动机的，由…推动的
- daydream [ˈdeɪdriːm] *n.* 白日梦 *vi.* 做白日梦
- plethora [ˈpleθərə] *n.* 过剩，过多；多血症
- boredom [ˈbɔːdəm] *n.* 厌倦
- cultivation [ˌkʌltɪˈveɪʃən] *n.* 培养，教养；耕作
- assembly-line 流水作业线
- undermine [ˈʌndəˈmaɪn] *vt.* 逐渐损害
- independent [ɪndɪˈpendənt] *n.* 中立派，无党派者 *adj.* 独立自主的
- underfed [ˌʌndəˈfed] *adj.* 未喂饱的；营养不良的
- digest [ˈdaɪdʒest] *n.* 分类，摘要 [daɪˈdʒest] *vt.* 消化，融会贯通
- foster [ˈfɔstə] *vt.* 养育，抚育 *n.* 养育者，鼓励者

如今的孩子们，除了正常的学习外往往还要参加补习班。请问补习班的正面和负面的影响分别是什么？你如何看待补习班？

在中国，人们谈论减轻孩子的学习负担都谈了好几年了。但是，学生们的书包还是一年比一年沉重。现在孩子们一个星期有六天半在学校度过，课外补课一堂接着一堂，这已经是很普遍的事情了。

尽管教育部明令禁止课外补课，但是大部分老师和家长还是认为课外补课是有好处的。对他们来说，越多越好。课堂时间越多，学生们的成绩就能一定程度地提高。课外时间则可用来做那无止境的考试或练习。而且，在学校补课可以防止学生浪费时间。放学以后，学生们就开始近乎报复性地放松，成天玩电脑游戏，或者看电视。对于那些缺乏自觉性的学生来说，补课尤其有作用。

但是，补课有时候却不是效果很大。学习关键是要看质量，而不是数量。事实上，许多学生在补课的时候睡觉。有些则大半时间思想在开小差。课程过多只会使他们更加反感。我们都知道，培养兴趣对学生来说是很重要的。而且，学生有时需要根据自己的兴趣来学习。这种生产线模式的教育抹煞了学生们的独立思考。在课堂上所有学生学习的都是同样的东西，个性没有得到丝毫体现。事实上，好学生和一般学生学习的步伐是不一样的。前者觉得没学够，而后者则感觉课堂上学的东西难以消化。

我强烈反对补课。事实上，我希望学生能减少一些课业负担。兴趣是最好的老师。补课是很难培养起兴趣的。

特别提醒

教育问题，历来都是雅思写作考试中的热门话题。雅思写作考试中，关于教育的写作题目大致可以分为三大类：1. 教育的内容（教育应该包含哪些内容、教育应该重点传授职业技能还是人文知识）；2. 教育的方式（混班教学 VS 男 / 女校、集体学习 VS 单独辅导）；3. 教育的意义（为什么要接受教育）。

推荐指数 ★★★★★

相关题目 5, 7, 26, 27, 28, 47, 49, 50, 54, 75, 81, 84, 85, 87, 89, 109

写作点拨

这道题目要求考生分别阐述补习的正面和负面影响，并指出自己的看法，是典型的“叙述＋观点”类雅思作文题。范文使用了最中规中矩的议论文的写法，全文分为四段：第一段引入话题；第二、三段介绍了补习的正面和负面影响；第四段指出作者自己的看法，摆明观点。

句型升级

-ing 形式充当伴随状语

普通版 It is common now for kids to spend six and a half days in school each week because they have to sit through one extra class after another.

升级版 It is common now for kids to spend six and a half days in school each week, sitting through one extra class after another.

注释：巧妙地使用动词的-ing 形式来充当伴随状语，可以让原本平淡的句式变得与众不同起来。

ESSAY 58

Young children should stay in kindergartens or nursery schools so that their mothers can return to work earlier. Do you agree?

Though equal, men and women have different roles in society. It has always been the wife's responsibility and hopefully pleasure to take care of the kids. Fortunately, kindergartens and nursery school can now relieve some of the burden of caring for the young.

By sending kids to nursery schools, mothers have the chance to continue their full-time jobs. It is too great a sacrifice for women to abandon their career for the sake of their children. Indeed, raising a child and working full-time need not interfere with each other. It can be easily managed by taking kids to kindergartens in the morning and picking them after work. There is no harm done if mothers and their children spend some time apart.

In fact, even for those mothers without career ambition, kindergartens would still be a good choice because most of them are staffed by professional nurses and instructors whose expertise is unmatched by most mothers. It will be perfectly safe to entrust a child to a nursery school. Actually, those schools are better prepared than most mothers to cope with emergencies. Some first-time mothers lack the knowledge and experience to provide adequate child care.

The time spend in a kindergarten also makes educational sense. Kindergarten is a good preparation for school. By partaking in various lessons and activities, children cannot only acquire some knowledge but also get a taste of what school is like. Besides, by mingling with other kids on a daily basis they can improve their social skills, the absence of which would severely hinder their future development.

Though emotionally demanding, it would be wise for mothers to send their kids to kindergartens where the children are in professional hands. Kindergartens can be viewed as an extension of and preparation for primary schools.

单词注释

- kindergarten [ˈkɪndəgɑːtn] *n.* 幼儿园
- nursery [ˈnɜːsəri] *n.* 托儿所
- relieve [rɪˈliːv] *vt.* 减轻，解除
- care for 照顾，照料
- sacrifice [ˈsækrɪfaɪs] *n.* 牺牲
- abandon [əˈbændən] *vt.* 放弃，舍弃
- interfere [ˌɪntəˈfɪə(r)] *vi.* 干涉，干预
- ambition [æmˈbɪʃn] *n.* 野心，雄心
- staff [stɑːf] *vt.* 为…配备人员
- professional [prəˈfeʃənl] *n.* 专业人员 *adj.* 专业的
- expertise [ˌekspəˈtiːz] *n.* 专家的意见；专门技术
- unmatched [ˌʌnˈmætʃt] *adj.* 无比的，无法匹敌的
- entrust [ɪnˈtrʌst] *vy.* 委托
- partake [pɑːˈteɪk] *vi.* 参与，参加
- mingle [ˈmɪŋgl] *v.* (使)混合；相交往
- hinder [ˈhɪndə] *vt.* 阻碍，打扰
- extension [ɪksˈtenʃn] *n.* 延长，扩充；范围
- primary school 小学

家长应该把孩子送到幼儿园或托儿所，从而让妈妈们能够更早地重返自己的工作。你是否同意这样的观点？

虽然男女平等，但是男人和女人在社会中的角色不同。照顾孩子总被当作是妻子的责任，希望她们也能以此为乐。幸运的是，现在幼儿园和托儿所能够减轻一些母亲的负担了。

把孩子送到托儿所，母亲们就可以有机会继续她们的全职工作了。如果因为孩子的缘故，女性不得不放弃自己的事业，那对女性来说，牺牲就太大了。事实上，抚育孩子和追求事业并不矛盾。只要把孩子送到幼儿园，早上送去，晚上接回来，这样就能两全了。母亲和孩子每天分开一些时间，也没有什么害处。

事实上，即使是对于那些不想追求事业的母亲来说，幼儿园也是一个很好的选择，因为那里的工作人员都是经过专业训练的，其专业水准是大部分母亲无法比拟的。把孩子送到托儿所是非常安全放心的。比起大部分的母亲来说，那些专业的护理机构能够更有效地应付突发事件。有些第一次做母亲的女性缺乏照顾孩子的知识和经验。

把孩子送到幼儿园还有助于将来的教育。幼儿园为将来上学作了一个很好的准备。在幼儿园，通过上课和参加各种活动，孩子们不仅学到了一些知识，而且还提前体验了一下将来上学的感觉。另外，每天和其他孩子的交往和接触，还可以培养孩子们的社交能力。缺乏这种能力的培养对孩子将来的发展是很不利的。

尽管在感情上可能有些难以割舍，但是把孩子送到幼儿园，由专业人员看护，对母亲来说是一个明智的选择。幼儿园可以看作是小学的准备和延伸。

特别提醒

儿童的教育问题，是雅思考试中最热门的话题之一。本书收集了10道以上关于儿童教育的雅思写作题目，涉及儿童教育的方方面面。请用心整理这些文章中常见的论据以及相应的英文表达。

推荐指数 ★★★ **相关题目** 33, 61, 90, 92, 105, 112

写作点拨

这道题目要求考生就“家长是否应该把孩子送到幼儿园或是托儿所”这一问题发表自己的看法，是典型的观点类雅思作文题。范文使用了最中规中矩的议论文的写法，全文分为五段：第一段引入话题，即应该把孩子送到幼儿园或托儿所；第二、三、四段介绍了应该把孩子送到幼儿园或托儿所的三个原因；第四段总结全文，重申作者的观点。

论据积累

应该把儿童送去幼儿园的理由：

1. 如果因为孩子的缘故，女性不得不放弃自己的事业，牺牲就太大了。
   It is too great a sacrifice for women to abandon their career for the sake of their children.
2. 幼儿园的工作人员的专业水准是大部分母亲无法比拟的。
   Kindergartens would be a good choice because most of them are staffed by professional nurses and instructors whose expertise is unmatched by most mothers.
3. 幼儿园为将来上学作了一个很好的准备。
   Kindergarten is a good preparation for school.

ESSAY 59

People now spend much time and money on their appearance and pay more attention to their dressing. Give reasons and your opinion on this.

It is reported that the money spent on cosmetic in the United States each year amounts to $ 200 billion, which is enough to feed all the people in Africa for two months. Alas, Africans go on starving to death despite all the talks about relieving poverty. Why is appearance so much regarded by some people?

Though it may sound harsh, the driving force behind the undue emphasis on one's appearance is vanity. Understandably, everyone is attracted to beauty and repelled by ugliness. None of us would wish to become less attractive. But our vanity may lead to excessive attention to our face and figure. Some even resort to plastic surgeries to beautify themselves, often at the risk of their health or even life. As it often happens, time and money are spent and pains are endured for no nobler reasons than to satisfy their vain self-esteem.

The changes in social mores also shape our attitude toward appearance. Different cultures treat appearance differently. In Muslim countries for example, women are covered up in shawls when they go out; men all wear similar clothes. Naturally, they don't care much about how they look. In other societies, however, women are judged by their appearance. Women are supposed to be attractive and sexy while men should be virile and worldly. There is no contending with social expectation and peer pressure: most people have no choice but conform.

The inordinate attention paid to appearance and dressing is deplorable to me. I regard it as shallow and vain. The pursuit of beauty should be carried out in our mind but not over our face or body. What really counts is not what meets the eye. Priorities should be given to things of real importance. It pains me to see that so many of us get distracted by this lopsided emphasis on appearance.

单词注释

- cosmetic [kɔz ˈmetɪk] *n.* 化妆品 *adj.* 化妆用的
- alas [əˈlæs] *int.* 唉
- appearance [əˈpɪərəns] *n.* 出现，露面；外貌
- harsh [hɑːʃ] *adj.* 粗糙的；荒芜的；苛刻的
- undue [ˌʌnˈdjuː] *adj.* 不适当的
- vanity [ˈvænɪti] *n.* 空虚，虚荣
- understandably [ˌʌndəˈstændəbli] *adv.* 可理解地
- repel [riˈpel] *vt.* 击退，抵制
- ugliness [ˈʌglɪnəs] *n.* 丑陋
- excessive [ɪkˈsesɪv] *adj.* 过多的，过分的
- resort [rɪˈzɔːt] *vi.* 求助；常去 *n.* 凭借，手段
- endure [ɪnˈdjʊə(r)] *v.* 耐久，忍耐
- noble [ˈnəʊbl] *adj.* 高贵的，华丽的
- vain [veɪn] *adj.* 徒然的，无益的；虚荣的
- esteem [ɪsˈtiːm] *vt.* 把…看作；尊敬 *n.* 尊敬，尊重
- mores [ˈmɔːreɪz] *n.* 风俗，习惯
- Muslim [ˈmʊzlɪm] *n.* 穆斯林，穆罕默德信徒
- shawl [ʃɔːl] *n.* 披肩，围巾
- virile [ˈvɪraɪl] *adj.* 男性的，男的
- worldly [ˈwɜːldli] *adj.* 世间的
- contend [kənˈtend] *v.* 斗争，竞争；主张
- peer [pɪə(r)] *n.* 同等的人；贵族 *vi.* 凝视，窥视
- conform [kənˈfɔːm] *vt.* 使一致，使遵守，使顺从 *adj.* 一致的
- inordinate [ɪnˈɔːdɪnət] *adj.* 过度的
- deplorable [dɪˈplɔːrəbl] *adj.* 可叹的
- shallow [ˈʃæləʊ] *adj.* 浅的，浅薄的
- priority [praɪˈɒrɪti] *n.* 优先，优先权
- lopsided [ˌlɒpˈsaidid] *adj.* 倾向一方的，不平衡的

如今人们越来越看重着装，在外表方面花费了大量的时间和金钱。请给出造成这种现象的原因以及你对此的看法。

据说，现在美国人每年花在购买化妆品上的钱高达2000亿美元，足够维持整个非洲人民生存两个月。天哪！尽管国际社会整天嚷着要消除贫困，非洲人民依然在饥荒线上挣扎。为什么有人要把外表看得这么重要呢？

也许这么说有些苛刻，但对外表的过分注重是虚荣心的体现。可以理解，每个人都有爱美之心，厌恶丑恶。我们都不想变得难看。但是我们的虚荣心可能导致我们过分关注我们的容貌和身材。有些人甚至冒着健康，甚至是生命危险，通过整容手术去使自己变得美丽。花了金钱和时间，付出了痛苦的代价，但并不是为了什么高尚的理由，而只是为了满足虚荣心，这种事情经常在我们的社会发生。

社会风气的变化改变了我们对外貌的态度。不同的文化对待外貌的态度不同。比如，在穆斯林国家，妇女出门的时候总是要蒙上面纱，而男性的穿着也几乎类似。很自然，他们就对外表不是很在意。但是，在别的国家，对待女性，往往是以貌取人。女性必须是迷人性感的，而男性则必须是刚毅成熟的。人们无法对抗社会的期望和同伴的压力，大部分人都只好屈从这种标准。

我很讨厌这种对外貌和衣着的过分关注。我觉得这是浅薄和虚荣的表现。对美的追求应该在内心，而不是体现在外表。外在的东西其实并不重要。我们应该关注那些真正重要的东西。令我悲哀的是，有太多的人过分关注他们的外表了，却忽视了那些真正重要的东西。

特别提醒

外表和服饰的问题，曾经一度是雅思考试中的热门话题，但是近年来在雅思考试中出现的频率有所下降，考生仅需要做一般参考。

推荐指数 ★★★　　**相关题目** 66, 69, 76

写作点拨

这道雅思写作题目要求考生解释人们日益看重外表和服饰这一现象的原因，同时给出自己的看法，是典型的“原因＋观点”类的雅思作文题。范文侧重解释造成该现象的原因，全文分为四段：第一段引入话题；第二、三段介绍了造成该现象的两个不同的原因；第四段表达作者个人的看法。

词汇升级

注意，关心

普通版 *Too much attention paid to appearance* and dressing is deplorable to me.

升级版 *The inordinate attention paid to appearance* and dressing is deplorable to me.

attention: full(全部的), rapt(全神贯注的), undivided(专心的), assiduous(勤勉的), meticulous(极度关心的), inordinate(过度的), scrupulous(小心翼翼的), unwanted(不必要的), unwelcome(不受欢迎的)

ESSAY 60

Many people believe that we have developed into a 'throw-away society' which is filled with plastic bags and rubbish. Do you agree or disagree?

It is indeed true that everything comes at a price. We are paying through the nose in terms of environmental damage for the conveniences we enjoy nowadays. The world is becoming a throw-away society, where the amount of garbage is increasing daily.

Of course, disposable items have to be used under some circumstances. Indeed, it is imperative to use disposable needles and syringes in hospitals to prevent contagion among patients. It would also be preferable if throw-away plates and spoons are used in restaurants out of sanitary consideration. At present those low-cost disposable plates and spoons are far from comfortable and biodegradable. Even so, they are used on a huge scale in China and many other countries.

Yet, disposable items are not only used in the medical and catering industry. They are virtually everywhere. There was a time when things were built to last, when durability was highly regarded. Today, people don't want to use the same thing all the time even if it is in perfect order. We have become less sentimental or nostalgic, which reveals itself not only in our discarding of old things but also in our reduced reluctance to abandon old friends. To many, everything is dispensable.

Recycling seems the only way to prevent the total inundation of the planet by the garbage produced over generations. People are unlikely to give up their conveniences easily. The demand of goods will increase inexorably, putting more strain on garbage disposal. Therefore, recycling offers the best hope. Not only miraculous but also essential is the idea of turning wastes into treasures. It is estimated that 60 percent of rubbish can be recycled quite economically. With improved technology, recycling will make more economical and environmental sense in the days to come.

The throw-away society, as some call it, is mainly the result of technological development and our change of attitude. The conviction that nothing will last is reinforced by the constant changes brought by technology. Without going into the rights and wrongs of this attitude, I am convinced that recycling is essential to the survival of mankind in the future.

单词注释

- pay through the nose 支付高昂的价格
- syringe [ˈsɪrɪndʒ] *n.* 注射器
- disposable [dɪsˈpəuzəbl] *adj.* 可任意使用的
- imperative [ɪmˈperətɪv] *n.* 命令，诫命；需要 *adj.* 命令的，强制的
- contagion [kənˈteɪdʒən] *n.* 传染，传染病，蔓延
- preferable [ˈprefərəbl] *adj.* 更可取的，更好的
- sanitary [ˈsænɪtəri] *adj.* (有关)卫生的，(保持)清洁的
- biodegradable [ˌbaɪəudɪˈgreɪdəbl] *adj.* 能生物分解的
- catering [ˈkeɪtərɪŋ] 提供饮食
- durability [ˌdjuərəˈbɪləti] *n.* 经久，耐久
- sentimental [ˌsentɪˈmentl] *adj.* 感伤性的，感情脆弱的
- nostalgic [nɒˈstældʒɪk] *adj.* 乡愁的，怀旧的
- discard [disˈkɑːd] *vt.* 丢弃，抛弃
- reluctance [rɪˈlʌktəns] *n.* 不愿，勉强
- dispensable [dɪsˈpensəbl] *adj.* 不是必要的，可有可无的
- inundation [ˌɪnʌnˈdeɪʃn] *n.* 泛滥；洪水
- inexorably [ɪnˈeksərəbl] *adv.* 无情地，冷酷地
- disposal [disˈpəuzl] *n.* 处理，处置
- miraculous [mɪˈrækjələs] *adj.* 奇迹的，不可思议的
- conviction [kənˈvɪkʃn] *n.* 深信，确信；定罪
- reinforce [ˌriːɪnˈfɔːs] *vt.* 加强，增援，补充 *vi.* 求援
- survival [səˈvaɪvl] *n.* 生存，幸存，残存

很多人认为今天的世界到处充斥着一次性塑料袋和垃圾，我们的社会已经进入了“一次性社会”。你是否同意这样的看法？

世上凡事都有代价。我们现在享受了许多便利，但是却在环境方面付出了巨大的代价。这个社会已变成了一个“一次性”社会，产生的垃圾与日俱增。

当然，一次性用品在某些场合是必需的。的确，为了防止病人感染，在医院里必须使用一次性针头和注射器。即使不考虑卫生因素，餐馆使用一次性盘子、勺子等也能给顾客带来很多便利。但是，我们目前使用的一次性低成本餐具，用起来既不舒适，又无法生物降解。即使是这样，中国和许多其他国家，仍在大量使用一次性餐具。

但是，一次性用品不仅在医疗和饮食行业使用，它们几乎无处不在。以前生产的东西总是很耐用，那时大家也很看重产品是否耐用。今天，人们不想总是用同样的东西，哪怕它还完好如初。我们没有以前那么恋旧了。我们不仅对旧事物如此，对老朋友也是如此。对很多人来说，一切都是可抛弃的。

对废物加以回收利用似乎是防止我们的地球被一代又一代的垃圾淹没的唯一办法。人们总是不会轻易放弃所享受的种种便利。人们对产品的需求在急速增长，这给垃圾处理带来了极大的压力。所以，回收利用是最好的出路。变废为宝不仅是一个神奇的、而且也是必要的方法。据估计，60%的垃圾能够以较为经济的成本回收利用。将来随着技术的提高，回收利用将会有更多的经济意义和环境意义。

我们的社会被有些人称之为“一次性”社会，这主要是科技发展和我们态度改变的结果。技术带来的不断变化加剧了人们认为万物不会持久的信念。我们在此不谈论这种态度的对与错。我相信废物回收利用是人类将来能否生存的关键。

特别提醒

环境保护的问题，一直都是雅思考试中最热门的话题之一。本书收集的关于环保话题的雅思写作题目，涉及环境保护的方方面面。请用心整理这类文章中常见的论据以及一些重复出现的论据的英文表达方式。

推荐指数 ★★★★　　**相关题目** 30, 77

写作点拨

这道题目要求考生就“当今社会是否已经进入了一次性社会”这一问题发表自己的看法，是典型的观点类雅思作文题。范文的写法有别于议论文的常规写法，除了给出作者的观点以及相应的论据外，还特别用一段文字提出了解决这个问题的建议。实际考试中，考生可以在“有话可说”的时候采用这种写法。范文分为五段：第一段给出作者的观点，即社会的确已经进入了一次性社会；第二、三段列举不同方面的证据来证明一次性社会已经来临；第四段提出作者的建议；第五段在重申作者观点的同时总结全文。

词汇升级

付出高昂的代价

普通版 In terms of environmental damage, we are *paying a high price* for the conveniences we enjoy nowadays.

升级版 We are *paying through the nose* in terms of environmental damage for the conveniences we enjoy nowadays.

注释：在写作文章中适当地使用常见的俚语，不仅可以丰富考生的语言表达，而且还可以让考生的语言更显地道。

ESSAY 61

Some people agree that all kinds of jobs should be equally open to men and women. Others think that some jobs should only be suitable for men and women respectively. Discuss and give your opinion.

Many of us would be a little amused at the sight of a male nurse and be upset by the presence of a female soldier. Yet, even the last bastion of male dominance—the navy is giving way to equal rights consideration. The stereotype male and female roles at workplace seem to be fading.

Equal rights advocates are hailing the fact that more jobs are opening to both men and women. In their opinion, it is a manifestation of equality. Why should women be barred from some jobs merely because of their gender? It is blatant discrimination against the underprivileged sex, which is rooted in the male chauvinistic view that men are superior to women. As it often turns out, women can do just as well, if not better, in virtually all kinds of work. Tasks requiring physical strength can now be done by machines, so female's weaker physique is not an issue here. Conversely, of course, there is no such a job that only a woman can do. What dissuades men from taking certain jobs is often stereotyped male self-perception, which deems certain professions as below their dignity. Indeed, a lot of talent is wasted when one sex choose not to pursue certain careers. Unfortunately, in many fields such as science and politics, female is still sharply under-represented. How many Madam Curies can the world turn out if we dispose of this long-held unjustified attitude?

It must not be taken, however, that we should have equal number of males and females doing any kind of work. It is a matter of individuality rather than gender. Some people, male or female, are naturally unfit for politics; some may never make good athletes; still some will find teaching repulsive. Thus, before embarking on a career, both sexes need to take account of their interests, abilities, inclination, temperament and so on.

Equal job opportunity for both sexes is not so much desirable as unavoidable. Developed nations are feeling the strain as a large portion of their talents (usually females) remain untapped. Jobs should be offered to whoever qualified regardless of the gender.

单词注释

- amused [ə'mjuːzd] *adj.* 愉快的，开心的，好玩的
- bastion ['bæstiən] *n.* 堡垒，阵地工事
- dominance ['dɒmɪnəns] *n.* 优势；统治
- stereotype ['steriətaɪp] *n.* 陈腔滥调，老套
- advocate ['ædvəkɪt] *n.* 提倡者
  ['ædvakeɪt] *vt.* 提倡，鼓吹
- manifestation [ˌmænɪfes'teɪʃən] *n.* 显示，表现；示威运动
- equality [i'kwɒləti] *n.* 等同性，同等，平等
- gender ['dʒendə] *n.* 性别
- blatant ['bleitənt] *adj.* 显眼的；喧嚣的，吵闹的
- discrimination [dɪˌskrɪmɪ'neɪʃn] *n.* 辨别，区别，识别力
- underprivileged [ˌʌndə'prɪvəlɪdʒd] *adj.* 被剥夺基本权利的；穷困的
- chauvinistic [ˌʃəʊvɪ'nɪstɪk] *adj.* 盲目爱国的，沙文主义的
- superior [suː'pɪəriə(r)] *adj.* 较高的，上级的；优秀的 *n.* 长者，高手，上级
- physique [fi'ziːk] *n.* (男子的)体格，体形
- conversely ['kɒnvɜːsli] *adv.* 相反地，逆地
- dissuade [dɪ'sweɪd] *vt.* 劝阻
- perception [pə'sepʃn] *n.* 理解，感知，感觉
- deem [diːm] *v.* 认为，相信
- unjustified [ʌn'dʒʌstɪfaɪd] *adj.* 未被证明为正确的
- individuality [ˌɪndɪˌvɪdʒu'æləti] *n.* 个性，个人的特性
- repulsive [rɪ'pʌlsɪv] *adj.* 排斥的，令人厌恶的
- inclination [ˌɪnklɪ'neɪʃn] *n.* 倾斜，倾度；倾向
- temperament ['tempərəmənt] *n.* 气质，性情
- untapped [ˌʌn'tæpt] *adj.* 未打开的；未开发的

有人认为所有的职位都应该向男性和女性平等开放，但是也有人认为某些职位的确更加适合某一种性别。请讨论这个问题并给出你的看法。

如果看到男护士或者是女士兵，我们当中的很多人都会感到滑稽或惊讶。但是如今，即使是男性主宰的最后堡垒——海军，也被男女平等的大潮所攻克了。传统的男女分工模式已经渐渐离我们远去了。

现在越来越多的工作对男女同时开放了。这受到了男女平等支持者的热烈欢迎。他们认为这是平等的表现。为什么有些工作仅仅因为性别的原因就可以阻止女性进入呢？这简直是对女性的公然歧视。其根源是男性沙文主义在作怪，认为男性比女性要优越。但事实经常是，在几乎所有领域，女性往往也能和男性做得一样好，如果不是更好的话。现在那些需要体力的活可以由机器来做，所以女性体格方面的劣势并不带来任何影响。相反，也不存在只有女性能做、男性不能做的工作。有些工作男性不愿意做，那是因为老观念在作怪，认为有些工作男性做了有损男性尊严。事实上，工作上的性别歧视使得大量的才能被浪费了。不幸的是，在很多领域，比如科学和政治，女性的才能远没有得到应有的体现。如果我们能够摒弃多年以来的错误观念，我们将能见到更多的居里夫人。

但是，我们不能理解为每种工作的男女比例要相等。这是因人而异的问题，和性别本身无关。有些人，可能是男人，也可能是女人，天生就不适合搞政治。有些人可能永远也成为不了好的运动员。有些人可能天生就讨厌教书。所以，在决定从事某项职业之前，必须仔细考虑个人的兴趣爱好、能力、性格等。

男女工作平等不但是合情合理，而且是必须的。发达国家已经感受到了这种压力。在发达国家，有很大一部分才能(通常是女性的能力)没有得到应有的开发。工作应该给那些最胜任的人去做，而不应该考虑他们的性别。

特别提醒

男女平等的问题，是雅思考试中的传统话题之一，曾经以非常高的频率在雅思写作考试中出现。虽然这类话题如今在雅思考试中出现的频率已经大不如从前，但是还是不时地有雅思真题涉及这类话题，请认真复习。

推荐指数 ★★★★

相关题目 33, 58, 90, 92, 105, 112

写作点拨

这道题目要求考生就“是否所有的职位都应该向男性和女性平等开放”以及“是否某些职位的确更加适合某一种性别”展开讨论，并且给出自己的观点，是典型的“讨论＋观点”类雅思作文题。讨论类的作文题，一定要从正反两方面展开论证，列举两方面的论据。范文分为四段：第一段引入话题；第二、三段分别从正、反两方面列举证据，分别论证两种说法的正确性；第四段提出作者的观点并总结全文。

词汇升级

公然的

普通版 It is *obvious* discrimination against the underprivileged sex.

升级版 It is *blatant* discrimination against the underprivileged sex.

公然的：vociferous, blatant, boisterous, strident, clamorous

ESSAY 62

Nowadays college students or even high school students start to work at a younger age. Do you think that it is a positive or negative development?

Adults often regard their school years as the best time of their lives. However, mankind is apt to forget pain once it is passed. It was actually not easy to be a student, even more so nowadays. Skyrocketing tuition fees and slowing economy compel students to work harder and earlier.

It is a rather unsavory trend. Some students begin working part-time at the tender age of fourteen. Regardless of its legality, the job options can be reasonably expected. Most work as salespersons, which not only exhausts them physically, but also interferes with their study. Even for those under better working conditions, say private tutors, part-time jobs invariably rob them of their precious time.

However, be that as it may, I still regard this as a positive development. Some good must come out of our mental and physical exertions, provided that they are not excessive. By taking intellectually challenging jobs students learn to apply what they are taught in class to real life. Even pure manual work can cultivate students' hardiness, discipline and will power. Provided that competition is to get fiercer, they need to know what life is really like earlier rather than later, a taste of which can be got through working. In addition, these early working experiences are conducive to their future career. Part-time jobs often lead to internship and eventually to full-time employment. The work experience is valuable in itself. It teaches a person how to fit into an organization, how to work with others and how to deal with disgruntled customers. Working is often a most demanding yet rewarding experience.

Sooner or later, we have to fend for ourselves. So why wait until the last minute? Working on a part-time basis prepares us to step out of the Ivory Tower and into the real world.

单词注释

- positive [ˈpɒzətɪv] *adj.* 肯定的，积极的
- negative [ˈnegətɪv] *n.* 否定；负数；底片 *adj.* 否定的
- apt [æpt] *adj.* 易于…的，有…倾向的
- skyrocket [skaɪrɒkɪt] *v.* 猛涨
- tuition [tjuˈɪʃn] *n.* 学费
- compel [kəmˈpel] *vt.* 强迫，迫使
- unsavory [ˌʌnˈseɪvəri] *adj.* 令人讨厌的；难吃的
- tender [ˈtendə] *adj.* 嫩的，温柔的，软弱的
- legality [liːˈgæləti] *n.* 合法；墨守成规，法律上的义务
- reasonably [ˈriːzənəbli] *adv.* 适度地，相当地
- salesperson [ˈseɪlzpɜːsn] *n.* 售货员
- tutor [ˈtjuːtə(r)] *n.* 家庭教师，(大学)指导教师
- invariably [ɪnˈveəriəbli] *adv.* 不变地，总是
- be that as it may 尽管如此
- exertion [ɪgˈzɜːʃn] *n.* 尽力，努力；发挥；行使，运用
- excessive [ɪkˈsesɪv] *adj.* 过多的，过分的，额外
- manual [ˈmænjuəl] *n.* 手册，指南 *adj.* 体力的，手动的
- cultivate [ˈkʌltɪveɪt] *vt.* 培养；耕作
- hardiness [ˈhɑːdɪnəs] *n.* 耐久力，顽强
- fierce [fɪəs] *adj.* 凶猛的；激烈的
- conducive [kənˈdjuːsɪv] *adj.* 有益于…的
- internship [ˈɪntɜːnʃɪp] *n.* 〈美〉实习医师，实习医师期
- valuable [ˈvæljuəbl] *adj.* 贵重的，有价值的，颇有价值的
- disgruntled [dɪsˈgrʌntld] *adj.* 不满的，不高兴的
- demanding [dɪˈmɑːndɪŋ] *adj.* 过分要求的，苛求的

如今，大学生甚至是高中生往往都提前开始工作了。你认为这是个好的现象，还是个不好的现象？

成年人通常把学校时光看作是他们一生当中最美好的回忆。人们的天性总是好了伤疤忘了疼。其实，学生时代的日子也不是那么好过的。现在的学生更是辛苦。学费飞涨、经济发展缓慢，这些都迫使现在的学生更努力地学习、更早地开始工作。

这种趋势是不容乐观的。有些学生仅 14 岁就开始做兼职工作了。先不说这是否合法，这种年龄能干的工作种类可想而知。大部分是做销售工作。这不仅劳累，而且还影响他们的学习。即使是那些工作条件好一些的兼职工作，例如家教，也总是要占用学生们宝贵的学习时间。

但是，尽管如此，我还是认为这是一种积极的事态发展。身体和精神上的锤炼，只要不过度，对我们总是有好处的。通过从事那些要求智力的兼职工作，学生们能够把所学理论用于实践。即使是纯体力活，也可以锻炼学生的毅力、纪律性和意志力。现在社会竞争越来越激烈，他们需要更早而不是晚些懂得生活的艰辛。通过兼职工作，学生们可以对生活有所体验，而且兼职工作经历对他们以后的职业发展也是有好处的。兼职工作经常可以转变为实习机会，甚至是全职工作。工作经验是很有价值的。它可以让人学会如何融入一个组织、如何与他人相处、如何应付投诉的客户等。工作往往是一种要求最高、但回报也是最大的人生经历。

我们迟早要自立，所以为什么要等到最后一分钟呢？兼职工作为我们走出象牙塔、走入社会做了一个很好的准备。

特别提醒

教育问题，历来都是雅思写作考试中的热门话题。雅思写作考试中，关于教育的写作题目大致可以分为三大类：1. 教育的内容（教育应该包含哪些内容、教育应该重点传授职业技能还是人文知识）；2. 教育的方式（混班教学 VS 男、女校、集体学习 VS 单独辅导）；3. 教育的意义（为什么要接受教育）。

推荐指数 ★★★

相关题目 44

写作点拨

这道题目要求考生就“学生提前参加工作是好事还是坏事”这一问题发表自己的看法，是典型的观点类雅思作文题。范文的写法有别于议论文的常规写法，除了给出作者的观点以及相应的论据外，还特别用一段文字提出观点的反面也有其正确性，起到了让步的作用。在实际考试中，让步段可以极大地加强论证的说服力和可信度。范文分为四段：第一段引入话题；第二段是让步段，列举出学生提前参加工作的种种弊端；第三段指出学生提前参加工作的合理性和必要性；第四段重申作者观点。

词汇升级

趋势

普通版 It is a rather *bad trend*.

升级版 It is a rather *unsavory trend*.

trend（趋势）：*adj*: adverse（不利的）, disturbing（令人烦扰的）, worrying（令人担忧的）, unfortunate（不幸的）, apparent（明显的）, discernible（显著的）, dominant（主导的）, prevailing（主流的）, accelerating（加速的）

ESSAY 63

Some people think that bicycle is the best way to travel from place to place. Discuss the advantages and disadvantages of the bicycle.

Nowhere are bikes more widely used than in China. About 300 million bikes are being used daily around the country, mainly for transport purposes. Indeed, I would certainly cycle to work if I lived nearer to my workplace.

Riding a bike contributes to our health. At the very least, cycling burns calories. In fact, it does much more. Cycling helps to train our hand-eye-feet coordination and sharpens our sense of balance. It is easy to learn and not physically demanding. It is probably the best sport for overweight people. Besides, the air will be a lot cleaner if more people choose to use bikes instead of cars. Bicycle is the most environment-friendly means of transport except for walking, which has the intolerable downside of being too slow. Actually, due to traffic congestion, cycling is often the quickest way to reach your destination. Apart from being clean and quick, cycling is safe. This means safety for ourselves and others. In light of the actual speed at which a bike usually travels, the likelihood of a collision with pedestrians and fellow cyclists is minimal. Even in the event of such an accident, people involved usually get away with a few scratches at the worst.

Having said that, a more critical rider may find a bike less than satisfactory. For example, it can't shield against rain or dust; the saddle is often uncomfortable. Besides, bikes are unfit for long distance travel. After all, most people can't ride more than 20 miles at a stretch.

Taken all together, the bicycle is indeed a brilliant human invention. Unlike many other devices, bike reinforces our reliance on ourselves both physically and mentally. This never fails to fascinate me.

单词注释

- nowhere [ˈnəʊhweə(r)] *adv.* 无处，到处都无
- calorie [ˈkæləri] *n.* 卡路里
- overweight [ˌəʊvəˈweit] *n.* 超重
- intolerable [ɪnˈtɒlərəbl] *adj.* 无法忍受的，难耐的
- downside [ˈdaʊnsaɪd] *n.* 底侧，下降趋势 *adj.* 底侧的
- congestion [kənˈdʒestʃn] *n.* 拥塞；充血
- collision [kəˈlɪʒən] *n.* 碰撞，冲突
- pedestrian [pəˈdestriən] *n.* 步行者
- scratch [skrætʃ] *n.* 乱写；刮擦声；抓痕
- shield [ʃiːld] *n.* 防护物，护罩，盾
- saddle [ˈsædl] *n.* 鞍，鞍状物 *v.* 承受
- stretch [stretʃ] *v.* 伸展，伸长 *n.* 一段时间
- reinforce [ˌriːɪnˈfɔːs] *vt.* 加强，增援，补充
- fascinate [ˈfæsɪneɪt] *vt.* 使着迷，使神魂颠倒

有人认为自行车是最方便的交通工具。请讨论自行车的利和弊。

中国是世界上自行车使用最多的地方。全国每天大概使用三亿辆自行车，而且大多数都是用于运输目的。事实上，如果我住的地方离我工作的地方不远的话，我都想骑自行车上班。

骑车对我们的健康有很多好处。至少骑车可以燃烧卡路里。事实上，骑车的益处还远不止如此：骑车可以锻炼我们的眼、手、脚的协调，并且可以增强我们的平衡能力。骑车很容易学，而且对身体素质的要求也不高。这可能是那些减肥人士最好的运动方式。另外，如果人们愿意骑车并且放弃开车的话，那么我们的空气将会变得更加清新。除了走路，自行车是最环保的交通方式了。但走路实在是太慢了，这一点很难让人接受。事实上，由于交通堵塞，自行车往往是到达目的地的最快方式。除了快捷和环保之外，自行车还很安全，而且是对人对己都安全。由于受到速度的限制，自行车撞人或与别的自行车相撞的机会很小。即使撞上了，最严重也不过是一些皮外伤而已。

尽管如此，挑剔的人还是能找出自行车的不足。例如，自行车不能挡风遮雨、不能挡灰尘，而且坐垫也不怎么舒服。另外，自行车不适合长距离旅行。毕竟大部分人不能一口气骑上 20 公里。

综合来看，自行车不愧是人类的一项伟大发明。与其他发明不同，自行车使得我们在体力上和意志上更加坚强。骑车总能让我心旷神怡。

特别提醒

交通问题，曾经是雅思写作考试中最热门的话题之一。雅思写作考试中，关于交通的写作题，大致可以分为两大类：1.各种交通工具的利和弊；2.如何改善交通状况。

推荐指数 ★★★ **相关题目** 12, 38

写作点拨

这道题目要求考生叙述自行车的利和弊，是典型的“正反叙述”类雅思作文题。实际考试中，推荐考生使用这篇范文所采用的这种传统的“四段法”来写这类文章：第一段引入话题；第二段列举自行车的各种优势；第三段列举自行车的各种弊端；第四段给出作者自己的观点或喜好。

论据积累

自行车的利弊

利：1. 有利于健康

Riding a bike contributes to our health.

2. 最环保的交通方式之一

Bicycle is the most environment-friendly means of transport except for walking.

3. 交通堵塞时，自行车是到达目的地的最快方式

Due to traffic congestion, cycling is often the quickest way to reach your destination.

弊：1. 不能挡风遮雨和挡住灰尘

Bicycles can't shield against rain or dust.

2. 不适合长距离旅行

Bicycles are unfit for long-distant traveling.

… gives people more free time, but actually they are busier than before. Do … disagree?

… me, most people are busy all day long. There never seems to be a free moment. It is indeed …nic that the so-called time-saving devices actually take up more of our time. We are reluctant to turn everything off and take a moment with ourselves.

Mankind is unlikely to lead a more leisurely life in the foreseeable future because science and technology won't ease our burden too much. Though touted as energy-saving, touch-button devices, most of inventions only open up the possibility of performing certain tasks simultaneously. Before the advent of cell phone, people wouldn't think of calling others while walking. Thus, they didn't have to endure the annoyance of answering the phone in the middle of something. It seems that technology makes our lives more efficient but not necessarily more leisurely, far from it actually. The moment we push the ' print ' key, we don't lean back and relax but turn our attention to something else.

Then, an optimist would laugh at the above assertion. Can't we just relax and call it a day? We are in control of our own schedules. We don't need to do extra work if we don't want to do so. But the truth is far from that. Contrary to common belief, a large portion of what we do is not determined by ourselves. At work, we are told what to do; at home we are influenced by family members. In short, we are influenced by peer pressure and social expectation. Even if one is strong-minded enough to turn off everything, he usually can't afford to do so because of the competition he faces. Very few can remain indifferent to what is embraced by all and what is expected of them. Besides, new technologies can be very alluring. They bring about conveniences and even wonders. Once hooked, few can resist the urge to use them to the full.

Fortunately or unfortunately, mankind is always pushing for something better. Tantalizing successes always loom ahead. Having tasted the wonders of advanced technologies, we cannot do without them. Hence we become increasingly busy.

单词注释

- ironic [aɪəˈrɒnik] *adj.* 说反话的，讽刺的
- tout [taʊt] *v.* 吹捧
- simultaneously [ˌsɪmlˈteɪniəsly] *adv.* 同时地
- assertion [əˈsɜːʃn] *n.* 主张，断言，声明
- call it a day 完成一天的工作，收工
- peer [pɪə(r)] *n.* 同等的人；贵族
- indifferent [ɪnˈdɪfərənt] *adj.* 冷漠的
- embrace [ɪmˈbreɪs] *vt.* 拥抱；包含
- alluring [əˈlʊərɪŋ] *adj.* 迷人的，吸引人的，诱惑的
- push for 为…奋力争取，强烈地要求
- tantalizing [ˈtæntəlaɪzɪŋ] *adj.* 非常着急的
- loom [luːm] *v.* 隐现；迫近
- hence [hens] *adv.* 因此，从此

现代科技为人们节省了大量的时间，但是人们却比过去更加繁忙了。你是否同意这样的说法？

大部分人像我一样成天忙个不停，好像就没有闲下来的时候。那些所谓节省时间的装置，事实上占用了我们更多的时间，这的确很有讽刺意味。人们总是不愿意把这些所谓的省时的玩意儿关了，自己享受一下片刻的闲暇。

在可预见的将来，人们不可能过上悠闲的生活，因为将来的科技并不会给我们减轻多少负担。尽管有很多的所谓节省时间、只要按一下按钮就行的玩意儿，但是这些东西中的大部分仅仅是使我们能够一心多用、同时干很多件事情而已。在手机发明之前，人们不会想到要边走路边打电话，所以也不会出现在干着别的什么事情时还必须接电话的情况。看来科技是使我们的生活更高效了，却未必是更悠闲了。事实上，我们的生活还远谈不上悠闲。按下打印键之后，我们不是靠在椅子上休息，而是又把注意力集中到别的事情上去了。

也许乐天派的人会对本文题目中的观点嗤之以鼻。为什么我们不可以坐下来放松放松，不要工作了呢？我们可以自己控制自己的日程安排。如果我们不想加班，我们可以不加。实际情况远非如此。和普遍存在的观点不同，人们所做的事情，在大部分情况下都不是自己能决定的。在工作的时候，上司安排我们的工作；在家里，我们的行为受到家庭其他成员的影响。总之，我们承受着同伴的压力以及社会期望所带来的压力。即使意志力很顽强的人也不可能完全与社会切断联系，因为激烈的竞争不允许他这样做。很少有人能够对大家都接受的东西或是别人对他的期望无动于衷。此外，新科技总是很吸引人的。它们带来了便利，甚至是创造了奇迹。一旦喜欢上新科技，很少有人能够不把这些东西大加利用的。

人们总是在追求更好的东西，不知这是人类的幸运还是不幸。总有成功的影子不断地在前方的不远处诱惑着人类。品尝了科技的滋味后，我们已经离不开它们了。因此，我们注定了会变得越来越忙了。

特别提醒

现代科技的问题，是雅思考试中最热门的话题之一。本书收集了近10道关于现代科技题材的雅思作文题目，其中大部分题目都涉及现代科技对人类生活和工作所造成的影响。

推荐指数 ★★★★★　　**相关题目** 5, 14, 15, 16, 20, 21, 25, 103, 110

写作点拨

这道题目要求考生就“现代科技为人们节省了大量的时间，人们却比过去更加繁忙了”这一观点发表自己的看法，是典型的观点类雅思作文题。这篇范文将题目所给的观点拆分为两个小的观点，再用两段文字分别讨论这两个小的观点，有别于议论文的常规写法。范文分为四段：第一段在引入话题的同时给出作者的观点，即人们的确比过去忙了；第二段论证现代科技并没有为人们节省大量的时间，指出题目给出的第一个小观点有误；第三段指出人们比过去更忙的原因；第四段重申作者观点。

词汇升级

即将到来的

普通版 The *coming* successes always loom ahead.

升级版 *Tantalizing* successes always loom ahead.

即将到来的：approaching, imminent, impending, tantalizing

ESSAY 65

Many people think that education is losing its value. Do you agree or disagree?

The number of college students is increasing yearly despite the increasing tuition fees, which are clearly beyond the means of low income families. This kind of investment in terms of time and money seems to have given sufficient proof to the value of college education. Yet, it is feared that education, or at least college education, is ‘devaluating’.

The claim can be justified only in a narrow sense. It is true that college graduates are experiencing trouble landing decent jobs and that the financial return of the investment in college education seems to be declining. It is also said that many students play truant regularly and only cram before final exams. They attend a university only to get a degree or even to have a good time. Yet, all these are simply the students' own fault or that of poor education quality. A good education is always invaluable.

College is a place where one can pursue one's own interests. There are professors to guide and inspire you; there are laboratories to provide first-hand experience; there are numerous books waiting to be perused. Prior to college, students often focus on acquiring a general knowledge of various subjects, but college allows them to dive into their majors. Deep and enduring interest can never be cultivated by merely scratching the surface. Besides, students are grouped with like-minded classmates, the interaction with whom adds impetus to their academic pursuit. By talking, sharing and cooperating with one's peers, one often gets inspired and encouraged and acquires a different perspective.

Education can bring personal improvement in ways other than scholastic achievement. Look at the huge difference between the educated and illiterate. Education is not merely the imparting of knowledge but also the cultivation of the mind, with the latter being more intangible and subtle. The uneducated tend to be ill-mannered, rude or even vulgar. We acquire our moral sense when we are taught the heroic deeds of great men and the atrocities caused by evil ones. Left to ourselves, we often subscribe to the pragmatic view of ‘ends justify means’ and regard nobility and sacrifice as hypocritical.

Therefore, instead of losing its value, education will become all the more essential in a world where we are in danger of being overwhelmed by the conflicts and competitions among ourselves.

单词注释

- devaluate [diːˈvæljʊeɪt] *v.* (使)贬值
- decent [ˈdiːsnt] *adj.* 正派的，体面的；有分寸的
- truant [ˈtruːənt] *n.* 逃避责任者
- cram [kræm] *v.* 填满
- pursue [pəˈsjuː] *vt.* 追求；从事
- peruse [pəˈruːz] *v.* 细读
- cultivated [ˈkʌltɪveɪtɪd] *adj.* 耕耘的；有教养的
- impetus [ˈɪmpɪtəs] *n.* 推动力，促进
- perspective [pəˈspektɪv] *n.* 观点；洞察力
- scholastic [skəˈlæstɪk] *adj.* 学校的，学校教育的
- illiterate [ɪˈlɪtərɪt] *n.* 文盲 *adj.* 不识字的，没受教育的
- impart [ɪmˈpɑːt] *vt.* 给予；传授；告知，透露
- intangible [ɪnˈtændʒəbl] *adj.* 难以理解的；无形的
- subtle [ˈsʌtl] *adj.* 狡猾的；敏感的，微妙的
- vulgar [ˈvʌlgə(r)] *adj.* 粗俗的，庸俗的；普通的
- atrocity [əˈtrɒsɪti] *n.* 残暴，暴行，凶恶
- subscribe [səbˈskraɪb] *v.* 捐款；订阅；签署(文件)；赞成
- pragmatic [prægˈmætɪk] *adj.* 务实的；实用主义的，实际的
- hypocritical [ˌhɪpəˈkrɪtɪkl] *adj.* 伪善的，伪善者的
- all the more 更加

很多人认为教育正在贬值。你是否同意这种说法？

虽然大学学费居高不下，低收入家庭无法承受，但是大学生的人数还是在持续增加。家庭投入的大量金钱和学生付出的大量时间，似乎都体现了大学教育的价值。但是，有人担心教育，尤其是大学教育，正在贬值。

这种说法是片面的。诚然，大学毕业生毕业后很难找到好工作，大学教育的投资回报不断下滑。有部分大学生常常逃课，在考试前则突击复习。很多学生读大学只是为了混个文凭，甚至是为了消磨时光。但是这一切都可以归因为学生自己的问题以及教学质量不过关。良好的学校教育永远是无价的。

学生们在大学里可以发展自己的兴趣。大学里有教授对学生进行指导和鼓励；学生可以在实验室里自己动手操作；图书馆里有无数的书籍供学生阅读。在上大学之前，学生的重点是打一个全面的基础；然而上大学后，学生可以钻研自己的专业。浅尝辄止是培养不出持续和浓厚的兴趣的。此外，学生们"人以群分"，彼此兴趣相投，可以互相促进。通过和同伴的交谈、分享以及合作，学生可以互相启发和激励，学会从不同的角度看问题。

教育带来的不仅仅是学业上的成就。受过教育和未受教育的人之间存在着巨大的差异。教育不仅仅传授知识，而且陶冶情操。后者往往更加潜移默化。未受过教育的人往往举止不雅，甚至有点粗鲁。我们在学校学习历代英雄人物的丰功伟绩以及千古罪人的滔天罪行。如果任我们自由发展的话，我们往往会变得自私自利，为达目的不择手段，把高贵和牺牲看作是伪善。

因此，在一个竞争和冲突不断加剧的社会里，人们常常不知所措。教育不但没有贬值，反而变得更为至关重要了。

特别提醒

教育问题，历来都是雅思写作考试中的热门话题。历年的雅思写作考试中所出现教育类的作文题，大致可以分为三大类：1. 教育的内容（教育应该包含哪些内容、教育应该重点传授职业技能还是人文知识）；2. 教育的方式（混班教学 VS 男、女校，集体学习 VS 单独辅导）；3. 教育的意义（为什么要接受教育）。这道雅思作文题目就是第三种类型的教育类文章。

推荐指数

★★★★★

相关题目

2, 6, 14, 24, 43, 44, 49, 68, 93

写作点拨

这道题目要求考生就"教育是否正在贬值"这一问题发表自己的看法，是典型的观点类雅思作文题。范文使用传统的议论文写作方法，分为五段：第一段开门见山地提出作者的观点，即教育并没有贬值；第二、三、四段例举不同方面的论据，有力地支持了作者的观点；第五段重申作者观点。

句型升级

定语从句

普通版 Besides, students are grouped with like-minded classmates. Their interaction with these classmates adds impetus to their academic pursuit.

升级版 Besides, students are grouped with like-minded classmates, the interaction with whom adds impetus to their academic pursuit.

注释：巧妙地使用定语从句，不仅可以达到变换句式的目的，而且还可以将一些句型结构过于简单的句子合并成一个长句。

ESSAY 66

Shopping has become a favorite pastime for some young people. Do we need to encourage the young to do something more useful in their free time? What is your opinion?

Ever larger shopping malls are propping up everywhere in cities to accommodate a growing number of shoppers consisting mainly of young people. For some, shopping is no longer something we do because we need something, but a recreation, an end in itself. Some even spend hours each day roaming from one store to another. It is a consolation this pastime is still largely confined to the fair sex.

Shopping for its own sake is a waste of both time and money. Indeed, most men cannot understand or endure the 'pleasure' of shopping. With nothing particularly in mind, women forge ahead tirelessly or even effortlessly, with their long-suffering boyfriends or husbands trailing behind and asking vainly to take a break. Since there is no apparent aim, women often try on numerous dresses, shoes or perfumes without buying anything. What possible good can come out of this? Some might argue that they can improve their taste and become more fashion-savvy. But it is not worth the time and energy.

Apart from stealing our time, shopping has a more insidious effect. It advocates a luxurious lifestyle. Ever glitzy are those shopping malls with a plethora of goods often beyond the means of ordinary consumers. Hence, most of us go window-shopping to admire those flashy things with exorbitant prices. The more shopping we do, the more we long for those luxuries. We start to envy those rich enough to enjoy luxuries. Making money becomes our primary goal. When we can't get it by legitimate means, some of us will get it by hook or crook. 'We desire what we can see' as the famous line in *The Silence of the Lamb* aptly puts it. So why get ourselves daily tempted?

There are worthier things to do than shopping. I would recommend reading. Read whatever you like as much as possible. Personally, I prefer biography and history books. Then we should do more community service. Instead of focusing on what we want, we should concentrate on what others want. As it often turns out, happiness comes from our harmonious relationships with others rather than material prosperity.

单词注释

- prop [prɒp] *v.* 支撑
- accommodate [əˈkɒmədeɪt] *vt.* 供应；能容纳
- recreation [rekrɪˈeɪʃn] *n.* 消遣，娱乐
- consolation [ˌkɒnsəˈleɪʃn] *n.* 安慰，起安慰作用的人或事物
- confined [kənˈfaɪnd] *adj.* 被限制的
- the fair sex 女性
- forge [fɔːdʒ] *v.* 稳步前进；铸造；伪造
- long-suffering *adj.* 坚韧的；能忍耐的
- perfume [ˈpɜːfjuːm] *n.* 香味，芳香；香水
- savvy [ˈsævi] *n.* 知道，了解
- insidious [ɪnˈsɪdiəs] *adj.* 隐伏的；阴险的
- glitzy [ˈglɪtsi] *adj.* 闪光的，耀眼的，眩目的
- plethora [ˈpleθərə] *n.* 过剩，过多；多血症
- flashy [ˈflæʃi] *adj.* 浮华的
- exorbitant [ɪgˈzɔːbɪtənt] *adj.* 过度的，过高的，昂贵的
- legitimate [lɪˈdʒɪtɪmət] *adj.* 合法的，合理的；正统的
- hook [huk] *n.* 陷阱；钩
- crook [kruk] *n.* 骗子；钩状物
- by hook and crook 不择手段地
- aptly [æptli] *adv.* 适当地，适宜地
- biography [baɪˈɒgrəfi] *n.* 传记
- prosperity [prɒsˈperəti] *n.* 繁荣

购物已经成为了很多年轻人最热衷的休闲活动。我们是否应该鼓励年轻人去做一些更加有意义的事情？你的观点是什么？

为了容纳不断增加的购物者(以年轻人居多)，大型商场如雨后春笋般到处涌现。对某些人而言，购物已经成为了一种消遣，购物的初衷不是缺什么东西，而是为了购物而购物。有些人每天花上几个小时逛商店。值得庆幸的是，购物这一消遣还主要是女性的专利。

单纯的购物是在浪费时间和金钱。其实，很多男性都无法忍受购物的"乐趣"。女性逛街的时候往往没有明确的目的，只是一味地闲逛；她们的男友或丈夫们却要跟在后面，想要休息也得不到批准。由于女性们没有明确的目的，所以她们往往会不断地试衣服、鞋子、香水等，最后却什么都不买。这样的闲逛有什么好处呢？有人可能会说这样可以提高个人品位，跟上潮流。但是这值得我们花费这么多的时间和精力吗？

浪费时间不说，购物还会带来其他的问题。购物导致人们追求奢靡的生活。商场里的货品五光十色、琳琅满目，但却往往非一般人所能消费得起。因此，我们大部分人只能橱窗购物，饱饱眼福。购物越多，人们就越向往那些奢侈品。人们开始羡慕那些有钱享受奢侈的人，挣钱成了他们的唯一目标。当通过合法手段挣不到钱的时候，有些人就会不择手段。《沉默的羔羊》里有一句经典对白：眼有所见，心有所想。何必要每天都诱惑自己呢？

有很多比购物更有意义的活动，比如说读书。想读什么就读什么，越多越好。我个人比较喜欢历史和传记类书籍。此外，我们还可以多参与社区服务。我们应该多考虑别人需要什么，而不要只考虑自己需要什么。幸福往往不来自物质财富，而来自和他人的和睦相处。

特别提醒

迷恋购物的利弊，是近年来雅思写作考试中新出现的话题。历年的雅思写作考试中所出现的关于人们的业余生活的写作题，无一例外地要求考生指出某一种消遣方式(例如旅游)的利弊，并且同时给出自己的建议。

推荐指数 ★★★★

相关题目 59, 69, 76

写作点拨

这道题目要求考生就"年轻人是否应该在空闲时间做一些比购物更有意义的事情"这一问题发表自己的看法，是典型的观点类雅思作文题。范文分为四段：第一段比较隐晦地提出作者的观点；第二、三段列举不同方面的论据，有力地支持了作者反对购物的观点；第四段在重申作者观点的同时，还给出了作者的建议。

论据积累

反对过度沉迷于购物的理由：

1. 购物的目的不是因为缺什么东西，而是为了购物而购物。

   Shopping is no longer something we do because we need something, but a recreation, an end in itself.

2. 购物导致人们追求奢侈的生活。

   Shopping advocates a luxurious lifestyle.

3. 购物让人们羡慕有钱人，让挣钱成了唯一目标。

   People start to envy those rich enough to enjoy luxuries and making money becomes their primary goal.

ESSAY 67

Is it necessary to forbid smoking? State your opinion and reasons.

Despite the knowledge that smoking is a potential killer, cigarette use is on the rise in most countries. Indeed, people are lighting up at a younger age. Twenty per cent of boys in secondary schools in Guangzhou smoke occasionally. Though unlikely to ban cigarette smoking altogether, it is imperative to forbid public smoking.

Public smoking is a health threat to others, especially the non-smokers. It is scientifically verified that second-hand smokers are four times more likely to develop lung cancer than smokers and 20 times more likely than non-smokers. Smokers may have the right to inflict their own bodies but must not impair the health of others. Indeed, some people, asthma sufferers for example, are allergic to tobacco smoke. Then we have many ladies who simply cannot stand the smell of cigarettes. In exercising one's own liberty, one must never infringe on that of others.

Additionally, smoking is a potential fire hazard. It is estimated by the National Fire Department that 30 per cent of fire was caused by unextinguished cigarette butts. How many lives have to be lost and houses burnt down before we come to our senses and realize that from time to time some people will manage to discard an unextinguished cigarette butt in the wrong place and at the wrong time? Given the fallible nature of mankind, it is always safer to ban public smoking altogether.

Moreover, even private smoking should be dissuaded. People smoke out of many reasons. Some do it because it is cool; some do it out of curiosity; still some smoke to keep their weight down. However, smoking is never the solution it promises to be. Its perceived benefits are illusionary and transient. The euphoria produced by cigarette is akin to that generated by alcohol or drugs, an escape from reality at best.

Thus it is in the interest of the public and the smokers themselves that public smoking should be banned. Those against the using of drugs should be able to see the rationale of forbidding smoking.

单词注释

- imperative [ɪmˈperətɪv] *adj.* 命令的，强制的
- inflict [ɪnˈflɪkt] *v.* 使遭受(损伤等)
- impair [ɪmˈpeə] *v.* 损害
- asthma [ˈæsmə] *n.* 哮喘
- allergic [əˈlɜːdʒɪk] *adj.* 过敏的，患过敏症的
- infringe [ɪnˈfrɪndʒ] *v.* 破坏，侵犯；违反
- cigarette butt 烟头
- unextinguished [ˈʌnɪksˈtɪŋgwɪʃt] *adj.* 未扑灭的，未止息的
- fallible [ˈfæləbl] *adj.* 易错的，可能犯错的
- dissuade [dɪˈsweɪd] *vt.* 劝阻
- perceive [pəˈsiːv] *v.* 察觉；感知，感到
- transient [ˈtrænziənt] *adj.* 短暂的 *n.* 瞬时现象
- euphoria [juːˈfɔːriə] *n.* 欣快
- akin [əˈkɪn] *adj.* 同族的，类似的
- at best 最多
- rationale [ˌræʃəˈnɑːl] *n.* 基本原理

你认为有必要禁止吸烟吗？请给出你的观点以及相应的理由。

虽然吸烟是个隐形杀手，大部分国家的香烟消费仍在不断增长。事实上，吸烟的人群越来越低龄化。在广州，有20%的中学生偶尔吸烟。尽管完全禁止吸烟是不可能的，但是我们有必要禁止在公众场所吸烟。

在公众场所吸烟会危害他人的健康，尤其是那些不吸烟的人的健康。科学已经证明，吸二手烟的人患上肺癌的可能性是吸一手烟的人的四倍，是不吸烟的人的二十倍。吸烟的人有权利损害自己的身体，但是绝不能危害他人的健康。事实上，有些人，比如哮喘病人，对香烟过敏。许多女士也不能忍受烟味。在行使自己的自由的时候，我们不能侵害他人的自由。

另外，吸烟还容易引起火灾。据国家消防总局估计，有30%的火灾是由于未熄灭的烟头引起的。究竟要让火灾夺去多少性命，烧毁多少房屋，我们才会意识到时不时地总是会有人把未熄灭的烟头在错误的时间扔在了错误的地点？人非圣贤，所以必须禁止在公共场所吸烟，我们的社会才会更安全。

即使是私下里吸烟也是不值得提倡的。人们吸烟可能出于多种原因。有些人吸烟是因为觉得吸烟很酷，有些人则是出于好奇，还有些甚至是为了减肥。但是，吸烟并不能解决问题。它的效果只是虚假和暂时的。同喝酒和吸毒一样，吸烟所带来的快感充其量也只是一种对现实的逃避。

所以，禁止在公共场所吸烟，对公众和吸烟者本身来说，都是有好处的。如果你能理解为什么要禁毒，你就能理解为什么要禁烟。

特别提醒

吸烟的问题，曾经多次出现在雅思写作考试中，在G类考试中出现的频率甚高。这篇文章指出了吸烟的各种危害，请用心整理这些经典论据，以及相应的英文表达方式！

推荐指数 ★★★★

写作点拨

这道题目要求考生就“是否有必要禁止吸烟”这一问题发表自己的看法，是典型的观点类雅思作文题。范文使用了最传统的观点类议论文的写作方法，分为五段：第一段开门见山地给出作者的观点；第二、三、四段列举不同方面的论据，有力地支持了作者“禁烟非常有必要”的观点；第五段重申作者的观点。

论据积累

禁烟的理由：

1. 抽烟危害他人的健康；在行使自己的自由的时候，我们不能侵害他人的自由。

   Public smoking is a health threat to others, especially the non-smokers. In exercising one's own liberty, one must never infringe on that of others.

2. 吸烟还容易引起火灾。

   Smoking is a potential fire hazard.

3. 吸烟所带来的快感与酗酒和吸毒一样，充其量也只是一种对现实的逃避。

   The euphoria produced by cigarette is akin to that generated by alcohol or drugs, an escape from reality at best.

ESSAY 68

Education used to be a period of schooling. But now people regard it as a lifelong process. Do you agree or disagree?

The word education usually refers to formal education, starting from primary school to college or further still. But learning is something we do all the time and at all ages. So in a larger sense, education, or learning, should last a lifetime.

To really master a subject one needs to devote his whole life to it. In nearly all fields, the accumulation of knowledge through the generations makes it impossible for any individual, even the most gifted ones, to become an expert in just a few years. Any academic or scholastic achievement requires years of hard work and persistence. Even if we have no scholastic pursuits and just do an ordinary job, we still need years to perfect certain skills to excel or even to survive at the workplace because all the repetitive work are now handled by machines and we are supposed to tackle tasks that require a certain amount of skill and knowledge.

Besides, science and technology is advancing at breathtaking speed. It is estimated that the total amount of knowledge doubles every 20 years and the speed is accelerating. Fifty percent of what we learn at college will become outdated in ten years' time. Indeed, change is omnipresent. It can overwhelm us if we don't learn to adapt. If a man a century ago were revived today, he would not be able to perform many of the daily tasks. He has to learn how to use the TV, the computer, the ATM, etc.

In fact, lifelong education is desirable to many people. It is not an unavoidable chore but a pleasure. This kind of education need not be very formal and rigid. We can pick up a book and read a few pages at our leisure; we can turn on the computer and watch a live demonstration. It depends on us and can be a refreshing experience. It is human nature to explore and satisfy our seemingly insatiable curiosity.

It is indeed never too old to learn. The changing world and intensifying competitions require it. Besides, mankind is inherently curious and knowledge-hungry.

单词注释

- accumulation [əˌkjuːmjəˈleɪʃn] *n.* 积累，堆积
- scholastic [skəˈlæstɪk] *adj.* 学校的，学校教育的
- breathtaking [ˈbreθteɪkɪŋ] *adj.* 惊人的，惊险的
- accelerate [əkˈseləreɪt] *v.* 加速，促进
- omnipresent [ˌɒmnɪˈprezənt] *adj.* 无所不在的
- overwhelm [ˌəʊvəˈwelm] *vt.* 淹没；制服，压倒
- adapt [əˈdæpt] *vt.* 使适应
- revive [riˈvaiv] *v.* (使)苏醒，(使)复兴，(使)复活
- chore [tʃɔː] *n.* 家务杂事
- at one's leisure 在闲暇时
- refreshing [rɪˈfreʃɪŋ] *adj.* 提神的，凉爽的；使人喜欢的
- rigid [ˈrɪdʒɪd] *adj.* 刚性的，严厉的
- insatiable [ɪnˈseɪʃəbl] *adj.* 不知足的，贪得无厌的
- curiosity [ˌkjʊərɪˈɒsəti] *n.* 好奇心
- intensify [ɪnˈtensɪfaɪ] *v.* 加强；强化
- inherently [ɪnˈhɪərəntli] *adv.* 天性地；固有地

过去教育通常指的是一段时间的校园教育，而如今人们却把教育当成是一个终生学习的过程。你是否同意这样的观点？

教育通常指的是我们在学校里接受的正规教育，从小学到大学甚至更高。但是学习则是我们时时刻刻、不管在什么年纪都可以进行的。从更广的意义上来说，教育或者说学习，都应该是终生的。

要想真正掌握一门专业，往往需要付出一生的精力。几乎在所有的领域，由于知识的历代积累，即使最具天赋的人也不可能在短短几年内成为专家。任何学术上的成功都需要多年的钻研。即使我们不从事学术研究而只是从事普通工作，我们仍然需要某些技能才能胜任甚至才能生存。这是因为现在所有的重复性劳动都被机器代劳了，一般的工作都要求具备一定的技能和知识。

此外，如今科技正以惊人的速度发展。据估计，人类的知识总量每20年就翻一番，而且增长速度还在加快。10年后，我们在大学所学的知识50%都会过时。事实上，变化是无处不在的。如果我们不能适应这个社会的瞬息万变，我们就会无法在社会上生存。如果一个一百年前的人复活，现在的许多工作他都将无法胜任。他必须学会如何使用电视机、电脑、自动提款机等。

实际上，终生教育对很多人来说都是大有裨益的。不能把它当作是一种不可避免的任务，而是要当作一种乐趣。这种教育并不需要很正式和很严格的。我们可以在闲暇时拿起一本书看上几页。我们也可以打开电脑，看上一段视频演示。这种学习完全可以由我们自己掌握，并且会是一种令人愉悦的体验。不断探索以满足我们未被满足的好奇心是人类的天性。

"活到老，学到老"，这是我们这个瞬息万变的社会以及日益激烈的竞争所要求的。此外，人类的本性也是好奇和渴求知识的。

特别提醒

教育问题，历来都是雅思写作考试中的热门话题。历年的雅思写作考试中所出现的教育类的作文题，大致可以分为三大类：1. 教育的内容（教育应该包含哪些内容、教育应该重点传授职业技能还是人文知识）；2. 教育的方式（混班教学 VS 男、女校，集体学习 VS 单独辅导）；3. 教育的意义（为什么要接受教育）。这道关于终生教育的雅思写作题属于第二种类型的教育类作文题。

推荐指数 ★★★★★

相关题目 2, 6, 14, 24, 43, 44, 49, 65, 93

写作点拨

这道题目要求考生就"教育是否是一个终生的过程"发表自己的看法，是典型的观点类雅思作文题。范文使用了最传统的观点类议论文的写作方法，分为五段：第一段开门见山地给出作者的观点；第二、三、四段例举不同方面的论据，有力地支持了作者"终生教育非常有意义"的观点；第五段重申作者的观点。

论据积累

终生教育的理由：

1. 要想真正掌握一门专业，往往需要人付出一生的精力。

   To really master a subject one needs to devote his whole life to it.
2. 如今科技正以惊人的速度发展。

   Science and technology is advancing at breathtaking speed.
3. 终生教育不是一种不可避免的任务，而应是一种乐趣。

   Lifelong education is not an unavoidable chore but a pleasure.
4. 活到老，学到老。

   It is indeed never too old to learn.

ESSAY 69

People have different hobbies such as collecting stamps or wood carving. Why are hobbies important to us? How can we benefit from having hobbies?

Former British Prime Minister Sir Winston Churchill once said that to be really happy and safe one ought to have two or three hobbies. Hobbies usually vary from person to person. However, this doesn't prevent us from reaping its benefits.

Hobbies are beneficial because they are a genuine source of fun and pleasure. Many people are doing uninteresting jobs for the sake of money. Work gives them no satisfaction apart from financial reward. They need to find some interest in life to absorb their attention and energy and above all to have fun. This kind of fun cannot be had by going to the cinema or taking a trip abroad, which brings nothing more than fleeting sensual pleasure. Real hobbies and interests can bring about abiding happiness.

A hobby is also an antidote to stress. Due to increasing social competition, most of us are victims of stress-related problems. We keep worrying about problems at work even outside working hours. A hobby serves to alleviate our stress and anxiety by engrossing our attention. We often forget our problems when we are preoccupied with our hobbies, which also increase our self-esteem. Low self-esteem is usually caused by our inability to pursue our dreams, to follow our hearts. When trapped in an unworthy job, we subconsciously blame ourselves for the lack of courage to break the shackles of society and seek freedom. Thus we need a hobby to be ourselves.

To best avail ourselves of our hobbies, we should associate with others who have similar hobbies. It is said that man can never be happy all by himself because the loneliness would be too much to bear if he has not a soul to share with. Hence, try to form genuine friendship, broaden your interests and become less self-centered.

单词注释

- hobby [ˈhɒbi] *n.* 业余爱好
- reap [riːp] *v.* 收获
- uninteresting [ʌnˈintrəstɪŋ] *adj.* 无趣的，令人厌倦的
- absorb [əbˈsɔːb] *vt.* 吸收，吸引
- fleeting [ˈfliːtɪŋ] *adj.* 飞逝的；短暂的
- sensual [ˈsenʃuəl] *adj.* 感观的
- abiding [əˈbaɪdɪŋ] *adj.* 持久的
- antidote [ˈæntɪdəʊt] *n.* 矫正方法
- victim [ˈvɪktɪm] *n.* 受害人，牺牲者
- alleviate [əˈliːvieɪt] *vt.* 减轻
- stress [stres] *n.* 重压，逼迫
- engrossing [ɪnˈgrəʊs] *v.* 吸引
- preoccupied [priˈɒkjupaɪd] *adj.* 全神贯注的
- pursue [pəˈsjuː] *vt.* 追赶，追踪
- shackle [ˈʃækl] *n.* 手铐，脚镣，桎梏
- avail onself of 利用
- genuine [ˈdʒenjuɪn] *adj.* 真实的，真正的

不同人有不同的爱好：有人喜欢集邮，有人钟意木雕。为什么业余爱好对我们如此重要？我们如何从业余爱好中受益？

前英国首相丘吉尔曾经说过，要想真正快乐，人必须有两三样嗜好。业余爱好因人而异。但是，我们可以从各自的爱好中得到快乐。

业余爱好之所以对我们有益，是因为它是快乐的源泉。很多人为了钱做着乏味的工作。工作除了可以带来工资之外，并不能给他们带来别的方面的满足。他们需要在生活当中另觅爱好，来消耗他们工作外的精力，当然更主要的是带来快乐。这种乐趣不是去看一场电影，或者出国旅游一趟能相比的。那些都只能带来一时的快乐。真正的爱好可以带来持久的乐趣。

爱好还能够很好地消除压力。由于社会竞争越来越激烈，我们大部分人都或多或少出现了与压力有关的毛病。即使在下班时间我们还是担心着工作。业余爱好可以转移我们的注意力，从而减轻我们的压力和焦虑感。我们沉浸在嗜好当中的时候，就忘却了我们的问题和烦恼，提升了我们的自我感觉。自我感觉不好往往是因为我们的梦想不能实现，我们想做的事情不能去做。当我们不得不从事一项没有意义的工作时，我们往往会下意识地责怪自己没有打破社会枷锁、追求自由的勇气。所以，我们需要有自己的嗜好来回归自我。

要想更好地从事我们的爱好，我们应该和有相同嗜好的人多交流。一个人是不能独自快乐的，因为没有他人分享的孤独是很难承受的。所以，尽量培养真诚的友谊，开阔你的视野，不能太以自我为中心。

特别提醒

这道关于业余爱好的益处的文章，曾经多次出现在雅思移民类的写作考试中。本书有若干篇关于人们的业余生活以及娱乐消遣的文章，这些文章多着重于各类娱乐消遣活动的利弊，因此论据基本通用。阅读本篇范文时，请多留意这些论据的英文表达方式！

推荐指数 ★★★★　　**相关题目** 59, 66, 76

写作点拨

这道题目要求考生就“为什么业余爱好对我们如此重要”发表自己的看法，并且指出“我们如何从业余爱好中受益”，属于“观点＋建议”型的雅思作文题。范文分为四段：第一段开门见山地给出作者的观点；第二、三段例举了业余爱好的不同益处；第四段指出如何才能从业余爱好中受益，回答了题目的第二个问题。

论据积累

业余爱好的益处：

1. 业余爱好是快乐的源泉。

   Hobbies are beneficial because they are a genuine source of fun and pleasure.

2. 业余爱好能够很好地消除压力。

   A hobby is also an antidote to stress.

3. 业余爱好让我们和有相同嗜好的人更多地交流。

   Hobbies enable us to associate more with others who have similar hobbies.

ESSAY 70

What are the advantages of marrying at an early and old age respectively?

It is China's official policy to advocate late marriage. In fact the minimum marriage age is 20 for woman 22 for man. Such an age limit is non-existent in some countries where people get married as young as 13 and as old as 90 years old. There is no optimal age for marriage.

An early marriage is usually based on genuine love. Even if the couple is not each other's first boyfriend or girlfriend, he or she usually regards love as the paramount reason for marriage. They are not likely to be swayed by financial or political considerations. By marrying young, people can get the kind of emotional support earlier rather than later. A happy marriage can provide the most happiness. Emotionally secured, the young couple can focus more on their careers and other undertakings. And if they choose to, they can have kids and enjoy the pleasure of watching them grow.

Meanwhile, a late marriage is also rewarding. By allowing oneself more time to choose one's ideal partner, one is more likely to find the right person, thus reducing the likelihood of divorce. With the passing of each year, one gets more mature and less inclined to rash actions. They have waited so long, so they would get it right. Besides, they are often financially secured and relatively successful in their career. They are in a better position to start a family than when they were young.

More often than not, when and where you get married depends on things beyond your control. Most people are seeking the right person and the right time. But when it comes, don't hesitate.

单词注释

- respectively [rɪˈspektɪvli] *adv.* 分别地，各个地
- advocate [ˈædvəkeɪt] *vt.* 提倡，鼓吹
- optimal [ˈɒptɪməl] *adj.* 最佳的，最理想的
- genuine [ˈdʒenjuɪn] *adj.* 真实的；真正的
- paramount [ˈpærəmaʊnt] *adj.* 极为重要的
- sway [swei] *v.* 摇摆，摇动
- consideration [kənˌsɪdəˈreɪʃn] *n.* 体谅；考虑
- secure [sɪˈkjʊə(r)] *v.* 保护，使安全
- rewarding [rɪˈwɔːdɪŋ] *adj.* 有回报的，有益的
- ideal [aɪˈdɪːəl] *n.* 理想 *adj.* 理想的
- mature [məˈtʃʊər] *adj.* 成熟的
- inclined [ɪnˈklaɪnd] *adj.* 倾向…的
- rash [ræʃ] *adj.* 轻率的，匆忙的
- hesitate [ˈhezɪteɪt] *v.* 犹豫，不愿

早婚和晚婚的优势分别是什么？

中国提倡晚婚。事实上，中国婚姻法规定女性的最低结婚年龄是 20，男性是 22。这种规定在别的一些国家并不存在，这些国家的人早到 13 岁就可以结婚，晚到 90 岁结婚的也有。结婚是没有最佳年龄的。

过早结婚通常是建立在真爱的基础上的。即使并非对方的初恋，他们也把爱情当作是婚姻的最终原因，而不会被经济或政治因素所影响。早些结婚的话，双方就能早些得到情感上的互相支持。幸福的婚姻能够带来最大的幸福。情感上有了寄托后，双方就能够更专注于事业等其他方面。如果夫妇双方愿意的话，他们还可以要孩子，然后看着孩子快乐地成长。

然而，晚婚也有好处。给自己更多的时间寻找一生的伴侣，这样更能找到合适的人选，减少离婚的可能。随着年龄的增长，人变得越来越成熟，不容易冲动。他们既然已经等了这么久，就一定要稳扎稳打。另外，晚婚的人通常经济实力雄厚些，事业成功些。他们这个时候组建家庭要比年轻时更合适。

但是，一个人什么时候在什么地方结婚，往往非己力所能控制。大部分人都在努力寻找合适的人和合适的时间。但是找到时，千万不要犹豫。

特别提醒

或许是考虑到相当比例的雅思考生尚未到适婚的年龄，雅思写作考试中很少涉及婚姻的问题。这道关于早婚和晚婚的作文题算是一个特例。不过请特别注意，婚姻以外的其他家庭生活问题一直是雅思写作考试中的热门话题。

推荐指数 ★★★ **相关题目** 111

写作点拨

这道题目要求考生分别指出早婚和晚婚的优势，属于“优劣势”型的雅思作文题。范文分为四段：第一段引入话题；第二、三段分别介绍了早婚和晚婚的优势；第四段总结全文，指出结婚的时间往往并不能控制。

词汇升级

最好的，最佳的

普通版 There is no *best* age for marriage.

升级版 There is no *optimal* age for marriage.

最好的，最佳的：superlative, unapproached, prime, optimal

ESSAY 71

Should people doing different jobs have holidays at different time of the year? What is your opinion?

More and more people choose to avoid the holiday seasons to go traveling because tourist sites are invariably overcrowded during public holidays. To enjoy yourselves you need to take a vacation when most people are working. Apart from public holidays, employees should be allowed an annual holiday at the time they choose.

The idea of people in different professions having holidays at different time is often out of necessity. Places such as hospitals, fire departments and even restaurants should be in operation all year long. Thus, their employees must partake in some kind of rotating vacation system, whereby each of them takes some days off by turn and on an irregular basis. Besides, some jobs are only seasonal. Teachers, for example, enjoy summer and winter holidays. In many lines of business, there is a peak season and a trough season. It is only reasonable to allow workers to take some days off when the business is slack.

In addition, this kind of liberal attitude toward holidays can reduce the strains on public facilities during the holiday seasons. As things stand now, it is a nightmare to travel during public holidays, for there will be throngs of people everywhere. It is hard to get tickets, book rooms or even to find decent eateries. The infrastructure is not adequate enough to cope with the influx of tourists swarming to certain numbers of scenic spots. With separate holidays becoming the norm, people can better enjoy their vacations.

The ideal way would be for the employees to decide the time and duration of the holidays, provided that it doesn't interfere with the running of the business. People themselves know when they would most enjoy a vacation. It is ultimately a personal matter and should be left to our own discretion if possible.

单词注释

- invariably [ɪnˈveərɪəbli] *adv.* 不变地，总是
- overcrowd [ˌəʊvəˈkraʊd] *vt.* 容纳过多的人，使过度拥挤
- annual [ˈænjuəl] *adj.* 一年一次的，每年的
- profession [prəˈfeʃn] *n.* 职业；专业
- operation [ˌɒpəˈreɪʃn] *n.* 运转，操作，实施
- partake [pɑːˈteɪk] *vt.* 分担，共享
- irregular [ɪˈregjʊlə(r)] *adj.* 不规则的，无规律的
- slack [slæk] *adj.* 冷清的，萧条的
- liberal [ˈlɪbərəl] *adj.* 不拘泥的
- strain [streɪn] *n.* 过度的疲劳；紧张
- nightmare [ˈnaɪtmeə(r)] *n.* 梦魇，噩梦
- throng [θrɒŋ] *n.* 群集
- decent [ˈdiːsnt] *adj.* 正派的；端庄的
- eatery [ˈiːtəri] *n.* 〈美〉餐馆，食堂
- infrastructure [ˈɪnfrəstrʌktʃə(r)] *n.* 基础设施
- influx [ˈɪnflʌks] *n.* 流入
- swarm [swɔːm] *v.* 涌往
- scenic [ˈsiːnɪk] *adj.* 景色优美的
- norm [nɔːm] *n.* 标准，规范
- duration [djuˈreɪʃn] *n.* 持续时间，为期
- interfere [ˌɪntəˈfɪə(r)] *vi.* 干涉，干预
- discretion [dɪˈskreʃn] *n.* 判断力

从事不同职业的人是否应该在不同的时间休假？请给出你的看法。

越来越多的人选择避开节假日去旅游，因为在节假日旅游景点总是很挤。要想玩得尽兴，你就必须在别人上班的时候去度假。除了公共假日外，应该允许员工自己选择时间来休年假。

让从事不同职业的人在不同的时间休假，这个想法是必要的。有些地方，比如医院、消防队、餐馆，一年到头都必须营业。所以，这些地方的员工就应该采用某种轮休制，按照一定的规律大家轮流休假。另外，有些工作具有季节性。比如，教师有寒暑假。许多行业也存在着旺季和淡季。应该让员工在淡季休假，这样才合理些。

此外，这种对节假日的宽松态度能够极大地减轻公共设施在公共假期期间所承受的压力。目前，在节假日出游简直是受罪，因为到处都是人。车票难买，酒店难订，甚至连像样的吃饭的地方都难找。有些旅游景点，游客蜂拥而至，其基础设施难以应付如此多的游客。如果分开休假这种观念被大家接受了的话，人们就能够更好地度假了。

最理想的方式是，在不影响工作的情况下，由员工自己来决定度假的时间和长度。只有人们自己才知道自己什么时候最想去度假。度假毕竟是个人的事情，如果可能的话，最好由我们自己来做主。

特别提醒

虽然度假的问题在雅思写作考试中的出现频率并不是特别高，关于旅游、节假日安排等的话题，还是不断地在雅思考试中出现。这道关于不同行业的工作人员的节假日安排的作文题，曾经让很多考生感到"无话可说"。请留意范文的观点及其对应的论据。

推荐指数 ★★★★　　**相关题目** 1, 13, 44, 86, 95

写作点拨

这道题目要求考生就"从事不同职业的人是否应该在不同的时间休假"发表自己的看法，是典型的观点类雅思作文题。范文的写法与最传统的观点类议论文写作方法有细微的不同。范文分为四段：第一段开门见山地给出作者的观点，即应该灵活安排假期；第二、三段列举不同方面的论据，有力地支持了作者的观点；第四段在重申作者的观点的同时，还给出了相应的建议。

词汇升级

态度

普通版 This kind of *relaxed attitude* toward holidays can reduce the strains on public facilities during the holiday seasons.

升级版 This kind of *liberal attitude* toward holidays can reduce the strains on public facilities during the holiday seasons.

attitude（态度）: carefree（轻松的）, casual（轻松的）, flexible（可通融的）, laid-back（懒散的）, conservative（保守的）, inflexible（顽固的）, rigid（顽固的）, uncompromising（强硬的）, prevailing（普遍的）, ambivalent（摇摆不定的）, sympathetic（赞成的）, conciliatory（调和的）

ESSAY 72

Some people like to risk their lives in some dangerous sports such as mountain climbing. Some say rescuers need not risk their own lives to save those trapped on mountain peaks and that people should be responsible for their own lives. What is your opinion?

People are indeed different. Some are not brave enough to play football while others are attracted to danger and excitement. However, dangerous sports can really live up to its name. People get injured or killed in these sports. Are they heroes or eccentrics asking for trouble?

Most of them don't choose extreme sport for fame or money. They do it because it fascinates them. They are certainly brave but not necessarily heroes. Like anyone else, they should be responsible for their own choice and look after themselves shall they ever in danger. However, this doesn't mean we need not try to rescue them at all cost.

After all, it is not their fault that they are trapped on a mountain side. It may be attributed to adverse weather condition or some mechanical malfunction. They should not be blamed for things beyond their control. It is true that they are responsible for their lives, but we have a duty to help each other. It is a moral issue. Our humanity demands that we render a helping hand to whoever in need whenever we can. That is what makes us human—indeed even animals of different species sometimes assist each other.

When it comes to whether we should risk our lives to save their lives, no one should be required to risk his or her life no matter how worthy the cause is. Those who choose to take the risk do it out of their nobility and decency. It is the highest form of moral virtue when people do something because it is right despite the risks involved. Hats off to those heroes who willingly risk their lives for others. We should take every precaution to ensure a smooth rescue operation, but we shouldn't forbid them to make the greatest sacrifice for the sake of others.

There will always be those who inadvertently cost other people's lives. And there will always be those who trade their own lives for those of others. To be saved is human; to save, divine.

单词注释

- rescuer [ˈreskjuːə] *n.* 救助者
- trap [træp] *vt.* 使落入险境，使陷入困境
- responsible [rɪˈspɔnsəbl] *adj.* 有责任的，负责任的
- eccentric [ɪkˈsentrɪk] *n.* 行为古怪的人
- extreme [ɪksˈtriːm] *adj.* 极端的
- fame [feɪm] *n.* 名声，名望
- fascinate [ˈfæsɪneɪt] *vt.* 使着迷
- rescue [ˈreskjuː] *vt.* 援救，营救
- adverse [ˈædvɜːs] *adj.* 不利的，有害的
- mechanical [məˈkænɪkl] *adj.* 机械的，机械制的
- malfunction [ˌmælˈfʌŋkʃn] *n.* 故障
- moral [ˈmɒrəl] *adj.* 道德的，精神的
- humanity [hjuˈmænəti] *n.* 人性；人类
- decency [ˈdiːsnsi] *n.* 庄重
- precaution [prɪˈkɔːʃn] *n.* 预防，警惕，防范
- inadvertently [ˌɪnədˈvɜːtəntli] *adv.* 不注意地
- divine [dɪˈvaɪn] *adj.* 神的，神圣的

有些人宁愿冒着生命危险去从事诸如登山之类的危险性运动。有人认为救援人员不需要冒生命危险去拯救那些被困在山顶的登山者，人们应该为自己的生命负责。请给出你的看法。

人与人是很不同的。有些人连足球都不敢踢，而有些人却热衷于危险和刺激的运动。但是，危险的运动有时候的确是名副其实的。人们经常会在这些危险运动中受伤甚至死亡。他们是英雄呢，还是自找苦吃的怪人呢？

大部分从事极限运动的人不是为了名利，而是出于对运动的狂热。他们当然是勇敢的，但不一定是英雄。和别人一样，他们必须对自己的选择负责，在处于危险当中时自己要照看好自己。但是，这并不是说，当他们遇到危险的时候，我们不需要去千方百计地救助他们。

毕竟，被困在山腰上也不是他们的错。也许是恶劣的天气条件，或者是机械故障的缘故。这些都是他们控制不了的因素，不能把责任归咎到他们身上。的确，他们要为自己的生命负责，但我们也有互相帮助的责任。这是个道德问题。我们的人性要求我们在可能的情况下向任何需要帮助的人伸出援助之手。这就是我们人类之所以为人的关键所在。甚至不同种类的动物之间有时都会互相帮助。

至于是否要冒着生命危险去救别人，没有人有义务一定要冒着自己的生命危险去救别人，不管出于多么高尚的理由。那些愿意舍己救人的英雄们之所以这么做，是为高尚的道德所驱使。这种不顾危险、只求道义的行为是最高尚的道德的体现。向那些舍己救人的英雄们致敬！我们在救人的时候当然要做足防范措施，但是我们也不能阻止他人冒着自己的生命危险去救人的壮举。

这个世界上，总是有人不经意地夺去他人的生命，又总是有人用自己的性命去换取他人的生命。被拯救的是人，拯救人的是神！

特别提醒

体育是雅思考试中的热门话题之一，几乎每年的雅思考试中都会出现一两道关于体育的写作题。本书收集了若干道关于体育的雅思作文题目，涉及包括奥运、运动员薪资、体育安全等体育问题的方方面面。

推荐指数 ★★★★

相关题目 11, 34, 102

写作点拨

这道题要求考生就“人们是否应该参加高危运动”以及“人们是否应该冒生命危险去拯救那些参加高危运动的人”两个问题发表自己的看法。范文分为四段：第一段引入话题，却没有给出观点；第二、三段从不同方面证明参加高危运动的合理性，表明了有关题目中第一个问题的观点；第四段讨论了拯救被困人员的问题，回答了题目中的第二个问题；最后一段在重申作者的观点同时，还给出了相应的建议。

词汇升级

天气

普通版 It may be attributed to *bad weather* condition or some mechanical malfunction.

升级版 It may be attributed to *adverse weather* condition or some mechanical malfunction.

weather（天气）：beautiful（很好的），superb（极好的），glorious（宜人的），adverse（不利的），appalling（可怕的），atrocious（恶劣的），awful（糟糕的），dismal（阴沉的），dreadful（可怕的），foul（恶劣的），gloomy（阴郁的），inclement（严酷的），inhospitable（不适合居住的），wretched（恶劣的），nasty（令人不快的），rotten（非常坏的）

ESSAY 73

Radio will be replaced by other forms of mass media such as TV or the Internet. Do you agree or disagree?

It is some people's pastime to make predictions about the future. But actually no one can be absolutely certain about what tomorrow will bring. As per my experience, some aspects of our life change, but slowly. Listening to the radio, for instance, will remain with us for a long time to come.

Radio is not likely to be replaced soon or at all because it is the most convenient way to acquire information. You don't have to be literate and you don't have to stare at a screen. Even if you are visually impaired, your enjoyment of it will not be affected a bit. Unlike TV or even newspaper, radio is never intrusive. We can focus on our main task and listen to the radio simultaneously without being distracted. Its presence is like that of a gentleman, ever in the background and responsive to our needs.

By providing audio information only, radio leaves much room for imagination. When we watch TV, we passively take in the moving images. Though pictures are more direct and detailed, they fail to excite our thoughts or imagination. The photo of the Great Wall can show us how it looks like from the angle of the photographer, whereas our imagination can conjure up a really majestic construction (though perhaps inaccurate), its history, its function, and its builders—there is no limit to our imagination. To really experience something in a vicarious way, one has to image it.

On a more tangible side, radio has its unique advantages. It is cheap and portable. Some radio can now be fitted into a pen and carried around all the time, conveying a variety of programs. The best radio costs no more than a thousand yuan.

It is undeniable that radio is facing increasing competition from other forms of media. It needs to improve in terms of program variety and reception quality. But its longevity is beyond doubt.

单词注释

- pastime [ˈpɑːstaɪm] *n.* 消遣，娱乐
- prediction [prɪˈdɪkʃn] *n.* 预言，预测
- as per 按照
- literate [ˈlɪtərɪt] *adj.* 有文化的，有读写能力的
- visually [ˈvɪʒuəli] *adv.* 在视觉上地，真实地
- impair [ɪmˈpeə] *vt.* 损害；使弱
- intrusive [ɪnˈtruːsɪv] *adj.* 打扰的；插入的
- simultaneously [ˌsɪmlˈteɪniəsli] *adv.* 同时地
- conjure [ˈkʌndʒə] *v.* 变戏法；想像
- majestic [məˈdʒestɪk] *adj.* 宏伟的，庄严的
- vicarious [vɪˈkeəriəs] *adj.* 间接感受到的
- tangible [ˈtændʒəbl] *adj.* 切实的
- portable [ˈpɔːtəbl] *adj.* 轻便的；手提(式)的，便携式的
- undeniable [ˌʌndɪˈnaɪəbl] *adj.* 不可否认的
- longevity [lɒnˈdʒevəti] *n.* 寿命；持久

广播将被电视、互联网等其他形式的大众传媒代替。你是否同意这样的观点？

一些人以预测未来为消遣。事实上，没有人可以绝对肯定地说出明天会发生什么。根据我自己的经验，生活的某些方面虽然发生了改变，速度却非常之慢。听广播将在未来的很长时间内依然是大多数人的选择。

广播不可能在短期内被其他形式的大众传媒彻底取代，因为广播是所有获取信息的方式中最方便的一种。你不需要识字，也不需要盯着屏幕。即使你的视力受损，你从广播中获得的快乐也丝毫不会受到影响。和电视甚至是报纸所不同的是，广播从来不会对我们构成干扰。我们可以一边干着我们的工作一边听着广播，丝毫不会感到自己被干扰。这种感觉就好比身后永远有一位绅士，每时每刻都满足着我们的需求。

广播仅仅提供了声音，因此给我们留下了无穷大的想像空间。看电视的时候，我们被动地接受了画面。尽管画面往往更加直接和详实，它们却很少能够激发我们的思维和想象力。万里长城的画面仅仅提供了摄影师眼中的长城，而我们的想像却能够魔法一般地构造一座极其雄伟的建筑。虽然这种想像往往不那么精确，我们却可以无穷无尽地在想象的世界里遨游——长城的历史、长城的功能以及长城的建造者。想以间接的方式真切地感受某一样东西，我们必须展开丰富的想像。

从现实的角度来说，广播也有着独一无二的优势。收音机不仅价格低廉，而且还方便携带。如今有一些收音机可以被安置在钢笔中，因此可以轻易地随身携带，收听各种各样的节目。即使是最贵的收音机，售价往往也不超过一千元人民币。

诚然，今日的广播正面临着其他形式的大众传媒所带来的激烈竞争。我们需要增加广播节目的多样性，并且提高节目的接收质量。但是，毋庸置疑，广播将长期存在。

特别提醒

大众传媒是雅思考试中最热门的话题之一，几乎每年的雅思考试中都会出现若干道关于大众传媒的写作题。本书收集了近10道关于大众传媒的雅思作文题目，涉及传媒的发展方向、传媒对青少年的影响、政府对传媒的监控等方方面面。

推荐指数 ★★★★

相关题目 4, 17, 23, 32, 45, 51, 56, 98

写作点拨

这道题目要求考生就“广播是否会被其他形式的大众传媒代替”发表自己的看法，是典型的观点类雅思作文题。范文使用了最传统的观点类议论文的写作方法。范文分为五段：第一段开门见山地给出作者的观点，即广播不会被取代；第二、三、四段例举不同方面的论据，有力地支持了作者的观点；第五段在重申作者的观点同时，还给出关于广播如何改善自身的建议。

句型升级

普通版 Even if *your vision has been impaired*, your enjoyment of it will not be affected a bit.

升级版 Even if *you are visually impaired*, your enjoyment of it will not be affected a bit.

注释：巧妙地使用副词，不仅可以将很多过于冗长的句子变短，而且可以让语言更加地道。

ESSAY 74

What are the problems for people living and working in the countryside? What should the government do to solve them?

City residents often crave for a life in the countryside, where the air is purer and people friendlier. But when one does settle in the rural area, he starts to complain, sometimes guiltily, about the downsides of a rural life. I regret to say the countryside has more to offer besides the idyllic pleasures.

Those living outside cities must be content with fewer career opportunities. Businesses and industries are largely concentrated in major cities; even small cities don't have much of a share, let alone the countryside. The job options in the countryside are rather limited, often having something to do with agriculture. Even if one wishes to open a business by himself, he is less likely to succeed because of the poor business environment in rural regions.

Then some would say that the countryside is a place to live not work in. But it doesn't do very well even in this respect. Though possessing superior natural environment, the countryside is often notorious for its lack of amenities, facilities and public service. Without the concentration of a large population, it is not economically viable to provide large-scale public service or build facilities that are commonplace in urban areas. For instance, one may have to wait for days before a plumber comes to fix a ruptured water pipe or drive hours to reach a clinic. In fact, rural inhabitants are known for their hardiness and self-reliance.

Isolation and loneliness are often associated with a rustic life. The countryside is still sparsely populated, with people living miles away from each other. You are lucky to see a soul or two a day. All too often you only have your family and pets for company. Although the telephone and Internet allow you to contract the outside world, you will still feel alienated for lack of face-to-face interaction.

For those seeking a quiet life, the countryside is the best place. But for most people, the outlook is not so rosy. As it often turns out, a sojourn in the countryside from time to time allows you to get the best of both worlds.

单词注释

- crave for 渴望
- guiltily [ˈɡɪltɪli] *adv.* 有罪地；自责地
- downside [ˈdaʊnsaɪd] *n.* 不利方面
- idyllic [ɪˈdɪlɪk] *adj.* 田园的；简朴且无忧无虑的
- be content with 满足于
- superior [suːˈpɪəriə(r)] *adj.* 较好的，更好的
- notorious [nəʊˈtɔːriəs] *adj.* 声名狼藉的
- amenity [əˈmiːnəti] *n.* 宜人，舒适
- facility [fəˈsɪləti] *n.* 设备，设施
- viable [ˈvaɪəbl] *adj.* 可行的
- plumber [ˈplʌmbə] *n.* 水管工人
- rupture [ˈrʌptʃə(r)] *v.* 破裂，裂开
- hardiness [ˈhɑːdɪnəs] *n.* 耐久力；顽强
- self-reliance [ˌselfrɪˈlaɪns] *n.* 自立
- isolation [ˌaɪsəˈleɪʃn] *n.* 隔绝，孤立，隔离
- sparsely [ˈspɑːsli] *adv.* 稀疏地，稀少地
- rosy [ˈrəʊzi] *adj.* 光明或愉快的；乐观的
- sojourn [ˈsɒdʒən] *n.* 逗留

在农村工作和生活的问题是什么？政府应该采取什么措施去解决这些问题？

城市的居民往往无比渴望乡村的生活，因为乡村的空气更加纯净，居民也更加友好。但是很多人刚在乡村里定居，就开始抱怨乡村生活的很多不足。我非常遗憾地认为，乡村生活远不只是田园意境。

生活在城市之外的人必须能够忍受工作机会的减少。工商业往往聚集于主要的大城市。即使是在小城市，工商业的比例都不是很高，更不要说乡村了。乡村的工作选择非常有限，大多数工作机会都与农业相关。即使你打算自己做生意，也很有可能失败，因为农村的商业环境并不好。

或许有人会说乡村是适合生活的地方，不是工作的地方。事实上，乡村也并不那么适合生活。尽管乡村有更好的自然环境，但往往缺少生活的便捷性、各种设备以及公共服务。由于缺乏大量的人口，乡村往往不能承受城市里有的大规模公共服务以及公共设施。比方说，如果家里的水管破裂，你或许要等上好几天才有水管工人上门来修理；如果你生病了，恐怕要开好几个小时的车去看医生。事实上，乡村的居民历来以顽强和自立著称。

乡村生活往往充满了孤独和寂寞。在广大的乡村，人烟稀少，居民也分散在各地。一两天之内能见到一个人就已经很幸运了。很多时候，陪伴你的仅仅是你的家人和你的宠物。虽然电视和网络极大地方便了人们和外界的沟通，在一个缺乏面对面的交流的环境里，人们依然很容易感到孤独。

对于那些喜欢宁静生活的人来说，乡村或许是最佳的居住地。但是对于大多数人而言，乡村生活的前景却过于暗淡。事实上，时不时地去乡村度假，就能够享受到乡村和城市生活所提供的一切。

特别提醒

乡村生活和城市生活的比较曾经一度是雅思考试中的热门话题。虽然最近几年这类话题在雅思考试中出现的次数锐减，每年的雅思考试中都依然会出现若干道涉及各种生活方式的比较的写作题。请留意本文中出现的一些经典论据，并在自己的作文中适当地引用。

推荐指数 ★★★★　　**相关题目** 37, 91

写作点拨

这道题目要求考生叙述乡村生活的不足，并且指出政府应该采取的措施，是典型的“叙述＋建议”类雅思作文题。范文分为五段：第一段引入话题；第二、三、四段指出乡村生活在不同方面的不足；第五段给出关于如何解决这些问题的建议。

词汇升级

不足，劣势

普通版 But when one does settle in the rural area, he starts to complain, sometimes guiltily, about the *disadvantages* of a rural life.

升级版 But when one does settle in the rural area, he starts to complain, sometimes guiltily, about the *downsides* of a rural life.

不足，劣势：drawback, handicap, downside, shortcoming, flaw, deficiency, imperfection

ESSAY 75

Some people say that we should not encourage sports games among schools because they lead to competition rather than cooperation. To what extent do you agree with it?

Sports games among schools are common nowadays. Most schools have football, basketball and other teams to take on the challenges of other schools. Unfortunately there have been reports on hostility and even violence resulting from inter-school sports events. But this is not reasonable enough to ban sports games among schools.

The claim that sports lead to competition rather than cooperation is only a lame argument. It is true that students often go all out to beat their opponents and feel mortified when defeated. But when the game is over they often shake hands or even hug each other because there is no ill will, no disdain or condescension. Everything is done fair and square. When they part with each other, they are left with respect for the other side and maybe the wish for another game. The much-dreaded vicious competition and animosity are always the result of unfair games or rogue teams, which are few and far between and don't represent the whole picture.

On the contrary, those games are conducive to cooperation and progress. When such an event is organized, all students often participate in one way or another. They are united by a single aim: to defeat the opponents and have a good time. They start to cooperate and help each other; a sense of community begins to grow. In addition, given the nature of mankind, no great progress is to be expected without some external or internal pressure. Competition is often desirable because it leads to progress. The desire to win is a strong incentive to push for one's limit. The sense of honour acts as a powerful drug to assuage pain and fatigue.

Measures should be taken to curb the occasional violence related to inter-school games. But we need not have any qualms about championing such events, for the competitions on the sports field always contribute to progress and cooperation.

单词注释

- hostility [hɒsˈtɪləti] *n.* 敌意，恶意；对抗
- lame [leɪm] *adj.* 无说服力的
- mortify [ˈmɔːtɪfaɪ] *v.* 使丢脸，使经受羞辱
- hug [hʌg] *v.* 拥抱
- ill will 憎恶，恶意
- disdain [dɪsˈdeɪn] *n.* 轻蔑，蔑视，鄙弃
- condescension [ˌkɒndɪˈsenʃn] *n.* 谦虚，屈尊
- vicious [ˈvɪʃəs] *adj.* 可恶的；凶残的
- animosity [ˌænɪˈmɒsəti] *n.* 仇恨，憎恶
- conductive [kənˈdʌktɪv] *adj.* 有传导性的；能传导的
- desirable [dɪˈzaɪərəbl] *adj.* 合意的；令人想要的
- incentive [ɪnˈsentɪv] *n.* 动机
- assuage [əˈsweɪdʒ] *vt.* 缓和，减轻；镇定
- fatigue [fəˈtiːg] *n.* 疲乏，疲劳
- curb [kɜːb] *v.* 抑制，控制
- qualm [kwɑːm, kwɔːm] *n.* 疑虑
- champion [ˈtʃæmpiən] *v.* 捍卫，支持

有人认为我们应该少鼓励学校间的体育比赛，因为这些比赛往往会导致学生之间的竞争，而不是合作。你是否同意这样的说法？

如今，校际的体育比赛非常普遍。大多数学校都有足球、篮球或其他的球队，随时接受其他学校发起的挑战。不幸的是，关于校际间比赛所引发的敌对甚至是暴力的报道时有见报。然而，这些却不足以成为禁止校际体育比赛的理由。

认为体育促发了竞争而不是合作的观点是站不住脚的。诚然，学生热衷于和别的学校的学生打比赛，而且失败的时候经常感到羞愧难当。但是比赛结束的时候学生们往往会握手甚至是拥抱，因为一切都是公平的——没有人胸怀恶意，也没有人会轻视对方或是贬低自己。当选手们离开的时候，他们往往心怀对对手的敬意，或许还会希望下一次比赛尽快到来。造成仇恨和恶意的往往是那些不公平的比赛。事实上，这样的比赛很少，不足以代表全部的事实。

与人们的看法相反的是，体育比赛事实上可以促进合作和进步。当学校组织体育比赛的时候，所有的学生都会以各种形式参与进来。学生们为同一个目标——打败对手享受比赛而团结起来。学生们往往会互相帮助并且通力合作，集体意识随之得到了增长。此外，人类的天性决定了如果没有外部或内部的压力，就不可能获得进步。竞争是可取的，因为它会促使我们进步。获胜的欲望可以极大地鼓励我们挑战自己的极限。荣誉感可以极大地减少我们的痛苦和疲劳。

我们必须采取措施去控制校际比赛偶尔引发的暴力行为，但是我们决不可以动摇我们对这些比赛的支持，因为体育赛场上的竞争往往会促进学生的合作和进步。

特别提醒

合作还是竞争，是雅思考试中的热门话题之一，曾经以不同的形式多次出现在雅思考试中。本书收集了若干道这类题材的雅思作文题目。请留意这些文章里出现的一些相通的论据，并适当地借鉴。

推荐指数 ★★★★　**相关题目** 5, 7, 26, 27, 28, 47, 49, 50, 54, 57, 81, 84, 85, 87, 89, 109

写作点拨

这道题目要求考生就“是否应该减少校际间体育比赛”发表自己的看法，是典型的观点类雅思作文题。范文使用了最传统的观点类议论文的写作方法。范文分为四段：第一段开门见山地给出作者的观点，即不应该反对校际间体育比赛；第二、三段例举不同方面的论据，证明了体育比赛并不会引发学生之间的恶意竞争；第四段在重申作者的观点同时，还给出了相关的建议。

词汇升级

论据，论点

普通版 The claim that sports lead to competition rather than cooperation is only a *incorrect* argument.

升级版 The claim that sports lead to competition rather than cooperation is only a *lame* argument.

argument（论据，论点）：spurious（不合理的），tenuous（站不住脚跟的），weak（不牢固的），lame（无说服力的），powerful（有力的），valid（有根据的），sound（可靠的），convincing（令人信服的），compelling（非常有说服力的），persuasive（有说服力的），plausible（似是而非的）

ESSAY 76

Some people regard animals as pets while others see them as a source of food and clothing. What is your opinion?

It is sometimes hard to comprehend the true nature of our existence until we let ourselves loose into the wilderness, where species of all kinds co-exist in good order. Then we will realize that mankind is but a part of nature, being only one species among the myriad of creatures.

Bearing this in mind, I would regard animals as my fellow creatures and treat them on an equal basis. Just as we have our human rights, animals should also enjoy animal rights. I, for one, won't take unfair advantage of an animal. Only a bully would shoo off a dog standing in his way. Wherever possible there need not be any use of force between humans and animals. Understandably, the relationship between man and his fellow creatures is a complex one, just like the relationship among people. Some animals will become our friends and companions; some will turn into our foes; still many may never come into contact with any of us.

However, there is one role that can only be played by plants and animals: being our food. This is actually a very poignant issue. Some religions, Buddhism for instant, explicitly forbid the killing and eating of animals. Vegetarians also preach the sanctity of animal life. These assertions, however, cannot bear close analysis. If the sanctity of life is indeed universally valued then we must starve to death because the life of vegetables should not be forfeited either. Thus revealed was the inconsistence of those absolute moralists. Alas, it is rather ironic that to maintain one life, some lives have to be sacrificed.

We have superior powers over most animals. We are on top of the food chain. We have the capacity to exterminate an entire species. On the other hand we can choose to treat animals as equals. Indeed, I would advocate equal treatment to all things, living or unliving. There should be no destruction of anything unless absolutely necessary.

单词注释

- comprehend [ˌkɒmprɪˈhend] *vt.* 领会，理解
- loose [luːs] *v.* 从…的压力或义务中解放出来
- wilderness [ˈwɪldənəs] *n.* 荒野，荒地
- myriad [ˈmɪriəd] *n.* 无数
- bully [ˈbuli] *n.* 欺凌弱小者
- understandably [ˌʌndəˈstændəli] *adv.* 可理解地
- complex [ˈkɒmpleks] *adj.* 复杂的
- companion [kəmˈpæniən] *n.* 同伴，共事者
- foe [fəʊ] *n.* 反对者，敌人
- poignant [ˈpɔɪnjənt] *adj.* 令人痛苦的；辛辣的；尖锐的
- Buddhism [ˈbʊdɪzəm] *n.* 佛教
- vegetarian [ˌvedʒəˈteəriən] *n.* 素食者
- preach [priːtʃ] *v.* 鼓吹
- sanctity [ˈsæŋktəti] *n.* 神圣；尊严
- assertion [əˈsɜːʃn] *n.* 断言，声称
- forfeit [ˈfɔːfɪt] *vt.* 没收；丧失
- moralist [ˈmɒrəlɪst] *n.* 道德家，卫道士
- ironic [aiˈrɒnɪk] *adj.* 说反话的，讽刺的
- exterminate [ɪkˈstɜːmɪneɪt] *v.* 消除

有人视动物为宠物，而别的人却认为动物仅仅是食物和服装的来源。请给出你的看法。

只有当我们抛开一切包袱漫步于野外、看到各种物种井然有序地和平共处时，我们才能够真正理解生存的本质。也只有在这个时候，我们才能真正地意识到，人类仅仅是大自然里无数生物中的一种，不过是大自然的一部分。

想到这些，我就会认为动物是和我们生活在同一个世界的物种，人类应该平等地对待它们。正如人类享有人权，动物也有它们的权利。我自己就不会不平等地对待动物。只有欺凌弱小者才会驱赶挡路的小狗。不管在哪里，人类和动物之间都没有必要动用武力。可以理解的是，正如人类之间的关系，人类和动物之间的关系也是非常复杂的。一些动物会成为人类的伙伴，另外一些却成了人类的敌人。还有一些动物，似乎从未和人类有丝毫的关系。

然而，有一种角色只有动物和植物才可以扮演：成为人类的食物。事实上，这是一件非常令人痛心的事情。一些宗教，例如佛教，明确禁止杀害和进食动物。素食主义者也大力鼓吹动物的生命尊严。但这些论断往往经不起仔细推敲。如果任何生命的尊严都要受到尊重，人类就注定会饿死，因为蔬菜也有生命，它们的生命也不能被剥夺。绝对的道德观的矛盾由此就暴露出来了。极其讽刺的是，为了维护一条生命，别的生命必须被牺牲。

相对于大多数动物，人类拥有更大的力量。我们在食物链的最顶端。我们有能力让别的物种彻底灭绝。然而，我们可以选择平等地对待动物。事实上，我主张平等地对待一切事物，不论是有生命的还是没有生命的。除非万不得已，我们不应该破坏任何事物。

特别提醒

动物保护虽然不是雅思考试中的热门话题，却也曾经以不同的形式多次出现在雅思考试中。本书收集了若干道动物题材的雅思作文题目。这篇范文中提出了一些相对新颖的观点，请认真整理和借鉴。

推荐指数 ★★★★

相关题目 106

写作点拨

这道题目要求考生就“应该视动物为宠物还是食物来源”发表自己的看法，是典型的观点类雅思作文题。范文的写法有别于传统的观点类议论文的写作方法。范文分为四段：第一段引入话题；第二、三段分别论证尊重动物以及视动物为食物来源两种截然不同的观点都有各自的合理性；第四段在发表作者的观点的同时，还给出了相关的建议。

词汇升级

消除，根除

普通版 We have the capacity to *get rid of* an entire species.

升级版 We have the capacity to *exterminate* an entire species.

消除，根除：annul, eliminate,extirpate, kill, eradicate, uproot, get rid of, dispose of, wipe out

ESSAY 77

Some people believe that damage to the environment is an inevitable consequence of the improvement of living standards. What is your opinion?

The city where I live is increasingly teeming with high-rise apartment buildings. As can be expected, trees are cut down to make room for those constructions. People are daily plagued by air and noise pollution as a result of the booming economy. As things now stand, we are paying too dear a price for the development.

Even the most developed countries are troubled by environmental issue. In fact, the more developed a nation is, the severer the problem. To sustain a prosperous economy, factories and companies have to be in full operation and the workforce putting in long hours. Industrial wastes cost a lot to be disposed of. The huge energy consumption depletes the natural resources at an unsustainable rate. There is every sign that the environment must be sacrificed to some extent for the sake of world economy. However, we are making a blunder by equating economic prosperity with better living standards.

A better life should be a life closer to nature. What we are now working so hard for is a mass-produced, standardized, seemingly comfortable life. It is true that we can now have computers, cars and larger houses, but something more valuable is being lost. We can no longer breathe clean air, have a quiet walk in the woods or even look at the stars because they are being obscured by smog and artificial light at night.

Hence, we need to curb the frantic pace of development in order to protect the environment and ironically to improve the quality of life. Our science and technology should be directed to creating harmony between mankind and nature. A better environment means much more than material comforts. Besides, by slowing down a little bit, people's lives become less stressful. To have a better life, we need to take it easy.

The currently environmental damage is the consequence of our misguided conception that material wealth is tantamount to a better life. Environmental protection won't stand in the way of our pursuit of a really better life.

单词注释

- teem [tiːm] *v.* 充满；大量出现
- plague [pleɪg] *vt.* 折磨，使苦恼
- booming [ˈbuːmɪŋ] *adj.* 急速发展的
- severe [sɪˈvɪə(r)] *adj.* 严重的
- deplete [dɪˈpliːt] *vt.* 耗尽，使衰竭
- unsustainable [ˌʌnsəsˈteɪnəbl] *adj.* 无法支撑的，无法维持的
- blunder [ˈblʌndə] *n.* 大错，失误
- equate [ɪˈkweɪt] *vt.* 使相等，视为平等 *vi.* 等同
- standardized [ˈstændədaɪzd] *adj.* 标准的；定型的
- artificial [ˌɑːtɪˈfɪʃl] *adj.* 人造的
- frantic [ˈfræntɪk] *adj.* 狂乱的，疯狂的
- ironical [aiˈrɒnɪkl] *adj.* 讽刺的，用反语的
- misguided [ˌmɪsˈgaɪdɪd] *adj.* 被误导的，误入歧途的
- tantamount [ˈtæntəmaʊnt] *adj.* 等价的

有人认为环境破坏是改善生活水平所不可避免的后果。你是否同意这样的观点？

在我所生活的城市，高层居民楼如雨后春笋般拔地而起。为了给这些建筑提供空间，树木被大量砍伐。随着经济的高速发展，人们日益受到空气和噪音污染的影响。事实证明，我们为发展付出了高昂的代价。

即使是最发达的国家也为环境的问题所困扰。事实上，往往国家越发达，环境问题就越严重。为了保持经济繁荣，厂矿往往要开足马力，长时间地工作。处理工业制造的污染需要付出很高的成本。大量的能源消耗使自然资源以一种不可扼制的比例削减，有迹象表明，为了全球经济的发展，人类正在逐渐牺牲环境。我们以为经济繁荣直接等于更高的生活质量。事实上，这是一个严重的错误。

贴近自然的生活才是真正更好的生活。而如今我们努力去追求的却是一个大批量生产的、标准化的、看起来舒适的生活模式。我们的确拥有了电脑、汽车以及更宽敞的房子，但却失去了一些更加宝贵的东西。我们不再有机会呼吸清新的空气，不再有机会漫步于宁静的树林间，甚至不再有机会看到天上的繁星。雾气和人造的灯光模糊了我们的视野。

为了保护环境进而改善我们的生活水平，我们必须抑制过快的发展步伐。我们应该让科技在人类和大自然之间制造和谐。好的生活环境远不仅仅意味着物质方面的舒适。此外，如果我们稍微放慢一点自己的节奏，我们就可以舒缓生活的压力。只有变得更加从容，我们才能获得更好的生活。

现今的环境破坏，是因为我们误以为更加美好的生活直接等于有更多的物质财富。环境保护绝对不会妨碍我们获得更加美好的生活。

特别提醒

环境保护是雅思考试中最热门的话题之一，每年的雅思考试中都会出现若干道涉及环保题材的文章。本书收集了若干道环境题材的雅思作文题。请用心阅读这些范文，并归纳整理环保类文章中常见论据的英文表达。

推荐指数 ★★★★　　**相关题目** 36, 60

写作点拨

这道题目要求考生就"环境破坏是改善生活水平所不可避免的后果"发表自己的看法，是典型的观点类雅思作文题。范文的写法有别于传统的观点类议论文的写作方法。范文分为五段：第一段引入话题；第二段指出人们往往错误地认为生活水平的提高直接等于物质条件的改善；第三段指出真正美好的生活应该是贴近大自然的生活；第四段就如何应对当前的环境问题给出了作者的建议；第五段重申作者的观点。

词汇升级

步伐，步调

普通版 Hence, we need to curb the *fast* pace of development in order to protect the environment and ironically to improve the quality of life.

升级版 Hence, we need to curb the *frantic* pace of development in order to protect the environment and ironically to improve the quality of life.

pace（步伐，步调）：blistering（极快的），breakneck（极快的），breathtaking（惊人的），brisk（轻快的），cracking（快的），frantic（狂暴的），frenetic（发狂的），frenzied（狂热的），furious（狂暴的），hectic（忙乱的）

ESSAY 78

The spread of English and growth of international tourism have some negative effects on countries' languages and traditional culture. To what extent do you agree or disagree?

English is now spoken, with various degrees of accuracy, in more than 60 countries. In China alone, more than 200 million people are engaged in the learning of the language, which is made easier by the interaction with millions of traveling native speakers of English. There is no need to be alarmed by the enthusiasm for English or the influx of tourists.

The dominance of our mother tongue will not to be detracted by the spread of English. We learn English out of academic, diplomatic, commercial or other practical considerations because English is the preferred language when communicating with most foreigners. Few of us deem it superior to Chinese. No one will forgo Chinese and concentrate on English only. In fact, we use Chinese all the time among ourselves. Besides, if need be, one is totally capable of being bilingual. Many people in Northern Europe are bilingual or even multilingual. Actually, learning a foreign language helps one to appreciate his or her native tongue. Without comparison, many of us would never see the beauty and uniqueness of Chinese.

The development of international tourism is in line with globalization. It will certainly affect our culture but not necessarily for the worse. Tourists from all over the world bring with them their cultures and traditions, many of which may seem exotic and appealing. Some of it will no doubt be picked up by the locals. This is regarded by some as an encroachment on our traditions. But I'd rather call it the enrichment of our culture. After all, culture is and should not be static; it is constantly changing even without outside influence. There is no need to blindly stick to traditional culture; whatever is outdated or obsolete needs to go.

As the daily world integrates, we need to communicate and travel around. The assimilation of the new doesn't necessarily result in the loss of the old. Foreign culture and language and its national counterpart actually complement each other.

单词注释

- accuracy [ˈækjərəsi] *n.* 精确性，正确度
- enthusiasm [ɪnˈθjuːziæzəm] *n.* 狂热，热心
- influx [ˈɪnflʌks] *n.* 流入，汇集
- detract [dɪˈtrækt] *v.* 转移
- diplomatic [ˌdɪpləˈmætɪk] *adj.* 外交的，老练的
- multilingual [ˌmʌltiˈlɪŋgwəl] *adj.* 使用多种语言的
- uniqueness [juˈniːknəs] *n.* 唯一性，独特性
- exotic [ɪgˈzɔtɪk] *adj.* 异国情调的，外来的
- appealing [əˈpiːlɪŋ] *adj.* 吸引人的，令人心动的
- encroachment [ɪnˈkrəʊtʃmənt] *n.* 侵蚀，侵犯
- enrichment [ɪnˈrɪtʃmənt] *n.* 丰富
- integrate [ˈɪntɪgreɪt] *v.* 结合
- assimilation [əˌsɪmɪˈleɪʃn] *n.* 同化
- counterpart [ˈkaʊntəpɑːt] *n.* 相似物，对应的人（东西）
- complement [ˈkɒmplɪment] *vt.* 补助，补足

英语的广泛传播以及跨国旅游的增长，对各国的语言和传统文化造成了很大的负面影响。你是否同意这样的看法？

虽然各个国家的水平有所不同，如今全球有超过60个国家使用英语。仅在中国，就有超过2亿人在学习英语。与来华旅游的外国游客交流，方便了国人的英语学习。我们完全没有必要因为国人英语学习的狂热或是外国游客的大量涌入而感到惊恐。

无论英语如何传播，母语的主导地位都不会发生改变。英语是在和外宾交流过程中最方便使用的语言——无论我们出于学术、外交、商业或是其他的实用目的而学习英语。不大会有人认为英语凌驾于汉语之上。没有人会彻底放弃汉语，只使用英语。事实上，在内部交流的时候，我们使用的依然是汉语。此外，在必要的时候，人们完全有能力使用双语。很多北欧人就可以使用两种甚至是多种语言。学习英语可以让我们更深地发现母语的优势。如果没有比较，我们很难发现汉语的优美和独特。

跨国旅游的发展符合全球一体化的趋势。这种发展势必会对我们的文化产生影响，但却未必是负面的影响。世界各国的游客们带来了各种充满异国风情的文化习俗，其中的一些习俗逐渐为国人所接纳。有些人认为这是文化入侵。我却认为这是文化的丰富和互补。毕竟，文化不是静态的，即使没有外部的影响，文化也是在不断变化之中的。过时的东西自然要被淘汰，盲目地坚持传统文化是毫无意义的。

随着当今世界的日益一体化，我们应该加强交流和互访。接受新的东西不等于一定要失去旧的。外国的文化和语言与本土的文化和语言事实上可以互为补充。

特别提醒

语言和文化的问题是近年来雅思考试中的热门话题之一。本书收集了若干道语言和文化题材的雅思作文题目。这道写作题，就曾经多次在雅思考试中出现，请认真阅读范文。

推荐指数 ★★★★　　**相关题目** 8, 35, 53

写作点拨

这道题目要求考生就“英语的广泛传播以及跨国旅游的增长是否对各国的语言和传统文化造成了很大的负面影响”发表自己的看法，是典型的观点类雅思作文题。由于题目涉及“英语的传播”以及“跨国旅游的增长”两方面的问题，范文的写法有别于传统的观点类议论文的写作方法。范文分为四段：第一段引入话题；第二段指出英语的传播不会影响到母语的地位，并且给出相应的论据；第三段论证了跨国旅游的增长对本土文化所起的补充作用；第四段重申作者的观点。

句型升级

普通版 It will certainly have some effects on our cultures. However, these effects may not necessarily be bad effects.

升级版 It will certainly affect our culture but not necessarily for the worse.

注释：使用动词affect以及介词短语for the worse，两个原本平淡无奇的句子就可以合并成一个句式结构颇有特点的句子。

ESSAY 79

Traditional art is a sign of civilization. Do you think government should subsidize musicians, painters, actors or opera companies? What should the government do?

China has a long history of over 5000 years and a fine tradition of art and literature. Deplorably, much of it has been irrevocably lost. There is something that the government can do to reverse the trend.

Some forms of subsidy should be given to those artists and organizations who are dedicated to traditional art. Though generally highbrow, many traditional art forms have lost their popularity and are facing extinction. There were formerly around 300 types of operas across China, including the well-known Beijing Opera, Cantonese Opera and so on. Regrettably, they cannot compete with imported popular arts and only a handful of them are occasionally performed and watched mainly by those over 40 years old. Their total demise would be an incalculable loss because they are the highest forms of art, incorporating singing, dancing and stage fighting. And this is just one of those art forms that are endangered due to the altered popular taste and competition from imported arts. Financial aid from the government is needed to ensure the survival of those arts.

Apart from providing subsidies, more measures can be taken to facilitate the development of traditional arts. Effective education and promotion can make a difference. Most of the young don't have the slightest idea of what traditional art is owing to the lack of education in this respect. The mass media is saturated with popular arts and offers no alternative. People's taste is largely shaped by the mass media. Given a taste of traditional arts, many would start to appreciate them. It is wrong to suppose that traditional arts have no place in the modern world. In many countries where they are given due attention, tradition arts are still flourishing or even dominant. The popularity of popular arts has much to do with the enormous amount of money spent on its promotion.

It is not viable nor sensible to preserve all tradition art forms. When its time comes, no elixir can save it. But those that have stood the test of time and have real artistic values should be preserved and promoted.

单词注释

- deplorable [dɪˈplɔːrəbl] *adj.* 可叹的
- irrevocably [ɪˈrevəkəbli] *adv.* 不能取消地，不能撤回地
- reverse [rɪˈvɜːs] *vt.* 颠倒，倒转
- subsidy [ˈsʌbsədi] *n.* 补助金，津贴
- dedicate [ˈdedɪkeɪt] *vt.* 献(身)，致力
- highbrow [ˈhaɪbraʊ] *adj.* 关于正统艺术思想的
- popularity [ˌpɒpjuˈlærəti] *n.* 普及，流行；声望
- extinction [ɪksˈtɪŋkʃn] *n.* 消失，消灭
- regrettably [rɪˈgretəbli] *adv.* 遗憾地，可悲地
- incalculable [ɪnˈkælkjʊləbl] *adj.* 数不尽的
- incorporate [ɪnˈkɔːpəreɪt] *v.* 合并
- saturate [ˈsætʃəreɪt] *vt.* 使饱和；使充满
- alternative [ɔːlˈtɜːnətɪv] *n.* 可供选择的东西
- due [djuː] *adj.* 应得的
- viable [ˈvaɪəbl] *adj.* 可行的
- elixir [ɪˈlɪksə(r)] *n.* 不老长寿药，万能药

传统艺术是文明的标志。你是否认为政府应该赞助音乐家、画家、演员以及戏剧公司？你认为政府应该做什么？

中国有长达5000年的历史以及艺术和文学方面的优良传统。令人叹息的是，我们的很多传统都已经失传了。政府应该采取措施来扭转这种趋势。

政府应该向致力于传统艺术的艺术家或机构提供某种形式的资助。虽然通常被人们视为阳春白雪，很多传统艺术形式都逐渐失去受众而濒临灭绝。中国曾经有近300种戏剧，其中包括著名的京剧和粤剧。然而这些剧种却很难和外来的流行艺术相抗衡。如今，仅仅只有几种戏剧偶尔还有表演，观众也多为40岁以上的人。这些剧种的集体消失将是无法统计的巨大损失，因为这些剧种融合了歌唱、舞蹈和舞台打斗，是艺术的最高形式。戏剧仅仅是因流行文化趋势的改变以及外来文化的竞争而濒临灭绝的诸多艺术形式中的一种。保护这些艺术形式，政府的财政资助是不可或缺的。

除了提供资助，政府还可以采取各种措施来扶持传统艺术的发展。有效的教育和推广可以极大地改变现状。由于缺少传统艺术方面的教育，大多数年轻人对传统艺术完全没有概念。流行艺术充斥着大众传媒，成了人们唯一的选择。人们的品味和喜好在很大程度上是由大众传媒所引导的。一旦偶尔有机会接触到传统艺术，很多人会开始欣赏和喜欢这些艺术形式。那种认为传统艺术在现代世界里已经没有容身之地的想法是绝对错误的。在那些传统艺术受到足够重视的国家，这些艺术形式依然可以繁荣发展，有些甚至处于主导地位。流行艺术之所以如此受欢迎，很大程度上是因为人们在流行文化的推广方面所付出的巨额成本。

试图保护所有的传统艺术形式是不理智的，也是不可行的。万事万物皆有自己衰退的那一天。时间到了，任何灵丹妙药都无法挽回这个结局。但是那些经受住了时间的考验、真正拥有不朽的艺术价值的艺术形式，应该受到保护和推广。

特别提醒

传统文化的保护问题，是雅思考试中最传统的话题之一。本书收集了近10道语言和文化题材的雅思作文题目。这道写作题，就曾经多次在雅思考试中出现，请认真阅读范文。

推荐指数 ★★★　　**相关题目** 40, 80

写作点拨

这道题目要求考生就“政府是否应该资助传统艺术”发表自己的看法，并且指出政府应该采取的措施，是典型的“观点＋建议”类雅思作文题。由于题目涉及“观点”以及“建议”两方面的问题，范文的写法有别于传统的观点类议论文的写作方法。范文分为四段：第一段引入话题；第二段指出政府应该资助传统艺术，并且给出相应的理由；第三段指出除了提供资助外，政府应该采取的其他措施；第四段重申作者的观点并且总结全文。

词汇升级

充斥，充满

普通版 The mass media *is full of* popular arts and offers no alternative.

升级版 The mass media *is saturated with* popular arts and offers no alternative.

充斥，充满：be flooded with, be saturated with, be rife with, be full of, be teeming with

ESSAY 80

Many people think that painting and music do not directly improve the quality of people. Therefore, government should not spend too much money on artistic projects. Do you agree or disagree?

The government is entrusted by the people to act for the common good. An ideal government should take care of all its citizens. When this could not be done, the government should try to address the pressing needs of most of its people. Hence, artistic projects should not be its priorities.

Art may be the highest form of enjoyment. It addresses our psychological, mental and spiritual needs. It cannot be replaced by anything else. However, it should not take precedence when other more pressing needs are left unattended. Hunger, poverty, crime and regional conflicts are still plaguing millions around the world. Even in developed countries people are still troubled by social injustice and environmental problems. It is hard to exalt our soul when our body is being tormented. Let us first tackle the problems of the body.

To eradicate poverty should be a global priority. Millions in African alone starve to death each year not because of natural disasters but simply because they cannot afford any food. If the developed and so-called civilized nations would only allocate one percent of their gross domestic product to alleviate poverty, the poor would all be guaranteed adequate food. Alas, they choose not to do so, claiming they have other priorities. What could possibly be more important than saving lives? Refusing to prevent death is almost equal to committing homicide. In addition, poverty often breeds other evils: child labour, social unrest, violent crimes and so on.

To ensure equality among people should be another priority. Equality is a recognition that we are all created by the miracles of the universe. The brotherhood of mankind demands equal treatment of each individual. Discrimination and injustice are the bane of society. They breed hostility and hatred among people. Its damage even exceeds that of poverty. When people feel repressed and exploited, they will want to rebel and to assert their due status. Revolution and war would ensue, as happened time and again in our recorded history.

It is in vain to preach about art to refugees, who would most like to be fed first. Basic problems should be tackled first before we take on the lofty undertaking of art.

单词注释

- entrust [ɪnˈtrʌst] *v.* 委托
- address [əˈdres] *v.* 处理
- pressing [ˈpresɪŋ] *adj.* 紧迫的
- priority [praɪˈɔrəti] *n.* 优先，优先权
- psychological [ˌsaɪkəˈlɒdʒɪkl] *adj.* 心理(上)的
- unattended [ˌʌnəˈtendɪd] *adj.* 没人照顾的；未被注意的
- injustice [ɪnˈdʒʌstɪs] *n.* 不公平
- plague [pleɪg] *vt.* 折磨，使苦恼
- exalt [ɪgˈzɔːlt] *v.* 提高，提升
- torment [ˈtɔːment] *v.* 折磨
- eradicate [ɪˈrædɪkeɪt] *v.* 根除
- adequate [ˈædɪkwət] *adj.* 适当的；足够的
- homicide [ˈhɒmɪsaɪd] *n.* 杀人
- unrest [ʌnˈrest] *n.* 动荡的局面
- miracle [ˈmɪrəkl] *n.* 奇迹，奇事
- brotherhood [ˈbrʌðəhʊd] *n.* 手足情谊，兄弟关系
- bane [beɪn] *n.* 祸根
- repress [rɪˈpres] *vt.* 抑制；镇压
- preach [priːtʃ] *v.* 鼓吹
- lofty [ˈlɔfti] *adj.* 高耸的；崇高的
- undertaking [ˌʌndəˈteɪkɪŋ] *n.* 事业，企业

很多人认为美术和音乐并不能够直接提高国民素质，所以政府不应该在艺术项目上投入太多的资金。你是否同意这样的观点？

政府受人民所托，为全体人民造福。成功的政府，应该关爱每一位百姓。如果不能够顾及每一位百姓的需要，政府就应该尽全力满足大多数人的需求。因此，艺术项目不应该成为政府的工作重心。

艺术为人们提供了最高形式的享乐，满足了人们在心理、脑力和精神方面的需求。艺术不能为其他任何事情所取代。但是，当我们还有更重要的问题需要解决的时候，艺术就应该退居其次了。全球依然有数以百万的民众正遭受着饥饿、贫穷、犯罪和区域冲突之苦。即使在发达国家，人们也同样为社会公正以及环境保护等问题所困扰。如果我们的肉体正在遭受痛苦，提升灵魂就根本无从谈起。我们当然应该先解决身体的问题。

全球最应该重视的问题是彻底消除贫困。仅在非洲，每年就有数以百万计的居民被活活饿死。造成这种状况的原因并不是天灾，而是人祸——他们无力购买任何食物。如果发达国家，或是所谓的"文明"国家，能够将自己的国内生产总值的百分之一用于消除贫困，所有的穷人就能够获得足够的食物。令人叹息的是，这些国家却没有选择这样做，而且还口口声声说他们有更重要的事情要做。有什么比拯救生命更重要呢？拒绝挽救他人的生命，无异于杀人。贫困常会引发别的问题：童工、社会动荡、暴力犯罪等等。

另外一件人们应该重视的事情，是确保人人平等。确保人人平等，就是承认每一个人都是宇宙的神奇力量所创造的个体。人类手足情深，理应平等对待每一个个体。歧视和不平等是社会的毒瘤所引发的人与人之间的敌意和对抗，危害远胜贫困。当人们受到镇压和剥削的时候，他们就会反抗，以获取自己的社会地位。正如历史一再表明的那样，革命和战争自然会随之而来。

向一群难民宣传艺术，无疑是徒劳的。因为对于他们来说，当务之急是填饱自己的肚子。我们应该先解决那些基本问题，然后才能够开展艺术之类的崇高事业。

特别提醒

艺术创作的问题，曾经是雅思写作考试中的热门话题；在各种关于艺术的雅思写作题中，关于艺术的价值以及艺术创作是否需要绝对自由的文章出现的频率最高。这篇范文涉及政府应该如何处理艺术的问题，是近年来雅思考试中的热门话题，请考生用心阅读。

推荐指数 ★★★★　　**相关题目** 40, 79

写作点拨

这道题目要求考生就"政府是否应该在艺术方面投入大量资金"发表自己的看法，是典型的观点类雅思作文题。范文采取了最传统的观点类议论文的写作方法。范文分为五段：第一段开门见山地给出作者的观点，即政府不应该过于重视艺术；第二、三、四段给出相应的理由，并指出政府应该重点解决的问题；第五段重申作者的观点并且总结全文。

词汇升级

需求，需要

普通版 When this could not be done, the government should try to *meet the pressing needs* of most of its people.

升级版 When this could not be done, the government should try to *address the pressing needs* of most of its people.

need(需求，需要)：respond to(回应), address(满足), cater for(满足), cover(满足), fulfil(满足)

ESSAY 81

Today, many students take the course International News in secondary school. Some say it is a waste of time. Discuss and state your opinion.

Students in China are often too busy to watch TV or read newspapers to the extent that many of them don't have the faintest ideas about what is happening in other countries. Some people are alarmed by this and urge students to study International News at high school, but others regard it as an unnecessary burden for the students.

Many claim that students are doing all right without much knowledge about the outside world. Events in other nations are not relevant and thus to distract students from their academic pursuit. Besides, many of the international news are nothing but government propaganda aiming to deceive the international community for political reasons, for the freedom of press is denied in many nations. Moreover, today's news reports are largely profit-driven. Sensationalism and tabloid journalism become increasingly prevalent. Events with real newsworthiness are left out because they do not cater to popular tastes.

However, despite all its imperfections, it is still well worth students' time to study International News, provided that worthy events are reported with a fair degree of accuracy. Our understanding of the world would be incomplete if we are ignorant of the happenings around the globe. Globalization and integration lead to more interdependency among nations. A local event is likely to have global repercussions. As potential pillars of society, high school students must not live in this insular condition, which often leads to bigotry and narrow-mindedness. Cooperation among different peoples starts with mutual understanding. Additionally, the knowledge of the outside world often leads to deeper insight into our own society. We start to cherish peace and prosperity when we see reports on war and famine tormenting millions in other lands. News about presidential elections help students understand our democracy better.

An insular life inside Ivory Towers could only turn out graduates with utopian ideals for and distorted ideas about our world. To find out the truth, one has to open his eyes to what's really happening in the world.

单词注释

- faint [feɪnt] *adj.* 暗淡的，模糊的
- alarm [ə'lɑːm] *vt.* 恐吓，警告
- propaganda [ˌprɒpə'gændə] *n.* 宣传
- profit-driven *adj.* 追求利润的
- sensationalism [sen'seɪʃənəlɪzm] *n.* 哗众取宠；危言耸听
- tabloid ['tæblɔɪd] *n.* 小报
- prevalent ['prevələnt] *adj.* 普遍的，流行的
- cater ['keɪtə] *v.* 迎合
- accuracy ['ækjərəsi] *n.* 精确性，正确度
- integration [ˌɪntɪ'greɪʃən] *n.* 结合
- interdependency [ˌɪntədɪ'pendənsi] *n.* 互相依赖
- repercussion [ˌriːpə'kʌʃn] *n.* 弹回；反响
- pillar ['pɪlə(r)] *n.* 柱子，栋梁
- insular ['ɪnsjələ(r)] *adj.* 与世隔绝的
- bigotry ['bɪgətri] *n.* 固执，顽固
- narrow-mindedness *n.* 气量小，小心眼
- famine ['fæmɪn] *n.* 饥荒
- torment ['tɔːment] *n.* 痛苦 *v.* 折磨
- presidential [ˌprezɪ'denʃl] *adj.* 总统的
- utopian [juː'təʊpiən] *adj.* 乌托邦的，理想化的
- distort [dɪs'tɔːt] *vt.* 扭曲，歪曲

如今，很多中学生都开始修读国际新闻课。有人认为这纯属浪费时间。请讨论这个问题，并给出你的看法。

中国的大多数学生都忙于学业，很少有时间看电视或是读报纸，以至于他们当中的很多人对其他国家所发生的事情毫无所知。有些人意识到了这个问题的严重性，因此敦促高中生修读国际新闻之类的课程，而别的人却认为修读这样的课程会给学生造成负担。

很多人认为，学生不太了解外面的世界也没什么。其他国家发生的事情，与高中生的生活几乎不相关，因此不应该为此分散他们的注意力。此外，大多数国家并没有实现新闻自由，所以相当一部分国际新闻报道都只不过是政府出于政治目的、为欺骗国际社会而捏造的宣传内容。更严重的是，如今大多数新闻报道都是为商业利益所驱动的。炒作和八卦新闻日益流行。真正有新闻价值的消息，往往因不符合大众的口味，而直接被删除了。

尽管国际新闻有种种缺陷，只要有价值的消息能够被精确地报道，学生花一定的时间学习国际新闻依然是值得的。如果我们对外面发生的事情一无所知，我们对整个世界的看法就是不完整的。全球一体化让国家之间日益变得相互依赖。一个地方性的事件，也很有可能会引起很大的国际反响。作为社会的栋梁之才，学生不应该生活在与世隔绝的环境中，因为这种环境往往会导致偏激和狭隘。不同民族之间的合作，开始于彼此的了解。此外，对外部社会的了解，往往也可以让我们对自己的社会有更深的了解。当我们看到关于其他国家的战争和饥荒的报道时，我们就会更加珍惜我们所拥有的和平与繁荣。关于总统大选的新闻，可以让学生们更好地理解我们的民主体制。

象牙塔里与世隔绝的生活，只会让学生对世界的看法变得过于理想化或是直接被歪曲。为了获得事情的真相，我们必须睁大眼睛了解这个世界正在发生什么。

特别提醒

这道雅思作文题所涉及的新闻传媒以及中学教育问题，都是雅思写作考试中的热门话题。本书收集了近20道大众传媒或教育方面的雅思写作题，这两类话题在雅思考试中出现频率之高由此可见一斑。用心阅读这些范文，并适当地整理一些常用的论据。

推荐指数 ★★★★

相关题目 5, 7, 26, 27, 28, 47, 49, 50, 54, 57, 75, 84, 85, 87, 89, 109

写作点拨

这道题目要求考生就“中学生是否应该修读国际新闻课发表自己的看法，是典型的观点类雅思作文题。范文的写法有别于最传统的观点类议论文的写作方法。范文分为四段：第一段引入话题；第二段为让步段，列出反对学生修读这门课程的各种理由；第三段给出大量的理由，指出学生其实还是应该修读这门课程；第四段重申作者的观点并且总结全文。

词汇升级

一无所知，毫无了解

普通版 Students in China are often too busy to watch TV or read newspapers to the extent that many of them *don't know at all* what is happening in other countries.

升级版 Students in China are often too busy to watch TV or read newspapers to the extent that many of them *don't have the faintest ideas about* what is happening in other countries.

一无所知，毫无了解：be utterly ignorant of, be totally unaware of, don't have the faintest idea about, be kept in dark about

ESSAY 82

If you have enough money, will you use it to buy a house or to start a business?

If I am wealthy enough to afford either a house or a business, I will definitely choose to buy a business for the simple reason that business investment means a lot more to me than a secured living place does.

A house brings with it all the comforts of and amenities of modern architecture, but a business promises much more. A business means an opportunity to make more money and to taste the joy of success. If I have invested in a business, I will strive to make the undertaking a success. During the process I may experience ups and downs, the happiness of gaining new customers and the frustration of losing profits. Yes, there are risks involved. I may be able to make a fortune but there is also the possibility of going bankrupt, but that's exactly the way I will choose to live—to make the best of what I have.

The relaxing environment of a house discourages me to meet new challenges and compels me to settle for an easy and secured life. After I have invested most of my savings in a business, I will be driven to try my uttermost; otherwise I may wind up having no place to live in. It is obvious that a business is something that puts me in an insecure position. But such a feeling of insecurity will in turn goad me to explore my full potential and struggle for prominence.

A business is evidently a better option for me than a house, for I am still young and need to strive rather than to relax. I prefer the excitement of running a business to the comfort of staying at home.

单词注释

- afford [əˈfɔːd] *vt.* 提供；买得起，供应得起
- definitely [ˈdefɪnətli] *adv.* 明确地，确切地
- investment [ɪnˈvestmənt] *n.* 投资，可获利的东西
- secured [sɪˈkjʊəd] *adj.* 安全的，可靠的
- amenity [əˈmiːnəti] *n.* 令人愉快的事物；舒适
- strive [straɪv] *v.* 努力，奋斗，力争
- frustration [frʌsˈtreɪʃn] *n.* 挫败，挫折；受挫
- bankrupt [ˈbæŋkrʌpt] *n.* 破产者 *adj.* 破产的
- discourage [dɪsˈkʌrɪdʒ] *vt.* 使气馁；阻碍
- compel [kəmˈpel] *vt.* 强迫，迫使
- uttermost [ˈʌtəməʊst] *n.* 极端，最大限度
- insecure [ˌɪnsɪˈkjʊə(r)] *adj.* 不可靠的，不安全的
- insecurity [ˌɪnsɪˈkjʊərəti] *n.* 不安全，不安全感
- goad [ɡəʊd] *vt.* 用刺棒驱赶；驱策，激励
- explore [ɪksˈplɔː] *v.* 探险；探测，探究
- prominence [ˈprɒmɪnəns] *n.* 突出，显著；突出物
- prefer [prɪˈfəː] *vt.* 更喜欢，宁愿

如果你有足够多的钱，你会选择买一套房子还是创业呢？

如果我有钱买房或者创业的话，我一定会选择创业。原因很简单，创业比起拥有一个安乐窝来说要有意义得多。

房子能给你带来现代建筑的种种舒适和乐趣，但创业能带来更多的东西。创业意味着有机会挣取更多的钱财并享受成功的滋味。在创业过程中，我能经历各种起起伏伏，既有获得新客户的欣喜，也有亏损的沮丧。是的，创业有风险。我可能赚大钱，也可能破产，但这正是我想要的生活方式——最有效地利用自己现有的东西。

房子给人带来的放松气氛会使我不愿接受新的挑战，还会迫使我安于现状。如果我把大部分的钱都用于创业，我就不得不尽我最大的努力。否则的话，我就可能要留宿街头。很显然，创业使我时刻面临危机。但正是这种危机感才能驱使我去发掘自己所有的潜能，为成功而努力。

所以，很显然，和买房相比，创业对我来说是一个更好的选择。因为我还年轻，需要的是奋斗，而不是懈怠。我宁愿面对创业的紧张刺激，也不舒适地待在安乐窝里。

特别提醒

这道雅思写作题涉及生活观念的问题，颇有点哲学意味。雅思写作考试中，类似的与生活观有关的写作题其实并不多，所以要特别留意这篇文章的写法！

推荐指数 ★★★

相关题目 31, 42, 88, 94, 100

写作点拨

这道题目要求考生就“买一套房子还是创业”发表自己的看法，是典型的观点类雅思作文题。范文使用了最传统的观点类议论文的写作方法。范文分为四段：第一段开门见山地给出作者的观点，即应该选择创业；第二、三段从不同方面给出应该创业而不是买房子的理由；第四段重申作者的观点并且总结全文。

词汇升级

明显地，显而易见地

普通版 A business is *obviously* a better option for me than a house.

升级版 A business is *evidently* a better option for me than a house.

明显地，显而易见地: apparently, evidently, markedly, visibly

ESSAY 83

It is better to be a member of a group than to be the leader of a group. Do you agree or disagree with the statement? Give your reasons.

Every organization consists of a leader and some members. Each of them plays an important yet different role in the group. As an individual, I find it more beneficial to be a leader than a member of the group. The reasons are quite obvious.

Being a leader is more conducive to personal growth. The role of a leader involves much responsibility and decision-making. This means you must engage yourself in a wide range of activities and learning. In doing so, your ability to tackle difficult problems and handle complex situations can be developed. Take myself for example. Before I was promoted to Branch Manager three years ago, I was only an ordinary teacher with little responsibilities or accomplishment. But the experience of being a manager has turned me into a capable and efficient leader.

Moreover, as a leader, one can establish more rewarding connections with influential people. Managers and department heads, for the nature of their work, tend to have more interactions with their peers or superiors, who are themselves leaders. These connections with influential people can lead to more career opportunities and pave the way for their future career. Besides, by consorting with people with superior minds or experiences, one often gets inspired and acquires different perspectives of and insights into things. By contrast, a member of a group often lacks these kinds of opportunities.

Without losing sight of the importance of teamwork and the contribution made by each member of a group, we should give due credits to the leader of the group. He is the one that holds the group together and in turn he reaps the benefits of his position in terms of personal growth and career development.

单词注释

- consist [kən'sɪst] *vi.* 由…组成，在于
- individual [ˌɪndɪ'vɪdjuəl] *n.* 个人，个体
- beneficial [ˌbenɪ'fɪʃl] *adj.* 有益的，受益的
- conducive [kən'djuːsɪv] *adj.* 有益于…的
- involve [ɪn'vɔlv] *vt.* 包括
- tackle ['tækl] *vt.* 固定；应付
- accomplishment [ə'kɒmplɪʃmənt] *n.* 成就，完成；技艺
- capable ['keɪpəbl] *adj.* 有能力的，能干的
- rewarding [rɪ'wɔːdɪŋ] *adj.* 有回报的，有益的
- influential [ˌɪnflu'enʃl] *adj.* 有影响的，有势力的
- peer [pɪə(r)] *n.* 同等的人，同龄人
- pave [peɪv] *v.* 铺(路)
- consort ['kɒnsɔːt] *vi.* 陪伴，结交
- perspective [pə'spektɪv] *n.* 观点，看法
- contrast [kən'trɑːst] *vt.* 使与…对比，使与…对照
- lack [læk] *vt.* 缺乏，没有
- opportunity [ˌɒpə'tjuːnəti] *n.* 机会，时机
- reap [riːp] *v.* 收割；收获

在一个团队里，当一名普通成员往往比担任领导更好。你是否同意这样的观点？请给出你的理由。

每一个组织都由一名领导者和一些成员组成。在团队中，每个人都扮演着重要却不同的角色。我个人认为，当一个团队的领导者比当普通成员更有益处。原因很明显。

当领导者对个人的成长更有好处。当领导者就必须承担大量的责任，做许多的决策。这就要求你必须更广泛地参与活动和学习。这样做能够培养你处理难题、应对复杂局面的能力。就拿我来说吧。三年前，那时我还没有担任教研室主任，只是一个普通的老师，没什么重要职责和成绩。但是担任了教研室主任后，我逐渐成长为一个有能力、有效率的领导。

而且，作为领导，你有机会和更多有影响力的人结识。这种人际关系是很有用的。由于他们的工作性质，经理与主管们经常要和他们的同事或者上级打交道，而这些人本身也是领导。和那些有影响力的人物交往，能够带来更多的职业发展机会，为将来的职业生涯打好基础。另外，经常和高素质的人物来往，你会得到启发，获得观察事物的新的角度和洞察力。相比而言，普通成员就没有上述种种机会。

在关注团队中其他成员的贡献以及团队的作用的同时，我们应该对团队领导的作用给予充分的肯定。是他们把这个集体凝聚在一起。当然，领导者本身也因为他(她)的领导位置而在个人与职业发展方面获得了不少益处。

特别提醒

竞争还是合作，领导还是服从？近年来的雅思写作考试中，不时出现这种二选一的问题。这类文章的写作方法非常有规律，所以请特别留意这篇文章的写法，以不变应万变！

推荐指数 ★★★　　**相关题目** 82

写作点拨

这道题目要求考生就“领导还是服从”发表自己的看法，是典型的观点类雅思作文题。范文使用了最传统的观点类议论文的写作方法。范文分为四段：第一段开门见山地给出作者的观点，即应该选择做领导；第二、三段从不同方面给出应该选择做领导而不是团队中的一个成员的原因；第四段重申作者的观点并且总结全文。

词汇升级

由…组成，包括…

普通版 Every organization *includes* a leader and some members.

升级版 Every organization *consists of* a leader and some members.

由…组成，包括…：include, consist of, be composed of, be constituted by, comprise

ESSAY 84

Some people say that children should spend their leisure time on educational activities. Some people believe it is dangerous to put too much pressure on children. What is your opinion?

Compared with their parents, children today are very lucky. An average school student spends some 25 hours per week on leisure activities, not to mention the summer and winter vacations. But competition is getting fiercer, both at school and in the job market. These children really need to spend more time on their study if they wish to succeed in life. From my point of view, more educational activities will benefit the kids in at least two aspects.

For one thing, better academic performance contributes a great deal to children's future careers. Ours is a world full of competitions. In China, only 40 percent of high school graduates are admitted to universities and still less college graduates can land decent jobs after graduation. Even within a company, people vie with one another for better positions. In order to survive and prevail in all these competitions, children need to work the hardest they can when they are young. The knowledge and skills they obtain will give them a big competitive advantage at the workplace.

For another, studying a wide range of subjects leads to an earlier start in one's career. Everyone is inherently gifted in one area or another. But the gift often lay dormant until stumbled upon and cultivated with conscious efforts. If children are encouraged to study more in their leisure time, they will expose themselves to various disciplines. Such exposure helps identify their career interest earlier than other kids. With such a head start, these children are more likely to succeed in life.

It might be argued that it is dangerous to put too much pressure on children. But actually educational activities are not necessarily associated with pressure or stress. Outdoor study tours and instructive games, for example, are welcomed by younger and older kids alike. When we incorporate an element of recreation into education, study can become great fun.

单词注释

- leisure [ˈleʒə(r)] *n.* 空闲，闲暇，悠闲，安逸
- competition [ˌkɒmpɪˈtɪʃn] *n.* 竞争，竞赛
- fierce [fiəs] *adj.* 凶猛的，猛烈的；热烈的
- admitted [ədˈmɪtɪd] *adj.* 被承认的，被确认无疑的
- decent [ˈdiːsnt] *adj.* 正派的，端庄的
- graduation [ˌgrædʒuˈeɪʃn] *n.* 毕业，毕业典礼；刻度
- vie [vaɪ] *v.* 竞争
- prevail [prɪˈveɪl] *vi.* 流行，盛行；获胜，成功
- obtain [əbˈteɪn] *vt.* 获得，得到
- inherently [ɪnˈhɪərəntli] *adv.* 天性地，固有地
- dormant [ˈdɔːmənt] *adj.* 睡眠状态的，静止的；隐匿的
- stumble [ˈstʌmbl] *v.* 绊脚；蹒跚而行
- cultivate [ˈkʌltɪveɪt] *vt.* 耕耘；培养
- instructive [ɪnˈstrʌktɪv] *adj.* 有益的；教育性的
- incorporate [ɪnˈkɔːpəreɪt] *vt.* 合并

一些人认为儿童应该利用空闲时间参加一些教育活动，而另一些人却认为太大的压力对儿童是非常不利的。请给出你的看法。

和他们父辈相比，现在的孩子算是非常幸运了。一名普通的学生每星期花在课余活动上的时间有 25 小时，这还没算上寒暑假。但是，现在不管是在学校还是在职场，竞争都越来越激烈。现在的孩子如果想要有所成就的话，就必须更努力地学习。我的观点是，至少在两个方面，更多的课余学习对孩子是有好处的。

第一，好的学习成绩对孩子将来的职业发展有很大帮助。我们的世界充满了竞争。在中国，只有百分之四十的中学生能够上大学。大学毕业后能够找到一份好工作的就更少了。即使在公司里，人们也为了升职而相互竞争。为了生存，为了在竞争中取胜，孩子们必须在小的时候就尽最大努力学习。他们学到的知识和技能能够给他们将来的职场竞争提供优势。

另一个原因是，广泛学习各门课程，有助于尽早开始一个人的事业。每个人都在某个领域有天赋，但是这种天赋往往是潜在的，有待发掘和培养。如果孩子们在课余时间能够更广泛地学习，他们就能接触更多的课程。这种广泛的接触能够帮助他们比别的孩子更早确定自己的兴趣所在。有了这种先发优势，孩子就更有机会在将来获得成功。

可能有人会说，给孩子太多的压力是很危险的。但是事实上，课余学习并不一定会带来压力或紧张。比如，户外考察或是有教育意义的游戏，都备受各个年龄段的孩子喜欢。只要我们把娱乐和学习结合起来，学习就会是一种乐趣。

特别提醒

儿童的教育问题是雅思考试中最热门的话题之一。本书收集了 10 道以上的关于儿童教育的雅思写作题，涉及儿童教育的方方面面，请用心整理这些文章中常见的论据以及相应的英文表达。

推荐指数 ★★★★　　**相关题目** 5, 7, 26, 27, 28, 47, 49, 50, 54, 57, 75, 81, 85, 87, 89, 109

写作点拨

这道题目要求考生就“学生是否应该利用空闲时间参加教育活动”发表自己的看法，是典型的观点类雅思作文题。范文使用了最传统的观点类议论文的写作方法。范文分为四段：第一段开门见山地给出作者的观点，即应该利用空闲时间参加教育活动；第二、三段从不同方面给出应该参加教育活动的原因；第四段重申作者的观点并且总结全文。

词汇升级

工作

普通版 In China, only 40 percent of high school graduates are admitted to universities and still less college graduates can *get* decent jobs after graduation.

升级版 In China, only 40 percent of high school graduates are admitted to universities and still less college graduates can *land* decent jobs after graduation.

job（工作）: apply for(申请), go for(申请), pack in(停止), resign from(辞职), give up(放弃), hold down(有), axe(解雇), cut(裁员), shed(解雇)

ESSAY 85

Some people think that in order to improve the quality of education, high school students should be encouraged to evaluate and criticize their teachers, but other people maintain that such evaluation and criticism may cause loss of respect for teachers and discipline. What do you think?

Students are nowadays regarded as the most important element of education. So students in some high schools now enjoy the right to evaluate and criticize their teachers to guarantee better teaching from the instructors. Naturally, such practice draws criticism from many conservatives who insist that evaluation and criticism from students interfere with the normal teaching process.

They do have their reasons. Firstly, teachers have a syllabus to follow and criticism from students may prevent it from being implemented. Second, negative evaluation from the students could harm the relationship between teachers and students. And excessive criticism may even breed resentment and hostility at schools.

Though not entirely groundless, these concerns are just unfounded worries. If students are not allowed to evaluate or criticize the teacher, it is hard for the teacher to find out what the students think or what they need. Without proper feedback from the students, the classroom becomes a place where students are crammed with knowledge considered useful, yet in fact, of little benefit or interest to them. Though the syllabus is set by the school authorities and has long been followed by most teachers, it may as well be altered if it no longer reflects the need of students. Besides, evaluation and criticism are themselves effective forms of communication, which should be welcomed by teachers because they will benefit a lot when their minds are open to the ideas and honest opinions of the youngsters. Those who feel ashamed to be criticized by their students or are afraid of losing their respect should adopt a more positive attitude instead of being excessively defensive and self-conscious.

Of course, students' assessments of their teachers may not always be objective or make sense, given that they are still young and impulsive. But I believe their opinions deserve our attention if we are to have a more effective and productive education system.

单词注释

- evaluate [ɪˈvæljueɪt] *vt.* 评价；估计
- maintain [meɪnˈteɪn] *vt.* 维持；维修；继续
- discipline [ˈdɪsɪplɪn] *n.* 纪律；学科
- instructor [ɪnˈstrʌktə(r)] *n.* 教师，〈美〉讲师
- conservative [kənˈsɜːvətɪv] *adj.* 保守的，守旧的 *n.* 保守派
- interfere [ˌɪntəˈfɪə(r)] *vi.* 干涉，干预，妨碍
- syllabus [ˈsɪləbəs] *n.* 课程提纲
- implement [ˈɪmplɪmənt] *vt.* 贯彻，执行
- excessive [ɪkˈsesɪv] *adj.* 过多的，过分的；额外的
- breed [briːd] *v.* (使)繁殖；教养
- resentment [rɪˈzentmənt] *n.* 怨恨，愤恨
- hostility [hɔsˈtɪləti] *n.* 敌意，恶意，不友善，敌对
- groundless [ˈgraʊndləs] *adj.* 无根据的，没有理由的
- unfounded [ʌnˈfaʊndɪd] *adj.* 没有理由的；未建立的
- cram [kræm] *v.* 填满
- alter [ˈɔːltə(r)] *v.* 改变
- youngster [ˈjʌŋstə(r)] *n.* 年青人，少年
- ashamed [əˈʃeɪmd] *adj.* 惭愧的，羞耻的
- excessively [ɪkˈsesɪvli] *adv.* 过分地，非常地
- assessment [əˈsesmənt] *n.* 估价
- impulsive [ɪmˈpʌlsɪv] *adj.* 冲动的

有人认为，为了提高教育质量，我们应该鼓励高中生对自己的老师进行评估；其他人却认为这种评估会造成不尊重教师、违反学校纪律的行为。请给出你的看法。

在现在的教育当中，学生被认为是最重要的因素。所以，为了保证教学质量，在有些中学里，学生有对老师进行评价和批评的权利。很自然，这种做法引起了一些保守派的反对，他们认为评价和批评老师会影响正常的教学进程。

他们的确有自己的理由。首先，老师要按照教学大纲来施教。来自学生的批评可能会妨碍教学大纲的实施。第二，来自学生的负面评价可能会损害老师和学生之间的关系。过度的批评甚至会在学校里引发憎恨和敌意。

尽管不是毫无依据，这些担忧还是站不住脚的。如果学生不能够评价或批评老师，那么老师就很难知道学生究竟在想些什么、需要什么。如果没有学生的适当反馈，那么教室就成了一个向学生灌输一些被认为有用、实际上对学生没有多大用处的知识的地方。虽然教学大纲是经过教育权威部门认定，为大部分老师所遵循，但是如果它不再能反映学生的需要，还是应该被修改的。另外，评价和批评本身也是一种有效的交流方式，应该受到广大老师的欢迎。通过听取学生的真实意见和想法，教师自己也能够受益匪浅。那些感觉被学生批评很难堪、害怕丧失尊严的老师，应该把心态放积极些，不要过于敏感，防范意识不要太强。

当然，学生对老师的评价并不一定总是客观、正确的，因为他们毕竟还年轻，容易冲动。但是，我相信他们的意见值得我们关注。这有助于改革我们的教育体制，使之变得更高效。

特别提醒

教育问题是雅思考试中最热门的话题之一。本书收集了近20道教育方面的雅思写作题，涉及儿童以及成人教育的方方面面。这道作文题所涉及的教育方面的内容，与其他的教育类雅思写作题有很大的不同，请用心整理文章中出现的论据及其英文表达。

推荐指数 ★★★★★

相关题目

5, 7, 26, 27, 28, 47, 49, 50, 54, 57, 75, 81, 84, 87, 89, 109

写作点拨

这道题目要求考生就“学生是否应该评估自己的老师”发表自己的看法，是典型的观点类雅思作文题。范文的写法有别于最传统的观点类议论文的写作方法。范文分为四段：第一段引入话题；第二段是让步段，列出反对学生对教师进行评估的理由；第三段从不同方面给出学生应该参与教师评估的原因；第四段重申作者的观点并且总结全文。

论据积累

学生评价老师的理由：

1. 通过评估，老师可以知道学生究竟在想些什么、需要什么。
   If students are not allowed to evaluate or criticize the teacher, it is hard for the teacher to find out what the students think or what they need.
2. 评价和批评本身也是一种有效的交流方式。
   Evaluation and criticism are themselves effective forms of communication.
3. 通过听取学生的真实意见和想法，教师自己也能够受益匪浅。
   Teachers will benefit a lot when their minds are open to the ideas and honest opinions of the youngsters.

ESSAY 86

Choosing a suitable career is a problem that faces many young people. What are the reasons? What suggestion would you give to them to help them make the right decision?

Each day, over a thousand job hunters swarm into the South China Employment Service (SCES), one of the largest placement services in town, either to present themselves to potential employers or to have their resumes entered in the database of SCES. In Guangzhou alone, there are about ten large-scale employment services and still many smaller ones, all of which are earning good money thanks to the growing number of job seekers in recent years.

Things were quite different thirty years ago, when most people hold one job all the time. Today, however, it is much harder to find a suitable job. The booming economy has created stark disparity in personal incomes, with some jobs considerably better paid than others. Hence, people change their jobs more often, in the hope of becoming better off with their new employers. What is more, the fierce competitions between business firms also lead to the dismissal of incapable employees. They have no choice but seek another job. All these contribute to the increase in the number of job-hoppers.

Outlined below are some of my suggestions to the young people who desire a successful career. To begin with, it is wise to remember that learning is a life-long process which is not limited to school education. Without constant learning, one may easily fall behind the times. Young people should understand that in addition to knowledge and skills, the ability to learn is also essential to their future development.

Besides, youngsters should get mentally prepared for the possible frustrations they may encounter while hunting for jobs. They may have to change a number of jobs before finding the most suitable one. While everybody is of some value to the society, it takes time for their value to be recognized by the community, or even by themselves. Provided that sustained effort is made, everybody will succeed in one profession or another.

Work is likely to become more demanding, and competition fiercer, but as long as we are fully prepared, the prospect looks good for all of us.

单词注释

- swarm [swɔːm] *v.* 涌往，挤满
- seeker [ˈsiːkə(r)] *n.* 搜索者，探求者
- suitable [ˈsuːtəbl] *adj.* 适当的；相配的
- booming [ˈbuːmɪŋ] *adj.* 急速发展的
- stark [stɑːk] *adj.* 刻板的；十足的
- disparity [dɪsˈpærəti] *n.* 不一致，不同，不等
- considerably [kənˈsɪdərəbli] *adv.* 相当地
- hence [hens] *adv.* 因此；从此
- dismissal [dɪsˈmɪsl] *n.* 免职，解雇
- incapable [ɪnˈkeɪpəbl] *adj.* 无能力的，不能的
- hopper [ˈhɒpə] *n.* 单足跳者
- outline [ˈaʊtlaɪn] *n.* 大纲，轮廓，略图 *vt.* 概述，略述
- mentally [ˈmentəli] *adv.* 精神上，智力上；在内心
- frustration [frʌsˈtreɪʃn] *n.* 挫败，挫折；受挫
- sustained [səsˈteɪnd] *adj.* 持续不变的，相同的
- demanding [dɪˈmɑːndɪŋ] *adj.* 过分要求的，苛求的
- prospect [ˈprɒspekt] *n.* 景色；前景，前途；期望

对于很多年轻人来说，选择一份合适的工作，是个不小的问题。请说明造成这种现象的原因并且给出如何做出正确的决定的建议。

每天都有一千多人涌入南方人才市场(SCES)——广州最大的人才市场之一。他们来到这里与潜在的雇主进行面谈，或者是把简历录入该市场的数据库。仅在广州就有大约十家这样的大型人才市场，当然还有许多小型的。它们都经营得很好，因为近些年来找工作的人越来越多。

仅在三十年前，情况就大不相同。当时，大部分人一辈子就干一份工作。但如今，人们更难找到一份合适的工作了。蓬勃发展的经济带来了巨大的个人收入差距，有些工作的收入大大高于其他工作。所以，人们更频繁地换工作，希望新的工作能带来更好的经济回报。而且，公司之间激烈的竞争常常导致那些能力不够的员工被解雇。他们没有办法，只好另找工作。所有这些因素共同导致了求职者的增加。

下面是我对那些渴望职业成功的年轻人的几点建议。首先，要记住，学习是终生的事情，不仅仅限于学校的学习。如果没有不断的学习，你就很容易落后于时代。年轻人应该明白，除了知识和技能，学习的能力对于他们将来的发展也是很重要的。

另外，年轻人应该做好思想准备，因为在他们求职的过程中难免会有挫折。也许在找到最适合的工作之前，要换好几次工作。尽管每个人对于社会来说，都有自己的价值。但是这种价值要为社会、甚至为自己所发现，都需要一定的时间。只要付出了不懈的努力，每个人都会在某个领域获得成功。

现在的工作对人的要求是越来越高了，竞争也越来越激烈了，但是只要我们做好充分的准备，每个人都会有个美好的前景。

特别提醒

工作问题，是雅思考试的传统话题之一，在近年的雅思考试中出现的频率有所提高。这道作文题所涉及的求职方面的内容，是近年来工作类的话题中雅思考试里出现频率最高的一种。请仔细阅读范文，并留意相关词汇！

推荐指数 ★★★★★　　**相关题目** 1, 13, 44, 71, 95

写作点拨

这道题目要求考生给出“年轻人难以找到合适的工作”的原因，并且给出相关的建议，是典型的“原因＋建议”类雅思作文题。这类文章的写作，最重要的是将重点放在“原因”上而不是“建议”上。范文有别于传统的写作方法，将重点放在了“建议”上。范文分为五段：第一段引入话题；第二段给出年轻人难以找到合适工作的原因；第三、四段从不同方面给出了相关的建议；第五段总结全文。

词汇升级

走

普通版 Each day, over a thousand job hunters *step into* the South China Employment Service, one of the largest placement services in town.

升级版 Each day, over a thousand job hunters *swarm into* the South China Employment Service, one of the largest placement services in town.

走：stroll(闲逛), saunter(漫步), prance(昂首阔步), strut(大摇大摆地走), swagger(昂首阔步), shuffle(拖着脚走), stumble(蹒跚), tramp(重步行走), plod(沉重地走), step(举步), stride(大步走), amble(缓行), swarm(蜂拥)

ESSAY 87

Many parents use punishment to teach their kids the differences between right and wrong. They think punishment is necessary in helping them learn the distinction. To what extent do you agree or disagree with these parents? What kind of punishments would you recommend?

Educating the children is a headache for many young parents. Some of them resort to punishment in order to hammer home some lessons to their kids. As far as I am concerned, while there are numerous other ways to educate a child, punishment is sometimes necessary.

It is true that commendation and incentives in return for good behavior can also help the child distinguish the right from the wrong. Yet by doing so, parents will be sending a misleading message to the kids that wrongdoings do not lead to punishment. Consequently, the kids never learn the lessons. Punishment is preferable because it leaves deep impressions on the wrongdoers. Such is human nature that we all strive to attain happiness in life and avoid pain and suffering; the latter is often the strongest driving force behind our behaviors. As often as not, we are willing to sacrifice happiness simply to minimize our ordeals. Thus punishment is more effective than any other disciplinary approach. Without the deterrent of punishment, the incentive may have little effect because the benefits that kids gain from behaving wrongly can be much more tempting than the award offered by their parents.

Given that punishment is essential in shaping a child's character, how can we do it properly? Physical punishment is out of the question because for one thing, children are too young to take full responsibility for their misbehaviors, for another, punishing children with violence will only lead to more violence, fear and traumas. It must be remembered that the purpose of punishment is not to hurt the kid, but rather, to point out the mistakes and prevent further recurrence or relapse. In fact, there are some kinds of harmless punishment that can carry the lessons home. For example, parents can forbid them to do things they really like such as playing games, watching TV, or going to parties, or make them do some housework like washing the dishes for a month. I believe these types of punishment will touch their soul instead of merely their bodies and thus can be more effective.

单词注释

- distinction [dɪsˈtɪŋkʃn] *n.* 区别，差别；级别；特性
- resort [rɪˈzɔːt] *vi.* 求助，诉诸，采取；常去
- hammer home 反复灌输
- commendation [ˌkɒmenˈdeɪʃn] *n.* 赞扬，称赞
- incentive [ɪnˈsentɪv] *n.* 动机 *adj.* 激励的
- misleading [mɪsˈliːdɪŋ] *adj.* 易误解的，令人误解的
- consequently [ˈkɒnsɪkwəntli] *adv.* 从而；因此
- preferable [ˈprefrəbl] *adj.* 更可取的，更好的，更优越的
- impression [ɪmˈpreʃn] *n.* 印象；感想
- wrongdoer [rɒŋduːə(r)] *n.* 做坏事的人
- as often as not 往往
- ordeal [ɔːˈdiːl] *n.* 严酷的考验，痛苦的经验，折磨
- disciplinary [ˈdɪsəplɪnəri] *adj.* 训练的，训诫的；规律的
- deterrent [dɪˈterənt] *n.* 威慑
- trauma [ˈtrɔːmə] *n.* [医] 外伤，损伤
- recurrence [rɪˈkʌrəns] *n.* 复发，重现；循环
- relapse [rɪˈlæps] *n.* 复发，回复原状

很多父母认为惩罚是帮助小孩明辨是非的必要措施。你是否同意这样的观点？你会推荐使用哪些方式的惩罚？

对于许多年轻父母来说，教育孩子是一件头痛的事情。有些父母诉诸惩罚，以此让孩子记住教训。我认为，尽管有许多教育孩子的方法，有时惩罚的确是必要的。

诚然，对孩子的好行为进行赞扬和激励，也能够让孩子明辨是非。但是，这样的做法会让孩子错误地认为干了坏事也不用受到惩罚。其结果是，孩子总是不会吸取教训。惩罚是必要的，因为只有这样，才能给犯错的孩子留下深刻的印象。人类的天性就是努力追求幸福快乐并避免痛苦，而后者往往是我们行为背后的强大驱动力。我们经常为了减少痛苦而宁可牺牲幸福。因此，惩罚是最有效的训诫方式。如果没有惩罚的威慑，激励机制也起不了多大作用，因为孩子从犯错当中得到的好处往往比父母提供的奖励要更有诱惑。

既然惩罚在塑造孩子的品行方面有重要的作用，那么我们应该如何适当地运用惩罚呢？体罚肯定是不行的。孩子毕竟还小，不应该为自己的不良行为负全责。另外，用暴力方式惩罚孩子，只会导致更多的暴力、恐惧和心灵创伤。必须记住，惩罚孩子的目的并非是要伤害孩子，而是要指出错误、防止再犯。事实上，有些无害的惩罚方式也能让孩子记住教训。比如，父母可以禁止孩子做一些他们很喜欢做的事情，例如玩游戏、看电视、参加派对等；或者让他们做家务，例如洗一个月碗。我相信，这些惩罚方式能触及孩子的内心，而不仅仅是肉体，因而更有效。

特别提醒

儿童教育问题是雅思考试中最热门的话题之一。本书收集了近10道儿童教育方面的雅思写作题，涉及儿童教育的方方面面。请用心整理范文中出现的论据并在考试中适当地借用！

推荐指数 ★★★★★　　**相关题目** 5, 7, 26, 27, 28, 47, 49, 50, 54, 57, 75, 81, 84, 85, 89, 109

写作点拨

这道题目要求考生就“惩罚是否是教育孩子明辨是非的必要方法”发表自己的看法，并且给出自己所推荐的惩罚方式，是典型的“观点＋建议”类雅思作文题。由于题目要求考生给出自己所推荐的惩罚方式，所以考生最好采取正面观点，即同意惩罚是教育孩子明辨是非的必要方法。范文分为三段：第一段在引入话题的同时给出作者的观点，即惩罚的确是必要的；第二段列各种理由来说明惩罚的必要性；第三段给出作者的建议，回答题目的第二个问题。

词汇升级

区别

普通版 It is true that commendation and incentives in return for good behavior can also help the child *tell* the right from the wrong.

升级版 It is true that commendation and incentives in return for good behavior can also help the child *distinguish* the right from the wrong.

ESSAY 88

Some people say that telling the truth is not always essential, and that it is necessary to tell lies sometimes. To what extent do you agree or disagree with this statement? Give specific reasons to support your ideas.

'Liar, liar, pants on fire,' goes an old saying. We have been told not to lie since childhood, but as we grow up, we find that everybody tells lies from time to time. In fact, I believe lies do seem a sensible choice on some occasions.

Some white lies certainly serve some purposes. We all have had experience of toiling at something for a long while but making no apparent progress. What we need in such circumstances is encouragement, which may sometimes come from lies instead of the truth. Take language learning for example. The process of learning a language, especially a foreign language, is a long and arduous one. The learner may often feel that no progress has been made despite all his efforts. If, at this point, someone tells him that his English is much better than before—even though it may not be true—he will soon regain his confidence and continue his learning with a more positive attitude. But if what he hears is the harsh truth—little progress can be seen in his English—chances are that he will soon lose heart and give it up altogether. Thus we see that telling lies can sometimes be beneficial.

Lies may also be told so as to cushion the blow or shield people from harsh realities. It is, for example, often wiser not to tell some terminally ill patients that they are dying in three weeks and nothing could be done to prolong their lives because many would be devastated by the news and even suffer a nervous breakdown, which often leads to further deterioration. 'Ignorance is kind' goes the old saying.

Of course, we should not lie unless absolutely necessary. Before telling untruth, we need to ask ourselves: am I doing this for the sake of other or out of our own consideration? Will others thank us for being so considerate or will they feel betrayed? We need to be very careful about telling lies because nobody enjoys being lied to and dishonesty often ruins long-established relationships.

单词注释

- sensible [ˈsensəbl] *adj.* 有感觉的；明智的
- toil [tɔɪl] *n.* 辛苦，苦工 *vi.* 苦干
- apparent [əˈpærənt] *adj.* 显然的；外观上的
- arduous [ˈɑːdjuəs] *adj.* 费劲的，辛勤的；险峻的
- despite [dɪsˈpaɪt] *prep.* 不管，尽管，不论
- regain [rɪˈgeɪn] *v.* 收回，恢复；重新获得
- confidence [ˈkɒnfɪdəns] *n.* 信心
- positive [ˈpɒzətɪv] *adj.* 肯定的；积极的
- harsh [hɑːʃ] *adj.* 粗糙的；荒芜的；苛刻的
- altogether [ˌɔːltəˈgeðə(r)] *adv.* 完全地，总而言之
- beneficial [ˌbenɪˈfɪʃl] *adj.* 有益的，受益的
- cushion [ˈkʊʃən] *n.* 垫子 *v.* 加衬垫；减缓；保护
- blow [bləʊ] *n.* 殴打，突然的打击
- terminally [ˈtɜːmɪnli] *adv.* 末尾；一定时期地
- prolong [prəˈlɒŋ] *vt.* 延长，拖延
- devastate [ˈdevəsteɪt] *vt.* 毁坏
- breakdown [ˈbreɪkdaʊn] *n.* 崩溃；衰弱
- deterioration [dɪˌtɪəriəˈreɪʃn] *n.* 变坏，退化，堕落
- ignorance [ˈɪgnərəns] *n.* 无知，不知
- untruth [ˌʌnˈtruːθ] *n.* 假话
- considerate [kənˈsɪdərət] *adj.* 考虑周到的
- dishonesty [dɪsˈɒnɪsti] *n.* 不诚实，不老实；欺骗，欺诈

有人认为没必要总是说实话，有些时候我们必须撒谎。你是否同意这样的观点？请给出具体的理由。

常言道：骗子，骗子，火烧裤子。我们从小就被教育不要说谎，但是我们长大后却发现每个人都会时不时地说一些谎话。事实上，我认为在有些时候，谎言是明智的选择。

一些善意的谎言能够起到一些好的作用。我们都有过这样的经历，费尽气力做某件事情，却收效甚微。这时候我们需要的是鼓励，而这种鼓励有时就来自谎言，而不是实话。就拿学外语来说吧。学习外语的过程漫长而艰辛。学习者有时候感到尽管努力，但是没有取得任何成效。如果在这个时候，有人告诉他，他的英语比以前好了很多，尽管这不是真的，但他可能就会重获信心，以一种积极的态度继续学习。但是，如果他听到的是事实——他的英语没什么进步，那么他很可能就会灰心丧气、甚至彻底放弃。所以，我们可以看到，有时候说些谎话也是有好处的。

谎言有时候也可以用来缓冲，或者让人们免受残酷事实的打击。例如，告诉一个病入膏肓的病人，他(她)只能活三个星期了，没有办法延长他(她)的生命了，这样做显然是不明智的。因为很多人在这种情况下都会经不住打击，甚至会崩溃，进而导致病情的进一步恶化。有句古语说得好，“无知是福”。

当然，除非万不得已，我们不要说谎。在说谎之前，我们必须先问问自己：我说谎的原因是为别人考虑，还是为了自己？如果别人发现了，他们会觉得我考虑周到呢，还是觉得我欺骗了他们呢？对于说谎我们必须非常谨慎，因为没有人喜欢被欺骗，谎言经常会毁了深厚的友谊。

特别提醒

近年来，雅思考试中不时出现一些颇有哲学意味的写作题，涉及“什么是幸福”、“什么是成功”等大家经常思考的哲学问题。这道关于人们是否可以撒谎的作文题就曾多次在雅思考试中出现，请特别留意这类“哲学风格”的雅思作文题应该如何展开论述。

推荐指数 ★★★

相关题目 31, 42, 94, 100

写作点拨

这道题目要求考生就“撒谎是否是必要的”发表自己的看法，是典型的观点类雅思作文题。范文采用了最传统的观点类议论文的写作方法。范文分为四段：第一段在引入话题的同时给出作者的观点，即某些时候撒谎的确是必要的；第二、三段列出有些时候的确应该撒谎的理由；第四段重申作者的观点的同时适当地让步，指出除非万不得已，不然还是不要撒谎。

论据积累

有时需要撒谎的理由：

1. 一些善意的谎言能够起到一些好的作用。

   Some white lies certainly serve some purposes.

2. 用谎言来缓冲，或让人免受残酷事实的打击。

   Lies may also be told so as to cushion the blow or shield people from harsh realities.

3. 有些谎言，即使被他人识破了，他们也会觉得我们考虑得很周到。

   Some lies, once detected, lead others to thank us for being so considerate.

ESSAY 89

Some say that students with similar academic abilities should be put in one class. Others believe a class should include students with different academic performances. Discuss.

In most schools students are grouped randomly into classes. No account is taken of their academic performances or personal preferences. This practice has been widely hailed as reflecting the principle of equality. It is also asserted by school authorities that most students benefit from these arrangements.

The class certainly becomes more diversified when students with dissimilar talents are put together. It helps to prevent the classroom from turning into a dull place, where people all have the same predilections and abilities. There is more chance of cooperation among these youngsters because they are often masters in some subjects and laymen in others. They complement each other and often reach win-win solutions by rendering each other help in separate fields. Moreover, such an array of different talents rarely fails to offer new perspectives, which are otherwise unattainable. When a math student sees a circle, he thinks about its diameter and things like that, but an art student would ponder on its symbolic meaning of being a completion.

However, grouping together students with similar proficiency has its unique appeals. It will be easier to meet the needs of all students since they are similarly inclined. The teachers won't have to take into account the receptive ability of each individual and adjust his syllabus and lesson schedule to ensure no one is left behind. This kind of adjustment often leads to lukewarm class participation from top students. Besides, with students performing on the same level, harmony is often guaranteed among students. No one would be jeered at for being obtuse or foolish. Students can easily get along with each other on equal terms.

Neither arrangement can accommodate the needs of all students, and it seems hard to get the best of both worlds. A sensible approach would be to take into account students' academic performance and personality.

单词注释

- randomly [ˈrændəmli] *adv.* 随便地，未加计划地
- hail [heɪl] *vt.* 致敬，招呼
- equality [iˈkwɒləti] *n.* 等同性，同等，平等
- assert [əˈsɜːt] *v.* 断言，声称
- diversified [daɪˈvɜːsɪfaɪd] *adj.* 多变化的，各种的
- dissimilar [dɪˈsɪmɪlə(r)] *adj.* 不同的，相异的
- predilection [ˌpriːdɪˈlekʃn] *n.* 爱好，偏袒
- layman [ˈleɪmən] *n.* 外行
- complement [ˈkɒmplɪment] *vt.* 补助，补足
- render [ˈrendə(r)] *vt.* 呈递；归还；实施
- perspective [pəˈspektɪv] *n.* 远景；前途；看法，观点
- unattainable [ˌʌnəˈteɪnəbl] *adj.* 难到达的，做不到的
- diameter [daɪˈæmɪtə(r)] *n.* 直径
- ponder [ˈpɒndə(r)] *v.* 沉思，考虑
- symbolic [sɪmˈbɒlɪk] *adj.* 象征的；符号的
- proficiency [prəˈfɪʃnsi] *n.* 熟练，精通；熟练程度
- inclined [ɪnˈklaɪnd] *adj.* 倾向…的
- receptive [rɪˈseptɪv] *adj.* 善于接受的，能接纳的
- syllabus [ˈsɪləbəs] *n.* 课程提纲
- lukewarm [ˌluːkˈwɔːm] *adj.* 冷淡的
- harmony [ˈhɑːməni] *n.* 协调，融洽
- jeer [dʒɪə(r)] *v.* 嘲弄，戏弄
- obtuse [əbˈtjuːs] *adj.* 钝的，愚蠢的，迟钝的
- accommodate [əˈkɒmədeɪt] *vi.* 适应
- personality [ˌpɜːsəˈnæləti] *n.* 个性，人格；人物

有人认为我们应该将学习成绩差不多的学生编入同一个班级，其他人却认为同一个班级里应该有各种学习成绩的学生。请讨论这个问题。

在大部分学校，学生都是随机分班的，没有任何成绩和个人偏爱方面的考虑。这一做法得到了广泛的欢迎，因为这反映了平等的原则。而且校方也表示，这样的安排对大部分学生是有好处的。

把具有不同才能的学生聚集到一起，这样定能使班级更具多样性。如果大家的爱好、能力都一样的话，这样的班级势必太沉闷。由于孩子们各自的专长不同，他们合作的机会就更多。他们互补，在不同的领域相互帮助，从而获得双赢的结果。而且，把多种才能的人聚集在一起，还能够提供在其他情况下难以获得的新视角。一个擅长数学的学生看到一个圆，他想到的是这个圆的直径等；但是一个学艺术的学生看到了一个圆，他可能想到的就是圆象征着圆满。

但是，把具有相似才能的学生聚集在一起也有其独特的好处。既然他们有许多相似性，那么就更容易满足他们的要求。老师就不必因为要考虑学生不同的接受能力而调整教学大纲，以保证所有学生都跟得上。这样做的结果往往是那些好学生上课的积极性不高。另外，由于学生水平都差不多，他们之间就更容易建立起和谐的关系。没有人会被嘲笑是愚蠢或迟钝的。学生们能够在平等的基础上和睦相处。

没有哪一种安排能够满足所有学生的需要，很难两全其美。一种合理的办法就是充分考虑学生的学习成绩和个性。

特别提醒

教育问题历来都是雅思写作考试中的热门话题。雅思写作考试中，关于教育的题目大致可以分为三大类：1. 教育的内容（教育应该包含哪些内容、教育应该重点传授职业技能还是人文知识）；2. 教育的方式（混班教学 VS 分班教学，集体学习 VS 单独辅导）；3. 教育的意义（为什么要接受教育）。这道关于学校是否应该混班教学的作文题目，属于第二大类，曾经以不同的形式在雅思写作考试中多次出现。

推荐指数 ★★★★ **相关题目** 5, 7, 26, 27, 28, 47, 49, 50, 54, 57, 75, 81, 84, 85, 87, 109

写作点拨

这道题目要求考生就“学校应该分班教学还是混班教学”这一问题展开讨论，是典型的讨论类雅思作文题。写这类作文时，考生不能仅仅给出自己的观点以及相应的理由，而是应该从正、反两面展开论述，指出正、反两面的合理性。范文分为四段：第一段引入话题，并且亮出作者的观点，即支持混班教学；第二、三段分别介绍了混班教学和分班教学的优点；第四段在总结全文的同时重申了作者的观点。

词汇升级

声称，断言

普通版 It is also *claimed* by school authorities that most students benefit from these arrangements.

升级版 It is also *asserted* by school authorities that most students benefit from these arrangements.

声称，断言：claim, hold out, profess, purport, affirm, allege, assert, asseverate

ESSAY 90

Some say it is impossible for a woman to work full-time and remain a good mother. So they should be paid by the government to stay at home to raise the children. What is your opinion?

Asked to choose from one's family and career, men often pick the latter whereas women opt for the former. Women are often devoted mothers if not wives. Many career women are somewhat estranged from their children. But actually working full-time and being a good mother is not incompatible.

Of course, in child's infancy, the mother needs to be there to feed and care for the baby. As a matter of fact, most companies offer maternity leave of up to one year to female employees. After the first precarious year when even the slightest mistake or negligence on the mother's side might lead to permanent damage to the baby's health or development, mothers can safely entrust their children to a grandparent, a babysitter or a nursery. Actually, compared with first-time mothers, a nursery is better at providing child care because it is often staffed with professional nurses and instructors, whose expertise is unmatched by most mothers.

Being a good mother doesn't mean being there all the time. The amount of time spent with your children is not what counts most; the quality of it is. There is no need to stay with your children all the time; they need to be left alone sometimes and spend time with their pals. Time spent apart may actually bring the mother and the child closer because children after the age of two or three don't often always prefer the company of their mothers; they like to mingle with their peers. Hence, for working mothers, a day care center seems the best place to send their children to.

Mothers are just as entitled to career advancement as fathers. Working mothers have every chance of being good mothers, as proven by countless single mothers who are doing very well working and caring for their children at the same time. Financial and other forms of assistance should be given by the government to all mothers.

单词注释

- opt [ɒpt] *vi.* 选择
- estranged [ɪˈstreɪndʒd] *adj.* 疏远的，不和的
- incompatible [ˌɪnkəmˈpætəbl] *adj.* 性质相反的，矛盾的
- infancy [ˈɪnfənsi] *n.* 幼年
- maternity [məˈtɜːnəti] *n.* 母性 *adj.* 孕妇的，产妇的
- precarious [prɪˈkeəriəs] *adj.* 不稳定的
- negligence [ˈneglɪdʒəns] *n.* 疏忽
- permanent [ˈpɜːmənənt] *adj.* 永久的，持久的
- nursery [ˈnɜːsəri] *n.* 托儿所
- expertise [ˌekspɜˈtiːz] *n.* 专家的意见；专门技术
- unmatched [ˈʌnˈmætʃt] *adj.* 无比的，无匹敌的；不相配的
- mingle [ˈmɪŋgl] *v.* (使)混合
- entitled [ɪnˈtaɪtld] *adj.* 有资格的

有人认为妇女不可能在从事全职工作的同时当一个称职的妈妈，政府应该资助妇女留在家里抚养小孩。请给出你的看法。

如果要在家庭和事业两者中选择一个，男人通常会选后者，而女人则往往选前者。女性即使不是一个尽责的妻子，也往往是一个尽责的母亲。有许多职业女性由于工作的原因疏忽了自己的孩子。但是，职业女性和好母亲这两者并非真的不能相容。

当然，在孩子的婴儿时期，母亲需要喂养孩子。事实上，大部分公司都会给与女员工最多可达一年的产假。在关键的第一年，即使是母亲最微小的失误和忽视，都可能会给孩子的健康和成长造成永久性的伤害。第二年开始，母亲们就可以安全地把孩子交给爷爷奶奶、保姆或者保育院。实际上，对于第一次做母亲的女性来说，保育院更会照看孩子。因为那里的工作人员往往都是经过训练的，他们的专业技能是大部分母亲所不能比拟的。

当一位好母亲并不一定要时时刻刻守在孩子身边。和孩子在一起多长时间并不是最重要的，最重要的是这段时间的质量。没有必要时时刻刻看着孩子，他们有时需要单独待一会儿，有时需要和小伙伴在一起。分开一段时间其实可以使母子(母女)关系更近，因为孩子到了两三岁以后并不都想和妈妈待在一起，他们想和同伴们在一块儿。对于需要工作的母亲来说，托儿所是一个很好的选择。

母亲们也和父亲们一样，有追求事业的权利。无数事实证明，工作的母亲同样也可以是一位好母亲。尤其是有许多单亲母亲在照顾好孩子的同时，事业也发展得很好。政府应给所有母亲提供经济和其他方面的帮助。

特别提醒

职业妇女的问题，是近年来雅思写作考试中新出现的话题，在移民类的考试中出现的频率较高。这道关于职业妇女是否能同时当个好妈妈的写作题，多次以不同的形式在雅思写作考试中出现，请认真阅读范文并适当借鉴。

推荐指数 ★★★　　**相关题目** 33, 58, 61, 92, 105, 112

写作点拨

这道题目要求考生就“职业妇女是否能同时当个好妈妈”给出自己的观点，是典型的观点类雅思作文题。范文采取了最正统的议论文写作方法，全文分为四段：第一段开门见山给出观点，即职业妇女也可能是个好妈妈；第二、三段分别阐述了职业妇女可以成为称职的母亲的两个原因；第四段总结全文，同时重申作者的观点。

词汇升级

享有…权利

普通版 Mothers *have the same right for* career advancement as fathers do.

升级版 Mothers *are just as entitled to* career advancement as fathers.

享有…权利：be entitled to, enjoy the right to, be empowered to, be authorized to

ESSAY 91

Your character is strongly influenced by the place where you grew up. In what ways can growing up in a city or in the countryside influence one's character? Please give your view.

Where you are dropped, as the saying goes, is who you are. Though possessing individuality, people often share some collective traits unique to the place where they live. The English are known for being conservatives; the French for being romantic; the Italian, optimistic. Places make people.

Growing up in the countryside helps to cultivate one's self-reliance. Infrastructure and public service being inadequate, rural residents often do things for themselves. It is not uncommon to see them fix their own cars, mend fences or even build their own houses. Self-dependence grows out of necessity into a habit. Compared with city dwellers, people from the countryside are less ambitious as a result of the slower pace of life. There is no rival business to compete with, no constant fear of losing your job. You only focus on the land, the crops and the harvest. It is a simpler, less complicated life. But there is also a downside. A rural life often leads to provincialism. Villagers tend to become conservative and biased because they seldom mingle with people from all walks of life. Change seems to them unnecessary and threatening; they prefer to do things the old way.

People raised in a city are often competitive and ambitious. They have been engaged in competitions with their peers since an early age: vying with others to enter a better school, scrambling for a better seat on the bus, striving to get a promotion. To survive and get ahead in the generally overcrowded cities, they must be aggressive or at least assertive. Money and fame mean a lot to them. And due to this kind of constant struggle, they are prone to selfishness and snobbishness. They are compelled to look out for their own interest first and then maybe that of others. The disparity in income and position reinforces people's class consciousness. The upper class, that is the rich and powerful, are respected; the lower class are often despised, inwardly at least. Seeing phony beggars on the roadside every day, most people are hardened into indifference.

These generalizations are accurate only to certain degrees. People's character can be attributed to many factors, the environment being only one of them. Our conscious efforts can make the biggest difference. As the saying goes, we are molded by our own hands.

单词注释

- individuality [ˌɪndɪˌvɪdʒuˈæləti] *n.* 个性，个人的特性
- trait [treɪt] *n.* 显著的特点，特性
- optimistic [ˌɒptɪˈmɪstɪk] *adj.* 乐观的
- reliance [rɪˈlaɪəns] *n.* 信任，信心；依靠
- infrastructure [ˈɪnfrstrʌktʃə(r)] *n.* 基础设施
- dweller [ˈdwelə(r)] *n.* 居住者，居民
- rival [ˈraɪvl] *v.* 竞争，对抗，相匹敌
- downside [ˈdaʊnsaɪd] *n.* 不利的方面
- provincialism [prəˈvɪnʃlɪzəm] *n.* 地方风尚
- vie [vaɪ] *v.* 竞争
- scramble [ˈskræmbl] *vi.* 攀缘；争夺
- assertive [əˈsɜːtiv] *adj.* 断定的；过分自信的
- prone [prəʊn] *adj.* 倾向于
- snobbishness [ˈsnɒbɪʃnəs] *n.* 势利
- disparity [dɪˈspærəti] *n.* 不一致，不同，不等
- reinforce [ˌriːɪnˈfɔːs] *vt.* 加强；增援；补充
- consciousness [ˈkɔnʃəsnəs] *n.* 意识，知觉；自觉，觉悟
- despise [dɪsˈpaɪz] *vt.* 轻视
- inwardly [ˈɪnwədli] *adv.* 在内部地；思想上，本质上
- phony [ˈfəʊni] *adj.* 假冒的 *n.* 假冒者
- indifference [ɪnˈdɪfrəns] *n.* 不关心
- generalization [ˌdʒenərəlaɪˈzeɪʃn] *n.* 一般化，概括；广义性
- mold [məʊld] *n.* 模子，铸型 *vt.* 浇铸，塑造

一个人的性格在很大程度上会受到成长的环境的影响。在城市或是农村长大会对一个人的个性产生什么影响呢？请阐述你的看法。

常言道：一方水土养一方人。尽管每个人都有自己的个性，但一个地方的人通常都会有一些这个地方所特有的特质。英国人很保守，法国人很浪漫，意大利人很乐观等。环境造就人。

在农村长大的人自力更生的能力强。由于缺乏基础设施和公共服务，农村居民什么都靠自己。自己修车辆，自己建围墙，甚至自己盖房子。条件所限，有必要自力更生，后来这种必要成为了一种习惯。和城市居民相比，因为生活节奏的缓慢，农村居民更满足于现状。在农村，你不必担心有生意上的对手和你竞争，不必总是担心失业。你只要管好你的田地、庄稼和收成就行了。这样的生活更简单、朴素。但是，这也有它不好的一面。农村生活容易导致地方主义。村民们往往很保守，而且有偏见，因为他们很少和各行各业的人交往。变化对他们来说是不必要的，甚至是危险的。他们喜欢墨守成规。

城市里长大的人则更具竞争意识和野心。他们从小就和同伴竞争：上学要竞争才能进入一所好的学校，坐公车要争一个好位子，工作要争取升职等。城市通常都人满为患，为了生存和出人头地，你必须要有闯劲，至少要充分自信。城市的人们太看重名利。由于经常性的竞争，使得人变得自私和势利。他们总是先考虑自己的利益，然后才是别人的。收入和地位的差异，使得城市人的阶层意识明显。上流社会，即那些有钱有权的人，普遍受到尊重。下层人群则经常受到蔑视。表面上可能没有表露出来，但至少在心里是这样的。天天看到那些假乞丐，大多数人的心也变得越来越冷漠了。

上面的归纳，只在一定程度上成立。人们的性格形成受到很多因素的影响，环境只是其中的一个。我们的主观努力所起的作用最大。俗话说：命运掌握在我们自己手中。

特别提醒

成长环境对一个人的影响，是近年来雅思写作考试中新出现的话题；农村和城市的比较，却是雅思写作考试中最传统的话题之一。这道关于农村和城市的成长背景对人的个性的影响的写作题，其采用的论据别出一格。请认真阅读这篇范文并适当留意当中出现的论据。

推荐指数 ★★★

相关题目 37, 74

写作点拨

这道题目要求考生就“农村和城市的成长背景对人的个性的影响”展开论述，是典型的论述类雅思作文题。切记，这类文章一定要讨论题目所给出的正反双方的利弊，而不能仅仅就其中一方展开论述。范文分为四段：第一段引入话题；第二、三段分别阐述了农村和城市对人的个性的影响；第四段总结全文，同时指出环境对人的影响终究是有限的。

句型升级

普通版 The English are known for being conservatives; the French are known for being romantic; the Italians are known for being optimistic.

升级版 The English is known for being conservatives; the French for being romantic; the Italian, optimistic.

注释：在并列句中，各个句子中重复出现的部分可以省略，从而让语言更加简洁和地道。

ESSAY 92

Many people believe that women make better parents than men and that is why they have greater role in raising children in most societies. Others claim that men are just as good as women at parenting. State your point of view.

Women are thought to be better parents, but nowadays many daughters are closer to their fathers. To me, this is not the result of Electra complex but because males can also excel at parenting.

It must be admitted that women are generally better parents. This has something to do with their disposition. Women are usually caring, gentle and patient. Their special bond with the children often cannot be understood by men. Their better verbal and communication skills also help to endear them to the children, especially when they are young. So it is easy for a mother to outdo her husband at raising children. However, their victory is not always guaranteed.

Men can also be tender and loving. They often entertain deep affection towards their kids though they may not show it in an explicit way. They may seem cold, strict and uncaring, but when they are really understood, they gain kids' love and respect. Unlike a mother's love which is tender and profuse, a father's love is subtle and profound. The time spent between a father and his children may be brief but productive, and often involves some heart-to-heart talk about work, people and life.

In fact, male influence is essential but sometimes lacking because fathers are often busy supporting the family. Kids raised by a single mother often suffer from a lack of confidence. They often feel insecure. The courage and hardiness of a father can nourish similar traits in a child.

Fathers are often not very much involved in raising children because of their work. In fact, they are just as capable of becoming good parents. They can often exert a unique influence on their children.

单词注释

- Electra complex 恋父情结
- disposition [ˌdɪspəˈzɪʃən] *n.* 气质，性情
- caring [ˈkerɪŋ] *adj.* 关心的，有同情心的
- verbal [ˈvɜːbl] *adj.* 口头的
- endear [ɪnˈdɪə(r)] *vt.* 使亲密，使受钟爱
- outdo [ˌaʊtˈduː] *v.* 胜过
- explicit [ɪksˈplɪsɪt] *adj.* 外在的，清楚的；直率的
- profuse [prəˈfjuːs] *adj.* 极其丰富的
- subtle [ˈsʌtl] *adj.* 微妙的，不易察觉的
- profound [prəˈfaʊnd] *adj.* 深刻的，意义深远的
- confidence [ˈkɒnfɪdəns] *n.* 信心
- insecure [ˌɪnsɪˈkjʊə(r)] *adj.* 无保障的，不安全的
- hardiness [ˈhɑːdɪnəs] *n.* 耐久力；顽强
- nourish [ˈnʌrɪʃ] *vt.* 滋养；培养

很多人认为女性比男性更擅长抚养孩子，这也正是为什么在大多数社会里，女性都在抚养孩子方面发挥最主要作用的原因；别的人却认为男性和女性抚养孩子的能力应该是一样的。请给出你的观点。

人们往往认为女性更善于抚育孩子，但其实如今很多女儿却和父亲更加亲近。我认为这不是因为"恋父情结"，而是因为男性在抚育子女方面同样出色。

必须承认女性往往更善于为人家长，这与她们的性情有关。女性往往温柔、体贴、有耐心。她们与子女的特殊联系往往令男性难以理解。女性的语言、交流能力均超过男性，容易亲近子女，尤其是在孩子们小的时候。因此，母亲在养育子女方面往往更加出色。但是，情况也并不总是这样。

男性也同样会温柔体贴。他们往往对子女怀有深切的感情，虽然很少直接表露出来。父亲们表面上似乎冷漠、严格、不关心子女，但是当子女真正理解父亲之后，他们会对父亲倍加敬爱。母亲的爱温柔而缠绵，父亲的爱含蓄而深沉。父亲同子女接触的机会可能不多，但是他们之间往往可以真心交流，畅谈工作、社会及生活。

实际上，父亲在子女成长过程中的地位十分重要，虽然父亲往往会因忙于养家糊口而没有太多时间照顾孩子。单亲母亲抚养的子女往往缺乏自信，没有安全感。父亲的勇气和坚毅往往能给子女培养出同样的品格。

由于工作的原因，父亲往往没有太多的时间教育孩子。实际上，他们同样可以成为好家长。他们对子女的影响是非常特殊的。

特别提醒

男女分工的问题，是近年来雅思写作考试中新出现的话题，在移民类的考试中出现的频率较高。这道关于男女谁更擅长抚养孩子的作文题目，曾经以不同的形式在雅思写作考试中多次出现，请认真阅读范文！

推荐指数 ★★★　　**相关题目** 33, 58, 61, 90, 105, 112

写作点拨

这道题目要求考生就"男性与女性谁更擅长抚养孩子"给出自己的观点，是典型的观点类雅思作文题。范文采取了最正统的议论文写作方法，全文分为五段：第一段开门见山给出观点，即男性也擅长抚养孩子；第二段为让步段；第三、四段分别阐述了男性也擅长抚养孩子的各种理由；第五段总结全文，同时重申作者的观点。

词汇升级

胜过，超过

普通版 To me, this is not the result of Electra complex but because males can also *do a better job* at parenting.

升级版 To me, this is not the result of Electra complex but because males can also *excel* at parenting.

胜过，超过：surpass, outdo, excel

ESSAY 93

There are lots of difficulties for the new students on the first day in a high school or college because they feel lonely. What are the difficulties they may face on the first day? What can the school or college do to solve these problems?

It is always hard to adapt to new environments. Children often have to be cajoled to spend their first day in elementary school. Even for high school or college students, the first day at school can still be a problem. Only a few can pass that day totally undisturbedly.

There is a lot to do on the first day. They must get registered, find their dorms, check out the class schedule and so on. These tasks can be exhausting because there are always queues to stand in. Being unfamiliar with the campus, those freshmen would have trouble finding their way around. Even with the help of parents, most of them take several days just to settle down.

Apart from those physical challenges, there are psychological ones. Loneliness is always experienced during the first few days. Having no friends, those freshmen will actually feel lonely. And this feeling is intensified by their unfamiliarity with the place. Everything seems strange to them. The more optimistic ones would set out to explore a bit, while others keep to themselves and begin to think about their old friends and schools.

Most of them are further troubled by a sense of uncertainty. Any change is likely to bring fear and worry. We are used to the old ways and naturally resent any alteration. Those students don't know if they can get along with their classmates or whether they can do well academically. They long for a better tomorrow but fear it will turn out worse than yesterday.

Those problems are natural but not unavoidable. Something can be done by the school as well as the students. It will make a great difference if the school can simplify the registration procedure and provide better orientation programs. Students can dispel their loneliness and get to know each other if the school can arrange some activities for each class.

单词注释

- adapt [əˈdæpt] *vt.* 使适应
- cajole [kəˈdʒəul] *vt.* 以甜言蜜语哄骗
- undisturbedly [ˌʌndɪˈstɜːbdli] *adv.* 没受到干扰地，安静地
- registered [ˈredʒɪstəd] *adj.* 已注册的，已登记的
- dorm [dɔːm] *n.* 宿舍(=dormitory)
- queue [kjuː] *n.* 行列，队列；长队
- psychological [ˌsaɪkəˈlɒdʒɪkl] *adj.* 心理(上)的
- intensify [ɪnˈtensɪfaɪ] *vt.* 加强 *vi.* 强化
- optimistic [ˌɒptɪˈmɪstɪk] *adj.* 乐观的
- resent [rɪˈzent] *v.* 愤恨，怨恨
- alteration [ˌɔːltəˈreɪʃən] *n.* 变更，改变
- academically [ˌækəˈdemɪkli] *adv.* 学术上，学理上
- unavoidable [ˈʌnəˈvɔɪdəbl] *adj.* 不可避免的
- procedure [prəˈsiːdʒə(r)] *n.* 程序，手续
- orientation [ˌɔːriənˈteɪʃn] *n.* 方向，方位；定位
- dispel [dɪˈspel] *vt.* 驱散，驱逐，使消散

很多学生在高中或大学入学的第一天会感到很寂寞，同时也会遇到很多问题。学生们第一天会遇到什么问题？学校应该采取什么措施来解决这些问题？

适应新环境总是很不容易。在小学一年级开学的第一天，家长往往要哄着孩子去学校。即便是对中学生或大学生而言，开学第一天也不是总那么顺利的。只有少数学生能够若无其事，“安然度过”开学第一天。

开学第一天的事情总是特别多。学生得去登记，找寝室，拿课表等等。几项下来学生往往就累坏了，因为每个地方都需要排队。由于不熟悉校园，他们往往很难找到路。即便有父母的帮忙，大部分人也往往要折腾几天才能安顿下来。

除了这些身体方面的挑战以外，学生还可能出现心理上的不适应。大部分新生在头几天都会感到非常寂寞，因为他们刚到学校，谁也不认识。人生地不熟，一切都显得很陌生。乐观的学生可能会出去逛逛，熟悉一下地形。其他的人则会待在寝室里，想念他们以前的朋友和学校。

大部分学生还会感到前途未卜。任何变化总是会带来一些恐惧和焦虑。人们习惯了旧的方式，往往会抵触任何变动。新生们不知道自己能不能和其他同学和睦相处，能不能把功课学好。他们希望明天会更好，但是又害怕光景会每况愈下。

这些问题非常自然，但并非不可避免。学生和校方都可以采取一定的措施。如果学校简化报名程序，提供更多的入校培训，那么情况将大为好转。如果学校组织各班同学参加集体活动，学生们就可以增进彼此的了解，消除寂寞。

特别提醒

教育问题历来都是雅思写作考试中的热门话题。雅思写作考试中，关于教育的题目大致可以分为三大类：1. 教育的内容（教育应该包含哪些内容；教育应该重点传授职业技能还是人文知识）；2. 教育的方式（混班教学 VS 男、女校；集体学习 VS 单独辅导）；3. 教育的意义（为什么要接受教育）。这道关于新生入学第一天会遇到哪些困难的作文题，并不属于上述三大常见的教育类作文题。因此，请特别留意这篇范文！

推荐指数 ★★★★

相关题目 2, 6, 14, 24, 43, 44, 49, 65, 68

写作点拨

这道题目要求考生就“新生入学第一天会遇到哪些困难”展开讨论，并且指出学校应该采取的措施，是典型的“叙述＋建议”类雅思作文题。范文分为五段：第一段引入话题；第二、三、四段分别介绍了新生入学第一天会遇到的各种困难；第五段指出了学校应该采取的措施，回答了题目中的第二个问题。

词汇升级

适应

普通版 It is always hard to *get used to* new environments.

升级版 It is always hard to *adapt to* new environments.

适应：adapt to, acclimatize oneself to, be seasoned with, accommodate oneself to

ESSAY 94

Some people think that their children's life will be different from their own. What is your opinion?

Things are constantly changing. Our life is no exception. It has been changing since our ancestors first walked the earth, and the pace is accelerating. The last two centuries has brought more changes to our life than all other centuries put together. However, that claim rather depends on what kind of change is being discussed.

Many elements of life remain constant throughout the history. Our children will still be attending school; they will still be working full-time after graduation; they will still be getting married and having kids. Our moral sense and value system will not change much in the near future. The political system is not likely to alter much when our children become adults. In some sense, life will be more or less the same.

However, some form of change is inevitable and often welcomed. The life of the children rarely resembles that of the parents because they often have different professions and place of residence. In China, for example, many people manage to move to the cities from the countryside, thus leading a rather different life from their parents. Besides, the level of education also determines our lifestyle. As a general rule, children are often better educated than their parents.

Apart from these specific reasons for a change in life, there are general ones. Scientific and technological advance will change our life in ways hard to predict now. One hundred years ago, no one could have envisaged the spread of the Internet. Likewise, even the most gifted science fiction writer can only guess what tomorrow will bring. Only change itself is guaranteed.

Life is going to change a lot externally, but internally it will remain pretty much the same. Any attempts to predict the future will be futile. But one thing is certain, that is, the future is in our hands.

单词注释

- exception [ɪkˈsepʃn] *n.* 除外，例外
- ancestor [ˈænsɪstə] *n.* 祖先，祖宗
- accelerate [ækˈseləreɪt] *v.* 加速，促进，催化
- moral [ˈmɒrəl] *adj.* 道德(上)的，精神的
- inevitable [ɪnˈevɪtəbl] *adj.* 不可避免的，必然的
- resemble [rɪˈzembl] *vt.* 像，类似
- residence [ˈrezɪdəns] *n.* 居住；住处
- envisage [ɪnˈvɪzɪdʒ] *v.* 想像，设想
- guarantee [ˌɡærənˈtiː] *vt.* 保证，担保
- externally [eksˈtɜːnli] *adv.* 外表上，外形上
- internally [ɪnˈtənəli] *adv.* 在内；在中心
- predict [prɪˈdɪkt] *v.* 预知，预言，预报
- futile [ˈfjuːtaɪl] *adj.* 无用的，无效果的

有人认为自己子孙的生活将会和自己的生活不一样。请给出你的看法。

世界无时无刻不在变化，我们的生活也不例外。从古至今，我们的生活在不断地改变，并且，变化速度不断加剧，上两个世纪的改变超过以前所有世纪改变的总和。但是，我们对改变的看法取决于我们的视角。

生活中的一些因素亘古不变。我们的孩子还是要上学；他们毕业以后还是要参加工作；他们还是要结婚生子。我们的道德体系和价值体系在不久的将来也不会有太大的变化。当我们的孩子长大成人时，政治体系也不大可能改变。在一定意义上来说，生活将保持不变。

然而，另外一些变化往往是不可避免的，也是为人所欢迎的。孩子们的生活往往都不同于其父母，因为他们的职业、住所往往不同。以中国为例，很多农村的孩子走进城市，开始了全新的生活，他们的生活自然与其父母大相径庭。此外，教育水平也决定了人们的生活方式。一般来说，子女受教育的程度都高于他们的父母。

除了这些个人的原因以外，还有一些社会的原因也导致我们生活的改变。科技的进步给我们带来的影响难以估量。一百年前，没有人能够想像全球互联网会如此普及。同样，即便是最有天赋的科幻小说家对未来世界的面貌也只能是加以猜测。我们可以肯定的只有变化本身。

我们的物质生活变化很大，但是我们的精神生活仍相对恒定。预测未来往往是徒劳的，但是我们可以肯定的是：未来掌握在我们自己手中。

特别提醒

未来生活的变化，是近年来雅思写作考试中的新话题，在考试中出现的频率并不是很高。在雅思写作考试中，这道作文题目出现的可能性非常小，所以请特别留意这道题目！

推荐指数 ★★★

相关题目 31, 42, 88, 100

写作点拨

这道题目要求考生就“下一代的生活是否会和自己的生活不一样”给出自己的观点，是典型的观点类雅思作文题。范文中加入了让步段，因此有别于最传统的观点类议论文的写作方法，全文分为五段：第一段引入话题；第二段为让步段，指出生活中的一些部分是不会发生改变的；第三、四段例举各方面的理由，强有力地证明下一代的生活的确会和我们自己的生活不一样；第五段在总结全文的同时重申作者的观点。

词汇升级

无用的，徒劳的

普通版 Any attempts to predict the future will be *useless*.

升级版 Any attempts to predict the future will be *futile*.

无用的，徒劳的：useless, bootless, in vain, unsuccessful, ineffective, fruitless

ESSAY 95

Today some people have to work away from their family. What are the advantages and disadvantages?

For most people, sacrifices have to be made in order to do jobs. To earn a living, we force ourselves to stick to dull jobs. To keep our position, we do what is required and go wherever needs to be. It is common for people to leave their families and work elsewhere.

People become more concentrated on their work when they are away from home. Apart from making a few calls to make sure everything is all right, one is not distracted by the day-to-day family concerns. There won't be any kid nagging him to play basketball together or any wife demanding some quality time together. Having no family members to spend time with, one often stays longer at the workplace and gives more thought to his work at hand. Moreover, this kind of separation from one's family often motivates him to excel at work in the hope of ending this separation by getting a promotion or a transfer. The desire to be reunited with one's spouse or kids can be a strong incentive for better job performance.

However, while enjoying better performance at work, those working apart from their family are subject to attacks of loneliness. When the work is done, they often return to their empty apartment alone, with no loved ones to greet or open the door for them. Spending time with friends can only slightly alleviate their nostalgia, which can be trying from time to time. To combat nostalgia, most people turn to work. They put in longer hours and stay at the office on weekends. Gradually, they become workaholic. This, we should note, is rather innocuous compared with other possible consequences of long-term separation. Living in separate places for a stretched period of time is likely to cause family crisis. Without proper management, distance often leads to alienation. This is true for husbands and wives as well as parents and kids. As time goes by, their feelings toward each other gradually fade; they begin turning to someone else for solace.

Whenever possible we should avoid working away from home. For those unfortunate enough to work this way, more attention should be given to maintaining family ties instead of reaching career goals.

单词注释

- concentrated [ˈkɒnsentreɪtɪd] *adj.* 全力以赴的
- distracted [dɪsˈtræktɪd] *adj.* 心烦意乱的
- nagging [ˈnægɪŋ] *adj.* 唠叨的 *n.* 唠叨
- separation [sepəˈreɪʃn] *n.* 分离，分开
- reunite [ˈriːjuːˈnaɪt] *v.* (使)再结合
- spouse [spaʊz] *n.* 配偶(指夫或妻)
- incentive [ɪnˈsentɪv] *n.* 激励
- alleviate [əˈlɪːvieɪt] *vt.* 使易于忍受；减轻
- nostalgia [nɒsˈtældʒə] *n.* 思乡，乡愁
- workaholic [ˌwɜːkəˈhɒlɪk] *n.* 工作狂，工作迷
- innocuous [iˈnɒkjuəs] *adj.* 无害的，无伤大雅的
- stretch [stretʃ] *v.* 延续；伸长
- alienation [ˌeɪliəˈneɪʃn] *n.* 疏远
- solace [ˈsɒləs] *n.* 安慰，慰藉

如今，很多人要离开家庭去外地工作。请指出这种工作形式的利弊。

大部分人往往都要为了工作而做出一些牺牲。为了维持生计，我们强迫自己从事无聊的工作。为了保住职位，我们东奔西走，竭尽全力。如今很多人都背井离乡到外地工作。

在外地工作可以让人全心投入工作。在外地工作的人平时只是给家里打打电话，得知一切安好之后便不再为家庭日常事务分心。孩子们不会缠着他们要求一起打篮球，妻子也不会要求他们共度好时光。由于不用花时间陪伴家人，他们往往会延长工作时间，对工作中的问题多加思考。而且，和家人分居往往促使他们更加努力工作，争取事业获得升迁或调动，早日和家人团聚。这种激励往往让他们工作更加出色。

然而，虽然工作业绩有所提高，异乡工作的人往往会感到孤独。下班以后，他们独自回到空荡荡的住所，没有亲人给他们开门。同朋友聚会也往往于事无补，思乡之情总会时时袭来。为了避免思乡，很多人转向工作。他们大量地加班，甚至周末也不回去。他们逐渐变成工作狂。成为工作狂还是小事，长期分居还有可能带来更多的问题。长期分居可能导致家庭危机。如果处理不当，距离会带来隔阂。夫妻之间、父母子女之间皆是如此。随着时间的推移，彼此间的感情会渐渐淡化；双方都会开始向第三方寻求慰藉。

可能的情况下，我们都应该避免去异地工作。对于那些没有办法非去不可的人来说，他们应该加倍重视家庭关系的维护，而不仅是事业上的成就。

特别提醒

关于工作的写作题，是近几年雅思考试的大热门。本篇作文就在2007年的雅思考试中出现过。本书收集了许多与工作有关的作文题目，请认真参考并适当练笔！

推荐指数 ★★★★

相关题目 1, 13, 44, 71, 86

写作点拨

这道题目要求考生叙述离开家到外地工作的利弊，是典型的利弊叙述类雅思作文题。范文使用了利弊叙述类作文题最传统的写法，全文分为四段：第一段引入话题；第二段叙述离开家到外地工作的有利之处；第三段叙述其弊端；第四段在总结全文的同时提出作者的建议。

词汇升级

令人难受的，令人烦恼的

普通版 Spending time with friends can only slightly alleviate their nostalgia, which can be *annoying* from time to time.

升级版 Spending time with friends can only slightly alleviate their nostalgia, which can be *trying* from time to time.

令人难受的，令人烦恼的：wretched, irksome, annoying, distressing, afflictive, pathetic

ESSAY 96

Foods are produced more cheaply today by using improved fertilizers and machinery. However, some of the methods used in agriculture are dangerous to human health and local communities. To what extent do you agree or disagree with this view?

The way we produce and preserve food is becoming increasingly efficient. In developed countries, only two percent of the population is engaged in agriculture, yet they are able to feed the entire nation. However, this kind of technology-intensive agriculture also has its side effects.

The extensive use of pesticides and other chemicals poses alarming health threats. Needless to say, pesticides are poisons strong enough to kill pests but supposedly safe enough to be swallowed by men. But, it is not actually the case. Even after we banned the use of evidently noxious chemicals such as DDT, those commonly used pesticides still send thousands of people to hospitals each year. There is no such a thing as an edible pesticide. That is why we should always wash before eating any fresh vegetable or fruit. However, not all pesticides are soluble to water. So, good luck!

Other more insidious effects are emerging recently. Scientists have established the correlation between the declined fertility rate and the use of fertilizer. It turns out that fertilizer and fodder contain certain hormones that are largely responsible for the increased infertility rate among men. In addition, those hormones also lead to precocity. The potential health threats posed by some novel food technologies such as genetically engineered food are hard to determine.

Large-scale farming is becoming unsustainable because it is not energy efficient and damages the environment. Farm machines consume huge amount of gasoline or diesel each year. This accelerates the depletion of unrenewable energy sources. Furthermore, like other vehicles, farm machines cause pollution. The rivers, forests and air are being polluted by the fuel-burning machines on farms.

As far as food is concerned, quantity should not be the only thing we aim at. Sadly, we are producing ever larger amount of junk food each year. Modern faming methods need to be closely examined and improved because our health is at stake here.

单词注释

- preserve [prɪˈzɜːv] *vt.* 保存，保持
- intensive [ɪnˈtensɪv] *adj.* 密集的
- extensive [ɪksˈtensɪv] *adj.* 广大的，广泛的
- pesticide [ˈpestɪsaɪd] *n.* 杀虫剂
- supposedly [səˈpəʊzdli] *adv.* 据说，据传
- swallow [ˈswɒləʊ] *vt.* 咽 *vi.* 吞下，咽下
- noxious [ˈnɒkʃəs] *adj.* 有害的
- edible [ˈedɪbl] *adj.* 可食用的
- soluble [ˈsɒljəbl] *adj.* 可溶的，可溶解的
- insidious [ɪnˈsɪdiəs] *adj.* 潜在的，隐状的
- correlation [ˌkɒrəˈleɪʃn] *n.* 相互关系，相关(性)
- fertility [fəˈtɪləti] *n.* 可生育性
- fertilizer [ˈfɜːtəlaizə(r)] *n.* 肥料
- fodder [ˈfɒdə] *n.* 饲料，草料
- hormone [ˈhɔːməʊn] *n.* 荷尔蒙，激素
- infertility [ˌɪnfəˈtɪləti] *n.* 不肥沃；不育
- precocity [prɪˈkɒsɪti] *n.* 早熟，早成
- novel [ˈnɒvəl] *adj.* 新奇的
- unsustainable [ˌʌnsəˈsteɪnəbl] *adj.* 不能持续的，无法维持的
- diesel [ˈdiːzl] *n.* 柴油
- depletion [dɪˈpliːʃn] *n.* 损耗
- unrenewable [ˌʌnrɪˈnjuːəbl] *adj.* 不可更新的
- junk [dʒʌŋk] *n.* 垃圾

化学肥料和机械化生产让食物的成本大为下降，然而，农业中一些方法的使用却对人体健康以及当地的生态环境造成了很大的危害。你是否同意这样的说法？

人们生产以及保存食物的方法变得日益高效。在很多发达国家，从事农业生产的人口只占总人口的百分之二，但是却可以养活整个国家。然而，这种技术密集型农业也并非百利而无害。

大量使用杀虫剂及其他化学品严重危害着人们的健康。显而易见，杀虫剂就是那些能够杀死害虫但据说又对人体无害的化学品。但事实并非如此。在禁止使用 DDT 等强毒性的杀虫剂之后，杀虫剂的使用还是导致每年有很多人住院。根本就没有什么“无害杀虫剂”。这就是为什么我们在吃水果和蔬菜的时候要先洗一洗。不幸的是，并不是所有杀虫剂都能溶于水。祝你好运！

其他一些潜在的危害最近也浮出了水面。科学家们已经证实了生育率下降和化肥的使用有联系。原来，化肥、饲料里含有的某些激素导致了男性不育现象的增加。而且，那些激素还会导致儿童早熟。新的食品技术如转基因技术所带来的健康问题目前还难以确定。

大规模的农业变得不可持续发展，因为能源的利用效率不高，并且有害环境。农场机器设备每年都要消耗大量的汽油或柴油，加速了不可再生能源的枯竭。而且，和其他车辆一样，农场机器也会带来污染。它们会污染河流、森林和空气。

就食物而言，数量不是我们追求的唯一目标。不幸的是，我们的垃圾食品产量连年上升。我们应该好好地审视和提高现代农业技术，因为这关系到我们的健康。

特别提醒

食品是雅思写作考试中的传统话题之一。食品类的雅思作文题，大致可以分为食品生产方式、食品种类的选择以及传统食物的保护三大类。这篇作文就属于第一大类。食品类的雅思作文中的很多观点，完全可以用在很多其他话题的雅思作文中。请认真阅读范文并适当归纳其中的英文表达！

推荐指数 ★★★　　**相关题目** 10

写作点拨

这道题目要求考生就“化学肥料和机械化生产是否对人体健康以及生态环境造成了很大的危害”给出自己的观点，是典型的观点类雅思作文题。范文使用了最传统的观点类议论文写作方法，全文分为五段：第一段引入话题并给出作者的观点，即支持题目的看法；第二、三、四段指出化学肥料和机械化生产对人体健康以及生态环境所造成的各种危害；第五段总结全文。

词汇升级

影响

普通版 Other *negative effects* are emerging recently.

升级版 Other *insidious effects* are emerging recently.

effect（影响）：adverse（不利的），catastrophic（灾难的），crippling（有害的），debilitating（削弱力量的），deleterious（有害的），destructive（破坏性的），detrimental（有害的），devastating（破坏性的），traumatic（伤害性的），domino（连锁反应）

ESSAY 97

Many old buildings are protected by law because they are part of a nation's history. However, some people think they should be knocked down to make way for new ones because people need houses and offices. How important is it to maintain old buildings? Should history stand in the way of progress?

For countries with a long history there is always some conflict between the new and the old. In cities in particular, buildings are constantly torn down and replaced with higher ones so as to accommodate the ever increasing population. Unfortunately, many historic buildings become victims of these development projects.

Demolishing old buildings often leads to irreparable loss. Architecture from the past is often linked with certain historic events, the description of which may sometimes be found in history books. But our understanding of such episodes would be greatly improved by visiting the tangible remnants from the past. Buildings are part of the legacy bestowed by our ancestors to whom we show our respect by preserving their constructions. Once torn down, those legacies are gone for ever.

Besides, most ancient buildings are of great artistic and aesthetic value. The sheer fact that they have stood the vicissitudes of centuries says something about its building technique. Indeed, the construction method of the Pyramid and the Great Wall has baffled modern architects. Many of the art works inside those buildings fill people with wonder and attract tourists from around the globe. The grandeur of those buildings is still unsurpassed today.

Actually, the old and the new need not be in mortal conflict. They can co-exist in harmony. Of course, those buildings without historic or artistic value should be torn town. The rest may need some restoration to rule out safety problems. The world would be a duller place if there were only modern buildings, which more or less resemble one another.

单词注释

- accommodate [ə'kɒmədeɪt] *vt.* 为…提供住处
- demolish [dɪ'mɒlɪʃ] *vt.* 毁坏，拆毁
- irreparable [ɪ'repərəbl] *adj.* 不能挽回的
- episode ['epɪsəʊd] *n.* 一段情节；一个事件
- tangible ['tændʒəbl] *adj.* 切实的；可见的
- remnant ['remnənt] *n.* 残余
- legacy ['legəsi] *n.* 遗赠(物)，遗产
- bestow [bɪ'stəʊ] *vt.* 给予；安放
- aesthetic [iːs'θetɪk] *adj.* 美学的，审美的
- sheer [ʃɪə(r)] *adj.* 全然的，纯粹的
- vicissitude [vɪ'sɪsltjuːd] *n.* 兴衰；枯荣；变迁
- baffle ['bæfl] *vt.* 困惑；为难
- architect ['ɑːkɪtekt] *n.* 建筑师
- grandeur ['grændʒə] *n.* 庄严，伟大
- unsurpassed [ˌʌnsə'pɑːst] *adj.* 无比的，卓越的
- mortal ['mɔːtl] *adj.* 必死的；极端的
- harmony ['hɑːməni] *n.* 协调，融洽
- restoration ['restə'reɪʃn] *n.* 修整，修复
- resemble [rɪ'zembl] *vt.* 像，类似

很多古建筑受到法律的保护，因为它们是国家历史的一部分。然而，有人认为我们应该拆掉这些古建筑，因为我们需要住房和写字楼。保护古建筑究竟有多么重要？历史是否应该阻碍进步呢？

对于历史悠久的国家来说，总是会出现新旧互相冲突的现象。尤其是在城市里，为了给不断增长的人口提供住所，旧建筑被推倒，新建筑取而代之。不幸的是，许多历史遗址也成了大兴土木的牺牲品。

拆毁古建筑通常会造成不可挽回的损失。过去的建筑往往和某些历史事件联系在一起，这可以在历史书中得到验证。但是，通过参观这些看得见摸得着的历史遗迹，我们可以更好地理解这些历史事件。建筑是我们的先辈留给我们的遗产之一。我们保存好这些建筑，是对先辈的尊敬。一旦推倒这些历史遗产，它们就永远离我们而去了。

另外，大部分的古建筑都极具艺术价值和审美价值。它们能历经数个世纪的历史变迁而屹立不倒，这本身就证明了其建筑工艺的高超。事实上，金字塔和长城的建筑技巧，即使是现代的建筑师也为之倾倒。那些古建筑内的众多艺术工艺令人惊叹不已，吸引了来自全球的许多游客。那些古建筑的风采至今仍是不可超越的。

实际上，新旧事物之间并不一定是你死我活的争端。它们能够和谐共存。当然，那些没有历史和艺术价值的旧建筑应该被拆除，有些则需要重建和修复以排除安全隐患。如果全世界到处都是大同小异的现代建筑，那么这个世界将变得更单调。

特别提醒

这道关于保护古建筑的雅思写作题是雅思写作考试中最新的题目之一。保护传统文化、传统建筑以及传统习俗，一直都是雅思写作考试中的热门话题。这篇范文中的很多观点，完全可以用在其他涉及保护传统的话题的雅思作文中。请认真阅读范文并适当归纳其中的论据！

推荐指数 ★★★

相关题目 9, 10, 48, 53, 78

写作点拨

这道题目要求考生论述“保护古建筑的重要性”，并且指出“进步是否应该让位给历史”，是典型的“叙述＋观点”类雅思作文题。范文分为四段：第一段引入话题；第二、三从不同方面论证了保护古建筑的重要性；第四段论证历史和发展之间的关系，回答了题目中的第二个问题。

句型升级

普通版 Buildings are part of the legacy bestowed by our ancestors and by preserving their constructions we show our respect to our ancestors.

升级版 Buildings are part of the legacy bestowed by our ancestors to whom we show our respect by preserving their constructions.

注释：在恰当的时候使用定语从句，可以将一个原本结构平淡无奇的并列句变成一个结构颇有特色的句子。

ESSAY 98

The mass media, including television, radio and newspapers, have great influence in shaping people's ideas. To what extent do you agree or disagree with this statement? Give reasons for your answer.

Many of us like to think ourselves wise and unbiased because we are not gullible and view the world objectively. In fact, even for avid readers of books, 90 percent of their daily information comes from the mass media. The mass media has become the sole source of information for most people. No wonder we lack independent thinking.

Our reliance on the mass media is, to some degree, unavoidable. It is impossible for us to always acquire first-hand knowledge. In fact, there is often no such need. Knowledge is handed down from one generation to another. It is accumulative. This makes science possible. In fact our whole civilization is based on the cooperation and coordination of individuals who take care of their respective work. Thus, people in the mass media industry are entrusted by the public to provide and disseminate information. They are like an extension of our eyes, ears and hands.

The power of the media is more evident in democratic countries. In a country where freedom of speech and reporting is guaranteed, the mass media is often looked upon favorably. By and large, it plays a major role in promoting good causes and exposing wrongdoings of all sorts. Any decent organization, including the government, have to consider the public fallout before planning anything distasteful. Ideally, the mass media acts as a monitoring device, ready to expose any ugly business. Scandals such as the Watergate scandal would have been covered up without effective independent journalism. In the same way, momentum could be gathered for worthy undertakings.

Thanks to technological development, the mass media is becoming more convincing than ever. One may doubt something if he only reads it in the newspaper—the author may write whatever he likes, but to see it on TV leaves little room for doubting. There will be interviews with relevant people, a neighbor, a relative or a police officer, collaborating each other's statement. Then again, all major news agencies run similar stories. The audience have no reason to doubt the authenticity. Thus, we form our 'informed' opinion based on what we gather from media reports.

As I said before, our opinions have to be based on facts, which are always second-hand information. The mass media is the biggest information provider for most people. For better or worse, our opinion is going to be shaped by the mass media.

单词注释

- unbiased [ʌn'baɪəst] *adj.* 不带偏见的
- gullible ['gʌləbl] *adj.* 轻易相信他人的
- avid ['ævɪd] *adj.* 热衷的，酷爱的
- reliance [rɪ'laɪəns] *n.* 依赖
- accumulative [ə'kjuːmjələtiv] *adj.* 积累的
- respective [rɪ'spektɪv] *adj.* 各自的
- disseminate [dɪ'semɪneɪt] *v.* 传播
- decent ['diːsnt] *adj.* 体面的
- fallout ['fɔːlaut] *n.* 影响，后果
- authenticity [ˌɔːθen'tɪsəti] *n.* 真实性

包括电视、广播和报纸在内的各种大众传媒，对人们思想的形成产生了巨大的影响。你是否同意这样的观点？

人们往往认为自己非常明智、不易轻信他人，而且看待问题也公正客观、不偏不倚。事实上，即使是读过很多书的人，他们主要的信息来源也是大众传媒。对大部分人来说，媒体是他们唯一的信息渠道。难怪人们难以进行独立思考。

在一定程度上，我们对媒体的依赖是不可避免的。我们不可能总能获取第一手资料，而且有时也没有必要。人类的知识本来就是代代相传的。知识是累积而成的，也正因如此才产生了科学。实际上，人类文明就是以相互合作、各司其职为基础的。媒体界人士受到公众信任，肩负着提供和传播信息的重任。他们就相当于我们的眼睛、耳朵及双手的延伸。

在民主国家，传媒的力量更加显著。在言论和新闻自由的国度里，人们对大众传媒的态度是积极的，因为媒体往往可以推进公益事业、揭露不良行径。任何机构，包括政府在内，都必须考虑舆论压力，进而不敢轻易违规操作。在理想化的状态下，传媒能起到一个监督的作用，随时可以揭露丑恶现象。如果没有有效、独立的新闻报道，诸如水门事件之类的丑闻就得不到曝光。与此同时，媒体也可以为公益事业推波助澜。

科技的进步使得传媒更加令人信服。读者在报纸上读完某些报道后可能还会将信将疑，因为毕竟口说无凭。但是当读者通过电视看到相关画面后就不容易心生怀疑了。通过电视人们可以看到当事人的一言一行，人们不得不信。此外还会有对当事人的亲属、邻居、警察的采访，他们的说法互相一致。这些又进一步增加了报道的可信度。此外，各大通讯社都对事件进行相似的报道，进一步加深观众对事件真实性的信任。所以，我们所谓的客观、基于事实的观点其实是以媒体报道为基础的。

如前所述，形成我们观点的事实往往都是二手信息。大众传媒是公众最大的信息提供者。无论如何我们的观点都会受到传媒的影响。

特别提醒

这篇范文所涉及的大众传媒的问题，是雅思写作考试中的传统热门话题之一。雅思写作题目中，不仅有关于电视的题目，还有关于互联网、报纸等其他媒体形式的题目。关于各种媒体形式的优缺点的文章，其实有不少相通的观点和论据，请注意收集和整理。

推荐指数 ★★★　　**相关题目** 4, 17, 23, 32, 45, 51, 56, 73

写作点拨

这道题目要求考生就“大众传媒是否对人们思想的形成产生了巨大的影响”给出自己的观点，是典型的观点类雅思作文题。范文使用了最传统的观点类议论文的写作方法，全文分为五段：第一段开门见山地给出作者的观点，即支持题目的看法；第二、三、四段指出大众传媒对我们所产生的各种巨大的影响；第五段重申作者的观点。

论据积累

大众传媒为何影响如此之大：

1. 我们依赖大众传媒，因为我们不可能总能获取第一手资料。
   We have to rely on the mass media because it is impossible for us to always acquire first-hand knowledge.
2. 在言论、新闻自由的国家里，媒体可以推进公益事业，揭露不良行径。
   In a country where freedom of speech and reporting is guaranteed, the mass media plays a major role in promoting good causes and exposing wrongdoings of all sorts.
3. 科技的进步使得传媒更加令人信服。
   Thanks to technological development, the mass media is becoming more convincing than ever.

ESSAY 99

Surveillance cameras are now installed in many shops and supermarkets to prevent shoplifting. But many people are against this because they think it is a disregard of privacy. What are your views about this?

Troubled by shoplifting and various forms of sabotage, shop owners around the world are taking measures to guard their stores. Security guards are posted at entrances and exits; people are assigned to monitor surveillance cameras. But the omnipresence of those cameras is under growing criticism—it is seen as an intrusion upon one's privacy.

It is now hard to do things unobserved. Wherever you go, there is always some possibility that you are being watched and even recorded. It is quite embarrassing to be caught sneezing on camera for instance. And many people feel uneasy before a camera, let alone a hidden one. The fact that our every move is being monitored makes people nervous. What we do and how we act should be our own business so long as they are legal. Unsolicited filming is a violation of our privacy.

However, that claim is one-sided. If possible, it would be better not to have electronic surveillance. But as things now stand, it has become a necessary nuisance. It is ineffective and costly to use human surveillance, which was used up till now and commonly accepted. No one would criticize the watchful eyes of a shop assistant or grandly assert their right not to be monitored. Yet most people cannot tolerate video cameras. In fact, there is no justification for that. How can we deny the shop owners' right to watch the customers on their premises? They are entitled to protect their properties and should be allowed to any lawful means to do so.

The downside of video surveillance is often negligible. What is embarrassing in a social context remains so with or without overhead cameras. People should behave themselves in public places such as supermarkets. It is not the right place to have an intimate moment with your lover not because there are cameras but because it is a public place. Actually, aside from its role in combating crimes, video surveillance often does service to ordinary citizens. Many a time was a distraught customer given his lost keys because the whole thing was caught by the camera. And many lives were saved when some elderly people were struck by heart attacks and would have been left unattended to, had it not been for the sweeping gaze of a surveillance camera.

As I see it, video surveillance is another tool against crime and capable of being misused. But those cameras are necessary. By and large, they work against the criminals rather than the public.

单词注释

- surveillance [sɜːˈveɪləns] *n.* 监控
- shoplifting [ˈʃɒplɪftɪŋ] *n.* 冒充顾客在店里偷窃
- sabotage [ˈsæbətɑːʒ] *v.* 蓄意破坏
- assign [əˈsaɪn] *v.* 指派，分派
- omnipresence [ˈɒmniˈprezəns] *n.* 无处不在
- unsolicited [ˌʌnsəˈlɪsɪtɪd] *adj.* 不请自来的
- nuisance [ˈnjuːsns] *n.* 让人讨厌的东西
- premises [ˈpremɪsɪz] *n.* 经营场所
- intimate [ˈɪntɪmət] *adj.* 亲密的
- distraught [dɪˈstrɔːt] *adj.* 心急如焚的

为了防止偷盗行为，如今很多商店和超市都安装了监视器。很多人反对安装监控器，因为他们觉得自己的隐私受到了侵犯。请给出你的观点。

由于偷窃及其他破坏现象的存在，世界各地的店主们都在采取各种措施保护自己的商店。在商店的进出口处往往都设有保安人员，店内摄像头也有人日夜监视。但是随着店内摄像监视愈演愈烈，人们的批评也不断升温，因为大家认为这是对个人隐私的侵犯。

如今人们做任何事都可能会被他人监视。不管你走到哪里，你都有可能被监视，甚至被拍摄下来。在打喷嚏的时候被他人拍到是很尴尬的事情。很多人面对照相机就不自在，更不要说是隐蔽的摄像头。当我们的一举一动都被人监视的时候，我们往往会紧张起来。只要合法，我们的各种行为举止都是我们自己的事情，别人无权插手。非自愿的拍摄就是对隐私的侵犯。

然而，这种观点是片面的。可能的话，没有电子监控当然是皆大欢喜。但是就现实而论，电子监控乃是无奈之举。以前只有人力监控，但是人力监控往往效率低下且成本高。消费者对店内售货员警惕的目光似乎并不在乎，亦不会小题大做，也不会理所当然地强调自己有权不受店员的监视。奇怪的是，大部分人却无法容忍摄像监控。其实这两者并没有什么区别。我们不应剥夺店主监控自己店面的权利。他们有权保护自己的财产，可以为此而采取一切合法的手段。

摄像监控给人们带来的不便之处其实很少。不管有没有摄像头的存在，有些行为在公众场合都是令人尴尬的。在公共场合人们就应该注意自己的举止。比如，情侣不应该在公共场合过分亲热，不是因为有摄像头的存在，而是因为这是公共场所。实际上，除了有助于打击犯罪以外，摄像监控还常常有助于大众。经常会有顾客遗失钥匙，遍寻不着，满头大汗，结果店员却将钥匙交还给顾客，因为他们通过摄像机看到了顾客掉钥匙的地方。摄像监控还挽救了很多人的性命：很多时候老年人因为心脏病突发昏倒在地，要不是摄像监控，他们很可能不会被人发现，得不到及时救治。

在我看来，摄像监控是打击犯罪的又一利器，虽然有可能被滥用，却是必不可少的。总的来讲，摄像监控针对的是罪犯而不是公众。

特别提醒

这道关于超市里是否应该安装监视器的作文题，是雅思写作考试中历史最悠久的话题之一。早在上个世纪的九十年代，这类话题就已经多次出现在雅思写作考试中了。开始阅读范文之前，请确保认识 surveillance camera（监视器）这个英文单词，以免在考试中陷入读不懂题目的尴尬境地。

推荐指数 ★★★

相关题目 46, 52, 56, 101, 108

写作点拨

这道题目要求考生就“监视器是否侵犯隐私”给出自己的观点，是典型的观点类雅思作文题。范文使用了最传统的观点类议论文写作方法，全文分为五段：第一段引入话题却没有给出作者的观点；第二、三、四段指出应该安装监视器的各种理由；第五段重申作者的观点。

论据积累

安装监视器的理由：

1. 如今人们做任何事都可能会被他人监视。

   It is now hard to do things unobserved.
2. 人力监控往往效率低下且成本高。

   It is ineffective and costly to use human surveillance.
3. 摄像监控给人们带来的不便之处其实很少。

   The downside of video surveillance is often negligible.

ESSAY 100

It is sometimes said that borrowing money from a friend can harm or damage the friendship. Do you agree? Why or why not? Use specific reasons to explain your view.

There is an old Chinese saying to the effect that an accurate account of debts should always be kept even among brothers. In China at least, borrowing money has become a taboo subject: people steer clear of it whenever possible because one often gets humiliated by failing to borrow the money. Loaning money is becoming rare even among cronies.

Personally, I cannot accept the claim that one risks his friendship if he borrows money from his friends. The friends discussed here refer to real friends. By nature, friends are supposed to be there for you and help each other out. The assistance rendered to a friend can be as small as a gentle nudge or as great as saving one's life. All is done unconditionally and spontaneously. We don't object to borrowing our friends' car, yet somehow we treat money differently. In fact, there is no justification for this kind of special treatment. Money is just another favor your real friends are to grant you. They will lend you the money if they can reasonably do so, otherwise they will say sorry. There are no hard feelings.

If anything, this only serves to strengthen their friendship. Even real friends are sometimes not convinced of the authenticity of their friendship. They don't know how good a friend the other person is because there is never a chance to test their friendship. A friend in need is a friend indeed. Those who lend and repay you money are those to be trusted because money can bring out the best and worst in most people. I once lend RMB 30 yuan to a college classmate but was told by others that I wouldn't get the money back because he was notorious for not paying back. However, I thought he was an honest man by heart and trusted him. Sure enough, I got my money back and we became friends.

There are friends who fall out over disputes about money. However, can we call them real friends? It is over money matters that trust and friendship are built and reciprocated.

单词注释

- to the effect that 大意是
- taboo [tə'buː] *n.* 禁忌
- steer clear of 闪避
- humiliate [hjuː'mɪlieɪt] *v.* 羞辱
- crony ['krəʊni] 好友，密友
- spontaneous [spɒn'teɪniəs] *adj.* 自发的
- somehow ['sʌmhaʊ] *adv.* 不知何故
- justification [ˌdʒʌstɪfɪ'keɪʃn] *n.* 理由，辩护
- if anything 如果有什么的话
- notorious [nəʊ'tɔːriəs] *adj.* 恶名昭著的
- dispute [dɪs'pjuːt] *n.* 争论，争吵
- reciprocate [rɪ'sɪprəkeɪt] *v.* 回应

有时候借朋友的钱会破坏彼此之间的关系。你是否同意这样的说法？请给出具体的原因。

中国有句俗话：亲兄弟，明算账。在中国，借钱已成为一个禁忌的话题。人们尽量不提借钱，因为借不到钱是很尴尬的。即便在多年的老友之间，借钱也变得日益罕见。

我认为向朋友借钱并不会危害朋友之间的友谊。这里讨论的朋友是指真正的朋友。朋友本来就应该互相帮助、互相支持。对朋友的帮助可大可小：小到一个搀扶，大到救人一命。这种互助是自发的、无条件的。我们觉得向朋友借车一用无伤大雅，但是却对借钱另眼相看。其实我们没有必要对借钱加以区别对待。朋友将钱借给你也等于给你帮个忙，如果他们能借得出他们就会借，没有的话他们也无能为力。借钱与否，朋友之间都不会伤和气。

借钱不但不会伤和气，反而可以增进友谊。即使真正的朋友之间有的时候也不确定彼此间的友谊到底有多深，因为人们往往没有机会检验彼此的友谊。患难见真情。向你借钱而且能及时归还的人就是值得信赖的朋友，因为对金钱的态度往往能展现人的本性。我曾经借了30元钱给我的一个大学同学，但其他同学告诉我这钱肯定是有借无还，因为那位同学向来都不还钱。然而，我却觉得他在内心深处是诚实的，我信任他。果然，他如期还了钱，我们也由此成为了朋友。

有些朋友因为钱而闹得不欢而散，但是这样的朋友算得上真正的朋友吗？人们往往是在钱财问题上建立起彼此的友谊与信任的。

特别提醒

这道关于是否应该借钱给朋友的雅思作文题，算是雅思写作考试中最特殊的题目之一。生活中或许很多人都会思考这个问题，但是要用英文把自己的观点完整地表述出来，恐怕对很多人来说都不算一件易事。请留意范文中的观点及对应的英文表达！

推荐指数 ★★★　　**相关题目** 31, 42, 88, 94

写作点拨

这道题目要求考生就“借钱给朋友是否会破坏友谊”给出自己的观点，是典型的观点类雅思作文题。范文使用了最传统的观点类议论文的写作方法，全文分为四段：第一段开门见山地给出作者的观点，即借钱给朋友并不伤和气；第二、三段例举了借钱给朋友并不伤和气的各种理由；第四段总结全文。

词汇升级

密友

普通版 Loaning money is becoming rare even among *very close friends*.

升级版 Loaning money is becoming rare even among *cronies*.

密友：crony, chum, intimate, confidant

ESSAY 101

If a five-year old commits a crime, should his/her parents take the responsibility and how should the parents be punished? What should be the age of a child when parents no longer take the responsibility for his or her behavior?

I almost didn't believe it when I was told one wouldn't be prosecuted if he/she broke the law because he/she was only ten years old. Frankly speaking, I was a little exhilarated because I had just had a fight with a classmate and would very much like to do him some damage. But I finally decided against this because it was morally wrong and my parents would be punished on my behalf. It is a universal practice that the parents take the blow when their underage children commit crimes.

As guardians of their children, the parents should be responsible for their children's behavior. Children below a certain age often rely on their parents to distinguish between the right and wrong. They are significantly influenced by their parents and often imitate them. Apart from educating their children, the parents are also responsible for keeping the kids from bad company, for counseling and helping their children at the first sign of trouble to prevent any rash actions taken by their kids. The parents' failure to prevent kids from breaking the law constitutes negligence in itself and should therefore incur punishment. If parents were not responsible for their children's wrongdoing, some criminally inclined parents may exploit this and force their kids to commit crimes on their behalf, availing themselves of kids' immunity from prosecution.

It is hard to determine the proper punishment for the parents. They are not the ones who are actually breaking the law. They are only partially responsible for what happened. Classmates, teachers, friends, and the society at large all contribute something to the going astray of those juvenile delinquents. The parents have jobs to do and cannot watch the kids 24 hours a day. Kids may turn criminals despite all the teaching they get from their parents; the reasons are many-fold. Parents should not be singled out to assume full responsibility. Hence, each case should be carefully examined before proper punishment can be decided upon.

It is actually hard to decide when a person can be seen as entirely independent. The age may be different for each individual. The commonly accepted age 18 probably applies to most people. It is an age when we are fully developed intellectually, mentally and hopefully, psychologically. We are supposed to be sensible enough to consider the consequences of our own behavior. But as I said, individuality should be taken into account when making this kind of judgment.

单词注释

- prosecute [ˈprɒsɪkjuːt] *v.* 起诉
- exhilarated [ɪɡˈzɪləreɪtɪd] *adj.* 欣喜的
- underage *adj.* 未达到法定年龄的
- distinguish [dɪsˈtɪŋɡwɪʃ] *v.* 区分
- imitate [ˈɪmɪteɪt] *v.* 模仿
- negligence [ˈneɡlɪdʒəns] *n.* 失职，疏忽
- avail [əˈveɪl] *v.* 利用
- astray [əsˈtreɪ] *adv.* 误入歧途
- assume [əˈsjuːm] *v.* 承担
- intellectual [ˌɪntəˈlektʃuəl] *adj.* 智力的
- psychologically [ˌsaɪkəˈlɒdʒɪkli] *adv.* 心理上
- sensible [ˈsensəbl] *adj.* 明智的
- consequence [ˈkɔnsɪkwəns] *n.* 后果

如果一个五岁的小孩触犯了法律，他(她)的父母是否应该承担责任？他(她)的父母应该受到何种惩罚？当小孩多大的时候，父母就不再需要为他们的行为负责了？

当我听说一个人犯了法不用坐牢，因为他只有十岁的时候，我简直难以置信。坦白地说，我心里暗自高兴，因为当时我刚刚和同学打了一架，很想进行报复。但是最后我还是没有那样做，因为我知道那是不道德的，而且父母会因此受到惩罚。子女犯罪，父母往往都要承担法律责任。

作为孩子的监护人，父母必须对孩子的行为负责。一定年龄以下的孩子往往依赖父母来辨别是非。他们喜欢模仿父母，受父母的影响很大。除了教育孩子以外，家长还有义务管教孩子，使其不与坏人为伍。孩子一出现问题，家长就应该采取措施，避免孩子鲁莽行事。如果父母没能阻止孩子犯罪，这本身就构成了过失罪，应该受到惩罚。如果父母不必为孩子的行为负责的话，有些有犯罪倾向的父母甚至会利用孩子的豁免权，强迫孩子代替他们去从事犯罪活动。

裁定对父母的恰当惩罚方式具有一定的难度。他们本身毕竟没有犯法，他们只应该负连带责任。同学、教师、朋友以及整个社会都应对孩子走向犯罪负一定程度的责任。父母工作在身，不能一天 24 小时看着小孩。有些孩子不管父母如何苦口婆心地教育，还是会误入歧途。青少年犯罪的原因是多重的。父母不应该为此负全责。所以，每一个案件都要具体对待，量情而定。

要确定一个人是否完全独立也非易事。每个人走向独立的年龄不尽相同。一般来说，18 岁以上就算是成年了。这对大部分人是适用的，因为 18 岁时我们在生理上、智力上已经基本发育成熟。幸运的话，我们的心理届时也已经发育成熟。我们应该有能力考量自己行为的后果了。但是，个体差异也不应被忽视。

特别提醒

儿童教育问题，是雅思写作考试中最热门的话题之一。本书收集了大量儿童教育题材的雅思作文题目。这道题目和其他很多题目完全不同，因为题目中提出了三个问题，是雅思写作考试中非常罕见的现象。请特别留意这类“多问题型”作文的写法！

推荐指数 ★★★

相关题目 46, 52, 56, 99, 108

写作点拨

这道题目要求考生回答“父母是否应该承担责任”、“父母应该受到何种惩罚”以及“小孩多大时父母就不再需要为他们的行为负责了”三个问题。一口气向考生提出三个问题的雅思作文题并不常见。范文使用了非常中庸的写作方法，平均分配三个问题。范文分为四段：第一段开门见山地给出作者的观点，即父母应该为孩子的行为负责；第二段例举了父母应该负责的各种理由，回答了第一个问题；第三段指出父母应该接受的惩罚，回答了第二个问题；第四段指出当小孩年满 18 时父母就不再需要为他们的行为负责了，并且给出了相应的理由，回答了题目的第三个问题。

词汇升级

欣喜的，开心的

普通版 I was a little *pleased* because I had just had a fight with a classmate and would very much like to do him some damage.

升级版 I was a little *exhilarated* because I had just had a fight with a classmate and would very much like to do him some damage.

欣喜的，开心的：delighted, cheerful, exhilarated, blithe, lighthearted

ESSAY 102

Participating in a sport is as important for psychological health and social development as it is for physical conditions. What is your opinion?

A stroll around any park will bring you face to face with people doing exercises in early mornings. The young as well as the old are becoming more health-conscious and are spending more time in gyms after work. Doing sports is certainly beneficial in many ways.

The most obvious is the physical benefit. Sports make us fitter, quicker and stronger. Physical exertion is conducive to our health. It has been proven scientifically that regular exercise is a weapon against illness and aging. Indeed, many maladies are the results of lack of physical exercise.

The benefits do not end there. Sport is a character builder. Sport invariably involves some exertion and discomfort. It trains our willpower. To win a game we have to be determined and perseverant. To outdo others or ourselves, we have to push our limits and conquer all difficulties. We come to know that there is always room for improvement. Then, failures are also common in sport. We learn to adjust to new conditions, to assess our weaknesses and to gather strength from our defeats. The fast-moving nature of most sport also helps us to become quick-witted and decisive.

By participating in team sport, we learn to work with others. In sport fields, individual ambition takes second place to team objective. Every team member is working towards a common goal. To achieve this goal, cooperation and coordination are essential. Members must work as a team and achieve the maximum synergy even if that means someone has to make certain sacrifices. For instance, a cyclist may take the leading position for half of the game and then drop out so as to ensure the victory of his teammate.

Like art, sport is a good way to train ourselves psychologically as well as physically. I myself have often experienced the uplifting effects of sport.

单词注释

- stroll [strəul] *n.* 漫步
- conducive [kən'djuːsɪv] *adj.* 有益于…的
- malady ['mælədi] *n.* 疾病
- perseverant [ˌpɜːsɪ'vɪərənt] *adj.* 顽强的
- assess [ə'ses] *v.* 衡量，评价
- ambition [æm'bɪʃn] *n.* 野心
- coordination [kəʊˌɔːdi'neɪʃn] *n.* 协调，配合
- uplifting [ˌʌp'lɪftɪŋ] *adj.* 振奋的

参加体育运动可以保持身体健康，体育运动在保持心理健康和社会发展方面发挥了同样重要的作用。你是否同意这样的看法？

清晨到公园里走上一圈的话，我们会看到很多人在晨练。青年人和老年人一样都日益关注自己的健康，下班后他们经常去健身房健身。体育锻炼的益处颇多。

最明显的就是对身体有益。体育锻炼使我们更健康、更敏捷、更健壮。运动有益健康。科学已经证明经常锻炼是预防疾病、延缓衰老的有效武器。实际上，很多疾病都是由于缺乏运动引起的。

运动的益处远不仅如此。体育可以培养人的品格。体育运动必然会带来一些肉体上的痛苦和不适，这可以锻炼我们的意志。为了赢得比赛，我们必须目标坚定、坚韧不拔。为了超过对方或突破自我，我们必须克服困难、挑战极限。我们由此学会了不断进取。此外，失败也是体育中常有的事情。由此我们学会了如何调整自己、扬长避短，从失败中吸取教训。运动瞬息万变，这可以培养我们即时反应、当机立断的能力。

通过参与团队项目，我们学会了如何与人合作。在赛场上，团队的目标高于个人的目标。所有队员都齐心协力，为同一个目标而努力。为达到这个目标，队员间的协调合作是至关重要的。队员们必须形成一个整体，达到最大的合力，即使付出一些个人牺牲也在所不惜。例如，有的时候队里的某位骑车运动员可能在比赛的前半段骑在最前面，然后却退出比赛。其目的是确保队友的胜利。

和艺术一样，体育也是很好的训练方法，无论是在生理方面还是心理方面。我自己就经常体验体育振奋人心的效果。

特别提醒

体育和健身，是雅思写作考试中历史最悠久的话题之一。但是这道关于体育运动益处的雅思作文题目，却是近几年雅思写作考试中新出现的题目。体育类的雅思作文题目，其实可以使用不少相通的观点和论据，请注意收集和整理！

推荐指数 ★★★

相关题目 11, 34, 72

写作点拨

这道题目要求考生就“体育运动在保持心理健康和社会发展方面是否发挥了与保持身体健康同样重要的作用”给出自己的观点，是典型的观点类雅思作文题。范文使用了最传统的观点类议论文写作方法，全文分为五段：第一段引入话题并且给出作者的观点，即体育锻炼益处颇多；第二、三、四段指出体育运动的各种好处；第五段重申作者的观点。

论据积累

体育运动的益处：

1. 运动有益健康。
   Physical exercise is conducive to our health.
2. 体育可以培养人的品格。
   Sport is a character builder.
3. 通过参与团队项目，我们学会了如何与人合作。
   By participating in team sport, we learn to work with others.

ESSAY 103

The threat of nuclear weapons maintains world peace. Nuclear power provides cheap and clean energy. The benefits of nuclear technology far outweigh the disadvantages. Give reasons for your answer.

Nuclear technology is a two-edged weapon. Millions have benefited from nuclear energy. However, the world has seen its destructive power when two atomic bombs were detonated on the Japanese soil. Luckily for us, no further nuclear bombs have exploded in populated areas so far.

Nuclear weapon is bound to cut us sooner or later. Nuclear deterrent may seem effective but is ultimately hazardous. More than twenty countries now possess nuclear weapons and only a few of them have signed treaties that promise never to use nuclear weapons unless under nuclear attack. What if those countries get into wars against each other? Will they refrain from using nuclear bombs when conventional weapons fail to bring victory? There is no guarantee! Moreover, what if one of those bombs got into the hands of terrorists or fanatics? Would they hesitate to use the bomb when their demands are not met? Nuclear weapon is like a time bomb, which is bound to set off unless dismantled.

By its very nature, nuclear weapon will cause disasters. It is against other humans, not aliens from outer space nor wild animals on earth that nuclear weapons are designed. They are capable of wiping out an entire city or nation. No one should be entrusted with such great power because power is apt to be abused. We are always tempted to use the power we have for our own purposes. One way or another, we all give in to that temptation. God wields absolute power and he wiped out the entire mankind save the Noah's Ark. The stakes are too high here to allow even one mistake.

Nuclear energy is entirely another matter. Peaceful usage of nuclear technology means using the technology for the good of mankind not against it. There are, of course, problems at this stage such as waste disposal and safety problems. But with time, all those technical problems can be solved.

Technology itself is amoral. It can either serve or cut us. How we use it depends on ourselves. We need to guard ourselves from the urge to abuse excessive power because more often than not we are our own biggest enemy.

单词注释

- two-edged *adj.* 双刃的
- atomic [əˈtɒmɪk] *adj.* 原子的，原子能的
- detonate [ˈdetəneɪt] *v.* 引爆
- deterrent [dɪˈtɜːrənt] *n.* 威慑
- ultimately [ˈʌltɪmətli] *adv.* 根本上，基本上
- hazardous [ˈhæzədəs] *adj.* 危险的
- treaty [ˈtriːti] *n.* 条约
- dismantle [dɪsˈmæntl] *v.* 拆除
- alien [ˈeɪliən] *n.* 外星人
- apt [æpt] *adj.* 倾向于…的
- temptation [tempˈteɪʃn] *n.* 诱惑
- wield [wiːld] *v.* 掌握，拥有；行使
- amoral [ˌeɪˈmɒrəl] *adj.* 不分是非的

核武器的威慑力维持着世界和平，而且核能也为我们提供了廉价、清洁的能源。有人认为核技术给我们带来的益处远远超过了它所带来的危害。你是否同意这样的观点？请给出具体的理由。

核技术是一柄双刃剑。千百万人从核能源中受益，但是我们也曾经目睹了两颗原子弹在日本国土上爆炸所带来的巨大摧毁力。庆幸的是，此后没有哪个人口密集的地区遭到核武器袭击。

核武器迟早都会危害人类。所谓的核威慑可能有些作用，但是它本身就是对人类的威胁。目前有20多个国家拥有核武器，这些国家当中只有少数几个签署了“不首先使用核武器条约”。一旦这些国家之间爆发战争，后果将不堪设想。当常规武器无法取胜时，它们会不使用核武器吗？谁也无法保证！而且，万一核武器落入恐怖分子或狂热分子手中又将如何？他们在要求得不到满足的时候会不会毫不犹豫地使用核武器？核武器就像是一个定时炸弹，除非将其拆除，否则必然爆炸。

核武器的性质本身就决定了它必然带来灾害。人类设计核武器，用来对付的不是外星人，也不是飞禽猛兽，而是人类自己。核武器可以摧毁整座城市或整个国家。任何人都不应该拥有如此巨大的力量，因为力量是容易被滥用的。我们往往会受到权力的诱惑，使之为己所用。在一定程度上，所有人都抵受不住这样的诱惑。上帝拥有绝对的力量，他却曾经将生物全部毁灭，只剩下诺亚方舟。核武器问题关系到全人类的存亡，不可以出半点差错。

核能源就完全是另一回事了。核技术的和平开发对人类有益。当然，目前利用核能还存在一些问题，比如核废料处理、安全保障等。但是随着时间的推移，这些问题都能够得到解决。

科技本身并无道德问题可言——水能载舟，亦能覆舟。对科技的恰当使用取决于我们自己。我们必须克制自己，不要过度滥用自己的力量，因为我们是自己最大的敌人。

特别提醒

高科技的利弊，一直是雅思写作考试中最热门的话题之一。这道关于核技术利弊的雅思作文题目，是近几年雅思写作考试中的热点。高科技类的作文题，其实可以使用不少相通的观点和论据，请注意收集和整理！

推荐指数 ★★★

相关题目 5, 14, 15, 16, 20, 21, 25, 64, 110

写作点拨

这道题目要求考生就“核技术是否利大于弊”给出自己的观点，是典型的观点类雅思作文题。范文使用了中庸的观点，指出科技的利弊取决于人类自己的使用方式。范文分为五段：第一段引入话题并且指出核技术是一柄双刃剑；第二、三段指出核技术的各种危害；第四段指出核技术的各种益处；第五段重申作者的观点。

词汇升级

有利有弊

普通版 Nuclear technology has its *advantages and disadvantages*.

升级版 Nuclear technology is a *two-edged weapon*.

ESSAY 104

Are famous people treated unfairly by the media? Should they be given more privacy, or is the price of their fame an invasion into their private lives?

Press freedom allows journalists to report nearly everything. But nothing receives more press coverage than the famous: movie stars, top athletes, models and so on. This kind of inordinate attention intrudes upon their private lives and should be curbed.

People, including celebrities, have the right to keep their private life private, which should be respected by nosy reporters. It is their right not to tell you what kind of food they are eating or what books they are reading. They have the right to 'remain silent'. Who they are dating is their own business and they can choose whether or not to divulge that information. When they are not inclined to be interviewed or photoed, they should be left alone. The tragic death of Princess Diana reveals once again how much damage those nosy paparazzi can cause. There are many famous people being molested by incessant media attention.

The famous are often the victims of sensationalism and tabloid journalism. They are being used to attract more audience and to boost the sales. The stories about celebrities may have no newsworthiness in an objective sense but usually cater to popular tastes. People are naturally curious and particularly love to read about and see the rich and the famous. They like to find in them what is lacking in their own ordinary lives. They want to experience some vicarious pleasure and excitement of their trendy life. The intrusion upon the privacy of the rich is profit-driven on the side of mass media and a touch of voyeurism on the side of common readers.

There are, however, some people who do seek the limelight. They pride themselves on the amount of attention they get and would even create some scandals to get on the headlines. There is no need to protect their privacy. But for the vast majority, the famous or the common, privacy should not be intruded upon.

单词注释

- inordinate [ɪnˈɔːdɪnət] *adj.* 过量的
- intrude [ɪnˈtruːd] *v.* 侵犯
- divulge [daɪˈvʌldʒ] *v.* 透露
- paparazzi [ˌpæpəˈrætsi] *n.* 狗仔队
- incessant [ɪnˈsesnt] *adj.* 不断的
- sensationalism [senˈseɪʃənəlɪzm] *n.* 耸人听闻的手法，哗众取宠
- tabloid [ˈtæblɔɪd] *n.* 小报
- vicarious [vɪˈkeəriəs] *adj.* 间接感受到的
- trendy [ˈtrendi] *adj.* 流行的
- voyeurism [vwaɪˈɜːʊɪzəm] *n.* 窥探癖
- limelight [ˈlaɪmlaɪt] *n.* 公众焦点
- scandal [ˈskændl] *n.* 丑闻

名人是否受到了媒体的不公正对待？他们应该有更多的隐私，还是说失去隐私是成名的代价呢？

新闻自由使得记者们可以对几乎所有的事件进行报道，但是受到媒体报道最多的总是那些社会名人：电影明星、运动明星、模特等。对他们的过分报道侵犯了他们的隐私，应该受到遏制。

所有的人，包括名人在内，都有权利保护自己的私人生活，记者不应侵犯这种权利。名人们有权拒绝透露他们的饮食及阅读习惯，他们有权保持沉默。他们与谁约会是他们自己的事情，他们可以对此缄口不谈。当他们不想接受采访、不想被拍照的时候，记者们不应该强人所难。戴安娜王妃的车祸事件再一次说明了好探听隐私的狗仔队带来的潜在威胁有多么大。很多名人都受到媒体的不断骚扰。

名人常常是小报新闻和轰动新闻的受害者。媒体利用他们来吸引读者，提高销量。对名人的报道可能并没有真正的新闻价值，但是却能迎合公众口味。公众天性好奇，尤其喜欢了解那些富有的、出名的人。公众希望从他们身上得到一些自己的平淡生活里所没有的东西，希望间接体验他们时尚生活中的快乐和刺激。对名人私生活的侵犯是媒体追求利益的结果，同时也是公众“窥探心理”的产物。

然而也有一些人追求公众关注。他们以此为荣，甚至为了上报纸头条不惜自己制造丑闻。他们的隐私就没有必要保护了。但是对于大多数人来说，名人也好常人也罢，隐私是不容侵犯的。

特别提醒

大众传媒话题一直是雅思写作考试中最热门的话题之一。这道关于名人和大众传媒的关系的雅思作文题目，在托福和 GRE 的写作考试中都出现过，请仔细阅读范文并注意收集和整理相关的论据！

推荐指数 ★★★★

相关题目 4, 17, 23, 32, 45, 51, 56, 73, 98

写作点拨

这道题目要求考生就“大众传媒是否侵犯了名人的隐私”给出自己的观点，是典型的观点类雅思作文题。范文使用了最传统的观点类议论文写作方法，全文分为四段：第一段引入话题并且给出作者的观点，即媒体的过分报道侵犯了名人的隐私；第二、三段指出名人的隐私也不可以侵犯的原因；第四段重申作者的观点。

词汇升级

过量的

普通版 *Too much* attention intrudes upon their private lives and should be curbed.

升级版 This kind of *inordinate* attention intrudes upon their private lives and should be curbed.

过量的：excessive, extravagant, immoderate, inordinate

ESSAY 105

Some countries allow women to join the armed forces, while some others think that armed forces such as navy or army don't suit women. Do you agree or disagree?

In ancient times, women were thought to bring bad luck to the military and were not allowed anywhere near the army. Nowadays a small number of women work in organizations affiliated to the armed forces, but mainly involved in the logistics or other civilian work. As far as I am concerned, the army or navy is not suited for the fair sex.

A life in the army is physically demanding for a woman. Indeed, many men can hardly cope with the vigorous training and drilling. It is true that we have female athletes who undergo intensive training daily, but what is required in the army goes against women's nature. Being a soldier, you must learn how to kill other people. Most women would readily learn how to defend themselves but would balk when it comes to killing. Many are disturbed by the sight of blood and unable to handle a gun or dagger. Only under extreme circumstances would they find the nerve to pull the trigger. Only very few women can make good soldiers.

The psychological effects of a military career could be devastating. Combating experience is traumatic for most people. Many veterans suffer from post-war syndrome. The bloodiness and cruelty of war often haunts them for the rest of their lives despite their efforts to put the past behind. Even in times of peace, soldiers are trained for war. Daily exposure to the violence and harshness, which is routine in the army, may cause damage to their mental health.

War and fighting may be mankind's unavoidable folly. By and large, men are its executioners and victims. It is sad enough that men are being exposed to the worst in mankind: cruelty, violence, wickedness and so on. Let's spare our fair sex, as much as possible, the evil of the world. We must not all become desensitized and dehumanized. Some of us need to remain caring and gentle. The female is a balancing factor toward the good. Our children need to have at least one parent who is loving and considerate.

单词注释

- affiliated [əˈfɪlieɪtɪd] *adj.* 附属的
- logistics [ləˈdʒɪstɪks] *n.* 后勤
- fair sex 女性
- balk [bɔːk] *v.* 畏缩
- nerve [nɜːv] *n.* 勇气
- trigger [ˈtrɪgə] *n.* 扳机
- psychological [ˌsaɪkəˈlɒdʒɪkəl] *adj.* 心理的
- devastating [ˈdevəsteɪtɪŋ] *adj.* 破坏性的
- combat [ˈkɒmbæt] *v.* 战斗，搏斗，抗击
- traumatic [trɔːˈmætɪk] *adj.* 创伤的，痛苦的
- veteran [ˈvetərən] *n.* 老兵，退伍军人
- syndrome [ˈsɪndrəʊm] *n.* 症状
- bloodiness [ˈblʌdɪnɪs] *n.* 残酷，血腥
- cruelty [ˈkruːəlti] *n.* 残忍，残酷
- haunt [hɔːnt] *v.* 时常出现，萦绕
- harshness [ˈhɑːʃnɪs] *n.* 粗糙的事物
- folly [ˈfɒli] *n.* 愚蠢行为
- executioner [ˌeksɪˈkjuːʃənə] *n.* 死刑执行人，刽子手
- wickedness [ˈwɪkɪdnɪs] *n.* 邪恶，不道德
- desensitize [ˌdiːˈsensɪtaɪz] *v.* 变得不敏感
- dehumanize [diːˈhjuːmənaɪz] *v.* 使失去人性

一些国家允许女性入伍，别的国家却认为女性并不适合当军人。请给出你的看法。

在古代，人们认为女人会给军队带来厄运，因此不允许女人从军。现如今有很多女性在军队的附属机构工作，但是她们从事的主要是后勤等民事工作。就我个人而言，我认为军队不适合女性。

军队生活对女性来说对身体的要求太高。很多男性都应付不了军队里的高强度训练。虽然女运动员们同样要接受高强度训练，但是军队的训练和女性的天性相悖。作为军人，她们必须学习如何杀人。大部分女性愿意学习自我防卫，但是不愿意学习如何杀人。很多女性怕见血，不敢使用枪支、匕首。只有在极端的情况下她们才有勇气扣动扳机。能成为好士兵的女性少之又少。

军旅生涯带来的心理问题也非同小可。战斗经历会给大部分人带来创伤。很多老兵都患有战后综合征。尽管他们极力遗忘战争的经历，但是战争的残酷和血腥往往会不断地困扰着他们。即便在和平时期军人们也会接受训练，时时为战争做准备。在军队里，军人们每天都要接触残酷和暴力。这会给女性带来严重的心理问题。

战争可能是人类不可避免的蠢行。总的来说，男人是战争的参与者与受害者。人类最为阴暗的是残酷、暴力和邪恶。男性深受其害已经很令人遗憾了。请让女性免于承受世界的罪恶吧！不要让我们每一个人都变得麻木不仁、行尸走肉。我们当中必须有人保持仁爱和温柔。女性为人类世界的善行贡献力量。我们的孩子们需要温柔体贴的父母，至少其中一位应该这样。

特别提醒

女性话题，是雅思写作考试中最传统的话题之一。雅思考试中涉及女性的作文题目，多半与儿童抚养、职业女性是否需要出门工作之类的生活话题有关。这道关于女性是否适合参军的雅思作文题目，题材比较特别，请仔细阅读范文！

推荐指数 ★★★

相关题目 33, 58, 61, 90, 92, 112

写作点拨

这道题目要求考生就“女性是否适合参军”给出自己的观点，是典型的观点类雅思作文题。范文分为四段：第一段引入话题并且给出作者的观点，即女性不适合参军；第二、三、四段指出女性不适合参军的原因。

论据积累

女性不适合参军的原因：

1. 军队生活对女性来说对身体的要求太高。
   A life in the army is physically demanding for a woman.
2. 军旅生涯带来的心理问题也非同小可。
   The psychological effects of a military career could be devastating.
3. 女性应该免于承受战争之苦。
   Men should spare women, as much as possible, the evil of the war.

ESSAY 106

Many people think it's wrong to lock animals up in zoos because it is cruel and serves little purpose. But others think that the animals in zoos can bring happiness to people, especially the kids. What is your opinion?

It is now hard to find a city without a zoo. It is the place that you bring your kids to on weekends. The animals in zoos always appeal to people of all ages. But I regard zoos as a form of imprisonment for our fellow creatures.

Some might argue the life in a zoo is a secured and leisurely one: they are well protected and given enough to eat. What else could the animals want? Freedom! We are denying those creatures freedom, which we hold dearest to our heart. 'Give me liberty or give me death,' said Patrick Henry before the American Civil War. To be caged and fed is not what animals want but what is convenient for us. Animals long for their natural way of life even if that means to be eaten by their predators. To deprive them of that is cruelty on our part.

Besides, the caged animals in zoos are not what they really are. They look like wild animals but act like tamed ones. They have lost much of their instincts because they are not allowed to roam the land, to prey for food or to fend for themselves. They are removed from their natural habitats to man-made domiciles. A zoo is not a place where you can get a real glimpse of wild animals.

To put animals in zoos is another reflection of our wrongful attitude towards nature. We have no respect for nature, which is sacrificed and altered to our advantage. We cut down trees for timber and slaughter animals for food. When exploiting nature, we give no thought to its balance, the damage of which poses potential threat to our life. Global warming is a case in point. We need to curb our urge to do things our way and start to live in harmony with our fellow creature.

If we really want to see wild animals, we should go to them instead of imprisoning them. In fact, in some national parks animals do freely roam the land and people get a chance to see what they are really like.

单词注释

- appeal [ə'piːl] *v.* 吸引
- imprisonment [ɪm'prɪzənmənt] *n.* 关押
- secured [sɪ'kjʊəd] *adj.* 安全的
- liberty ['lɪbəti] *n.* 自由
- cage [keɪdʒ] *vt.* 关入笼中；放到笼里
- predator ['predətə] *n.* 掠夺者；食肉动物
- deprive [dɪ'praɪv] *v.* 剥夺
- cruelty ['kruːəlti] *n.* 残忍，残酷
- tame [teɪm] *vt.* 驯养；驯服
- instinct ['ɪnstɪŋkt] *n.* 本能
- roam [rəʊm] *v.* 奔驰
- prey [preɪ] *v.* 捕猎
- fend for oneself 照顾自己
- habitat ['hæbɪtæt] *n.* 栖息地
- domicile ['dɒmisaɪl] *n.* 住所，住宅
- glimpse [glɪmps] *n.* 一瞥，一看
- alter ['ɔːltə] *v.* 改变
- timber ['tɪmbə(r)] *n.* 木材
- slaughter ['slɔːtə] *v.* 屠宰；残杀
- curb [kɜːb] *v.* 抑制

有人认为把动物关在动物园里太过残忍，有些人却认为动物园可以给人们尤其是给孩子们带来快乐。请给出你的看法。

现在很少有城市没有动物园。周末，人们常常带着孩子去动物园玩。动物园里的动物往往博得男女老少的喜爱。但是我认为动物园是对动物的一种监禁。

有人可能会说动物在动物园里安全且悠闲：动物有吃有睡，无人侵扰。动物们还会有别的要求吗？它们要自由！我们自己珍视自由却剥夺动物的自由。帕特里克·亨利在美国独立战争前曾有一句名言：不自由，毋宁死。我们把动物关在笼子里喂养并不是因为动物们希望如此，而是为了我们自己方便罢了。动物渴望自然的生活方式，即使他们可能会被其他猎食动物吃掉。剥夺它们自然的生活方式是残忍的。

其次，关在笼子里的动物已经失去了其本来面目。它们貌似野兽，但其实也失去了野性。它们不能在旷野上奔走，不能捕食猎物，不能自我保护，已经失去了本性。它们离开了自然的栖息场所，被关进了人造囚笼。在动物园里我们是看不到动物的真面目的。

把动物关进动物园反映了我们对大自然的态度。我们肆意改造大自然，使之为我们所用。我们对大自然毫无敬意。我们砍伐树木获取木材，屠杀动物获取食物。我们利用大自然却从未考虑自然界的平衡。大自然失衡会危及人类的生存。全球气候变暖就是很好的例子。我们不能再一意孤行，我们要和世界万物和谐相处。

如果我们要观看野生动物的话，我们应该走到它们当中，而不该把它们关起来。实际上，在很多野生动物园里动物们可以自由走动，向我们展示它们的本来面目。

特别提醒

动物园的利弊，是近年来雅思写作考试中新出现的话题之一。这道关于把动物关在动物园里是否太过残忍的雅思作文题目，就曾经以不同的形式多次出现在近年的雅思写作考试中，请仔细阅读范文！

推荐指数 ★★★

相关题目 76

写作点拨

这道题目要求考生就"把动物关在动物园里是否太过残忍"给出自己的观点，是典型的观点类雅思作文题。范文使用了最传统的观点类议论文写作方法，全文分为五段：第一段引入话题并且给出作者的观点，即把动物关在动物园里的确太过残忍；第二、三、四段指出把动物关在动物园里的确太过残忍的原因；第五段重申作者的观点。

论据积累

反对动物园的原因：

1. 我们自己珍视自由却剥夺动物的自由。
   We are denying those creatures freedom, which we hold dearest to our heart.
2. 关在笼子里的动物已经失去了其本来面目。
   The caged animals in zoos are not what they really are.
3. 把动物关进动物园反映了我们对大自然的态度。
   To put animals in zoos is another reflection of our wrongful attitude towards nature.

ESSAY 107

Nowadays doctors can become very rich. Maybe they should not focus on profitable activities such as plastic surgery or looking after rich patients but concentrate more on all patients' health, no matter how rich they are. Give your view.

Doctors in China often envy the high income enjoyed by physicians in the west. In fact, qualified doctors are often amply rewarded financially. With the national medical bill increasing three folds in the past ten years, they have every chance to get really rich. But, money should never be their priority.

Being a doctor should not be merely a job but a sacred calling. Saving lives and curing patients should be doctors' duty and privilege because they are trained and entrusted to do so and are respected for doing so. Doctors are in a unique position to alleviate human sufferings. They are rewarded not only financially for doing this; they feel valued and appreciated when they see the smiling faces of cured patients and their families. Money cannot buy this kind of peace of mind. Indeed, money earned from treating rich patients while their destitute counterparts are denied medical treatment would always haunt doctors' conscience.

If money becomes their main objective, dire consequence will ensue. Professional ethics will be discarded in the pursuit of money. All too often we have seen risky but lucrative operations performed by unscrupulous doctors in order to pocket the fee. Unnecessary tests are often carried out because doctors who prescribe those test get part of the fee. In China, some doctors receive kickback from pharmaceutical companies for prescribing their medicines, leaving patients with exorbitant medical bills. These doctors are not only money-oriented but also law breakers. Of course, they are not representative of doctors in general. But if financial rewards become the sole objective of all doctors, similar practice will become rampant in the medical industry. Standards and services will be sacrificed for higher profits. Doctors will turn their attention to making money instead of honing their skills and doing research.

Greed for money often robs people of their humanity. Ample examples can be found in that respect. Who can guarantee that no deadly virus would be intentionally created by some rogue doctors so as to sell his anti-virus serum? Patients' well-being always should be the paramount consideration for the doctors.

单词注释

- plastic surgery 整形手术
- qualified [ˈkwɒlɪfaɪd] *adj.* 合格的
- priority [praɪˈɒrɪti] *n.* 优先权
- sacred [ˈseɪkrɪd] *adj.* 神圣的
- unique [juˈniːk] *adj.* 独特的
- alleviate [əˈliːvieɪt] *v.* 减少
- haunt [hɔːnt] *v.* 困扰
- dire [ˈdaɪə(r)] *adj.* 严重的
- ensue [ɪnˈsjuː] *vi.* 跟着发生
- lucrative [ˈluːkrətɪv] *adj.* 获利多的
- unscrupulous [ʌnˈskruːpjələs] *adj.* 无道德的
- prescribe [prɪˈskraɪb] *v.* 开药
- kickback [ˈkɪkbæk] *n.* 回扣，酬金
- pharmaceutical [ˌfɑːməˈsuːtɪkl] *adj.* 制药的
- exorbitant [ɪɡˈzɔːbɪtənt] *adj.* 过高的，昂贵的
- rampant [ˈræmpənt] *adj.* 泛滥的
- hone [həʊn] *v.* 磨炼，打造；使完美
- rogue [rəʊg] *n.* 流氓，无赖
- serum [ˈsɪərəm] *n.* 浆液
- paramount [ˈpærəmaʊnt] *adj.* 至高无上的

如今医生们已经进入了富裕阶层。或许医生们不应该在诸如外科整形手术以及照料有钱的病人之类赚钱的工作上花太多的精力，而应该不论贫贱，关注所有人的健康。请给出你的看法。

中国的医生常常羡慕西方医生们的高收入。实际上，医术高明的医生的收入也相当不菲。近十年来，全国的医疗支出增加了三倍，很多医生都跨入了富有阶级。但是，挣钱不应该成为医生的首要目标。

当医生不该只是一种谋生手段，而应该是一种神圣的职业。救死扶伤是医生的神圣义务和权利，因为他们接受了必要的训练，受到人们的信赖和尊敬。医生的地位特殊，应该以减轻人类痛苦为职业。他们救死扶伤得到的不仅仅是经济上的回报，当他们看到病人和家属们灿烂的笑容时，他们得到的是价值的实现、人们的认可。这种心灵的宁静是金钱无法买到的。实际上，对贫穷的病人置之不理，只去治疗富有的病人，这样得来的金钱会令医生受到良心的谴责。

如果挣钱成为医生的主要目标，其后果不堪设想。在对金钱的追逐中，职业道德会丧失殆尽。经常有医生昧着良心，为了挣钱，为病人实施一些危险的手术。有些医生为了检查费提成常常让病人去做一些没有必要的检查。在中国，有些医生收取医药公司的回扣，胡乱开药，使病人的医疗费用居高不下。这些医生不但是钻进了钱眼，而且还触犯了法律。当然，他们不具有代表性。但是如果经济回报成为医生的唯一目标的话，类似现象就会愈演愈烈。医疗标准及服务会因为追求利益而大打折扣。医生们会把精力放到挣钱上去，而不去钻研业务，从事科研。

对金钱的贪婪往往让人失去人性。这方面的例子比比皆是。谁能保证不会有黑心医生为了钱故意释放某种致命的病毒，然后再独家出售抗病毒血清呢？病人的健康永远都应该是医生的首要目标。

特别提醒

医疗话题，一直是雅思写作考试中的热门话题。但是雅思考试中涉及医疗的作文题目多半与政府应该如何支持医疗事业的发展有关。这道关于医生是否应该关注所有人的健康的雅思作文题目，题材比较特殊，请仔细阅读范文！

推荐指数 ★★★　　**相关题目** 3, 29

写作点拨

这道题目要求考生就“医生是否应该关注所有人的健康”给出自己的观点，是典型的观点类雅思作文题。范文分为四段：第一段引入话题并且给出作者的观点，即医生的确应该关注所有人的健康；第二、三、四段指出医生的确应该关注所有人的健康的原因。

论据积累

医生不应该只顾赚钱的原因：

1. 医生不该只是一种工作，而应该是一种神圣的职业。

   Being a doctor should not be merely a job but a sacred calling.

2. 如果挣钱成为医生或医院的主要目标，其后果将不堪设想。

   If money becomes the main objective of doctors or hospitals, dire consequence will ensue.

3. 医疗标准及服务会因为追求利益而大打折扣。

   Standards and services will be sacrificed for higher profits.

ESSAY 108

Should criminals be punished with lengthy jail terms or re-educated and rehabilitated, using community service programs for instance, before being reintroduced to society?

Crime is on the rise in most countries. No country is happily free of it. Laws are made to define criminal acts and determine proper punishment. Different crimes deserve different penalties, ranging from a fine to death penalty. But by and large, we should aim at reintroducing those inmates to the society upon release.

We need to make sure that criminals no longer pose threat to the society. Although there is no guarantee what an individual will do when he is out of prison, there are ways to minimize the risk. Death penalty would seem the safest way to protect the public, but it is cruel and should be the last resort. Life imprisonment should be meted out to those incorrigible felons unlikely to forgo criminal acts. But for the majority of the convicts, jail time is not the best option.

Lengthy time behind bars is not the best way to ensure public safety because most of the criminals will be released one day or another. Our goal to punish wrongdoers is not to seek revenge, which the victims' families and friends would certainly like, but to prevent further damage. There is no real revenge in the world; what is done cannot be undone; the perished loved one is gone forever whatever we do to the killer. Revenge is an emotional approach, not a sensible one. To be truly noble you must 'love thy enemy'. We need to do something to prevent similar tragedies from occurring. And re-education is our best bet.

We only increase criminals' bitterness and criminal inclination by locking them up or maltreating them. Most inmates can be re-educated through the right approach. By showing them the damages they have caused, the forgiveness from the victims and a totally different life they otherwise could have lead, many would repent their past. After all, given the alternative, no one would voluntarily seek a life of crime. Whenever possible they should be given a chance. To err is human; to forgive divine. They may once again become law-abiding citizens.

Of course, it is never easy to transform a fallen soul. It might be easier to just lock them up. But it is in our society's interest to re-educate the criminals.

单词注释

- criminal [ˈkrɪmɪnl] *n.* 罪犯
- lengthy [ˈleŋθi] *adj.* 漫长的
- jail term 服刑期
- rehabilitate [ˌriːəˈbɪlɪteɪt] *v.* 使（身体）康复，使复原
- deserve [dɪˈzɜːv] *v.* 应得
- inmate [ˈɪnmeɪt] *n.* 犯人
- pose [pəʊz] *v.* 构成
- minimize [ˈmɪnɪmaɪz] *v.* 最小化
- resort [rɪˈzɔːt] *n.* 凭借；手段
- imprisonment [ɪmˈprɪzənmənt] *n.* 关押
- mete out 给予
- incorrigible [ɪnˈkɒrɪdʒəbl] *adj.* 无可救药的，屡教不改的
- felon [ˈfelən] *n.* 重犯
- convict [ˈkɒnvɪkt] *n.* 罪犯
- revenge [rɪˈvendʒ] *v.* 报复
- bitterness [ˈbɪtənɪs] *n.* 苦味；辛酸，苦难
- inclination [ˌɪnklɪˈneɪʃən] *n.* 倾向，爱好
- maltreat [ˌmælˈtriːt] *vt.* 虐待
- repent [rɪˈpent] *v.* 忏悔
- err [ɜː(r)] *vi.* 犯错，做错
- divine [dɪˈvaɪn] *adj.* 神的，神圣的

我们应该用漫长的刑期来惩罚犯人，还是应该以社区服务的形式对他们进行再教育和改造，然后让他们回归社会？

在全球大部分国家，犯罪率都在上升。没有哪个国家没有犯罪。人们制定法律用以界定犯罪行为，并规定相应的惩罚。不同的犯罪的惩罚也不相同：从罚款到死刑。总的来讲，我们应该尽量地帮助罪犯们在刑满释放后融入社会。

我们必须确保罪犯们不再对社会构成威胁。虽然我们无法确保一个人出了监狱到底会干些什么，但是我们可以采取措施，将威胁降至最低。死刑似乎是保护公众安全的最佳方案，但是它太过残忍，实属下策。那些无药可救、无心悔改的罪犯应该终身监禁。但是对于大多数罪犯而言，坐牢并非上策。

把罪犯关进监狱并不是确保公众安全的最佳方法，因为罪犯们迟早是要放出来的。虽然受害者及其家属可能想报仇，但是我们惩罚犯人的最终目的不是为了报复，而是为防止他们再作恶。世间并没有真正意义上的报仇雪恨：覆水难收，人死不能复生，将凶手杀了又能如何？报仇是感情用事，不是明智之举。大贤者能够"博爱仇敌"。我们要采取措施，避免悲剧再次发生。再教育乃是上策。

将犯人关起来只会增加他们的仇恨及犯罪倾向。只要方法得当，大部分的犯人是可以再教育的。当犯人看到他们给他人所带来的痛苦时，当受害者原谅了他们时，当他们看到重新做人的曙光时，很多犯人都会痛改前非。毕竟，如果有其他选择的话，没有人会主动选择罪恶的一生。只要可能，我们都该再给他们一个机会。人非圣贤，孰能无过？他们可能再次成为遵纪守法的好公民。

当然，改造误入歧途的人并不容易。把他们关起来倒是省事，但是对罪犯进行再教育有利于整个社会。

特别提醒

犯罪的话题，在雅思写作考试中属于比较冷门的话题，出现的频率并不高。这道关于犯罪分子应该被送进监狱还是接受社区改造的雅思作文题目，题材非常特殊，请仔细阅读范文！

推荐指数 ★★★★ **相关题目** 46, 52, 56, 99, 101

写作点拨

这道题目要求考生就"犯罪分子应该被送进监狱还是接受社区改造"给出自己的观点，是典型的观点类雅思作文题。范文分为五段：第一段引入话题并且给出作者的观点，即犯罪分子不应该被送进监狱；第二、三、四段指出犯罪分子不应该被送进监狱的原因；第五段总结全文并且重申作者的观点。

论据积累

犯人不应该被送进监狱的原因：

1. 我们无法确保一个人出了监狱到底会干些什么。

   There is no guarantee what an individual will do once he is out of prison.

2. 惩罚犯人的最终目的不是为了报复，而是为防止他们再作恶。

   Our goal to punish wrongdoers is not to seek revenge, but to prevent further damage.

3. 将犯人关起来只会增加他们的仇恨及犯罪倾向。

   We only increase criminals' bitterness and criminal inclination by locking them up or maltreating them.

ESSAY 109

Many schools demand that the students should wear uniform. Some people think that such a practice undermines students' personality and individuality. What do you think?

Most schools in China mandate the wearing of uniforms, which are seen as a symbol of the schools. I started wearing them when I was in the fifth grade and enjoyed the experience.

Students are in no danger of losing their individuality by wearing uniforms. The kind of clothes we wear is only a slight indication of our personality, which is largely revealed by the way we speak and act. Our character is not likely to be affected by what we wear. Uniform is only a part of our external appearance. You can have quite different experience with similarly uniformed sales girls: one rude; the other patient. No matter what we wear, we will remain different from each other because each of us is unique.

Uniform gives the students a sense of community. All sorts of people wear uniforms: the police, the doctors, shop assistants, etc. It tells others and themselves who they are. Having others in similar attire makes it easy for us to fit in. Due to their age, students in particular feel the need to identify a community. They are afraid of being left alone. Wearing the same uniform is at least one thing in common they have with their peers.

Besides, students don't have to decide what is proper for school if they all wear uniforms. This saves them a lot of time and trouble. And students won't engage in some vain and vicious competition about who has got the best clothing. Moreover, uniform is especially beneficial to those underprivileged families with limited means. Kids from those families will not be jeered at for wearing inferior clothes.

Uniform acts as an equalizer, contributing to the equality among students. It also gives them a sense of identity. So it is worth the students' while to forgo their preference for certain clothes and put on a uniform.

单词注释

- undermine [ˌʌndəˈmaɪn] *v.* 破坏
- mandate [ˈmændeɪt] *v.* 要求
- individuality [ˌɪndɪˌvɪdʒuˈæləti] *n.* 个性
- slight [slaɪt] *adj.* 轻微的
- indication [ˌɪndɪˈkeɪʃn] *n.* 显示
- attire [əˈtaɪə(r)] *n.* 衣服
- vicious [ˈvɪʃəs] *adj.* 恶的，不道德的
- underprivileged [ˌʌndəˈprɪvəlɪdʒd] *adj.* 穷困的，下层社会的
- jeer [dʒɪə(r)] *v.* 嘲弄，戏弄
- inferior [ɪnˈfɪəriə(r)] *adj.* 低级的
- equalizer [ˈiːkwəlaɪzə] *n.* 使相等的东西，平衡装置
- forgo [fɔːˈgəʊ] *v.* 放弃

很多学校要求学生穿校服，但是有人认为穿校服会限制学生的个性。请给出你的看法。

中国很多学校要求学生穿校服，因为校服被看作是学校的象征。我是从五年级开始穿校服的，而且乐此不疲。

穿校服并不会导致学生失去个性。我们的衣着只能体现我们个性的很小的部分。我们的言行举止才真正体现我们的个性。我们的个性不会因为我们的衣着而改变。校服只是我们外表的一部分。 穿着同样制服的售货员给我们的感觉可能完全不同：一位耐心细致，另一位粗俗无礼。不管我们的衣着如何，我们都彼此不同，因为我们每个人都是与众不同的。

校服给学生以集体感。很多人都穿统一的制服：警察、医生、售货员等等。制服是他们身份的象征。所有人都衣着统一使他们更容易融入集体。由于学生年纪小，所以更需要一种归属感。他们害怕离开群体。穿同样的校服至少是学生与其同伴拥有的一个共同点。

此外，如果所有人都穿校服的话，学生就不必为穿衣而烦恼了。这给他们省了很多时间和麻烦。学生也不必为衣着而进行无谓的攀比。而且，对家庭条件不好的学生来说，校服无疑是雪中送炭。有了校服，这些孩子们就不会因为衣着朴素而被同学嘲笑了。

校服有助于营造学生之间的平等。校服还能给学生一种归属感。因此学生有必要将自己对某些服装的偏好搁置起来而选择穿校服。

特别提醒

学生是否应该穿校服，是雅思写作考试中最传统的话题之一。这道关于学生是否应该穿校服的雅思作文题目，曾经多次在雅思写作考试中出现，但近年来出现的频率并不高。

推荐指数 ★★★★ **相关题目** 5, 7, 26, 27, 28, 47, 49, 50, 54, 57, 75, 81, 84, 85, 87, 89

写作点拨

这道题目要求考生就“学生是否应该穿校服”给出自己的观点，是典型的观点类雅思作文题。范文分为五段：第一段引入话题并且给出作者的观点，即学生应该穿校服；第二、三、四段陈述学生应该穿校服的原因；第五段总结全文并且重申作者的观点。

论据积累

学生应该穿校服的原因：

1. 穿校服并不会导致学生失去个性，因为我们的衣着只能体现我们个性的很小的部分。
   Students are in no danger of losing their individuality by wearing uniforms as the kind of clothes we wear is only a slight indication of our personality.
2. 校服给学生以集体感。
   Uniform gives the students a sense of community.
3. 穿校服后，学生就不必为衣着而进行无谓的攀比。
   Students won't engage in some vain and vicious competition about who has got the best clothing.

ESSAY 110

Thanks to modern technology, people are living a longer life. Is it a good thing or a bad one? State your opinion.

Longevity is sought for by generation upon generation. Many emperors of the past even commissioned alchemists to produce elixir of life. While immortal life may be too much for us to handle properly, a long life is certainly in our best interest.

Advanced age doesn't necessarily mean senility. With more years after the usual span of life, the elderly can embark on whatever their heart desires. They have a lifetime of skills and experiences behind them and can use them to their advantage. In fact, most politicians are over 60. Ronald Reagan was still the President of the United States at 79. Goethe wrote *Foust* when he was 80. With time on their hand, they can pursue their own interest, do something for the community or simply enjoy life. Their senior years may be their happiest period because they have enjoyed the pleasures and sorrows of life and gained whatever insights that could be possible got. Never would they understand and enjoy life better.

Their prolonged life also benefits others. Senior citizens are often far from unproductive. Though usually retired, most of them often do things for the common good. They ask no pay and simply enjoy the sense of being needed and appreciated. With their insights and experiences, they are often good counsels to the young, cautioning them about the shortsightedness of some of their undertakings. Besides, their spending can also stimulate the economy.

It is true that elderly people are physically weaker and more vulnerable to diseases. But what counts is not the body but the mind. Except those with mental disease, the old are generally wiser than the young. Often enough, life begins at 60.

单词注释

- longevity [lɒnˈdʒevəti] *n.* 长命，长寿
- emperor [ˈempərə] *n.* 皇帝，君主
- commission [kəˈmɪʃn] *vt.* 委任，任命
- alchemist [ˈælkəmɪst] *n.* 炼金术士
- elixir [ɪˈlɪksə(r)] *n.* 不老长寿药，万能药
- immortal [ɪˈmɔːtl] *adj.* 不会死亡的
- senility [səˈnɪləti] *n.* 衰老
- span [spæn] *n.* 期限，一段时间
- embark [ɪmˈbɑːk] *v.* 采取行动
- prolong [prəˈlɒŋ] *vt.* 延长，拖延
- unproductive [ˌʌnprəˈdʌktɪv] *adj.* 无益的；产量少的
- counsel [ˈkaʊnsl] *n.* 忠告，建议
- vulnerable [ˈvʌlnərəbl] *adj.* 脆弱的，易受…伤害的

现代科技让人们的寿命得以延长。这是件好事还是件坏事？请给出你的看法。

人们世世代代都在追求长寿。古代的很多帝王甚至派炼丹士们炼制长生不老药。虽然长生不老之后，人们可能反而无所适从，但是长寿是有益无害的。

年老并不一定意味着衰老。长寿让老人们有时间去发展他们的兴趣爱好。他们有大量的经验和技能，可以大有所为。实际上，大部分的政治家都是在六十岁以上。里根 79 岁还就任美国总统。歌德 80 岁写出了《浮士德》。老人们有大量的时间，可以尽情做自己想做的事，为社区做贡献或者安享晚年。他们的晚年可能是他们最快乐的时期，因为他们已经尝尽了人世的酸甜苦辣、看尽了人世百态。他们在晚年最能理解生命并享受生命。

他们的长寿对他人同样有益。老年人并非对社会无用。他们虽然退休，但往往都会参与某些公益事业。他们不图报酬，为的是实现自我价值，得到他人的肯定。他们拥有敏锐的洞察力和丰富的经验，是年轻人的良师益友，并常常警告他们不要目光短浅。此外，老年人的消费还可以刺激经济发展。

诚然，老年人体力衰退，容易患病。但是真正重要的不是我们的身体而是我们的心灵。除了那些患有神经疾病的老人外，老年人往往比青年人更睿智。夕阳无限红，虽然近黄昏。

特别提醒

现代科技的问题，是雅思考试中最热门的话题之一。本书收集了雅思考试中已经出现过的全部有关现代科技的作文题，其中大部分题目都涉及现代科技对人类生活和工作所造成的影响。

推荐指数 ★★★★

相关题目 5, 14, 15, 16, 20, 21, 25, 64, 103

写作点拨

这道题目要求考生就"现代科技让人们的寿命得以延长是件好事还是件坏事"给出自己的观点，是典型的观点类雅思作文题。范文分为四段：第一段引入话题并且给出作者的观点，即现代科技让人们的寿命得以延长是件好事；第二、三、四段陈述这是件好事的原因。

词汇升级

开始着手做

普通版 With more years after the usual span of life, the elderly can *start to pursue* whatever their heart desires.

升级版 With more years after the usual span of life, the elderly can *embark on* whatever their heart desires.

开始着手做：embark on, get down to, start on, wade into

ESSAY 111

What are the advantages and disadvantages of getting married with a foreigner?

Cross-border marriages are becoming more common in China now. We often envy those who are married to foreigners. Marrying someone from another country does have its appeals.

Foreigners are often thought to be more romantic. French, for instance, are known for their knack to maintain romance after marriage; while people in China or many other Asian countries take a more practical approach to married life. Besides, cross-border marriages offer one unique insight into another culture and tradition. They allow people to understand each other and help to reduce the prejudice among people from different races. Those marriages also offer good prospects for their children, who will grow up enjoying the best of both worlds. They usually become bilingual, to say the very least. It is also said that mixed-blood often enjoy intellectual gifts.

However, there are downsides as well. Unless one of them is fluent in the other's language, the couple is going to encounter communication barriers, which often tend to be an easier obstacle for them to surmount. What is more insurmountable is their differences of opinions. Raised in different background and culture, their beliefs, ideas and attitudes are apt to differ. For instance, a Chinese mother may think her western husband callous when he cuts off financial support when their kids enter college. It is often hard to really understand, let alone to reach a compromise with each other. And the kids may be torn between these conflicting ideas. They may have a hard time finding their own identity. They seem unable to fit in either culture.

There is no guarantee that a marriage will work, whether it is one with a foreigner or not. But again, like anything else, marriage is not perfect. I won't even suggest that you weight the benefits against drawbacks because a marriage is not a financial deal where sensibility reigns.

单词注释

- cross-border [ˈkrɒsbɔːdə] *adj.* 跨国的
- appeal [əˈpiːl] *n.* 魅力，吸引力
- romantic [rəʊˈmæntɪk] *adj.* 浪漫的
- knack [næk] *n.* 诀窍
- approach [əˈprəʊtʃ] *n.* 方法
- insight [ˈɪnsaɪt] *n.* 洞察力
- reduce [rɪˈdjuːs] *v.* 减少
- prejudice [ˈpredʒudɪs] *n.* 偏见
- prospect [ˈprɒspekt] *n.* 前景
- bilingual [ˌbaɪˈlɪŋgwəl] *adj.* 能说两种语言的
- downside [ˈdaʊnsaɪd] *n.* 弊端
- insurmountable [ˌɪnsəˈmaʊntəbl] *adj.* 不可逾越的
- callous [ˈkæləs] *adj.* 无情的，冷淡的
- sensibility [ˌsensəˈbɪləti] *n.* 敏感性
- reign [reɪn] *vi.* 支配；盛行；占优势

请阐述和外国人结婚的利和弊。

在中国，跨国界婚姻变得日益常见。我们往往羡慕那些同外国人结婚的中国人。异国婚姻的确有其自身的魅力。

我们往往认为外国人更加浪漫。例如法国人的浪漫就举世闻名。他们能够在婚后还保持浪漫。中国及亚洲其他国家的人对婚姻的态度就比较实际。其次，跨国婚姻让人了解到异国的文化和传统。它能增强人们间的相互了解，减少偏见。跨国婚姻往往能为孩子们带来好的前景，因为孩子们能够了解两种文化。至少他们可以成为双语人才。据说，混血儿还往往比较聪明。

不过，异国婚姻也有弊端。除非夫妻一方精通另一方的语言，否则他们必然会遇到语言障碍，语言障碍还不是最严重的障碍。更难以克服的是观点的分歧。由于双方生长在不同的文化里，拥有不同的信仰，他们的观点、态度也很可能不同。例如，西方的父亲在孩子上大学之后往往不再给予经济支持，这在中国女性看来是不负责任的。往往双方很难真正地理解对方，更别说达成妥协了。孩子们也会因此不知所措。他们将难以找到自己的位置，很难有归属感。

我们无法确保某段婚姻必然成功，本国婚姻、跨国婚姻皆如此。但是，和世间万物一样，婚姻也是不完美的。我甚至不会建议大家在结婚前权衡利弊，因为婚姻并不是做交易，婚姻往往是感性而非理性的。

特别提醒

或许是考虑到相当比例的雅思考生尚未到适婚的年龄，雅思写作考试中很少涉及婚姻的问题。这道关于跨国婚姻的作文题目，算是一个特例。不过请特别注意，除了婚姻以外，其他家庭生活问题，一直是雅思写作考试中的热门话题。

推荐指数 ★★★　　**相关题目** 70

写作点拨

这道题目要求考生分别指出跨国婚姻的利和弊，属于利弊型的雅思作文题。范文分为四段：第一段引入话题；第二、三段分别介绍了跨国婚姻的利和弊；第四段总结全文，指出婚姻成功与否取决于很多因素。

词汇升级

克服(困难)

普通版 Unless one of them is fluent in the other's language, the couple is going to encounter communication barriers, which is often an easier obstacle for them to *overcome*.

升级版 Unless one of them is fluent in the other's language, the couple is going to encounter communication barriers, which is often an easier obstacle for them to *surmount*.

克服：conquer, defeat, upset, overpower, surmount, overcome

ESSAY 112

Are women suitable to become police officers? Give your reasons and examples.

Female police officers are not uncommon these days in many countries. Feminist movement certainly gives a boost to women's presence in the police force. And their job performances largely justify that presence.

In fact, unlike what is shown on TV, police work depends much more on our brain than on our brawn. It doesn't matter if you cannot run two miles under 15 minutes. If so, most officers after middle age would lose their jobs. What count here are the investigative skills and expertise, which can be cultivated in both sexes. Indeed, in many cases, policewomen outdo their male counterparts because they are more patient and pay more attention to details.

Female officers are also better at making inquiries. People are often taciturn before a burly policeman because they feel insecure and fear they might get into trouble. But the presence of a policewoman often reassures them and puts them at ease. Besides, women are often better listeners than men. They are better at extracting and taking in information from people.

Moreover, their sensitivity allows them to relate to people more easily. Men are inherently less sympathetic than women, especially after they are hardened by years of police work. Women, on the other hand, always show their sympathy toward the victims. They will bring a humanitarian touch to the police work and will get more cooperation from the public as a result.

Men certainly have superior physical strength, which may come handy when chasing the bad guys. But much of the police work is not that drastic. Women are often good at seeking cooperation, which is essential to police work. Therefore, a police force consisting of both male and female officers can best serve the public.

单词注释

- feminist [ˈfemənɪst] *n.* 女权主义者
- boost [buːst] *n.* 推动
- brawn [brɔːn] *n.* 体力
- cultivate [ˈkʌltɪveɪt] *v.* 培养
- counterpart [ˈkaʊntəpɑːt] *n.* 职位相当的人，对应的人或物
- inquiry [ɪnˈkwaɪəri] *n.* 询问
- taciturn [ˈtæsɪtɜːn] *adj.* 沉默寡言的
- burly [ˈbɜːli] *adj.* 魁伟的，结实的
- extract [ɪkˈstrækt] *vt.* 析取，吸取
- sensitivity [ˌsensɪˈtɪvəti] *n.* 敏感，灵敏性
- inherently [ɪnˈhɪərəntli] *adv.* 天生地
- sympathetic [ˌsɪmpəˈθetɪk] *adj.* 有同情心的
- humanitarian [hjuˌmænɪˈteəriən] *n.* 人道主义者
- handy [ˈhændi] *adj.* 唾手可得的，容易取得的
- drastic [ˈdræstɪk] *adj.* 激烈的
- consist [kənˈsɪst] *v.* 包含

女性是否适合做警察呢？请给出你的看法和具体的原因。

如今女警官并不少见，这多少得益于女权运动的发展。女警员的杰出表现让人们对她们的工作能力不再产生怀疑。

其实，警察的工作和电视里展现的大不相同。做好警务工作更多的是依靠大脑，而不是依靠体力。一个警官 15 分钟内能否跑完两英里并不重要，重要的是刑侦技巧和专业知识。而这些是男性和女性都可以培养的。实际上，在很多情况下女警官工作更出色，因为她们更加耐心细致，更注意细节。

女性警察更擅长于调查情况。面对高大的男警官很多人就缄口不言，因为他们觉得没有安全感，害怕惹上麻烦。女警官则能够缓和气氛，使人们放松戒备，不再感到紧张。而且女警官往往是更好的听众，她们更擅长从群众中获取信息。

此外，女警官更加敏感，更善于和人沟通。男性天生就没有女性那么富有同情心，尤其是那些从事了多年警察工作的警官更是如此。相反，女警官则总能表现出对受害者的同情。她们能使警察工作更富有人情味。因此她们可以得到更多群众的支持与配合。

男警官在体力方面占有优势，这在追捕罪犯时能够派上用场。但是，大部分的警务工作并没有这么激烈。女警官在获取群众支持和配合方面更加出色，而这一点恰恰是警务工作的关键。所以，一支由男女警官共同组成的警察队伍才能最好地为公众服务。

特别提醒

女性话题，是雅思写作考试中最传统的话题之一。雅思考试中涉及女性的作文题目多半与儿童抚养、职业女性是否需要出门工作之类的生活话题有关。这道关于女性是否适合当警察的雅思作文题目，题材比较特别，请仔细阅读范文！

推荐指数 ★★★

相关题目 33, 58, 61, 90, 92, 105

写作点拨

这道题目要求考生就“女性是否适合当警察”给出自己的观点，是典型的观点类雅思作文题。范文分为五段：第一段引入话题并且给出作者的观点，即女性适合当警察；第二、三、四段指出女性适合当警察的原因；第五段总结全文并重申作者的观点。

词汇升级

推动，促进

普通版 Feminist movement certainly *encourages* women's presence in the police force.

升级版 Feminist movement certainly *gives a boost to* women's presence in the police force.

推动，促进：promote, hoist, facilitate

ESSAY 113

Some people think that it is the responsibility of the government to ensure that people in the country have healthy lifestyles. Other people believe that individuals should be free to decide their own lifestyles. Please give your own opinion.

The last two decades witnessed an alarming rise in the proportion of adults with unhealthy lifestyles. Smoking, alcohol misuse and obesity have substantially increased the risk of developing some of the most debilitating chronic diseases. Most people understand the importance of a healthy lifestyle in the prevention of disease and the delay in the deterioration in their health. They also know that lifestyle changes and choices can be critical in determining their health and lifespan. Yet news reports reveal that less than 15% of the population around the globe practices a healthy lifestyle. Therefore, the role of the government in the promotion of a healthy lifestyle is difficult yet inescapable.

We know that unhealthy lifestyles may result from a lack of self-discipline. Nevertheless, many factors, including economic status, education, genetics, social factors, culture and media, contribute to the high number of people who have adopted lifestyles that undermine their health. The answer to the prevalence of unhealthy lifestyles lies beyond the scope of the influence of any individual citizen, any non-government organization or any sector to address on its own. The government of a country can play a stewardship role in public health, providing leadership and drawing in players from across many sectors. The government may also work collectively across departments and with other share holders on legislation, regulation and taxation levers, to support activities that promote healthy eating, physical activity and healthy weights.

Admittedly, governments should never curtail the freedom of the citizens to choose their own lifestyles. But too often people are unaware of the unhealthy habits they have acquired because they hardly stop to observe their own lifestyles. Government efforts are therefore essential to enhance citizens' healthy awareness.

On the basis of the above-mentioned arguments, we can conclude that government is well positioned to help citizens break the habits that undermine their health and thus it plays a key role in the promotion of healthy lifestyles.

单词注释

- alarming [əˈlɑːmɪŋ] *adj.* 使人惊慌的；令人担忧的
- alcohol [ˈælkəhɒl] *n.* 酒精，酒
- misuse [ˌmɪsˈjuːs] *n.* 误用，滥用
- obesity [əʊˈbiːsəti] *n.* 肥胖
- substantially [səbˈstænʃəlɪ] *adv.* 相当大地
- debilitate [dɪˈbɪlɪteɪt] *vt.* 使衰弱，使虚弱
- chronic [ˈkrɒnik] *adj.* 慢性的
- deterioration [dɪˌtɪəriəˈreɪʃn] *n.* 变坏，恶化
- genetics [dʒəˈnetɪks] *n.* 遗传特性
- prevalence [ˈprevələns] *n.* 流行
- stewardship [ˈstjuːədʃɪp] *n.* (服务员的)职位或工作
- collectively [kəˈlektɪvli] *adv.* 全体地，共同地
- shareholder [ˈʃeəhəuldə] *n.* 股东；利益相关者
- legislation [ˌledʒɪsˈleɪʃn] *n.* 立法
- regulation [ˌregjuˈleɪʃn] *n.* 规则，规章
- admittedly [ədˈmɪtɪdli] *adv.* 诚然，无可否认地
- curtail [kɜːˈteil] *vt.* 剥夺

有人认为政府应该确保民众拥有健康的生活方式；其他人却认为个人应该享有选择自己的生活方式的自由。请给出你的看法。

过去的二十年里，生活方式不健康的人群在日益扩大，情况令人担忧。抽烟、酗酒、肥胖极大地增加了一些对身体损伤巨大的慢性病的风险。大多数人都清楚地知道健康的生活方式可以防止疾病以及延缓身体的衰老，也同样知道生活方式决定了人的健康状况以及寿命。尽管如此，新闻报道依然指出全球仅有不到15%的人口拥有健康的生活方式。政府在推广健康生活方式方面所承担的任务因而变得艰巨而又不可逃避。

人们之所以会沾染不健康的生活习惯，很多时候是因为缺乏自制力。然而，经济状况、教育程度、遗传、社会因素、文化因素以及大众传媒都在一定程度上导致了人们的不良生活方式。任何个人、非政府机构或是政府部门都无法独立解决生活方式不健康这一广泛存在的问题。政府应该服务于公共健康，以领导的角色联合各方。政府同样可以让各个部门联手，在司法、规章以及税收层面支持那些促进健康饮食、体育锻炼以及控制体重的活动。

诚然，政府不可以剥夺国民自由选择自己生活方式的权利。但是很多时候人们丝毫没有察觉到自己的生活习惯已经威胁到了自己的健康，因为很少有人会停下来反思自己的生活方式。政府在促进大众健康方面的努力因而变得必不可少。

从以上的论述中，我们可以得出这样的结论：政府很适合帮助国民改掉不良的生活习惯，进而在推广健康生活方式方面发挥重要的作用。

特别提醒

生活方式和健康的话题，曾经一度是雅思写作考试中最热门的话题之一，但是近年来在雅思考试中出现的频率已经明显下降。这篇作文，曾在2008年中国大陆考区里难倒了很多考生。请认真参考并适当练笔！

推荐指数 ★★★★★

相关题目 3, 29

写作点拨

这道雅思写作题目要求考生就“政府是否应该确保民众拥有健康的生活方式”给出自己的观点，属于典型的观点类的雅思写作题，是近年来雅思中出现频率最高的一种类型。范文分为四段，第一段引入话题并摆出作者的观点，即政府应该在推动大众健康方面发挥重要作用；第二段立场鲜明地指出各种理由；第三段为让步段；第四段总结全文，重申观点。

论据积累

应该由政府负责大众健康的理由：

1. 很多时候人们丝毫没有察觉到自己的生活习惯已经威胁到了自己的健康。

   Too often people are unaware of the unhealthy habits they have acquired because they hardly stop to observe their own lifestyles.

2. 任何个人、非政府机构或是部门都无法独立解决生活方式不健康这一广泛存在的问题。

   The answer to the prevalence of unhealthy lifestyles lies beyond the scope of the influence of any individual citizen, any non-government organization or any sector to address on its own.

3. 政府同样可以让各个部门联手，在司法、规章以及税收层面支持那些促进健康饮食、体育锻炼以及控制体重的活动。

   The government of a country can play a stewardship role in public health, providing leadership and drawing in players from across many sectors.

《雅思词汇词根+联想记忆法(加强版)》
(附 MP3)　俞敏洪　编著

◎ 完整收录雅思常考词汇，大量真题例句
◎ “词根 + 联想”实用有趣，配有插图，加深记忆
◎ 按字母顺序编排，增加返记菜单，便于考生进行自测

定价：58 元　开本：16 开　页码：528 页

《雅思词汇词根+联想记忆法(乱序版)》
(附 MP3)　俞敏洪　编著

◎ 完整收录雅思常考词汇，大量真题例句
◎ “词根 + 联想”实用有趣，配有插图，加深记忆
◎ 增加返记菜单和索引，便于查找定位

定价：58 元　开本：16 开　页码：528 页

《雅思词汇词根+联想记忆法》
(附 MP3)　俞敏洪　编著

◎ 原汁原味的真题例句，收词全面，涵盖雅思四大题型词汇
◎ 标出听力、口语单词，有针对性进行记忆

定价：32 元　开本：32 开　页码：368 页

《雅思词汇词根+联想记忆法——写作》
(附 MP3)　俞敏洪　编著

定价：12 元　开本：64 开　页码：200 页

《雅思词汇词根+联想记忆法——听力》
(附 MP3)　俞敏洪　编著

定价：12 元　开本：64 开　页码：160 页

《雅思词汇词根+联想记忆法——口语》
(附 MP3)　俞敏洪　编著

定价：12 元　开本：64 开　页码：192 页

《雅思词汇词根+联想记忆法——阅读》
(附 MP3)　俞敏洪　编著

定价：12 元　开本：64 开　页码：232 页

◎ “词根 + 联想”实用有趣，配有插图，加深记忆
◎ 涵盖雅思阅读词汇，收词全面，分类科学

《雅思考官口语实战指导》
(附 MP3)　Mat Clark　编著

◎ 分析中国考生的成绩现状，阐释评分系统的逐项要求
◎ 详尽介绍考试三部分程式，收录最新问题与话题卡片

定价：35 元　开本：16 开　页码：212 页

《雅思听力胜经》(附 MP3)
新东方教育科技集团雅思研发团队　编著

◎ 以雅思听力真题为蓝本，细分常见题型和场景
◎ 提供大量听写和分项练习，帮助考生提高听力单项技能

定价：30 元　开本：16 开　页码：170 页

《雅思口语胜经》(附 MP3)
新东方教育科技集团雅思研发团队　编著

◎ 收录口语考试最新问题和卡片话题
◎ 精选口语考试常用词汇和句型

定价：35 元　开本：16 开　页码：216 页

《雅思阅读胜经》
新东方教育科技集团雅思研发团队　编著

◎ 词汇、语法、语篇三大层次剖析雅思阅读
◎ 精选 16 篇时文，全真模拟雅思阅读考试情境

定价：30 元　开本：16 开　页码：224 页

《雅思写作胜经》
新东方教育科技集团雅思研发团队　编著

◎ 系统说明写作准备过程及步骤
◎ 提供同题各档次作文比较，方便考生自测自学

定价：25 元　开本：16 开　页码：188 页